The Multi-level Governance of Space Mining

Aerospace Law and Policy Series

VOLUME 24

Editors

Pablo Mendes de Leon, Professor of Air and Space Law, and Tanja Masson-Zwaan, Assistant Professor of Space Law, Leiden University, The Netherlands.

Introduction

The *Aerospace Law and Policy Series* critically examines the fundamental changes that international aviation and space activities have undergone since the last century, growing up as mature industries while freeing themselves from traditional regulatory constraints and displaying a variety of innovative applications that call for creative legal solutions.

Objective

The objective of the Series is to make a contribution to legal thinking on public international air and space law and policy, and their implementation at the regional and national levels, responsibility and liability of public bodies and service providers, competition law, insurance law, company law, and the complex relationship between EU law and public international law.

Readership

Aviation and space lawyers, academics, representatives of governments, international organizations, and companies involved in aviation and space activities.

The titles published in this series are listed at the end of this volume.

The Multi-level Governance of Space Mining

Antonino Salmeri

Wolters Kluwer

Published by:
Kluwer Law International B.V.
PO Box 316
2400 AH Alphen aan den Rijn
The Netherlands
E-mail: lrs-sales@wolterskluwer.com
Website: www.wolterskluwer.com/en/solutions/kluwerlawinternational

Sold and distributed by:
Wolters Kluwer Legal & Regulatory U.S.
920 Links Avenue
Landisville, PA 17538
United States of America
E-mail: customer.service@wolterskluwer.com

ISBN 978-94-035-1856-5

e-Book: ISBN 978-94-035-1926-5
web-PDF: ISBN 978-94-035-1936-4

I dedicate this book to the everlasting memory
of my dearest grandfather, Andrea Ragusa,
whose life teachings made me the man
I hope he would be proud of today.

Table of Contents

List of Abbreviations

AA	Artemis Accords
ARRA	Agreement on the Rescue of Astronauts, the Return of Astronauts and the Return of Objects Launched into Outer Space
ARSIWA	Articles on the Responsibility of States for Internationally Wrongful Acts
AT	Antarctic Treaty
ATCM	Antarctic Treaty Consultative Meeting
ATS	Antarctic Treaty System
BB	Building Blocks for the Development of an International Framework for the Governance of Space Resource Activities
BR	Radiocommunication Bureau
BR IFIC	Radiocommunication Bureau International Frequency Information Circular
BSS	Broadcasting-Satellite Services
CCAMLR	Convention on the Conservation of Antarctic Marine Living Resources
CCAS	Convention on the Conservation of Antarctic Seals
CCC	Choice of Court Convention
CHM	Common Heritage of Mankind
CJEU	Court of Justice of the European Union
CoCoSL	Cologne Commentary on Space Law
COSPAR	Committee on Space Research
DIFC	Dubai International Financial Centre
EAGLE	Effective and Adaptive Governance for a Lunar Ecosystem
ECHR	European Convention for the Protection of Human Rights and Fundamental Freedoms

ECOSOC	Economic and Social Council
ECtHR	European Court on Human Rights
ESA	European Space Agency
EU	European Union
FSS	Fixed-Satellite Services
GEGSLA	Global Expert Group on Sustainable Lunar Activities
GPS	Global Positioning System
ICJ	International Court of Justice
IISL	International Institute of Space Law
ILC	International Law Commission
ILRS	International Lunar Research Station
ISA	International Seabed Authority
ISRU	In-Situ Resource Utilization
ISS	International Space Station
ITLOS	International Tribunal for the Law of the Sea
ITU	International Telecommunication Union
JAXA	Japan Aerospace Exploration Agency
JC	Convention on the Recognition and Enforcement of Judgments in Civil or Commercial Matters
JSRA	Japan Space Resources Act
LIAB	Convention on International Liability for Damage Caused by Space Objects
LSC	Legal Subcommittee of the UN Committee on the Peaceful Uses of Outer Space
LTS	Long-Term Sustainability Guidelines for Outer Space Activities
LUXSRL	Loi du 20 juillet 2017 sur l'exploration et l'utilisation des ressources de l'espace (Luxembourg Space Resources Law)
MA, MOON	Agreement Governing the Activities of States on the Moon and Other Celestial Bodies
MVA	Moon Village Association
NAFTA	North American Free Trade Agreement
NASA	National Aeronautics Space Administration
Non-GSO	Non-Geostationary
NYC	New York Convention on the Recognition and Enforcement of Foreign Arbitral Awards
OLF	Open Lunar Foundation
OSI	Outer Space Institute
OSSA	One Small Step to Protect Human Heritage in Space Act
OST	Outer Space Treaty
PCA	Permanent Court of Arbitration
PEPAT	Protocol on Environmental Protection to the Antarctic Treaty

REG	Convention on Registration of Objects Launched into Outer Space
RR	Radio Regulations of the International Telecommunication Union
SGAC	Space Generation Advisory Council
SRWG	United Nations Working Group on Legal Aspects of Space Resource Activities
ToR	Terms of Reference
UAEFLRSS	Federal Law on the Regulation of the Space Sector
UDIL	Unity and Diversity in International Law
UN	United Nations
UNCITRAL	United Nations Commission on International Trade Law
UNCLOS	United Nations Convention on the Law of the Sea
UNCOPUOS	United Nations Committee on the Peaceful Uses of Outer Space
UNGA	United Nations General Assembly
UNOOSA	United Nations Office for Outer Space Affairs
UNSC	United Nations Security Council
UNSG	United Nations Secretary General
USCLCA	Commercial Space Launch Competitiveness Act
USSR	Soviet Union
VCLT	Vienna Convention on the Law of Treaties
WHO	World Health Organization
WRC	World Radio Conferences
WTO	World Trade Organization

Foreword

The present book very successfully finalizes one period of the professional life of Antonino Salmeri. It was a period full of new encounters, new challenges, lots of writing and a brilliant defense of his doctoral thesis.

When I first met Antonino, he was a student in the Master's course in Space and Air Law at the University of Leiden. He approached me after my telecommunication lecture and asked about the conditions of doctoral studies at my University, the University of Luxembourg. After this meeting, I did not see him until the selection of new doctoral students, where he fully convinced the selection committee and was awarded one of the few prestigious places at the Luxembourg doctoral school.

Very fast, the subject of his thesis was chosen: Antonino had always been fascinated by Lunar exploration and exploitation; however, as the central theme of the doctoral school was the effect of legal norms, it was necessary to create a bridge between the exploitation of Lunar resources and this general subject. He managed to build that bridge with elegance and, together with his U.S. colleague and friend Marc Sundhal, developed a system of registration of space resources missions enabling the effective coordination of the activities of operators of space resources activities. No surprise that this model has been presented to the United Nations (UN) and discussed in several international fora.

After the initial search for the exact title of the thesis followed the time when Antonino was using every opportunity to learn and exchange his knowledge in Luxembourg and abroad. He became a very successful lecturer at the University, assisted the SES Chair in organizing its annual international workshops, took the lead in implementing a series of lectures on legal aspects of launching satellites, and published most intensively. Only his personal drive to face new and unexplored challenges resulted in his decision not to exploit the whole period of doctoral studies available, and—as an absolute exception among doctoral students—he submitted his doctoral thesis much earlier than required.

It was always a great pleasure to work with Antonino: he took initiatives, was always very fast in delivering outstanding results, and—if necessary—was able to pursue his goals in a most persistent and persuasive way. With a small team, we worked together on a Commentary on the Space Legislation of Luxembourg, and he was the first who delivered his contributions—well before the publication of the book in 2022. During the hardships of the COVID-19 period, he continued to work from his small Luxembourg flat, and the fewer opportunities there were for meeting friends and colleagues, the more he wrote and published. For me, he was not so much my doctoral student than an esteemed colleague.

I am firmly convinced that Antonino will pursue a most successful professional career: He is an excellent lawyer, a hard worker, and a wonderful colleague. My most sincere congratulations to your great book, Antonino, which I know so well and which you defended with such brilliance!

Professor Mahulena Hofmann
SES Chair in Space, SatCom and Media Law
University of Luxembourg
Luxembourg, October 29, 2022

Editor Preface

It is a great pleasure to include Antonino Salmeri's book in our series on Aerospace Law and Policy. The author obtained his LL.M. (cum laude) in Advanced Studies in Air and Space Law at the International Institute of Air and Space Law at Leiden University in 2018 where I taught him space law. Already at that time he demonstrated a deep scientific interest in the legal aspects of space resource activities, doing an internship at a space mining company and writing his LL.M. thesis on the subject. Antonino was a brilliant student and was always very engaged. His drive and passion for space law and policy also transpired in his active involvement with Space Generation Advisory Council, where he initiated an Advocacy and Policy Platform and led a lunar governance project resulting in the impactful EAGLE report ("Effective and Adaptive Governance for a Lunar Ecosystem"), which was presented to the United Nations Committee on the Peaceful Uses of Outer Space in 2021.

Antonino further perfected his knowledge of space law at the University of Luxembourg where I had the pleasure of sitting on his Ph.D. committee in July 2022. This book is the culmination of his research on the topic of space resources, focusing specifically on enforcement challenges of present and future norms applicable to space mining. The book presents a comprehensive study of the multifaceted aspects of regulating the novel space activity of commercially utilizing space resources. It will be a useful tool for lawyers, students, diplomats, policymakers and entrepreneurs interested in the future governance of space resource activities. It addresses public international law, international space law, national law and a comparative analysis with the regimes of the high seas and Antarctica, and presents realistic options for developing and enforcing a future regime in the most pragmatic manner.

The author continues his fascination with and commitment to lunar governance in his professional journey and I am eager to follow his next steps. This book aptly illustrates his academic capabilities which form the basis of his future endeavors. I am proud, as his former professor, his mentor and now his editor, that we were able to publish this important study in our series.

Tanja Masson-Zwaan
Co-editor

Author Preface

Raise your hand if you ever heard that space mining will be like the Wild West's gold rush. For years, public conversations on space mining have been misled by exaggerated narratives fantasizing about new trillionaires or interplanetary wars for the control of space resources. Next time someone tries to sell you that, please hand them over this book.

Even though there is certainly room for improvement, you can rest assured that space resource activities do not escape the rule of (international) law. From Apollo 11 to Chang'e-5 and Hayabusa 2, space agencies have successfully extracted and recovered space resources under the tenets of the Outer Space Treaty (OST), the "Magna Carta" of international space law, for over fifty years. While the involvement of commercial entities, as well as the increased scale and long duration of their planned mining endeavors, surely raise important legal and policy issues that have to be carefully addressed, ensuring the legality of their activities is not a question of if but "simply" of how.

Moving from this premise, this book analyzes the existing legal and policy landscape for space resource activities. From the OST to the recently approved Japan Space Resources Act, the book investigates the multi-level framework of space law, provision by provision, to assess relevant implications on the governance of space mining. The book also provides an overview of major policy initiatives discussing the development of new rules specifically designed to govern large-scale, long-term space resource activities conducted (also) by commercial entities, such as The Hague Building Blocks or the Effective and Adaptive Governance for a Lunar Ecosystem (EAGLE) Report on Lunar Governance. This analysis is further enriched with an assessment of the options available for enforcing the various norms that might become relevant. Such assessment serves the purpose of testing the practical relevance of the existing rules in view of their potential application in the next future. Building upon these studies, the book concludes by evaluating the tenure of the governance system and proposing three pragmatic correctives to stabilize it in the short, medium and long term.

Writing this book has been an incredibly rewarding journey for me. Over the past four years, I got the privilege and the pleasure of working with amazing colleagues from whom I distilled my own knowledge and understanding of space resources and lunar governance. The journey of this book is coming to an end, and new ones are about to begin. But none of these journeys would have been possible without the support and guidance of my mentors, my family, my friends and my colleagues. As I send this book off into the world, I would like to thank each and every one of them for the part they have played.

First, I want to thank my former Ph.D. supervisor, Professor Mahulena Hofmann, for her academic guidance and inspiring example of personal and professional virtues. This book would have never seen the light without her. A heartfelt "thank you" also goes to my first mentor, Professor Tanja Masson-Zwaan, for having introduced me to the space world and for her invaluable support in all stages of my professional life.

I want, of course, to thank my family, my north star in this exciting journey through space: my parents, Elena and Leonardo; my siblings, Andrea and Clara; my grandmother, Ninì; my cousins Martina and Sonya; my aunt and uncle Angela and Angelo, as well as the little Sofia.

You gave me the confidence to follow my heart and intuition even when it led me off the well-worn path, and that has made all the difference.

I would be nothing without the wonderful people that fill my days with love and laughter: la Banda Bassotti, il Team Dinamite, la MLAG Family, i Fantafanatici, the Bibbon Tutentin, the Falcon Heavy, the SSP19 crew and my dear Nat. Thank you for being part of my life and for the unforgettable moments we shared together across time and space.

Finally, I would like to acknowledge some of the most amazing humans that I have had the pleasure to work with in the space community: Chelsea, Jessy Kate, Jacob, Harshi and Heloise from the Open Lunar Foundation; Carlos, Jenna, Vinnie and Julien from ispace Luxembourg; Giuliana, Davide, Valentina, Harriet, Anthony, Hamza, Bram, Giulia, Sahba, Antonio, Morgane and Nicolas from the Space Generation Advisory Council; and PJ, Gabrielle, Federico and Laetitia from the former SES team at Unilu. Your passion and excellence constantly inspire me to be the best version of myself, and it is a true pleasure to work with you on a bright future in space for the benefit of all humankind.

Ad Astra
Your Antonino

Perseverance
will get you anywhere.
I hope this book inspires
all those who are struggling
through hard times in their lives.
I learned that oftentimes impediments
are actually opportunities in disguise.
Keep persevering, and rest assured,
at some point, you will emerge
to see the stars again.
All it matters is that
you don't just
give up.

Introduction

1 MULTI-LEVEL GOVERNANCE UP TO THE STARS: REGULATORY ASPECTS AND ENFORCEMENT OPTIONS OF SPACE MINING

Few contest that outer space is a special domain. Space activities are carried out in a three-dimensional, transparent and continuous medium. By their very nature, they are international, global and even extraterrestrial.[1] Therefore, no actor can perform them in isolation, no matter how powerful or technologically advanced. The international community grasped this reality from the very beginning, which is why already, in 1959, States have realized that the regulation of space activities was better concerted at the international level.[2] To this end, they established the United Nations Committee on the Peaceful Uses of Space[3] (UNCOPUOS) as a specialized committee of the UN General Assembly (UNGA) tasked with the development of international rules for the peaceful exploration and use of space.

1.1 The Origins of International Space Law

It is in this context that the rules of international space law were written during the 1960s through the fruitful diplomatic negotiations between the Western and Soviet blocks in UNCOPUOS.[4] To better understand this process, it is important to stress that despite ending up competing with each other, the United States (U.S.) and the Soviet Union (USSR) approached the negotiations with peace as a fundamental priority and

1. Pablo Mendes de Leon, *Crossing Borders in International Air and Space Law*, 3 (1) India Law Journal 2-3 (2010).
2. Isabella Diederiks-Verschoor, *An Introduction to Space Law* 23-24 (2008).
3. More info on UNCOPUOS can be found at https://www.unoosa.org/oosa/en/ourwork/copuos/index.html (accessed January 2021).
4. Diederiks-Verschoor, *supra* note 2.

international cooperation as a main guiding principle.[5] Looking at the *travaux préparatoires* of the OST,[6] we find that its drafters strongly believed in the importance of preventing predatory behaviors in space and built the nascent system of international space law upon international regulation and cooperation.[7]

Moving from these premises, diplomacy has then shaped the further development of the rules governing the exploration and use of space for the past sixty years. During this time, UNCOPUOS produced five international agreements and fifteen UNGA resolutions, collectively referred to as the *Corpus Iuris Spatialis.*[8]

Back at the roots of international space law, the exploration and use of outer space were the privileges of a restricted group of States,[9] so this set of norms has been developed with States being both the players and the regulators. For the first two decades, these norms have been almost exclusively developed at the international level. Starting from the 1990s, this practice has begun to change due to the dramatic transformation of the space industry.[10] From a government-driven sector, mostly focused on remote sensing activities, the space industry evolved into the *Global Space* economy,[11] a market which today is worth USD 469 billion.[12] Naturally, the increasing role played by private entities in the exploration and use of outer space has impacted the development of international space law in requiring a proportionate degree of involvement from national regulators.

To be sure, an increasing role for non-governmental entities in the future of space activities was already foreseen by the OST drafters, who discussed extensively first whether to permit and eventually how to regulate private activities in outer space. On the one hand, the USSR was skeptical about non-governmental space activities and was of the opinion that only a State conscious of its international responsibility should

5. Kai-Uwe Schrogl, *Space Law and Diplomacy*, 2016 (1) Proceedings of the International Institute of Space Law 3-4 (2016).
6. Treaty on Principles Governing the Activities of States in the Exploration and Use of Outer Space, Including the Moon and Other Celestial Bodies, *entered into force* October 10, 1967, 18 U.S.T. 2410, 610 U.N.T.S. 205 [hereinafter: "OST"].
7. Steven Freeland & Ram Jakhu, *Article II*, in *Cologne Commentary on Space Law: Vol. 1* 44-63 (Stephan Hobe, Bernhard Schmidt-Tedd & Kai-Uwe Schrogl eds., 2009—book hereinafter: "CoCoSL I").
8. For a historical overview on the creation of international space law, *see* Bin Cheng, *Studies in International Space Law* 150-211 (2004) and also Vladimir Kopal, *United Nations and the Progressive Development of International Space Law*, VII Finnish Yearbook of International Space Law 1-58 (1996). For contemporary assessments on the *Corpus Iuris Spatialis, see:* Mahulena Hofmann & Tanja Masson-Zwaan, *Introduction to Space Law* (2019); Francis Lyall & Paul Larsen, *Space Law: A Treaties* (2nd ed., 2018); Frans Von Der Dunk & Fabio Tronchetti (eds.), *Handbook of Space Law* (2015).
9. Ronald L. Spencer Jr, *International Space Law: A Basis for National Regulation*, in *National Regulation of Space Activities* 3 (Ram S. Jakhu ed., 2010).
10. For a comprehensive overview of these changes, *see* Andrew J. Butrica, *Beyond the Ionosphere: Fifty Years of Satellite Communication* (1997).
11. For a detailed analysis of the *New Space* economy, *see* Marco Ferrazzani, *The Development of a New Space Economy and of Mega Constellations*, in *Innovation in Outer Space: International and African Legal Perspectives* 93-104 (Mahulena Hofmann & P.J. Blount eds., 2018—book hereinafter: "Innovation in Outer Space").
12. Space Foundation, *The Space Report* 3 (2022).

engage in the exploration and use of space.[13] On the other hand, the United States already had plans for privately operated telecommunication satellites and strongly believed in opening the gates of space also to non-governmental entities.[14] Ultimately, a compromise between the two viewpoints was found in the text of Article VI OST, a provision of paramount importance in international space law.[15] This article enables non-governmental entities to engage in the exploration and use of outer space under the authorization and continuing supervision of the "appropriate State Party to the Treaty."[16] In this sense, Article VI OST is at the root of the obligation to nationally regulate private space activities since the responsible State must ensure that they are conducted in conformity with the OST provisions.[17] Article VI OST further implies an obligation of due diligence,[18] which means that States have to actively verify the legitimate conduct of private activities in outer space.[19] The mechanism foreseen in Article VI OST is the reason why international space law, in general, has become a multi-level regulatory system. The more private entities engage in space activities, the more relevant domestic law becomes.

1.2 The Multi-level Nature of Space Mining

This binomial is especially true for space mining. Even though States have been the very first entities engaging in extraterrestrial extraction activities through the conduct of various sample return missions from the Moon[20] or asteroids,[21] in recent times, space mining has increasingly captured the interest of commercial operators. In this regard, it is important to note that previous space resource missions have been generally conceived as one-time endeavors, exclusively driven by scientific purposes because States were not willing to invest the high sums required to develop the necessary technologies and capabilities for expanding them. The general opinion, in fact, is that private entities are better equipped for these purposes since their commercial mindset can increase both the efficiency and effectiveness of space resource activities. With these assumptions in mind, some States have decided to enact domestic legislation in order to provide an adequate legal framework that could foster the development of a national space mining industry. The first country paving the way for the national regulation of space mining was the U.S., which in 2015 passed the

13. Michael Gerhard, *Article VI OST*, in *CoCoSL I*, *supra* note 7, at 106.
14. *Id.*, at 105.
15. Diederiks-Verschoor, *supra* note 2 at 26.
16. Article VI OST, *supra* note 6.
17. Stephen Gorove, *Freedom of Exploration and Use in the Outer Space Treaty: A Textual Analysis and Interpretation*, 1 Journal of International Law and Policy 100 (1971).
18. Cheng, *supra* note 8 at 188; *see also* Antonio Cassese, *International Law* 168 (2005).
19. Tanja Masson-Zwaan, *Article VI of the Outer Space Treaty and Private Human Access to Space*, 2008 (9) Proceedings of the International Institute of Space Law 537 (2008).
20. For an overview of sample return missions from the Moon, *see* Allan H. Treiman & et al., *Sample Return from the Earth's Moon*, available https://www.lpi.usra.edu/decadal/captem/AllanTreimanMoon.pdf (last accessed October 2022).
21. The most important sample return missions from asteroids have been conducted by the Japan Aerospace Exploration Agency (JAXA) and are reported http://www.isas.jaxa.jp/en/topics/keywords/sample-return_mission/ on their website (last accessed October 2022).

Commercial Space Launch Competitiveness Act (USCLCA) as the first law ever allowing private entities to obtain certain rights in space resources.[22] Following the U.S. example, in 2017, Luxembourg became the first European State to pass legislation enabling the conduct of commercial space mining activities.[23] Over the last two years, these States have been joined by the United Arab Emirates and Japan.[24]

The low number of States nationally regulating space mining has its counterpart in the lack of prescriptive rules governing space mining at the international level. To be sure, this situation is only normal given the fact that the multi-level regulatory system of space mining has begun to develop only recently. While the topic has been discussed for years by scholars, States have not engaged in diplomatic discussions about a regulatory system for space mining since the adoption—and subsequent failure—of the Moon Agreement[25] (MA) in 1979. It was only after the enactment of the USCLCA that the Legal Subcommittee (LSC) of UNCOPUOS decided to introduce an agenda item dedicated to space mining.[26] Already from the first year of debates, some States have expressed concern about the involvement of private entities in space mining and the related multi-level framework that was initiated with the enactment of the USCLCA.[27] Since then, the LSC has been divided[28] between those demanding direct regulations at the international level[29] and those favoring a more prominent role, at least in the initial stages, for national legislation.[30] While the international debate continues,[31] the combination of Articles I and VI OST offers a clear legal basis for the further development of space mining as a multi-level regulatory system.[32] For the purpose of

22. Commercial Space Launch Competitiveness Act *entered into force* November 25, 2015, H.R.2262, 114th Congress (2015-2016) [hereinafter: "USCLCA"].
23. Loi du 20 juillet 2017 sur l'exploration et l'utilisation des ressources de l'espace, *entered into force* July 28, 2017, Lux Recueil de Legislation A674 (2017) [hereinafter: "LUXSRL"].
24. Respectively, for the UAE: Federal Law No. 12 of 2019 on the Regulation of the Space Sector, *entered into force* January 20, 2020, 669 UAE Official Gazette 111 (2019) [hereinafter: "UAEFL-RSS"]; and for Japan: Space Resources Act, *entered into force* December 23, 2022, 141 Japan Official Gazette 4 (2022) [hereinafter: "JSRA"].
25. Agreement Governing the Activities of States on the Moon and Other Celestial Bodies *entered into force* July 11, 1984, 1363 U.N.T.S. 3.
26. Resolution adopted by the General Assembly at its 71st Session, UN Doc A/RES/71/90 (December 6, 2016).
27. Report of the Legal Subcommittee on its 56th Session, held in Vienna from March 27 to April 7, 2017, UN Doc A/AC.105/1122 30-33 (2017).
28. Report of the Legal Subcommittee on its 57th Session, held in Vienna from April 9 to 20, 2018, UN Doc A/AC.105/1177 29-32 (2018); *see also* Report of the Legal Subcommittee on its 58th Session, held in Vienna from April 1 to 12, 2019, UN Doc A/AC.105/1203 32-36 (2019).
29. Working Paper from the Governments of Belgium and Greece, Proposal for the Establishment of an Working Group for the Development of an International Regime for the Utilization and Exploitation of Space Resources, UN Doc A/AC.105/C.2/L.311 (2019).
30. *See* both the 2018 and 2019 LSC Reports, *supra* note 28.
31. The latest update in the Legal Subcommittee saw the establishment of a dedicated working group on the legal aspects of space resource activities, which is set to begin its substantive activities in 2023. Report of the Chair and Vice-Chair of the working group established under the Legal Subcommittee agenda item entitled "General exchange of views on potential legal models for activities in the exploration, exploitation and utilization of space resources," UN Doc A/AC.105/C.2/2022/SRA/L.1, p. 1 (2022).
32. On the right of individual States to propose their own interpretation of international law, *see* Antonino Salmeri, *The Integration Between National and International Regulation of Space Resources Activities under Public International Law*, 43 (1) Journal of Space Law 60-84 (2019).

this book, it is assumed that this *status quo* will be generally maintained during the current decade, thus preserving the current multi-level dimension of space mining regulation. This is because of two reasons. First, even if States would decide to develop an international agreement regulating space mining, it is unlikely that every step of the regulatory process will be managed at the international level. Under Article VI OST, private activities in outer space will still need to be authorized and supervised by a State, which inevitably implies a role for domestic regulators.[33] Second, even in the remote hypothesis of a fully fledged international system, it can be reasonably assumed that its development will take years (if not decades) of negotiations and implementations. In the meantime, there would be nothing preventing States from authorizing and supervising commercial space mining activities under the terms of Article VI OST, as negotiating a new regulatory system does not affect the status of legal rights and obligations which are currently in force.

To be sure, space mining is only one of many multi-level regulatory systems that have recently emerged in the international arena. As is well-known, in contemporary times, the dramatic impact of globalization has made traditional governance mechanisms no longer able to properly tackle the problems of our contemporary society.[34] Nowadays, various actors interact at different levels across multiple jurisdictions, thus transcending the territorial and hierarchical dimensions that used to govern decision-making processes.[35] The nation-State is not anymore the gravity center around which all other actors orbit[36] and does not seem to be suited to solve the major problems of our world.[37] Climate change, migration movements, not to mention the COVID-19 pandemic and the Russian invasion of Ukraine all escape the grasp of individual governments unless they properly coordinate at the international level. Further, because of their complexity, certain global issues like those mentioned above can only be addressed with the contributions of all involved actors, including private ones.[38] Within this global context, space mining offers an interesting example of the difficulties faced by nation States in developing a regulatory system that could be at the same time legitimate and effective. While these regulatory issues have been increasingly explored in academic literature, related questions of enforcement have received little attention, despite their theoretical importance and practical relevance.

33. Article VI OST, *supra* note 6. Masson-Zwaan, *supra* note 19.
34. Robert Falkner, *Global Governance: The Rise of Non-state Actors—A Background Report for the SOER 2010 Assessment of Global Megatrend* 4 (2011).
35. Jan Zielonka, *Enlargement and the Finality of European Integration*, in *What Kind of Constitution for What Kind of Polity? Responses to Joschka Fisher* 151-160 (Christian Joerges, Yves Meny & Joseph H.H. Weiler eds., 2000).
36. Anne-Marie Slaughter, *Government Networks: The Heart of the Liberal Democratic Order*, in *Democratic Governance and International Law* 199 (Gregory Fox & Brad Roth eds., 2000). *See also* Gary Marks et al., *Competencies, Cracks and Conflicts: Regional Mobilization in the European Union*, in *Governance in the European Union* 40-41 (Gary Marks ed., 1996).
37. Michael Longo, *Reconceptualising Public International Law: Convergence with the European Union Model?*, 25 (1) University of New South Wales Law Journal 88-93 (2002).
38. Zielonka, *supra* note 35 at 161-162.

1.3 The Contribution of This Book to the Academic Debate on Space Mining and Multi-level Systems

The main goal of this book is to investigate the regulatory configuration of space mining as multi-level system and determine the relevant options available for its enforcement.

In recent times, questions related to the legality and governance of space resource activities have been increasingly discussed in space law literature. Moving from these initial studies, the present book contributes to the academic debate by offering an original, detailed assessment of how the systemic nature of international law, as well as the individual provisions of international space law, affect both the conduct and regulation of space resource activities. Further, and building upon this analysis of the regulatory aspects, the book also provides an original assessment of the options available for the adjudication and enforcement of the norms composing the system of space mining.

The topics discussed in the book can be grouped into four sets of questions:

(1) What is the relationship between space law and international law?
(2) What is the regulatory configuration of space mining as multi-level system?
(3) What are the options available for enforcing national and international provisions of space mining, and what is their legitimacy and effectiveness?
(4) How can we reinforce the multi-level system of space mining, taking inspiration from normative solutions adopted in comparable models?

Since these subjects involve the interaction between different actors at various governance levels, the conducted analysis combines international space law, public international law, space policy and general theory of law under a comparative approach. Structurally, the present book moves from general to particular, beginning with the status of international law as a legal order and ending with the specific options available for enforcing the norms applicable to space mining. Accordingly, the book is divided into three chapters. Since international space law constitutes a specialized system within the broader normative environment of international law, Chapter 1 analyzes their relationship in order to contextualize the subsequent assessment of the development and enforcement of space mining regulations. Following, Chapter 2 moves to consider the current configuration of the multi-level regulatory system of space mining as shaped by the applicable international and national norms. Based on this regulatory analysis, the third and final chapter of the book identifies potential enforcement options, assesses them in terms of effectiveness and legitimacy, and further proposes potential correctives for addressing identified deficiencies. Finally, the book concludes by revisiting its main findings to evaluate the overall tenure of space mining as multi-level system and indicate future perspectives for its sustainable and peaceful evolution and application.

CHAPTER 1

The Relationship Between Space Law and International Law

In order to properly assess the regulatory aspects and enforcement options of space mining as multi-level system, it is essential to begin first with a foundational assessment of the structure and dynamics characterizing the system of international space law itself. Because this system is part of the legal order of international law, it is important to understand its interactions with the broader normative environment surrounding it. After having identified the boundaries shaping the systemic development of space law, it will be possible to meaningfully analyze the regulatory aspects and enforcement options of the specialized portion dealing with space mining.

The present chapter is divided into two sections. Section 1 begins the analysis by considering the current status of the legal order of international law. To this end, it specifically discusses three fundamental aspects shaping its modern development: substantive diversification, functional differentiation and systemic integration. Based on these findings, section 2 moves to assess the relationship between international space law and the broader normative environment of international law in terms of both substantive and institutional integration.

1 THE LEGAL ORDER OF INTERNATIONAL LAW

One of the most defining elements of international law as a legal order is its normative development. As the wording itself suggests, normative development is defined as the process(es) by virtue of which juridical norms are developed.[1] In a positive legal order, the rules of normative development are laid down in special norms, which are usually

1. Bruno Romano, *Sulla Visione Procedurale Del Diritto: Saggio Sul Fondamentalismo Funzionale* 2-24 (2001).

located at the top (or, depending on one's perspective, at the foundations) of the legal system.[2] At the very minimum, these structural norms define who holds power to enact juridical norms, what are the effects of those norms and under what conditions the norm-making activity shall be exercised.[3] Given the complexity of our modern reality, the vast majority of modern legal systems distributes the power to create juridical norms among a variety of institutions.[4] While the actual distribution changes depending on the fundamental features of a given system, the allocation of norm-making power is usually done through the use of hierarchy and competence criteria.[5] Through the former one, institutions are traditionally organized under a vertical order, with the consequence that the rules made by a superior body trump those made at the lower level. According to the competence criteria, the norm-making power is further distributed per subject matter, usually following the principle of subsidiarity. Consequently, a certain domestic legal order can be divided into a number of legal systems that coexist and integrate with one another by virtue of certain structural rules. For instance, within the legal order of the Italian Republic, there are three legal systems—created by the State, the Regions and the Communes[6]—each producing norms in accordance with the rules that are established in the Italian Constitution.[7] Accordingly, the existence of structural rules makes sure that the normative development within a positive legal order follows a predetermined path in order to control the complexity of the system and ensure its ordered functioning.[8] Thanks to the structural rules of normative development, the legal order can only be divided into a predetermined number of legal systems, which is directly related to the number of institutions provided with norm-making power. To further strengthen the stability of the system, structural rules of normative development usually remain in force for rather long periods of time.[9] However, while this is true for most domestic legal orders, the same cannot be said for international law. In this legal order, there are no structural rules assigning the norm-making power to the competence of certain institutions.[10] Rather, this power is diffused through the international community of States,[11] which are free to create new systems with dedicated rules and institutions at any point in time.[12] This lack of structural rules for normative development is at the root of the substantive diversification, functional differentiation and systemic integration of international law.

2. Hans Kelsen, *General Theory of Norms* 26-30 (1991).
3. Ludovico Mazarrolli & Dimitri Girotto, *Diritto Costituzionale* 3-24 (2015).
4. Neil Maccormick, *Institutions of Law: An Essay in Legal Theory* 35-37 (2007).
5. Mazzarolli & Girotto, *supra* note 3 at 25-66.
6. Costituzione della Repubblica Italiana, Articolo 117.
7. Mazzarolli & Girotto, *supra* note 3 at 535-536.
8. Niklas Luhmann, *Potere e Complessita Sociale* 50 (1979).
9. The U.S. Constitution is the oldest constitutional document whose basic division of powers has been maintained for over 200 years.
10. Paola Gaeta, Jorge E. Vinuales & Salvatore Zappalà, *Cassese's International Law* 4-6, 181 (3rd ed., 2020) [hereinafter: "Cassese's IL"].
11. Alexidze Levan, *Legal Nature of Jus Cogens in Contemporary International Law* 245 (1987).
12. Henry G. Schermers & Niels M. Blokker, *International Institutional Law* 29-47 (5th revised ed., 2011) [hereinafter: "Schermers & Blokker"].

1.1 Substantive Diversification

Since time immemorial, the normative development of international law has never been entrusted to a predetermined set of institutions and remained the privilege of all States.[13] Albeit within certain limits, this means that they are, in principle, free to create and dismantle as many legal systems as they want. For centuries, States have barely used this faculty as the development of international law was mostly proceeding at the substantive level, through the conclusion of international agreements regulating certain matters.[14] However, since the conclusion of World War II, and especially after the fall of Berlin's wall in 1989, the *status quo* has changed. The spread of multilateralism, combined with the transformative action of globalization, have determined a dramatic increase in the number of legal systems within the legal order of international law.[15] This proliferation of multilateral regimes,[16] and especially of international judicial bodies,[17] convinced the then President of the International Court of Justice (ICJ), Gilbert Guillaume, to deliver a historical speech before the UN General Assembly (UNGA).[18] In his intervention, President Guillaume expressly criticized this phenomenon by stating that it could "jeopardize the unity of international law."[19] Following up on these concerns, the UNGA asked the International Law Commission (ILC) to tackle the problem. Over the subsequent years, the ILC did so through a series of studies ultimately finalized by Koskenniemi[20] and culminating in a final report presented in July 2006.[21] Needless to say, the ILC study on the "fragmentation" of international law was just the tip of an iceberg of many discussions elaborating on the potential demise of international law as a united legal order.[22] The debate on fragmentation, prompted

13. Cassese's IL, *supra* note 10 at 181-202.
14. *Id.*, at 20-37.
15. Robin Geib, *Non-state Actors: Their Role and Impact on the Fragmentation of International Law*, in *Unity and Diversity in International Law* 303, 318-320 (Andreas Zimmermann & Rainer Hofmann eds., 2006—book hereinafter: "UDIL"); *see also* Cassese's IL, *supra* note 10 at 37-44.
16. Jonathan Charney, *The Proliferation of International Tribunals: Piecing Together the Puzzle*, 31 (4) New York University Journal of International Law and Policy 697-708 (1999).
17. Karin Oellers-Frahm, *Multiplication of International Courts and Tribunals and Conflicting Jurisdiction: Problems and Possible Solutions*, in *Max Planck Yearbook of United Nations Law Vol. 5* 67-104 (Armin von Bogdandy & Rüdiger Wolfrum eds., 2001).
18. *The Proliferation of International Judicial Bodies: The Outlook for the International Legal Order*—Speech by His Excellency Judge Gilbert Guillaume, President of the International Court of Justice, to the Sixth Committee of the General Assembly of the United Nations, available https://ghum.kuleuven.be/ggs/events/2013/springlectures2013/documents-1/guillaume-proliferation-intnat-judicial.pdf (accessed February 2021) [hereinafter: "Fragmentation Speech"].
19. *Ibid.*
20. Report of the Study Group of the International Law Commission, Finalized by Martti Koskenniemi, *Fragmentation of International Law: Difficulties Arising from the Diversification and Expansion of International Law*, UN Doc A/CN.4/L.682 (April 13, 2006) [hereinafter: "ILC Study"].
21. Report of the Study Group of the International Law Commission, *Fragmentation of International Law: Difficulties Arising from the Diversification and Expansion of International Law*, UN Doc A/CN.4/L.702 (July 18, 2006) [hereinafter: "ILC Report"].
22. For the beginning of the debate *see, inter alia:* Pierre-Marie Dupuy, *L'unité De L'ordre Juridique International* (2002); Kalipso Nikoalidis & Joyce L. Tong, *Diversity or Cacophony? The Continuing Debate over New Sources of International Law*, 25 (4) Michigan Journal of International Law

by President Guillaume's remarks before the UNGA, has lasted for about two decades. While the present book is not the place to revive that debate, this section goes through its main elements with the goal of understanding the pluralist configuration of the legal order of international law.

An interesting aspect of the President's speech is that it focuses only on certain effects of the "fragmentation problem," i.e., the proliferation of international judicial bodies.[23] Interestingly enough, President Guillaume does not seem to be concerned with the actual cause of this proliferation, which is the lack of structural rules for the normative development of international law.[24] From his perspective, the fragmentation of international law was not problematic until it resulted in the development of various "competitors" to the jurisdiction of the ICJ. Consequently, some observers saw in the fragmentation speech a hegemonic attempt to preserve the unity of the jurisdiction of its court rather than of international law as a legal order.[25] This methodological deficit was later solved in the study and the report developed by the ILC.

1.1.1 The ILC Report on Fragmentation: Framing the Problem

The ILC report states that the fragmentation of international law raises both institutional and substantive problems.[26] Moving from the premise that "the issue of institutional competencies is best dealt with by the institutions themselves,"[27] the ILC decides to focus on the substantive problems. The scope of these problems is addressed in detail by the Commission in section B of the ILC study, where it discusses fragmentation as a phenomenon. From the very beginning of its analysis, the ILC acknowledges fragmentation as "an incident of the diversity of the international social world,"[28] thus revealing it as an almost inevitable feature of the globalized society. When understood as normative differentiation, the Commission also reveals fragmentation as an old feature of international law, which is not new to dealing with "tensions or conflicts between legal rules and principles."[29] From this argument, the ILC draws a distinction between "traditional" and "new" fragmentation. The Commission considers as "traditional" fragmentation the division of international law into "more or less autonomous territorial regimes called national legal systems."[30] Evidently, this idea of international law being divided into a variety of sub-systems comes from a "monist"

1349-1375 (2004); Mireille Delmas-Marty, *Le Pluralisme Ordonné* (2006); UDIL, *supra* note 15; Charney, *supra* note 16; Oellers-Frahm, *supra* note 17. For more recent contributions, *see:* Eirik Bjorge & Mads Andenas (eds.), *A Farewell to Fragmentation, Reassertion and Convergence in International Law* (2015) [book hereinafter: "Farewell to Fragmentation"]; Anne Peters, *The Refinement of International Law: From Fragmentation to Regime Interaction and Politicization* (2016); Tamar Megiddo, *Beyond Fragmentation: On International Law's Integrationist Forces*, 44 (1) Yale Journal of International Law 115-146 (2019).

23. As one can understand from its very title. Fragmentation Speech, *supra* note 18.
24. Cassese's IL, *supra* note 10.
25. Mario Prost, *The Concept of Unity in International Law* 202-209 (2012).
26. ILC Report, *supra* note 21 at 4-5.
27. *Ibid.*
28. ILC Study, *supra* note 20 at 15.
29. *Id.*, at 16.
30. *Id.*, at 15.

conception of the relationship between international and municipal law.[31] In essence, this theory regards international and municipal law as part of a universal legal order and emphasizes the supremacy of international law within it.[32] As is well-known, monism does not benefit from universal acceptance and is, in fact, contested by those promoting the dualist approach. Moving from Strupp's *jus positivism*, which stresses the sovereignty of States as founders and masters of international law,[33] the dualist theory argues that international law and municipal law are independent systems, separated from each other and with different spheres of application.[34] Because of this theoretical division, the notion of "traditional" fragmentation adopted by the ILC may very well be put into question. However, by carefully reading through the arguments of the Commission, it is possible to identify a second type of "traditional" fragmentation. This type of fragmentation is generated by the diffused normative development of international law and implicitly acknowledged by the ILC when reporting "the wealth of techniques in the traditional law for dealing with tensions or conflicts between legal rules and principles."[35] Notably, these techniques do not deal with the relations between international and municipal law. Rather, they address substantive conflicts which are exclusively internal to international law, and in particular: relations between special and general law (section C of the ILC Report), prior and subsequent law (section D), laws at different hierarchical levels (section E) and finally relations of law to its "normative environment" (section F).[36] According to the ILC, these techniques *(lex specialis, lex posterior, lex superior)* are perfectly capable of resolving the normative conflicts connected to the substantive application of international law.[37] Coherently with these remarks, it is possible to state that the substantive diversification of international law—as a form of "traditional" fragmentation—is an essential part of international law since time immemorial.

This brings the question of what are the elements of the "new" fragmentation brought up by President Guillaume and discussed by the Commission. In essence, the ILC defines this problem as the "splitting up" of international law into "specialized boxes," claiming autonomy from each other as well as from the general law.[38] Interestingly, at the core of this definition lays the presumed "rebellion" of specialized systems against the general one, as well as their tendency to overcome one another. To be sure, the aspiration to prevail against competing rules (either those of another "specialized box" or general international law) is what animates the development of a specialized system in the first place. In general, this goal is perfectly consistent with the

31. Malcom N. Shaw, *International Law* 98 (8th ed., 2017). *See also*, Elihu Lauterpacht, *International Law: Collected Papers* 151-177 (1957).
32. Alina Kaczorowska-Ireland, *Public International Law* 129 (5th ed., 2015).
33. Karl Strupp, *Les Regles Generales du Droit International de la Paix*, 47 Collected Courses of the Hague Academy of International Law 389 (1934). *See also* Dionisio Anzilotti, *Corso Di Diritto Internationale* 43 (3rd ed., 1928).
34. Kaczorowska-Ireland, *supra* note 32.
35. ILC Study, *supra* note 20 at 15-16.
36. *Id.*, at 2-5.
37. *Id.*, at 207.
38. *Id.*, at 13.

normative development of international law.[39] As we have seen above, the norm-making of international law is in the hands of individual States. The diffused nature of this process naturally translates into an increased differentiation as a legal order. Further, the rule that specific norms prevail over general ones is a well-established principle of international law, as also recognized by the ILC itself.[40] Nonetheless, according to the Commission, issues began when the newly established "specialized boxes"—or "self-contained regimes," as the ILC study also calls them—further developed secondary rules for managing the application of the substantive *lex specialis* created thereby.[41] In other words—and to answer our question—modern fragmentation arose when the internal configuration of international law as a legal order changed from a series of special *rules* to a series of special *systems*.

Within this context, the ILC Report identifies one particular issue posed by modern fragmentation: the development of special rules managing the response against a particular breach of international law.[42] As is well-known, the ILC itself has dealt with this very issue in its Articles on the Responsibility of States for Internationally Wrongful Acts (ARSIWA).[43] Within that work, which is considered to be declaratory of customary international law,[44] the ILC considered the general rules of international law sanctioning the violation of an international obligation. Therefore, the ILC is troubled by the "very large number" of specialized systems claiming precedence of their own sanctioning mechanisms against those identified in the ARSIWA.[45] To name some, the ILC references the European Union's (EU's) prohibition to adopt countermeasures between EU Member States or the various special "non-compliance mechanisms" developed under international environmental law.[46] According to the ILC, this approach risks undermining the unity of international law in at least two instances. First, whenever specialized systems conflict with rules of *jus cogens*, given that they do not tolerate any derogation. Second, whenever the legitimate aspiration of managing internal conflicts in a specialized fashion arises to the point of completely excluding the application of general international law. In the opinion of the Commission, the general

39. *Id.*, at 15.
40. Martin Koskenniemi, *Fragmentation of International Law: Topic (A)—The Function and Scope of the Lex Specialis Rule and the Question of Self-Contained Regimes—An Outline* 4, ILC Study Group on Fragmentation available https://legal.un.org/ilc/sessions/55/pdfs/fragmentation_outline.pdf (accessed February 2021) [hereinafter: "Koskenniemi Study Group"].
41. *Id.*, at 8-10.
42. ILC Report, *supra* note 21 at 5-6.
43. Resolution adopted by the General Assembly at its 56th Session, *Responsibility of States for Internationally Wrongful Acts*, UN Doc A/RES/56/83 (December 21, 2001). The consolidated text as adopted by UNGA Resolution 56/83 and corrected by UND OC A/56/49(Vol. I)/Corr.4 is available https://legal.un.org/ilc/texts/instruments/english/draft_articles/9_6_2001.pdf (accessed February 2021) [hereinafter: "ARSIWA"].
44. Cassese's IL, *supra* note 10 at 246; James Crawford, *Articles on Responsibility of States for Internationally Wrongful Acts* 3 (2012), available https://legal.un.org/avl/pdf/ha/rsiwa/rsiwa_e.pdf (accessed February 2021). Simon Olleson, *Internationally Wrongful Acts in the Domestic Courts: The Contribution of Domestic Courts to the Development of Customary International Law Relating to the Engagement of International Responsibility*, 26 (3) Leiden Journal of International Law 615-642 (2013).
45. Koskenniemi Study Group, *supra* note 40 at 10.
46. *Ibid.*

rules should always be able to intervene to either fill the gaps left by specialized systems or whenever those fail to function properly.[47]

To determine if a system may be deemed to have "failed" to function properly, the ILC Report references primarily factual elements such as persistent non-compliance from some of its parties as well as their withdrawal from the relevant legal instruments.[48] Against this background, in the following three sections of its report, the ILC examines the application of classic interpretation techniques like *lex specialis, lex posterior* and *lex superior* to resolve both traditional and modern fragmentation problems. As anticipated above, the Commission finds that all these techniques are perfectly capable of addressing the challenges posed by fragmentation—*rectius:* diversification—processes.[49]

1.1.2 The ILC Report on Fragmentation: The Role of Systemic Integration

The last section of the ILC Study sets out to discuss the application of a fourth technique which operates "in the background" of the others and can be expressed through the concept of "systemic integration."[50] Notably, the systemic nature of international law is consistently mentioned by the Commission as a foundational feature of its legal order. According to the ILC, the application of any technique for the solution of normative conflicts always requires to "situate" the provision under examination within the broader normative environment of international law.[51] After all, in order to decide whether the rule in question is "special" to the general norms or whether it comes "after" another special one, one needs to consider first which other norms of international law could be applied. Quite logically, this process is essential not only to solve a normative conflict but to actually establish the existence of a conflict in the first place since "rules appear to be compatible or in conflict *as a result of interpretation*" (emphasis added).[52] In support of systemic integration as logical precondition of the interpretation process, the Commission references Article 31 (3) (c) of the Vienna Convention on the Law of Treaties (VCLT).[53] According to this provision, the interpretation of a treaty shall take into account, together with the context, "any relevant rules of international law applicable in the relations between the parties."[54] As anticipated, the ILC identifies this article as the normative source of the principle of systemic integration within the legal order of international law.[55] Although there have been few

47. *Ibid.*
48. ILC Report, *supra* note 21 at 13.
49. ILC Study, *supra* note 20 at 207.
50. For further analysis on the principle, *see* Jean Combacau & Serge Sur, *Droit International Public* 175 (2004) as well as Campbell McLachlan, *The Principle of Systemic Integration and Article 31 (3) (c) of the Vienna Convention*, 54 International and Comparative Law Quarterly 279-320 (2005).
51. ILC Study, *supra* note 20 at 91, 94 and 243.
52. *Id.*, at 207.
53. Vienna Convention on the Law of Treaties, *entered into force* January 27, 1980, 1155 U.N.T.S. 331 [hereinafter: "VCLT"].
54. Article 31 (3) (c) VCLT, *supra* note 53.
55. ILC Report, *supra* note 21 at 13.

references to the article itself in judicial or State practice,[56] the importance of Article 31 (3) (c) VCLT is often overlooked as its practical application is taken for granted. As discussed above, it is only logical to search for other rules within the normative environment of international law in order to understand firstly whether there is a conflict and secondly how to solve it. This automatic, implicit application of the provision confirms the fundamental role that Article 31 (3) (c) VCLT plays within the legal order of international law. Given the universal acceptance of the VCLT and the status of Articles 31-32 as declaratory of customary international law,[57] Article 31 (3) (c) VCLT provides a tool that can be used in virtually any legal dispute which is governed by the rules of international law. In the quest for the determination of international law as a legal order, the existence of a universally accepted rule establishing that each rule needs to be interpreted in relation to the others is of the utmost importance.

To be sure, Article 31 (3) (c) VCLT has also not gone exempt from severe criticisms. In the Gabčikovo-Nagymaros case, one of the judges criticized the lack of clarity and preciseness concerning the substantive and temporal scope of the provision.[58] For this reason, the ILC undertakes a comprehensive analysis of Article 31 (3) (c) VCLT in order to determine its normative meaning and actual implications on the unity of international law as a legal order.[59] Despite the abovementioned criticisms expressed by Judge Weeramantry, the analysis conducted by the Commission reveals that the substantive scope of the provision is sufficiently clear already from its textual interpretation.

As mentioned, the text of Article 31 (3) (c) says that in the interpretation of a treaty, "there shall be taken into account, together with the context [...] any relevant rules of international law applicable in the relations between the parties."[60] Deconstructing this provision into its essential elements, the ILC makes the following considerations. Firstly, concerning the use of the term "rules" of international law, the Commission argues that this reference excludes the application of broader principles or practices which have not raised to the status of rules.[61] Secondly, concerning the meaning of "international law," the ILC argues that such a broader term has been purposely adopted to cover all sources of international law: treaties, customs and general principles.[62] Thirdly, regarding the term "relevant" rules, the Commission interprets it as referring to norms which are governing the same subject matter in

56. ILC Study, *supra* note 20 at 218.
57. For a comprehensive summary of state practice, jurisprudence and doctrinal writings on this matter *see* Mark E. Villiger, *Customary International Law and Treaties: A Study of Their Interactions and Interrelations with Special Consideration of the 1969 Vienna Convention on the Law of Treaties* 334-343 (1985). For more recent practice, *see* Territorial Dispute case (Libyan Arab Jamahiriya/Chad) 1994 I.C.J. Reports 6; Kasikili/Sedudu Island case (Botswana/Namibia) 1999 I.C.J. Reports 1059; LaGrand case (*Germany v. United States of America*) 2001 I.C.J. Reports 501, at para. 99.
58. Case concerning the Gabčikovo-Nagymaros Project (Hungary/Slovakia), (separate opinion of Judge Weeramantry), 1997 I.C.J. Reports 114.
59. ILC Study, *supra* note 20 at 213-244.
60. Article 31 (3) (c) VCLT, *supra* note 53.
61. ILC Study, *supra* note 20 at 214, 233-237.
62. *Id.*, at 215, 233-237.

question.[63] The fourth and final question addressed by the ILC concerns the meaning of the term "parties" within the expression "any relevant rules of international law applicable in the relations between the parties."[64] After a thorough analysis, the ILC concludes that the term must be referring to the *parties in dispute* and not to all the parties of a given treaty.[65] Therefore, reference to a rule from another treaty is permitted, provided that the parties in dispute are also parties to that other treaty. Accordingly, we can conclude that the substantive scope of Article 31 (3) (c) VCLT covers the use of all rules from the broader normative environment of international law, provided that they are relevant to the subject matter and legally binding upon the parties in dispute. This conclusion is further supported by the drafting history of the VCLT, which reveals universal consensus among the drafters on this particular meaning of Article 31 (3) (c) VCLT.[66] However, while this clarifies the substantive scope of the provision, the same cannot be said for the temporal one.[67] During the drafting of Article 31 (3) (c) VCLT, members of the ILC strongly debated concerning the inter-temporality of the provision.

A proposed version of the article even included an explicit reference to rules in force "at the time of the conclusion of the treaty"[68] but did not make it to the actual text. Based on this exclusion, and in light of the ICJ doctrine on the normative evolution of international law, we can infer that Article 31 (3) (c) does not refer *only* to the rules in force at the time of the conclusion of the treaty.[69] As the ILC points out, the temporal element will have to be determined on a case-by-case basis from the fundamental analysis of the parties' intentions.[70] Obviously, the rules in force at the time of the conclusion of a given treaty will always have to be considered, as those were the rules kept in mind by the treaty's drafters. However, some of these rules may very well evolve over time, and thus the parties must have been aware that certain meanings could have changed following the conclusion of the treaty itself.

From the above findings, Article 31 (3) (c) VCLT shows its fundamental role within the broader normative environment of international law. By requiring the interpreters and adjudicators of international law to take into account the systemic relations of a given norm with other applicable and relevant rules of international law, this article both preserves and fosters the unity of international law as a legal order.[71] On the one hand, Article 31 (3) (c) VCLT preserves unity as it ensures that existing connections among rules of international law are duly taken into account in their application. On the other one, the article further fosters unity in clarifying and strengthening the implicit relations among international norms as a result of their systemic interpretation. Without the principle of systemic integration, as enshrined in

63. *Id.*, at 215.
64. *Id.*, at 237-239.
65. *Id.*, at 238.
66. *Id.*, at 216-218.
67. *Ibid.*
68. Sir Humphrey Waldock, *Third Report on the Law of Treaties*, in *1964 Yearbook of the International Law Commission Vol. II* 55, UN Doc A/CN.4/SER.A/1964/ADD.1. (July 7, 1964).
69. ILC Study, *supra* note 20 at 240-243.
70. *Ibid.*
71. ILC Study, *supra* note 20 at 243-244.

Article 31 (c) VCLT, the centrifugal forces generated by the diffused normative development of international law would threaten to tear the legal order apart. If this has not happened, it is mostly thanks to the unifying processes developed in connection with the principle of systemic integration. Ultimately, this is the main argument that makes the ILC confident about a positive solution to the fragmentation problem and the future of international law as a legal order.[72]

1.1.3 The ILC Report on Fragmentation: Key Takeaways

To be sure, the above considerations merely scratch the surface of the complex study conducted by the ILC and finalized by Martin Koskenniemi. However, the purpose of this chapter is neither to synthesize nor to reassess the work done by the Commission. As mentioned, many scholars have engaged in this activity, and after two decades, very little remains to be added to the discussion. It is, however, important to acknowledge that international law managed to remain one legal order, albeit with many differentiations within it.[73] To a certain extent, this success may very well be owed to both the fragmentation speech and the following work of the ILC. In response to a potential threat to the legitimacy of international law as a legal order, the Commission provided the theoretical foundations to organize an adequate response. Building on these elements, the main normative actors of international law—States, multilateral institutions, international judges and scholars—each took their own measures directed at neutralizing the common threat.[74] Notably, this diffused reaction is a further argument confirming the nature of international law as a legal order. Even in the lack of centralized coordination among the various responses to fragmentation, besides perhaps the role played by the ILC report as common reference point, all of them went in the direction of reinforcing the systemic integration of international law.[75] This is because, albeit "competing" with each other to regulate certain "sections" of international relations, all these actors consider themselves as part of the same group. Therefore, when the legitimacy of the collective was threatened, they all reacted to defend it. Ultimately, if the purpose of specialized regimes was to become "self-contained"—as argued by President Guillaume—they would have seized the opportunity offered by the fragmentation debate to emancipate from general international law. If this has not happened, it is likely because the general aspiration of these regimes is not to depart but rather to be part of the legal order of international law.[76]

---

72. *Id.*, at 248-249.
73. *Ibid. See also* Erik Bjorge, *The Convergence of the Methods of Treaty Interpretation: Different Regimes, Different Methods of Interpretation?*, in *Farewell to Fragmentation, supra* note 22 at 533; Rainer Hofmann, *Concluding Remarks*, in *UDIL, supra* note 15 at 491. Peters, *supra* note 22 at 702-704.
74. Bjorge, *supra* note 73. Peters, *supra* note 22 at 680-681.
75. *Ibid.* The same conclusion can also be found in the ILC Study, *supra* note 20 at 218-232.
76. Mads Andenas, *Reassertion and Transformation of International Law*, in *Farewell to Fragmentation, supra* note 22 at 536-539.

1.2 Functional Differentiation

1.2.1 Functional Differentiation: Rationale

As pointed out by the ILC,[77] the "diversity" of international law is not only *substantive* but also *institutional.*[78] This is because certain problems are too complex to be addressed only through substantive diversification.[79] For instance, to properly tackle climate change, it is not sufficient to develop rules governing the emissions of carbon dioxides and then expect all States to comply. The high degree of complexity of international law, together with the often unforeseeable evolution of global circumstances,[80] demands a step-by-step approach that prioritizes issues in terms of foreseeability and essentiality.[81] This regulatory model is called *adaptive governance* and is successfully spreading around as an optimal tool to address modern global problems.[82] Based on the principle of adaptive governance, dedicated institutions are needed to oversee the application of the rules and adjust their application to the evolution of the circumstances. These specialized institutions guide and support States by clarifying meaning, monitoring compliance and solving disputes. Thus, the development of such institutions is not a threat to—but rather a safeguard for—the preservation of international law as a legal order. If global problems were left in the hands of States only, the inevitable failure in addressing them[83] would have perhaps been an argument *against* international law. Nowadays, different actors interact at various levels transcending the territorial and hierarchical dimensions that used to govern decision-making processes.[84] This is to say that multi-level systems created multi-level regulation and not the other way around. The nation-State ceased to be the gravity center around which all other actors orbit long before the development of multi-level regulatory systems.[85] In contemporary times, this phenomenon takes the name of multi-stakeholderism, a term encompassing a new governance model based on the open

---

77. ILC Report, *supra* note 21 at 4-5; ILC Study, *supra* note 20 at 247.
78. For a thorough analysis on international institutional law, *see* Schermers & Blokker *supra* note 12.
79. Cassese's IL, *supra* note 10 at 43.
80. Thomas Dietz et al., *The Struggle to Govern the Commons,* 302 (5652) Science (New Series) 1907-1912 (2003).
81. Dietz, *supra* note 80; Brian Walker et al., *Resilience, Adaptability and Transformability in Social-Ecological Systems,* 9 Ecology and Society 5 (2004).
82. Lisa Sharma-Wallace, *Adaptive Governance Good Practice: Show Me the Evidence!,* 222 Journal of Environmental Management 174-184 (2018).
83. Robert Falkner, *Global Governance: The Rise of Non-state Actors—A Background Report for the SOER 2010 Assessment of Global Megatrend* 4 (2011), available https://www.eea.europa.eu/publications/global-governance/download (last accessed October 2022).
84. Jan Zielonka, *Enlargement and the Finality of European Integration,* in *What Kind of Constitution for What Kind of Polity? Responses to Joschka Fisher* 151-160 (Christian Joerges, Yves Meny & Joseph H.H. Weiler eds., 2000).
85. Anne-Marie Slaughter, *Government Networks: The Heart of the Liberal Democratic Order,* in *Democratic Governance and International Law* 199 (Gregory Fox & Brad Roth eds., 2000). *See also* Gary Marks et al., *Competencies, Cracks and Conflicts: Regional Mobilization in the European Union,* in *Governance in the European Union* 40-41 (Gary Marks, Fritz Schaprf, Philippe Schmitter & Wolfgang Streeck eds., 1996).

dialogue among all major stakeholders to reach effective but also equitable solutions.[86] Due to the lack of dedicated international bodies dealing with space mining, this section looks at existing institutions of international law to identify which of them already play or could likely play a role within the multi-level regulatory system of space law. These findings will then be combined with the analysis conducted in the next chapter to provide the foundational basis for assessing related questions of enforcement.

1.2.2 Functional Differentiation: The Families of International Organizations

The concept of specialized regimes that has been previously discussed in this book may find its institutional counterpart in the term "family of international organizations."[87] This expression has been developed by Bastid with special reference to the United Nations[88] but can be used to describe also certain types of highly structured specialized regimes.

As discussed in the previous section, these specialized regimes can be recognized from the presence of secondary rules governing the update, application and adjudication of its own primary norms. Accordingly, Schermers and Blokker use this expression in their assessment of international institutional law to account for the division of the global institutional society into a myriad of families, of which the UN constitutes the bigger one.[89] Following this logic, the UN "family" includes all its seventeen specialized agencies[90] as well as a series of ten "minors"[91] acting without independent legal personality. Such an analysis is helpful in understanding the extreme complexity that the decentralized system of international law has also reached from an institutional perspective.

At the same time, the concept of "families" does not completely capture the kind of institutional diversification that the ILC was referring to at the beginning of its fragmentation report. Situated in that context, institutional diversification should be rather understood as *functional decentralization.*[92] In essence, this term refers to the distribution of tasks within the global society, which finds its basis in Chapters X and

86. Andras Rasche, *Global Policies and Local Practice: Loose and Tight Couplings in Multi-stakeholder Initiatives*, 22 (4) Business Ethics Quarterly 679-708 (2012). *See also* Julia Roloff, *Learning from Multi-stakeholder Networks: Issue Focused Stakeholder Management*, 82 Journal of Business Ethics 223-250 (2008).
87. Schermers & Blokker, *supra* note 12 at 1085.
88. Suzanne Bastid, *Sue Quelques Problèmes juridiques de coordination dans la famille des Nations Unies*, in *Le Droit International, Unité Et Diversité: Mélanges Offerts à Paul Reuter* 75-101 (Paul Reuter ed., 1981).
89. Schermers & Blokker, *supra* note 12 at 1085-1094.
90. As reported https://ask.un.org/faq/140935 by the UN (accessed February 2021).
91. Schermers & Blokker, *supra* note 12 at 1088-1089.
92. David Mitrany, *A Working Peace System*, in *The European Union: Readings on the Theory and Practice of European Integration* 77-79 (Brent Nelsen & Alexander Stabb eds., 1994). *See also* Cassese's IL, *supra* note 10 at 4; Geib, *supra* note 15 at 326-327.

XI of the UN Charter. According to Article 56 of the UN Charter,[93] "all Members pledge themselves to take joint and separate action in co-operation with the Organization for the achievement of the purposes set forth in Article 55."[94] Pursuant to this provision, Articles 57-60 address the development of "specialized agencies" as well as their relationship and coordination with the UN. These rather crucial activities are entrusted to the primary responsibility of the General Assembly,[95] which in turn relies on the support of the Economic and Social Council (ECOSOC).[96] Based on the UN Charter, *functional decentralization* indicates the development of separate and independent bodies tasked to administrate the application and adjudication of specialized regimes.[97] One example may help to clarify the difference between the vantage point of functional decentralization compared to the one of "institutional families." Using the latter concept, Schermers and Blokker consider the World Health Organization (WHO) as a part of the UN family, being one of its most important specialized agencies.[98] At the same time, according to the ICJ, the UN family is based on a clear division of roles.[99] In one of its two advisory opinions on the *Legality of the Use by a State of Nuclear Weapons in Armed Conflict* of 1996,[100] the Court rejected the request received from the WHO on the grounds that the responsibilities of the WHO "are necessarily restricted to the sphere of public 'health' and cannot encroach on the responsibilities of other parts of the United Nations system."[101] Such a rigid interpretation of functional decentralization is regrettable because of its implications on the phenomenon of fragmentation. One could argue that by taking a rather formalistic approach toward the division of competencies already within the UN family, the Court pushed specialized bodies more in the direction of institutional isolation rather than systemic integration. By holding that the WHO should not be concerned with "questions concerning the use of force, the regulation of armaments and disarmaments"[102] because those are "within the competence of the United Nations and lie outside that of the specialized agencies,"[103] the ICJ suggested that every specialized regime is like a silo.[104] To be sure, this is not to deny that different institutions have different competencies and responsibilities under contemporary international law. Naturally, this is a fundamental feature of any modern legal order, allowing for its ability to adequately address and govern the complexity of the global society. Understood in this sense, competencies' division serves the purpose

93. Charter of the United Nations, *entered into force* October 24, 1945, 1 UNTS 16 [hereinafter: "UN Charter"].
94. Which is dedicated to the creation of conditions of stability and well-being that are necessary for peaceful and friendly relations among nations. *Id.*, at Article 55.
95. Article 60 UN Charter, *supra* note 93.
96. Which is disciplined by Articles 61-72 UN Charter, *supra* note 93.
97. Cassese's IL, *supra* note 10 at 40.
98. Schermers & Blokker, *supra* note 12 at 1086-1087.
99. *Ibid.*
100. Legality of the Use by a State of Nuclear Weapons in Armed Conflict, Advisory Opinion requested by the WHO, (Advisory Opinion, July 8, 1996) 1996 ICJ Report 66-85.
101. *Id.*, at 81, para. 26.
102. *Ibid.*
103. *Ibid.*
104. This message is even the more striking when compared to the fragmentation speech delivered by the President of the very same Court no more than just five years later.

of incrementing efficiency and effectiveness by allocating the *primary* responsibility for dealing with a certain matter to the institution which is sought to be as best qualified or legitimized for it. Nevertheless, this *functional* division of competence should never be brought to the point of creating silos within the legal order itself. On the contrary, institutions should be encouraged and empowered to interact dynamically with each other in the exercise of their functions. Based on these premises, the next section discusses how international law has managed to remain a united legal order through various processes of systemic integration.

1.3 Systemic Integration

1.3.1 Upholding Systemic Integration: Techniques for Managing the Ordered Pluralism of International Law

In a thoughtful analysis of the refinement of international law, Peters addresses a number of "techniques" adopted to "channel fragmentation" for the purpose of enhancing the effectiveness and legitimacy of international law.[105] Moving from the results of that analysis, this section presents the available "toolbox" for managing the ordered pluralism of international law. Further elaborating on Peters' findings, the section differentiates between three types of instruments: binary criteria, integration mechanisms and political discourses. The first type includes both traditional and modern interpretation practices for normative conflict resolution.[106] The theoretical premise for the use of these tools comes from the establishment of a normative conflict, which then gets resolved through the use of binary criteria that identifies which norm should be applied in the case at hand.[107] Taking a step forward, the second type of instrument includes various integration mechanisms developed and used by lawmakers, law appliers and law adjudicators.[108] The theoretical premise for the use of these tools comes from the systemic nature of international law,[109] which gets concretized through the use of harmonization and integration techniques. Finally, the third type of instrument includes political discourses publicly contesting a certain regime before the global community.[110]

The theoretical premise for the use of this technique comes from a legitimacy argument according to which certain foundational conflicts should only be resolved through the global political discourse.[111] Naturally, each of these three types presents various diversifications and can be further divided into different sub-categories. The purpose of this section is to give an overview of these instruments by describing their

105. Peters, *supra* note 22 at 682-702.
106. As identified in the ILC Study, *supra* note 20 at 15-16. *See also* Cassese's IL, *supra* note 10 at 218-241.
107. ILC Study, *supra* note 20 at 17-25. Peters, *supra* note 22 at 682-685.
108. ILC Study, *supra* note 20 at 25-28. Peters, *supra* note 22 at 685-700; Cassese's IL, *supra* note 10 at 75.
109. ILC Report, *supra* note 21 at 6. Bjorge, *supra* note 73.
110. Peters, *supra* note 22 at 700-701.
111. ILC Study, *supra* note 20 at 245.

functioning and purpose as well as their systemic collocation within the ordered pluralism of international law.

1.3.2 *Upholding Systemic Integration Through Binary Criteria*

Binary criteria solve normative conflicts by determining which rule should apply within a set of competing norms. From the vantage point of the temporal evolution of international law, this category can be further divided into traditional and modern tools. Traditional tools are those enshrined in the customary conflict rules codified in the VCLT: *lex specialis, lex posterior* and *lex superior.*[112] Examples of "modern" binary tools can be found in Peters' analysis and include the "margin of appreciation" and "mutual recognition" techniques,[113] respectively developed by the jurisprudence of the European Court on Human Rights (ECtHR) and the Court of Justice of the European Union (CJEU).

i *Traditional Binary Criteria*

Traditional binary tools have been used by the western legal community since Roman times and, as such, are not specifically related to fragmentation. Nevertheless, the principles of *lex specialis, lex posterior* and *lex superior* still represent a valid defense against the "destructive" forces of fragmentation.[114] The first two principles resolve normative conflicts by applying the rule which appears to be vested with a (theoretically) higher potential of effectiveness. The *lex specialis* rule is based on the assumption that the norm which has been purposely devised for a specific situation is also the best equipped to regulate it.[115] Likewise, under the *lex posterior* criteria, the rule which has been enacted more recently should incorporate the experience developed in the meantime, and thus being more apt to regulate the case at hand.[116] On a different line of reasoning, the *lex superior* clause relies on the vertical hierarchy among the norms in question.[117] When applying this technique, considerations of effectiveness or efficiency are trumped by the legitimacy argument that certain rules are simply more important than others.[118] Needless to say, all three criteria are exposed to a series of inherent flaws limiting their actual application in practice. For instance, and relevant to our current analysis of the relationships between special regimes, a classic failure of the *lex specialis* rule arises when the many facets of a dispute determine a conflict between different rules equally constituting *lex specialis.*[119] In this case, the application of the principle is impeded by the difficulties in identifying which norm is the actual *lex*

112. *Id.*, at 15-16.
113. Although she does not explicitly list them as binary. Peters, *supra* note 22 at 685-687.
114. ILC Study, *supra* note 20 at 15-16.
115. Oriol Casanovas, *Unity and Pluralism in Public International Law* 246 (2001). For a comprehensive analysis on *lex specialis, see* Koskenniemi Study Group, *supra* note 40.
116. ILC Report, *supra* note 21 at 17-19.
117. *Id.*, at 20-25.
118. ILC Study, *supra* note 20 at 167.
119. *Id.*, at 62-64.

specialis compared to the others. Traditionally, at this point, the *lex posterior* comes into play by determining the application of the more recent rule. However, the use of the temporal criteria in international law is undermined by the fact that oftentimes the *lex posterior* has been developed by different parties.[120] In similar instances, where both the previous criteria have failed, a decisive aid could be offered by the *lex superior* by means of a hierarchical assessment. However, in the vast majority of normative conflicts, it is simply not possible to legally establish a hierarchical connection between the rules at hand.[121] This is because, in the decentralized legal order of international law, only a limited group of norms enjoy a higher status compared to the others.[122] Those rules however come into play very rarely,[123] and courts like the ICJ have been quite reluctant in resorting to their application.[124] From the above, we can conclude that despite the continuing relevance of the traditional criteria of *lex specialis, lex posterior* and *lex superior*, there is a significant number of instances where their application is either not possible or leads to unsatisfactory results.

ii *Modern Binary Criteria*

"Modern" binary criteria—the margin of appreciation and the principle of mutual recognition—have been developed in contemporary times by the jurisprudence of two influential European courts, the ECtHR and the CJEU. Because of their recent development, these two criteria are here marked as modern to distinguish them from the three ones examined above. The common element among all these criteria is that they all lead to binary conclusions, i.e., to the application of one rule at the expense of another. However, the rationale justifying the application of modern criteria is fundamentally different, as is their historical development. These criteria, in fact, originated at a regional level and, in time, have been "endorsed" by other systems to the point of acquiring the status of general rules for solving normative conflicts.[125] To begin with, the margin of appreciation has been developed by the ECtHR for scrutinizing the conformity of national measures adopted by States with their obligations under the European Convention for the Protection of Human Rights and Fundamental Freedoms (ECHR).[126] In essence, this tool refers back the scrutiny to the (limited) discretion of national courts. Within the ECHR framework, the rationale for such a

120. *Id.*, at 61-62, 121-122.
121. Ignaz Seidl-Hohenveldern, *Hierarchy of Treaties*, in *Essays on the Law of Treaties: A Collection of Essays in Honour of Bert Vierdag* 15-16 (Jan Klabbers & René Lefeber eds., 1998). *See also* Michael Akehurst, *The Hierarchy of Sources of International Law,* 47 British Yearbook of International Law 273-285 (1974-1975).
122. The ILC identifies three groups of "higher sources": the UN Charter, *jus cogens* and obligations erga omnes. ILC Study, *supra* note 20 at 166-205.
123. For an empirical analysis, *see* Erika De Wet & Jure Vidmar (eds.), *Hierarchy in International Law: The Place of Human Rights* (2012).
124. *Id.*, at 191.
125. Susanne K. Schmidt, *Mutual Recognition as a New Mode of Governance,* 14 (5) Journal of European Public Policy 667-681 (2007). *See also* Jean L. Cohen, *Globalization and Sovereignty: Rethinking Legality, Legitimacy, and Constitutionalism* 73 (2012).
126. Peters, *supra* note 22 at 685.

decision came from a combination of the principles of democracy and subsidiarity.[127] For the ECtHR, national courts are "better placed to evaluate local needs and conditions"[128] because of their direct democratic legitimacy and their proximity to the facts and interests at hand. *Mutatis mutandis,* this tool can be used to resolve situations of conflict between specialized regimes provided with dedicated law adjudicators. In such a scenario, the margin of appreciation can be used to leave room for the intervention of the "other" court whenever the latter's regime is considered to be more proximate to the case at hand. Needless to say, the margin of appreciation can only be used whenever there is a certain level of trust between the involved courts.[129] The decision to "renounce" ruling on the topic is primarily based on the confidence that the other court will self-restrain its own assessment not to trespass the given "margin." Within the ECHR framework, national courts are incentivized to behave properly because of the higher hierarchical position of the ECtHR.[130] However, a similar incentive would lack in the relations between international courts since they all operate from an equal foot.[131] Therefore, the decision to rely on the margin of appreciation will be based on strategic considerations and anticipations about what will the other court do if deferred the decision on the given issue.

The second criterion—the principle of mutual recognition—is also based on a minimum level of trust.[132] However, differently than the margin of appreciation, for mutual recognition to operate, trust needs to be placed not in another law adjudicator but rather in a different lawmaker.[133] This is because while the margin of appreciation operates in the relationship between courts, mutual recognition operates in the relationship between regimes. As is well-known, through this principle, the CJEU has fostered the development of the single market of the EU by pushing Member States to remove or harmonize internal barriers limiting the circulation of goods.[134] From the CJEU's jurisprudence, it is possible to define mutual recognition as a functional equivalence of norms originating from different sources. For example, in the famous *Cassis de Dijon* judgment, the CJEU held that the German rules affecting the selling of alcoholic beverages were not applicable to the beverages imported from another EU Member State, which in this case was France.[135] Conversely, the German authorities

127. *Ibid.*
128. Case of *Hatton and Others v. The United Kingdom* (Application no. 36022/97), (Judgment, July 8, 2003), 2003-VIII ECtHR Report 216, para. 97.
129. Peters, *supra* note 22 at 685.
130. Manifested in its quasi-supranational sanctioning powers. For a comprehensive analysis on this matter, *see* Giorgio Repetto (ed.), *The Constitutional Relevance of the ECHR in Domestic and European Law: An Italian Perspective* (2013).
131. On the relationship among international courts, *see* Philippa Webb, *International Judicial Integration and Fragmentation* (2013).
132. Schmidt, *supra* note 125; Peters, *supra* note 22 at 686-687.
133. Joined Cases C-404/15 and C-659/15 PPU (reference for a preliminary ruling), (judgment, April 5, 2016), CJEU Digital Reports ECLI:EU:C:2016:198, p. 13, para. 77.
134. Schmidt, *supra* note 125.
135. Case 120/78 (reference for a preliminary ruling), (judgment, February 20, 1979), 1979 E.C.R. 649-665.

had to presume that since the *cassis de Dijon* was legally distributed in France, it could have also been commercialized in Germany.[136]

In other words, mutual recognition determines the quasi-automatic application of a "foreign" rule by presuming its compatibility with those of the system at hand. At a closer look, this quasi-automatic application implies that mutual recognition solves potential normative conflicts at the expense of internal rules. Precisely for this reason, the application of this principle is only *quasi-automatic*, meaning that the "receiving" system can refuse to recognize the foreign rule provided that certain conditions are met.[137]

To stick with examples taken from the EU integration regime, in the *Tobacco* case, the CJEU upheld the Germans authorities' prohibition of foreign advertisements promoting cigarettes on the grounds that it was justified by the protection of public health.[138]

The *Tobacco* example shows that mutual recognition can solve only certain types of normative conflicts. When the level of contrast with the internal system is too high, the principle ceases to function. The rationale for this limitation is that mutual recognition is based on a relatively explicit set of shared values that all regimes are committed to respecting.[139] As long as those values are respected, then the receiving regime cannot refuse the application of the foreign rule. To ensure respect for this condition, receiving authorities retain the right to actively verify said compliance with the shared values in the case at hand. For the purposes of our analysis, this means that mutual recognition can only be used among specialized regimes sharing a similar set of values. A suitable example can be found in the relations between the EU and the ECHR. In the *Bosphorus* case,[140] the ECtHR ruled that obligations under EU law were, *in principle,* considered to be compatible with the ECHR in light of a fundamental equivalence between the two systems. At the same time, the Court specified that "any such finding of equivalence could not be final" and would remain "susceptible to review" by the Court itself.[141]Accordingly, whenever two regimes share similar values, the strategic features of mutual recognition (presumption of equivalence but prerogative to double check) would solve normative conflicts with a minimum dispersion of energies.[142] At the same time, the majority of specialized regimes are not willing to

136. *Id.*, at 664, para. 14.
137. Peters, *supra* note 22 at 686.
138. Case C-376/98 (reference for a preliminary ruling), (judgment, October 5, 2000), 2000 E.C.R. 8498-8534.
139. Peters, *supra* note 22 at 687.
140. Case of *Bosphorus Hava Yollari Turizm Ve Ticaret Anonim Şirketi v. Ireland,* (Application no. 45036/98), (Judgment, June 30, 2005), 2005-VI E.Ct. H.R. 107-171.
141. *Id.*, at 158, para. 155.
142. On the usefulness of mutual recognition as governance tool, *see also* Kalypso Nicolaidis & Gregory Shaffer, *Transnational Mutual Recognition Regimes: Governance Without Global Government,* 68 (3-4) Law and Contemporary Problems 263-317 (2005).

accept the significant renunciation of control implied in the quasi-automatic application of foreign rules.[143] Thus, mutual recognition remains a powerful but also not very popular technique of normative conflict resolution.[144]

1.3.3 Upholding Systemic Integration Through Integration Mechanisms

Beyond traditional and modern binary tools for normative conflict resolution lays the realm of integration mechanisms. This second type of instrument includes a plethora of techniques involving lawmakers, law appliers and law adjudicators.[145] The *red thread* shared by all these mechanisms is a fundamental theoretical premise: the systemic nature of international law as a legal order.[146] Moving from this starting point, these tools attempt to avoid the formation of normative conflicts by fostering—each in its own way—integration among the regimes at hand. In this author's view, from a methodological standpoint, these techniques of regime integration can be differentiated through the use of subjective and objective criteria. Applying the first one, this section classifies integration tools into three groups based on the main entity involved: lawmakers, law appliers and law adjudicators. Applying the second one, the analysis further distinguishes between passive and active tools as appropriate within each group.

i Integration Tools Primarily Involving Lawmakers

Let's begin with integration tools primarily involving lawmakers. In essence, these instruments attempt to reconcile a certain regime with either the broader normative environment of international law or another special regime, depending on the circumstances. Because the primary role is played by lawmakers, these tools generally work in a passive fashion. This expression is used to explain that these techniques "passively" integrate a regime without actively modifying its rules. One example might help to clarify. According to Article 2 (3) of the Cartagena Protocol,[147] "nothing in this Protocol shall affect in any way the sovereignty of States over their territorial sea established in accordance with international law."[148] These types of provisions are called *notwithstanding clauses*[149] and are a perfect example of passive regime integration established by a lawmaker. In essence, a provision like Article 2 (3) of the Cartagena Protocol removes any normative conflict between the rules of the Protocol and the sovereignty of States over their territorial sea insofar as it establishes that the

143. Schmidt, *supra* note 125 at 672.
144. Jacques Pelkmans, *Mutual Recognition in Goods: On Promises and Disillusions*, 14 (5) Journal of European Public Policy 699-716 (2007).
145. ILC Study, *supra* note 20 at 25-28. Peters, *supra* note 22 at 685-700; Cassese's IL, *supra* note 10 at 75.
146. ILC Report, *supra* note 21 at 6. Bjorge, *supra* note 73.
147. Cartagena Protocol on Biosafety to the Convention on Biological Diversity, January 29, 2000, 2226 U.N.T.S. 208 [hereinafter: "Cartagena Protocol"].
148. *Ibid.*
149. Peters, *supra* note 22 at 688.

two of them should be read in harmony. To be sure, notwithstanding clauses may ultimately result in setting aside the internal rules, and for this reason, they may look like a binary tool rather than an integration one. However, categorizing them as binary would not render justice to the correct application of such clauses. Their goal, in fact, is to guide the application of internal rules in order to prevent normative conflicts with the rules of another regime. Accordingly, notwithstanding clauses should be considered as a manifestation of the intent of the parties to guide the interpreter toward a certain interpretation that is in harmony with another relevant rule from a foreign regime.

Another integration tool frequently adopted by lawmakers consists in making explicit *cross-references* to a foreign regime.[150] Differently than notwithstanding clauses, cross-references determine the application *tout court* of selected rules from either the broader normative environment or another special regime. This technique is famously used in private international law under the name of renvoi to determine the applicability of foreign law within domestic judicial proceedings.[151] It should be noted that the practical impact of the regime's cross-references will always depend on how the renvoi is concretely expressed. A pertinent example that may help to clarify is Article III OST,[152] which determines the applicability of international law to the exploration and use of outer space. As will be further discussed in the next section,[153]Article III OST works in two ways. First, the provision limits the exercise of the freedom to explore and use outer space in order to prevent conflicts with applicable rules of international law.[154] In this way, the special regime of international space law is integrated with the broader normative environment of international law.[155] Second, Article III OST, in connection with Article I OST,[156] provides for the applicability of international law as a gap filler of space law[157] to govern situations which are not specifically addressed thereby.[158]

At the end of our analysis, on integration techniques primarily involving lawmakers, stand *balancing clauses.*[159] In essence, these clauses provide a combination of the two tools examined above. They still result in the application of foreign rules, but they do so by explicitly demanding that the concerned party makes reasonable efforts

150. *Id.*, at 689-690.
151. For a comprehensive analysis on the use of renvoi in private international law, *see* Jean Georges Sauveplanne, *Renvoi*, in *International Encyclopedia of Comparative Law: Volume 3—Private International Law* 3-37 (Kurt Lipstein chief ed., 1990).
152. Treaty on Principles Governing the Activities of States in the Exploration and Use of Outer Space, Including the Moon and Other Celestial Bodies, *entered into force* October 10, 1967, 18 U.S.T. 2410, 610 U.N.T.S. 205 [hereinafter: "OST"].
153. To which the reader is *renvoyé* for a thorough assessment of Article III OST.
154. "States Parties to the Treaty shall carry on activities in the exploration and use of outer space *in accordance* with international law, including the Charter of the United Nations." Article III OST, *supra* note 152.
155. As to which, *see* section 2.1 later in this chapter.
156. According to which "outer space [...] shall be free for exploration and use by all States [...] in accordance with international law." Article I OST, *supra* note 152.
157. For the role of international law as gap filler of specialized regimes, *see* Koskenniemi Study Group, *supra* note 40 at 8-10.
158. As to which, *see* section 2.1 later in this chapter.
159. Peters, *supra* note 22 at 688-689.

to reduce as much as possible any inconsistency with the internal ones. An example of balancing clauses is Article 104 of the North American Free Trade Agreement (NAFTA),[160] which allows for the prioritization of certain environmental agreements like the Montreal Protocol,[161] "provided that where a Party has a choice among equally effective and reasonably available means of complying with such obligations, the Party chooses the alternative that is the least inconsistent with the other provisions of this Agreement."[162] This safeguard serves the purpose of promoting the cumulative application of relevant rules by reducing the scope for a binary choice between them. Considered altogether, passive integration tools primarily involving lawmakers through the use of *notwithstanding clauses,* renvoi and *balancing clauses* appear as adequately promoting the systemic integration of international law. Above all, these clauses confirm not only that international lawmakers are aware of the risks posed by decentralized normative development but also that they intend to mitigate these risks in support of the unity of the legal order.[163]

ii *Integration Tools Primarily Involving Law Appliers*

A second group of integration tools includes those techniques primarily involving law appliers. In contrast with the ones belonging to the previous group, these instruments could be defined as *active* insofar as they foster integration through dynamic institutional dialogue or, as Crawford & Nevill call it, through *regime interaction.*[164] In essence, clauses of regime interaction determine a delegation of integration powers from lawmakers to law appliers. A lawmaker would choose this technique whenever it wants to go beyond the cumulative application determined by passive integration tools. Regime interaction ensures a higher degree of systemic integration by linking the dynamic evolution of the systems at hand. For instance, Article 3 (5) of the Agreement on the Application of Sanitary and Phytosanitary Measures[165] provides that its Committee on Sanitary and Phytosanitary Measures "shall develop a procedure to monitor the process of international harmonization and coordinate efforts in this regard with the relevant international organizations."[166] Young points out that this technique may be affected by a legitimacy deficit insofar as it could lead to the evolution of international law beyond the consent of its legitimate lawmakers (States).[167] To be

160. The North American Free Trade Agreement, *entered into force* January 1, 1994, 32 I.L.M. 289 (1993) [hereinafter: "NAFTA"].
161. Montreal Protocol on Substances that Deplete the Ozone Layer, *entered into force* January 1, 1989, 1522 U.N.T.S. 3 (1987).
162. Article 104 NAFTA, *supra* note 160.
163. Bjorge, *supra* note 73.
164. James Crawford & Penelope Nevill, *Relations Between International Courts and Tribunals: The "Regime Problem,"* in *Regime Interaction in International Law: Facing Fragmentation* 235 (Margaret A. Young ed., 2012) [hereinafter: "Regime Interaction"].
165. Agreement on the Application of Sanitary and Phytosanitary Measures, *entered into force* January 1, 1995, 1867 U.N.T.S. 493 [hereinafter: "SPS Agreement"].
166. *Id.*, at Article 3.
167. Margaret A. Young, *Trading Fish, Saving Fish: The Interaction Between Regimes in International Law* 255-256 (2011).

sure, handing over the integration process to law appliers determines the establishment of a classic *principal-agent* relationship.[168] Accordingly, there is a risk that the agent—in this case, the law applier(s)—may escape the control of its principal (the lawmaker) by pushing forward a degree or a type of integration that was not originally intended by the latter.[169] At the same time, a certain degree of autonomy is inherent to the establishment of any principal-agent relationship[170] because there would be no point in delegating a function to another entity if the latter is not provided with a minimum margin of *maneuver* to exercise it.[171] Conversely, the level of autonomy granted to law appliers should never reach the point of reshaping the normative system or frustrating its purposes. To control these risks, Young underlines the importance of inclusiveness and transparency as fundamental principles guiding the processes of regime interaction.[172] Since it is the responsibility of lawmakers to provide these assurances when empowering law appliers for integration purposes,[173] their absence may be interpreted as a manifestation of the intent to leave ample discretion to them. In sophisticated regimes like the EU, this lack of limits may even render invalid the delegation in the first place, as enshrined in the *Meroni* doctrine[174] developed by the CJEU.[175] As such, regime interaction can be a powerful and useful tool of integration, provided that it is kept within predetermined boundaries preventing law appliers from abusing it at the expense of the system's legitimacy.

iii Integration Tools Primarily Involving Law Adjudicators

The last group of integration tools includes those envisioning a primary role for law adjudicators like courts and tribunals. Because of the variety of techniques at the disposal of judges, this group includes both passive and active mechanisms. To begin

168. The principal-agent relationship is a concept that describes the institutional dynamics generated by delegation of power. Michael C. Jensen & William H. Meckling, *Theory of the Firm: Managerial Behavior, Agency Costs and Ownership Structure*, 3 (4) Journal of Financial Economics 305-360 (1976). In political science, the concept has been discussed by various authors either in the context of international relations, for which *see* Andrew Moravcsik, *Liberal Intergovernmentalism and Integration: A Rejoinder*, 33 (4) Journal of Common Market Studies 611-628 (1995)—or within the context of European Integration, for which *see* Geoffrey Garret and Barry Weingast, *Ideas, Interests, and Institutions: Constructing the EC's Internal Market*, in *Ideas and Foreign Policy* 173-206 (Judith Goldstein & Robert Keohane eds., 1993).
169. A classic example of an agent escaping control and promoting integration beyond the intent of its former principal is the Court of Justice of the European Union. For an excellent analysis on this topic *see* Karen J. Alter, *Who Are the "Masters of the Treaty"?: European Governments and the European Court of Justice*, 52 (1) International Organization 121-147 (1998).
170. Paul Pierson, *The Path to European Integration: A Historical Institutionalist Perspective*, 29 (2) Comparative Political Studies 123-163 (1996); Mark Pollack, *Delegation, Agency, and Agenda Setting in the EC*, 51 (1) International Organization 99-134 (1997).
171. Jensen & Meckling, *supra* note 168.
172. Young, *supra* note 167 at 279-280.
173. Alter, *supra* note 169.
174. Case 9/56 (annulment application), (Judgment, June 13, 1958), 1957-1958 E.C.R. 135-155 (English special edition).
175. For a comprehensive analysis on the EU institutionalization of the principal-agent problem, *see* Paul Craig, *EU Administrative Law* 151-198 (3rd ed., 2018).

with the first sub-group, Peters[176] underlines the importance of a classic ICJ interpretation maxim called *presumption of law-abiding intentions.*[177] Essentially, this maxim says that a legal text should be interpreted as intended to produce effects in accordance with—and not in violation of—existing applicable laws. The justification for such a maxim derives from the existence of a shared understanding of the systemic nature of international law among global actors.[178] Without this shared understanding, it would not be legitimate to presume that a legal document has been developed by its drafters with the intention of fitting within its broader normative environment. Besides the ICJ, the ECtHR has often made use of this maxim too. In the *Al-Dulimi* case,[179] the Grand Chamber of the Court used it to presume law-abiding intentions behind the decisions of the United Nations Security Council (UNSC). Through the use of this maxim, the ECtHR managed to harmonize certain UNSC resolutions with the human rights obligations established by the Convention. In the words of the Court, whenever the resolutions did not explicitly exclude or limit respect for human rights, "the Court must always presume that [its] measures are [meant to be] compatible with the Convention."[180] Interestingly, in the *Srebrenica* case,[181] the ECtHR used the same maxim for reaching the opposite result, setting aside the protection offered by the Convention. In this case, the Court presumed that States Parties to the ECHR did not intend to protect human rights at the expense of long-standing obligations of international law, such as—in that particular case—the duty to grant immunity to the United Nations.[182] Notably, in both cases, the Court could have resolved the case by adopting a hierarchical, binary approach in accordance or contrast with the supremacy clause laid down in Article 103 of the UN Charter. The Court chose the path of law-abiding intentions because it led to the same result but in a less controversial way. Specifically, through the use of this maxim, the ECtHR avoided the creation of a formal conflict with the UN Charter and took positive steps toward the harmonization of the Convention's regime with the broader normative environment of international law. Notwithstanding these positive aspects, Peters criticizes the use of this maxim by arguing that this tool is more similar to legal fiction.[183] Expanding on this criticism, one may argue that if a lawmaker wanted to avoid conflicts with a given regime, it would have said so. According to an old Roman adage, *ubi lex voluit, dixit; ubi noluit, tacuit—where the law wanted to achieve something, it said so; where it did not want it, it remained silent.* Nevertheless, this line of interpretation would reach the paradoxical result that whenever a treaty would not explicitly declare compatibility with other general or

176. Peters, *supra* note 22 at 690.
177. Right of Passage over Indian Territory (*Portugal v. India*), (Preliminary Objections, November 26, 1957) 1957 ICJ Rep. 125, 142.
178. Peters, *supra* note 22 at 691.
179. *Al-Dulimi and Montana Management Inc v. Switzerland,* (Application no. 5809/08) (Judgment of the Grand Chamber, June 21, 2016), available https://hudoc.echr.coe.int/eng#{%22itemid%22:[%22001-164515%22]} (accessed February 2021).
180. *Id.*, at para. 140.
181. *Stitching Mothers of Srebrenica and others v. The Netherlands,* (Application no. 65542/12), (Decision on Admissibility, June 11, 2013) 2013 ECHR 739.
182. *Id.*, at para. 139.
183. Peters, *supra* note 22 at 692.

special rules, then we must presume that the treaty intended to disregard them. Because it would be absurd to assume that every treaty is conceived in open opposition to the others, we can conclude that the presumption of law-abiding intentions builds upon an implicit intent of all lawmakers.

A second technique is *systemic interpretation* under Article 31 (3) (c) VCLT. Pursuant to this provision, the interpretation of a treaty shall take into account "any relevant rules of international law applicable in the relations between the parties."[184] Since this tool has already been addressed within section 1.1, it won't be discussed again here. For the purpose of the present analysis, it is sufficient to recall the famous expression developed by ICJ Judge Hanquin Shue, according to whom Article 31 (3) (c) VCLT is like a "master key to the house of international law."[185] The fundamental importance of this provision is reinforced every time a court makes a reference to a "foreign" rule of international law, being it from the "general" part or another specialized regime. Accordingly, without Article 31 (3) (c) VCLT, international law would be deprived of its very own normative justification as a unified legal order.[186]

Among the active tools of integration, we find the concept of *judicial dialogue*, a practice that sees international courts and tribunals taking into particular account "foreign" case law in the development of their own.[187] Similar to the use of Article 31 (3) (c) VCLT, the practice of judicial dialogue is based on a fundamental belief in the systemic nature of international law.[188] By taking into consideration each other's case law, international courts and tribunals acknowledge not only the existence of different regimes but, most notably, that these regimes are connected with each other. In doing so, these courts provide a significant contribution both to the development of international law and the preservation of its unity.[189] As Teubner puts it, through the practice of judicial dialogue, international courts transcend their individual perspective to contribute to the creation of the *ordre public transnational.*[190] Evidently, this operation depends on the existence of foundational shared values that make the various actors and regimes feel part of the same order.[191] In modern international law, these values have been codified in critical documents like the UN Charter or the VCLT, which are universally shared by all States. Although in a more indirect and uncertain way, such values are also expressed in those rules binding the international community as a whole: *jus cogens, customary international law* and *general principles of international*

184. Article 31 (3) (c) VCLT, *supra* note 53.
185. ILC Study, *supra* note 20 at 211.
186. As to which, *see* section 2.1 later in this chapter.
187. Antonios Tzanakopoulos, *Judicial Dialogue in Multi-level Governance: The Impact of the Solange Argument*, in *The Practice of International and National Courts and the (De)Fragmentation of International Law* 188-189 (Ole Kristian ed., 2014; book hereinafter: "The Practice of Courts").
188. For which *see* ILC Study, *supra* note 20 at 25-28; Peters, *supra* note 22 at 685-700; Cassese's IL, *supra* note 10 at 75.
189. William W. Burke-White, *International Legal Pluralism*, 25 Michigan Journal of International Law 963, 973 (2004).
190. Gunther Teubner, *Constitutional Fragments: Societal Constitutionalism in Globalization* 160-161 (2012).
191. On this shared sense of belonging to the legal order of international law, *see* Bjorge, *supra* note 73.

law.[192] By providing a common starting point, the foundational values of international law allow international courts and tribunals to look further than their own regime and do their part for the preservation of international law as a legal order. Ultimately, this "internalization of an outside perspective"[193] is perhaps the best safeguard against the potential dangers of fragmentation.[194] For these reasons, and despite what the name may suggest, judicial dialogue does not necessarily imply active communication among courts, although that would be, of course, the most prominent example of this practice. For instance, the International Criminal Tribunal for the former Yugoslavia used to rely on the ECtHR's case law for the definition of torture[195] but never "talked" to the ECtHR in its judgments. In the field of trade and investment law, the dispute settlement bodies of the World Trade Organization (WTO) heavily influence[196] and are also influenced[197] by the case law of parallel courts and tribunals, but they never engaged in actual "dialogues" with each other. Per its part, active judicial dialogue is scarcer because it requires an institutional framework legitimizing the discussion between the courts.[198] Therefore, it should not come as a surprise that most cases of active international judicial dialogue involve the CJEU. Given the institutional links provided by the preliminary ruling system foreseen in the EU treaties, the CJEU regularly "dialogues" with national courts from the EU Member States.[199] Beyond that institutional framework, the CJEU is much more careful in "calling out" other courts, despite making clear references to their regimes or jurisprudence, as exemplified, for instance, by its (in)famous Opinion 2/13.[200] To be sure, the lack of an institutional framework is one of the two fundamental problems traditionally associated with judicial dialogue. In the absence of an international preliminary ruling or advisory system,[201] this practice is entirely left in the hands of the judiciary. While this deficiency has not been a major problem so far,[202] it certainly represents a serious

192. ILC Study, *supra* note 20 at 166-205.
193. Peters, *supra* note 22 at 696.
194. Burke-White, *supra* note 189.
195. Until it then developed a more narrowed version for the purposes of criminal prosecution. *Prosecutor v. Krnojelac,* (Case No. IT-97-25-T), (Trial Chamber II, Judgment March 15, 2002) at para. 181, available https://www.icty.org/x/cases/krnojelac/tjug/en/krn-tj020315e.pdf (accessed February 2021).
196. Gabrielle Marceau, Arnau Izguerri & Vladyslav Labonnovy, *The WTO's Influence on Other Dispute Settlement Mechanisms: A Lighthouse in the Storm of Fragmentation*, 47 Journal of World Trade 481, 512-530 (2013).
197. Peters, *supra* note 22 at 697.
198. Some authors proposed to establish such framework in connection with the ICJ. Andrew Lang, *The Role of the International Court of Justice in a Context of Fragmentation*, 62 International & Comparative Law Quarterly 808 (2013).
199. For an overview of the relationship between the CJEU and European domestic courts, *see* Hjalte Rasmussen, *On Law and Policy in the European Court of Justice* (1986).
200. Opinion pursuant to Article 218 (11) on the Accession of the European Union to the European Convention for the Protection of Human Rights and Fundamental Freedoms, (Opinion, December 18, 2014), CJEU Digital Reports ECLI:EU:C:2014:2454 [hereinafter: "EU Opinion 2/13"].
201. Like the one proposed by Lang, *supra* note 198.
202. Peters, *supra* note 22 at 698.

structural vulnerability of the international legal order.[203] The absence of an institutional framework for judicial dialogue is a natural consequence of the decentralized normative development of international law.[204] Truth be told, it would hardly make any sense to develop structural connections between law adjudicators in the absence of previously established links among lawmakers.[205] At the same time, one can only acknowledge that international courts and tribunals have been playing a crucial role in preserving the unity of international law as a legal order.[206] This leads us to the second problem related to judicial dialogue: its lack of input legitimacy. If domestic courts are traditionally detached from direct democratic legitimacy in order to maintain their impartiality, international courts have basically no connection with the fundamental principle of democracy. Allowing these technical entities to play such a crucial role in the development of international law implicitly ratifies the failure of States to do so. Brought to its ultimate consequences, this leads us to the third and final type of instrument for channeling fragmentation: politicization.

1.3.4 Upholding Systemic Integration Through Politicization

According to Calhoun, politicization means the public contestation of a certain regime before the global community.[207] Behind this technique stands the legitimacy argument that fundamental conflicts among specialized regimes should be resolved through a global political discourse[208] because, as Oeter points out, regime collisions typically give rise to processes of political contestation.[209] Through these processes, global actors as well as specialized regimes *compete* for the attention and interest of the international community by showcasing how they better align with the broader general interest.[210] For these reasons, the politicization of international law could become a powerful tool of systemic integration by forcing its actors to reconnect with the foundational elements and drivers of the system.[211] At the same time, politicization is also difficult to achieve because of the significant resources required to be seen and recognized in the global arena. However, this should be a reason to further strengthen and consolidate its processes. Ultimately, a more *politicized*, more publicly discussed international law would also further promote its constitutionalization[212] to the benefit of every actor involved.

---

203. Yuval Shani, *One Law to Rule Them All: Should International Courts Be Viewed as Guardians of Procedural Order and Legal Uniformity?*, in *The Practice of Courts*, *supra* note 187.
204. Oellers-Frahm, *supra* note 17.
205. Rosalyn Higgins, *The ICJ, the ECJ, and the Integrity of International Law*, 52 International & Comparative Law Quarterly 1-20 (2003).
206. Burke-White, *supra* note 189; Teubner, *supra* note 190.
207. Craig Calhoun, *Politicization*, in *Dictionary of the Social Sciences* 369 (Craig Calhoun ed., 2002).
208. ILC Study, *supra* note 20 at 245.
209. Stefan Oeter, *Regime Collisions from a Perspective of Global Constitutionalism*, in *Contested Regime Collisions: Norm Fragmentation in World Society* 21 (Kerstin Blome et al. eds., 2016).
210. *Id.*, at 36-37.
211. Peters, *supra* note 22 at 701-702.
212. Oeter, *supra* note 209 at 40.

1.3.5 *Upholding Systemic Integration: Key Takeaways*

The previous sections discussed the current configuration of international law as an "ordered plurality."[213] Following the path indicated by the ILC in its fragmentation report, the conducted analysis looked at the normative development of international law and its substantive diversification. To complement those findings, the sections assessed how international law has managed to remain a united legal order, notwithstanding the lack of any centralized structure for lawmaking, law applying and law adjudicating.

As discussed, this result can be attributed to the efforts carried out by the main actors of the international legal order at these three levels. Each with its own tools and instruments, lawmakers, law appliers and law adjudicators have done their part in maintaining the unity of international law by promoting its systemic integration. Based on these premises, the next section discusses the consequences of the development and evolution of international space law.

2 THE RELATIONSHIP BETWEEN SPACE LAW AND INTERNATIONAL LAW

The implications of the general configuration of international law as a legal order on the relationship with the multi-level regulatory system of space mining are noteworthy. Twenty years after the fragmentation speech of President Guillaume, international law is now understood as "ordered pluralism"[214] or "*unitas multiplex.*"[215] These expressions have the great merit of capturing the combination of the two driving forces of international law: decentralization and systemic integration. These notions welcome the flexible diversity[216] of international law as a manifestation of its capacity to address global problems.[217] This capacity is only the more important in the context of the exploration and use of outer space and celestial bodies, considering that space issues are global in nature and can only be addressed through a plurality of integrated contributions.[218] Based on these findings, this section discusses the relationship between the system of space law and the legal order of international law from a substantive and institutional perspective.

2.1 Substantive Integration

The previous analysis of the nature and configuration of international law as a legal order found that systemic integration operates in two ways. On the one hand, it connects the many specialized systems of international law with one another. On the

213. Delmas-Marty, *supra* note 22.
214. *Ibid.*
215. Prost, *supra* note 25.
216. Hofmann, *supra* note 73.
217. Cassese's IL, *supra* note 10 at 41-43.
218. As to which, *see* section 1 earlier in the Introduction.

other hand, it links each and every one of them with the broader normative environment of international law. Needless to say, the system of space law is no exception to these trends. Therefore, the question is *how* the systemic integration between space law and international law happens in practice. Based on the analysis conducted in section 1, systemic integration can be promoted through different tools. Looking at the relationship between the system of space law and the legal order of international law with this lens, it is possible to formulate the following considerations. First and foremost, international space law has been integrated with the broader normative environment of international law through the open *renvoi*[219] laid down in Article III OST,[220] a provision of critical importance in international space law.[221] According to this article, space activities shall be conducted "in accordance with international law, including the Charter of the United Nations, in the interest of maintaining international peace and security and promoting international cooperation and understanding."[222] As anticipated earlier,[223] Article III OST makes an open and dynamic[224] renvoi to the broader normative environment of international law. Concerning the scope of the renvoi, in line with the ILC interpretation of Article 31 (3) (c) VCLT,[225] the normative meaning of the term "international law" within the OST should be defined in connection with Article 38 of the Statute of the ICJ,[226] which lists the sources of international law. In accordance with this provision, "international law" in Article III OST refers to international conventions, international custom and the general principles of law recognized by civilized nations[227] as applicable to exploration and use of space. Concerning the temporal element of the renvoi, it is possible to rely on the considerations expressed by the IhLC with reference to Article 31 (3) (c)[228] and the evolutionary interpretation of treaties. This method of interpretation has been recently

219. Within the context of this book, the term renvoi is used to indicate a tool for systemic integration primarily involving lawmakers, not to be confused with the homonym legal mechanism used in private international law.
220. Article III OST, *supra* note 152.
221. The importance and the meaning of Article III OST have been extensively discussed in literature. *Inter alia, see* Olivier Ribbelink, *Article III OST*, in *Cologne Commentary on Space Law: Vol. 1* 64-69 (Stephan Hobe, Bernhard Schmidt-Tedd & Kai-Uwe Schrogl eds., 2009—book hereinafter: "CoCoSL I"); Bin Cheng, *Studies in International Space Law* 150-211 (2004); Mahulena Hofmann & Tanja Masson-Zwaan, *Introduction to Space Law* (2019) 17; Frans Von Der Dunk, *International Space Law*, in *Handbook of Space Law* 29-32 (Frans Von Der Dunk & Fabio Tronchetti eds., 2015).
222. Article III OST, *supra* note 6.
223. As to which, *see* section 1.3.3 (i) earlier in this chapter.
224. Both qualities can be inferred from the use of the generic term "international law," following the same approach adopted by the ILC for the interpretation of Article 31 (3) (c) itself. ILC Study, *supra* note 20 at 215.
225. As to which, *see* sections 1.1.2 and 1.1.3 earlier in this chapter.
226. Statute of the International Court of Justice, *entered into force* August 31, 1965, 33 UNTS 993 [hereinafter: "ICJ Statute"].
227. Article 38, ICJ Statute. Subject to the provisions of Article 59 of the Statute, Article 38 also refers to judicial decisions and the teaching of the most highly qualified publicists as subsidiary means of interpretation.
228. As to which, *see* section 1.1.2 earlier in this chapter.

promoted by Bjorge[229] and is well grounded in the consolidated case law of the ICJ,[230] according to which when States Parties to a treaty make use of generic terms, they must be presumed to have given them an evolutionary meaning.[231] Thus, it can be concluded that Article III OST determines the application in outer space of the whole corpus of international law as applicable and relevant to the case at hand and as it stands in the present time.[232] As a consequence of this direct and dynamic applicability of international law, the rules of space law are "automatically" harmonized with the broader normative environment of international law.

The second part of Article III OST goes beyond the level of normative development and addresses how the freedom to explore and use outer space shall be exercised in practice. According to the last sentence of the provision, the exploration and use of outer space shall be conducted "in the interest of maintaining international peace and security and promoting international cooperation and understanding."[233] This explicit connection between space activities and international peace and security—as well as international cooperation and understanding—extends the application of international law also to the application, adjudication and enforcement phases. At a closer look, the provision reveals an almost *verbatim* quotation from Article I of the UN Charter, which defines the purposes and principles of the United Nations,[234] beginning with the maintenance of international peace and security.[235] Such a strong connection with the UN Charter is of essential importance to understand the relationship between the system of space law and the legal order of international law. As is well-known, one of the main priorities of the drafters of the OST was to ensure that outer space became neither the reason for nor the direct theatre of global conflicts.[236] To a certain extent, Article III OST serves this purpose even more than Article IV OST, notwithstanding the fact that the latter provision specifically addresses the peaceful uses of outer space and celestial bodies.[237] Arguably, this is because of Article III OST's direct references to Article I of the UN Charter.

By subjecting the freedom to explore and use outer space to the foundational purpose of the United Nations, Article III OST determines that every space activity threatening international peace and security does not constitute a valid exercise of the freedom to explore and use outer space. Based on the above analysis, it can be

229. Eirik Bjorge, *The Evolutionary Interpretation of Treaties* (2014).
230. Dispute Regarding Navigational and Related Rights (*Costa Rica v. Nicar.*), (Judgment, July 13, 2009), 2009 I.C.J. Reports 213, at para. 242 [hereinafter: "Navigational Case"]; Legal Consequences for States of the Continued Presence of South Africa in Namibia (South West Africa) notwithstanding Security Council Resolution 276, (Advisory Opinion, June 21, 1970), 1971 I.C.J. Reports 16 at para. 53 [hereinafter: "Namibia Case"].
231. Navigational Case and Namibia Case, *supra* note 230. *See also* Christian Djeffal, *Static and Evolutive Treaty Intepretation: A Functional Representation* 27 (2016); Bjorge, *supra* note 229.
232. Ribbelink, *supra* note 221 at 67.
233. Article III OST, *supra* note 152.
234. Article I UN Charter, *supra* note 93.
235. *Ibid.*
236. Stephan Hobe, *Historical Background of the Outer Space Treaty*, in *CoCoSL I*, *supra* note 221 at 1-14.
237. Article IV OST, *supra* note 152.

concluded that through Article III OST, the system of space law integrates an open-ended series of legal and political limitations to the freedom of exploration and use of outer space established under Article I OST.[238] Based on these findings, the next section discusses the institutional implications of these legal and political connections between space and international law.

2.2 Institutional Integration

Since the system of space law has not yet reached the point of formalizing a proper institutional structure,[239] its integration within the legal order of international law is particularly relevant for the application, adjudication and enforcement of its norms. The question of which of the many international institutions could "fill the gaps"[240] could be tackled from a variety of different angles[241] and even constitute the subject of a dedicated book. For the purposes of the present book, this question is addressed through the lens of functional decentralization and with specific reference to the general functions attributed to the principal organs of the UN as identified by Article 7 of the UN Charter: the General Assembly (UNGA), the UNSC, the ECOSOC, the Trusteeship Council, the ICJ, and the United Nations Secretary General (UNSG).[242] Within the framework established in the Charter, these organs are empowered to deal with any matter of international law.[243] By exclusion, any institution of international law which is not a principal organ of the UN is here included within the vast genus of specialized bodies. The importance of this distinction comes from the fluid nature of space mining as multi-level system, given that its institutionalization is still in progress.[244] At present, when looking at the application, adjudication and enforcement of space mining norms, it is hard to predict which institutions will be involved among the various specialized bodies of international law. In theory, such tasks could potentially fall under the competence of a myriad of different institutions. Singling out the principal organs of the UN has the merit of organizing this factual uncertainty at the

238. Stephan Hobe, *Article I OST*, in *CoCoSL I*, *supra* note 221 at 36-39. *See also*: Ram Jakhu, *Legal Issues Relating to the Global Public Interest in Outer Space*, 32 Journal of Space Law 31 (2006); Stephen Gorove, *Freedom of Exploration and Use in the Outer Space Treaty: A Textual Analysis and Interpretation*, 1 Journal of International Law and Policy 18 (1971); Cheng, *supra* note 221 at 3-87.
239. For an essential overview on space law's governance, *see* Hofmann & Masson-Zwaan, *supra* note 221 at 9-11.
240. On the role of international law as "gap filler" of specialized regimes, *see* Koskenniemi Study Group, *supra* note 40 at 10.
241. For some of the most interesting analysis *see* Frans Von Der Dunk, *International Organizations in Space Law*, in *Handbook of Space Law*, *supra* note 221 at 269-330, and Olga Stelmakh-Drescher, *Global Space Governance for Space Sustainability*, in *Innovation in Outer Space: International and African Legal Perspectives* 65-89 (Mahulena Hofmann & P.J. Blount eds., 2018—book hereinafter: "Innovation in Outer Space").
242. Article 7 UN Charter, *supra* note 93.
243. Cassese's IL, *supra* note 10 at 313-344.
244. For a comprehensive and recent overview on this process, *see* Olavo De Bittencourt Neto, Mahulena Hofmann, Tanja Masson-Zwaan & Dimitra Stefoudi (eds.), *Building Blocks for the Development of an International Framework for the Governance of Space Resource Activities: A Commentary* (2020).

theoretical level, making it readable and assessable. It allows to identify a certain group of international institutions that are already connected with the multi-level system of space law and will likely get involved in its specialized portion dealing with space mining, based on the legal and political links established with the UN Charter by Article III OST. And even if the regulation and enforcement of space mining would be entrusted to a specialized agency of the UN, following the example of the International Telecommunication Union[245] (ITU) within the domain of telecommunications,[246] the direct applicability of the UN Charter would always offer a sound legal basis for the intervention of the UN organs, if necessary. *Mutatis mutandis,* this legal basis would justify an intervention also in the event that a completely new international organization would be set up,[247] as well as in the opposite scenario where no international institutional framework is developed. This simple but effective prognostic assessment provides the present analysis with a starting point, allowing it to focus on the potential role that could be played by the principal organs of the UN, despite any further development that the system of space mining might encounter. Conversely, this assessment also offers a valid methodological reason to exclude from the scope of the analysis all the other specialized regimes populating the broader normative environment of international law.

2.2.1 The Role of the UN Principal Organs in the System of Space Law

The previous findings raise the question of whether and how the UN's principal organs—the UNGA, the UNSG, the UNSC, the ECOSOC, the UN Trusteeship, and the ICJ—already are or could get involved in the multi-level regulatory system of space mining. To begin with, we can immediately set aside the ECOSOC and the UN Trusteeship, given that their attributions under the Charter do not cross the realm of international space law.

i The General Assembly

Concerning the remaining four institutions, and starting with the UNGA, this institution plays a critical role in the normative development of international space law. In fact, the very foundations of the *Corpus Iuris Spatialis* have been laid down through the normative intervention of the General Assembly. In Resolution 1348 (XIII) of December 18, 1958, the Assembly recognized the need for international cooperation—to be governed by multilateral treaties—ensuring the peaceful uses of space. Less than a year later, UNGA Resolution 1472 (XIV) of December 12, 1959, established the UNCOPUOS

245. Constitution and Convention of the International Telecommunication Union *entered into force* July 1, 1994, 1825 UNTS 1 [hereinafter: "ITU Constitution and Convention"].
246. On the relationship between the ITU regime and international space law, *see* Mahulena Hofmann, *ITU Instruments under the Perspective of General International Law,* Proceedings of the 56th Colloquium on the Law of Outer Space 327-338 (2014).
247. As proposed by some authors like Philippe De Man, *Exclusive Use in an Inclusive Environment: The Meaning of the Non-appropriation Principle for Space Resource Exploitation* (2016).

as a permanent body tasked with the international regulation of space activities. Every year since then, UNCOPUOS has been reporting its progress to the Assembly, and the latter has been endorsing its work by enacting its Report in dedicated UNGA resolutions.[248] The status of UNCOPUOS as a specialized permanent committee of the UNGA leaves no doubts as to its involvement in the multi-level regulatory system of space mining. As a matter of fact, the Assembly has already played a crucial role through the enactment of A/RES/71/90 of 2016, where it endorsed UNCOPUOS' decision to adopt a dedicated agenda item on space mining. Since then, every progress made by UNCOPUOS in this field has been incorporated into the UN system within the annual UNGA resolution on international cooperation in the peaceful uses of space. In the future, should UNCOPUOS manage to develop any normative instrument contributing to the multi-level regulation of space mining, it will likely do so under the auspices and through the powers of the UNGA.

ii *The Secretary General*

Next in this analysis, based upon proximity to the system of space law, stands the UNSG. This institution is very much involved in the practical application of space law and is notably mentioned in all of the five treaties composing the *Corpus Iuris Spatialis*.[249] Among the many references, it is worth mentioning here the essential role played by the UNSG under the Registration Convention (REG). Building upon the foundations of Articles VIII OST[250] and XI OST,[251] the REG integrates the UNSG within the system of space law by entrusting this entity with the maintenance of an international Register for objects launched into outer space.[252] Due to the fundamental importance of registration for the peaceful and sustainable uses of space, the UNSG seems to be well integrated within the system of space law. For what concerns the multi-level regulation of space mining, the UNSG may very well play a critical role also

248. A comprehensive list is available https://www.unoosa.org/oosa/documents-and-resolutions/search.jspx?&view=resolutions on UNOOSA's website (accessed February 2021).
249. The UNSG is explicitly mentioned in: Articles V and XI OST, *supra* note 152; Article 1 of the Agreement on the Rescue of Astronauts, the Return of Astronauts and the Return of Objects Launched into Outer Space, *entered into force* December 3, 1968, 672 UNTS 119 [hereinafter: "ARRA"]; Article XV of the Convention on International Liability for Damage Caused by Space Objects, *entered into force* October 9, 1973, 24 U.S.T. 2389, 961 U.N.T.S. 187 [hereinafter: "LIAB"]; Articles II, III, IV, V, VI, VIII, XI of the Convention on Registration of Objects Launched into Outer Space, *entered into force* September 15, 1976, 28 U.S.T. 695, 1023 U.N.T.S. 15 [hereinafter: "REG"]; Articles 5, 7, 9, 12, 13, 15, 18, 20 of the Agreement Governing the Activities of States on the Moon and Other Celestial Bodies, *entered into force* July 11, 1984, 1363 UNTS 3 [hereinafter: "MA"].
250. Which lays down the legal basis for the registration of space objects: Article VIII OST, *supra* note 152.
251. Which entrusts the UNSG with the "immediate and effective" distribution of the information transmitted by States on the "nature, conduct, locations and results" of their space activities. Article XI OST, *supra* note 152.
252. Article III REG, *supra* note 249.

in that context.[253] Due to the current lack of coordination mechanisms for space resources activities, the UNSG may be instrumental in collecting and distributing essential information needed to avoid harmful interferences under the auspices of Article XI OST.[254] As will be seen later, it is important to note that the duties of the UNSG under the space treaties are discharged by the UN Office for Outer Space Affairs (UNOOSA).[255]

iii The Security Council

Moving to the UNSC, in theory, this institution has very tight connections with the system of international space law due to the strategic relevance of space activities for the maintenance of international peace and security. As discussed earlier,[256] this relevance has been formally expressed in Article III OST, according to which space activities shall be conducted "in the interest of maintaining international peace and security and promoting international cooperation and understanding."[257] By using the same language as Article 24 UN Charter—which entrusts the UNSC with the primary responsibility to maintain international peace and security[258]—Article III OST provides a sound legal basis for the UNSC to intervene in the practical application of international space law. Not by chance, this possibility has recently found explicit confirmation in the practice of the UNSC itself. In its Resolution 2087/2013, addressing some nuclear and ballistic missiles tests conducted by the Democratic People's Republic of North Korea,[259] the UNSC begins by "recognizing the freedom of all States to explore and use outer space in accordance with international law, *including restrictions imposed by relevant Security Council resolutions* [emphasis added]."[260] From the above, we can conclude the Council's role within the system of space law is that of a distant guardian that can always restrict States' freedom to explore and use outer space by virtue of its powers under Chapter VII of the UN Charter.[261] Concerning the potential involvement of the Council in the multi-level system of space mining, it is honestly hard to imagine how any space mining activity could—in itself —constitute a threat to international peace and security capable of triggering the exercise of the UNSC powers

253. Antonino Salmeri, *Developing and Managing Moon and Mars Settlements in Accordance with International Space Law,* 2020 (2) Proceedings of the International Institute of Space Law 107-120 (2020).
254. Article XI OST, *supra* note 152.
255. More information on UNOOSA's activities are available https://www.unoosa.org/oosa/en/aboutus/roles-responsibilities.html (last accessed October 2022).
256. As to which, *see* section 2.1 earlier in this book.
257. Article III OST, *supra* note 152.
258. Article 24 UN Charter *supra* note 93.
259. More information on the facts can be found https://spacenews.com/un-security-council-hits-north-korea-for-satellite-launch/ (last accessed October 2022). Recently, North Korea strongly protested against said—and subsequent—UNSC resolutions condemning its nuclear and missile tests, as reported http://www.koreaherald.com/view.php?ud=20201120000516 (last accessed October 2022).
260. Resolution 2087/2013 adopted by the Security Council at its 6904th meeting, UN Doc S/RES/2087 (January 22, 2013).
261. Articles 39-51 UN Charter, *supra* note 93.

under Chapter VII of the UN Charter.[262] More realistically, the global relevance of space resources activities could certainly generate tensions[263] justifying the UNSC intervention under Chapter VI of the UN Charter.[264] *Inter alia,* interferences or accidents among uncoordinated space mining activities,[265] as well as the excessive exploitation of space resources for exclusive national purposes by some countries,[266] are all possible scenarios that may begin a series of disputes "the continuance of which is likely to endanger the maintenance of international peace and security."[267] Accordingly, the UNSC may thus intervene to coordinate and foster peaceful means of dispute resolution. Finally, a third avenue for the intervention of the UNSC may come from the application of Article 94 of the UN Charter,[268] an often-overlooked provision addressing compliance with the decisions and judgments of the ICJ,[269] even though this hypothesis will be addressed in more detail later in this book.[270]

iv *The International Court of Justice*

The very possibility of legal disputes focused on space mining activities naturally leads to the potential involvement of the World Court. In this regard, the ICJ may be the UN organ with the lowest chance of playing a role in the multi-level system of space mining. This is for a number of reasons. First, the ICJ is the only organ among those examined in this section that has never been involved in space law. In almost seventy years of space activities, there has been not a single instance in which a State has considered beginning proceedings before the ICJ for a space law dispute.[271] While this is also due to the fact that there have been very few actual causes for disputing,[272] the reality is that States would prefer to solve such disputes by any means except

262. *Ibid.*
263. As recently reported https://spacenews.com/white-house-looks-for-international-support-for-space-resource-rights/ after U.S. President Trump enacted an executive order https://trumpwhitehouse.archives.gov/presidential-actions/executive-order-encouraging-international-support-recovery-use-space-resources/ apparently rejecting the legal status of outer space and celestial bodies as global commons (both links accessed February 2021). For a comprehensive overview of the discussions and tensions raised by the U.S. EO, *see* the collection of opinions published https://spacewatch.global/tag/president-donald-j-trump/ by Spacewatch Global (last accessed October 2022).
264. Articles 33-38 UN Charter, *supra* note 93.
265. Salmeri, *supra* note 253.
266. On these risks *see* Fabio Tronchetti, *Legal Aspects of Space Resources Utilization,* in *Handbook of Space Law, supra* note 221 at 769-792.
267. Article 33 UN Charter, *supra* note 93.
268. *Id.*, at Article 94.
269. On the role of Article 94 within the UN Charter, *see* Edgardo Sobenes Obregon, *Recourse to the Security Council under Article 94 (2) of the United Nations Charter,* in *Max Planck Encyclopedia of International Procedural Law* (2017).
270. As to which, *see* section 1.1.1 in Chapter 3.
271. For a comprehensive analysis of dispute resolution practice in space activities, *see* Maureen Williams, *Dispute Resolution Regarding Space Activities,* in *Handbook of Space Law, supra* note 221 at 995-1046.
272. For an overview on one of the few examples, *see* Tanja Masson-Zwaan, *Space Law and the Satellite Collision of 10 February 2009,* 174 Space Research Today 4-11 (2009).

international judicial proceedings.[273] The reason for this preference can be once again traced back to the highly strategic and political relevance of space activities. When brought before the courts, States lose all their political leverage and are not in control of the situation anymore.[274] The intrinsic uncertainty associated with judicial proceedings does not align with the delicate issues that would be a stake in a space law dispute. A second reason why the ICJ is not likely to play an active role in the multi-level system of space mining is because of its international competitors.[275] Echoing President Guillaume's fragmentation speech,[276] it is certainly true that the proliferation of international courts and tribunals has undermined the influence and importance of the ICJ.[277] Therefore, *if* States would suddenly become keen to solve their space disputes before an international judge, the ICJ would probably not be their first choice. The World Court would have to overcome the competition of the Permanent Court of Arbitration[278] (PCA) as well as of specialized bodies such as the proposed "Space Court,"[279] a new international arbitration tribunal for space activities that may be set up under the Dubai International Financial Centre (DIFC) Courts.[280] Concerning the first, it should be noted that in 2011 the PCA released an optional set of rules for the arbitration of disputes relating to outer space activities.[281] The combination of the presence of a dedicated set of rules, the flexibility of international arbitration—including the possibility of involving private companies[282]—and the international recognition enjoyed by the PCA makes the latter a particularly indicated adjudicator of space disputes.[283] For similar reasons, also the new "courts of space" initiative announced by the UAE is likely to represent a better option than the ICJ. This space court may be new, but it seems to be designed to provide a flexible, competent and discrete mechanism for dispute resolution,[284] all features that are usually much appreciated by States. Further to that, being incorporated within the DIFC, this new space court may be particularly attractive for private entities as well, given its expertise in business and contract law. Considering that space mining is so far intended to be

273. Hofmann & Masson-Zwaan, *supra* note 221 at 28; Williams, *supra* note 271 at 996.
274. On the weakening impact of legal proceedings on States, *see* Alter, *supra* note 169 at 133.
275. Williams, *supra* note 271 at 996.
276. Fragmentation Speech, *supra* note 18.
277. Higgins, *supra* note 205.
278. Convention for the Pacific Settlement of International Disputes *entered into force* September 4, 1900, 32 Stat. 1799.
279. As reported https://www.timesofisrael.com/dubai-creates-space-court-for-out-of-this-world-disputes/ (last accessed October 2022).
280. Information on the DIFC can be found https://www.difccourts.ae/ (last accessed October 2022).
281. Optional Rules for Arbitration of Disputes Relating to Outer Space Activities, Permanent Court of Arbitration, Effective December 6, 2011, available https://docs.pca-cpa.org/2016/01/Permanent-Court-of-Arbitration-Optional-Rules-for-Arbitration-of-Disputes-Relating-to-Outer-Space-Activities.pdf (last accessed October 2022).
282. Which nowadays is seen as a fundamental feature for any space law dispute resolution mechanism. Williams, *supra* note 271 at 1031.
283. Fausto Pocar, *An Introduction to the PCA's Optional Rules for Arbitration of Disputes Relating to Outer Space Activities*, 38 Journal of Space Law 171 et seq. (2011). For more on the PCA role *see* section 1.1.2 in Chapter 3.
284. As reported https://www.thenationalnews.com/uae/courts/dubai-launches-space-court-to-support-thriving-global-sector-1.1157474 (last accessed October 2022).

carried out mostly by private entities, it is only natural that they would prefer to see their disputes discussed before a court which offers them an autonomous legal standing and is specifically trained in the subject matter. There is, however, one scenario in which the ICJ could be involved in a space mining dispute. This would require a non-spacefaring nation proceeding against a spacefaring one which has previously declared acceptance of the compulsory jurisdiction of the Court.[285] The reason is that the arguments discouraging recourse to the ICJ are not as compelling when considered from the perspective of non-spacefaring countries. Such States, in fact, are not likely to reach any concrete result by means of diplomatic negotiations and would be better positioned before the ICJ than before an international tribunal specialized in space or business law. Interestingly, there is a number of spacefaring nations that would be exposed to this "risk," including countries like Germany, Canada, Italy, Japan, Luxembourg, Australia and the United Kingdom.[286] What is more, some of those States—like Luxembourg or Japan—are at the forefront of space mining regulations[287] and activities.[288] Should a State like to challenge the compatibility between their national laws on space mining and the principles of the OST before the ICJ,[289] both States would be bound to appear before the Court and argue the case. In this respect, it should be further added that the Luxembourgish declaration was made in the year 1930, and it is automatically renewed every five years.[290] In the absence of any documented renunciation, Luxembourg is currently bound by its declaration until the year 2025. Needless to say, whether to maintain or withdraw such a declaration is a strategic choice based on political, legal and international relations factors. Based on the above reasoning, it is possible to conclude that the acceptance by some spacefaring nations of the compulsory jurisdiction of the ICJ suggests that also the World Court may potentially play a role within the multi-level system of space mining.

---

285. For a condensed overview of the compulsory jurisdiction of the ICJ, *see* Raymond Ranjeva, *Global Justice: Compulsory Jurisdiction and the Role of the ICJ,* 17 (3) Harvard International Review 16-17, 73 (1995). For a critique, *see* Gary L. Scott & Craig L. Carr, *The ICJ and Compulsory Jurisdiction: The Case for Closing the Clause,* 81 (1) American Journal of International Law 57-76 (1987). For a contemporary re-assessment, *see* Brian Mcgarry, *Rethinking Compulsory Jurisdiction: The Case for U.S. Reentry into the ICJ's Optional Clause System,* in *American Society of International Law: Proceedings of the Annual Meeting (Vol. 111)* 313-316 (2017).
286. The updated list of States accepting the ICJ jurisdiction is available https://www.icj-cij.org/en/declarations on its website (last accessed October 2022).
287. As in the case of Luxembourg: Mahulena Hofmann, *Space Resources: Regulatory Aspects,* in *Innovation in Outer Space, supra* note 241 at 209-212.
288. As in the case of Japan: Kojiro Fujii, Shimpei Ishido & Atsushi Mizushima, *What Is an Appropriate Interaction Between International Law and Domestic Legal Systems to Promote Space Resources Development?,* 42 Air & Space Law 543, 546 (2017).
289. The contentiousness of the Luxembourgish Space Resources Law is discussed by Philippe De Mann, *Luxembourg Law on Space Resources Rests on Contentious Relationship with International Framework* (2017), working paper available https://ghum.kuleuven.be/ggs/publications/working_papers/2017/189deman (accessed February 2021). While the compatibility of the 2017 Space Resources Law with the rules of international space law will be addressed in the next chapter, for the purpose of the present analysis the very possibility of an assessment before the ICJ is already noteworthy.
290. Available https://www.icj-cij.org/en/declarations/lu (accessed February 2021).

The above analysis identified four international institutions enjoying direct connections both with the established system of space law and its evolving specialized portion dedicated to space mining: the UNGA, the UNSG, the UNSC and the ICJ. As anticipated, this identification is of fundamental theoretical importance since it allows us to frame the upcoming regulatory and enforcement assessments within some precise boundaries.

3 CONCLUSIONS

The legal and political links between space law and the broader normative environment of international law have been the main subject of this chapter. To begin with, section 1 presented the configuration of international law as a legal order. This section analyzed the normative development of international law by emphasizing the decentralized nature of international law. Moving from the famous fragmentation speech of ICJ President Guillaume and building upon the findings developed by the ILC in its subsequent report of 2006, the section discussed the substantive diversification as well as the functional differentiation of international law. The section found that while fragmentation has certainly been a serious threat, it did not actually compromise the unity of international law as a legal order. Despite the lack of centralized processes for lawmaking, law application and law adjudication, the main normative actors of international law—States, multilateral institutions, international judges and scholars—each took their own measures to neutralize the common threat to the legal order. Ultimately, the section argued that this was because, albeit "competing" with each other to regulate certain "sections" of international relations, all these actors consider themselves to be part of the same group and thus reacted to preserve it. Thus, section 1 continued its analysis by presenting the three types of instruments adopted to neutralize the fragmentation threat: binary criteria, integration mechanisms and political discourses. For each of these three groups, the section presented the relevant tools by analyzing their rationale and main features through the use of concrete examples from the current practice of international law. From the above analysis, the section concluded by praising the nature of international law as "ordered pluralism" (Delmas-Marty) or "*unitas multiplex*" (Prost): a legal order capable of preserving unity in diversity.

Based on this notion of international law, section 2 moved to discuss its relationship with the system of space law from the substantive and institutional viewpoints. To begin with, the section assessed the role of the open and dynamic renvoi laid down in Article III OST. First and foremost, the section found that this provision ensures that the normative development of space law proceeds in harmony with the legal order of international law. Further to that, the section argued that Article III OST provides a legal basis for a dynamic role of international law in the application, adjudication and enforcement of space law. At the same time, the section noted that due to the embryonal stage of space mining as multi-level regulatory system, it is necessary to focus the analysis on a specific group of rules and institutions that benefit from direct connections with the system of space law. Due to the relationship established by Article III OST with the UN Charter, section 2.1 identified these rules in the general norms of international law and these institutions in the principal organs of the UN. Therefore, section 2.2 moved to consider the involvement of the UN's principal organs in both the general system of space law and the specialized sub-system of space mining. The section began by excluding the ECOSOC and the UN Trusteeship from the analysis in view of their limited competencies under the Charter, thus placing the focus on the UNGA, the UNSG, the UNSC and the ICJ. Concerning the first, the section found that the UNGA has been and still is significantly involved in the normative development of space law, of which is the formal legislator. Under this normative competence, the Assembly has already begun to play an enabling role in the development of space mining regulations, as shown by UNGA Resolution 71/90 of 2016. Concerning the UNSG, the section noted that this organ is very well integrated into the system of space law. Like the UNGA, the UNSG is mentioned in all the five treaties composing the *Corpus Iuris Spatialis*, both in substantive and procedural provisions. Among the many references, the section focused on the critical role assigned to the UNSG by the REG for the maintenance of the UN Register of objects launched into outer space. Building upon the successful exercise of this function by the UNSG, the section further argued in favor of its involvement in the nascent multi-level system of space mining under the auspices of Article XI OST. For what concerns the UNSC, section 2.2 found important legal and political connections between space activities and the mandate of the Council, based upon Article III OST and the opinion expressed by the UNSC itself in its Resolution 2087/2013. Under this "executive" competence, the Council may very well become involved in space mining if and when any related dispute should be likely to endanger the friendly relations among nations or actually constitute a threat to international peace and security. Finally, section 2.2 turned to consider the potential involvement of the ICJ. Notably, the section found that the ICJ has (so far) never been involved in the multi-level system of space law. A role for the World Court seems to be precluded by both the traditional resistance of States to adjudicatory processes and the competition of arbitration tribunals. At the same time, section 2.2 noted that the inclusion of some spacefaring nations within those accepting the compulsory jurisdiction of the ICJ may trigger its intervention at the request of non-spacefaring nations. Especially within the context of space mining, these States may decide to initiate proceedings before the ICJ in case they would feel left out from the main benefits of these activities. Based on the above, the section concluded that the system of space law is very well integrated within the legal order of international law both from a substantive and institutional viewpoint.

This chapter assessed the connections between the system of space law and the international legal order with the goal to contextualize the subsequent analysis of the development and enforcement of space mining regulations. At the end of this foundational assessment, it is possible to conclude that the very nature of international law as a legal order, as well as its systemic integration with the multi-level regulatory system of space law, can create both challenges and opportunities. Accordingly, Chapter 2 complements this assessment by analyzing the current regulatory configuration of the nascent multi-level system of space mining.

CHAPTER 2

The Multi-level Regulation of Space Mining

This chapter assesses the current configuration of the multi-level regulatory system of space mining. To this end, it is divided into three sections. Section 1 begins the analysis by considering the applicable rules of international space law as laid down in the five international treaties composing the Corpus Iuris Spatialis: the Outer Space Treaty (OST),[1] *the Rescue and Return Agreement (ARRA),*[2] *the Liability Convention (LIAB),*[3] *the Registration Convention (REG)*[4] *and the Moon Agreement (MA).*[5] *In light of the fundamental role played by the OST,*[6] *the section primarily focuses attention on its impact on space mining activities and regulations. Following, section 2 moves to consider the only four existing examples of domestic legislation specifically dedicated to space mining: the U.S. Commercial Space Launch Competitiveness Act of 2015*[7] *(USCLCA), the Luxembourg Space*

1. Treaty on Principles Governing the Activities of States in the Exploration and Use of Outer Space, Including the Moon and Other Celestial Bodies, *entered into force* October 10, 1967, 18 U.S.T. 2410, 610 U.N.T.S. 205 [hereinafter: "OST"].
2. Agreement on the Rescue of Astronauts, the Return of Astronauts and the Return of Objects Launched into Outer Space, *entered into force* December 3, 1968, 672 UNTS 119 [hereinafter: "ARRA"].
3. Convention on International Liability for Damage Caused by Space Objects *entered into force* October 9, 1973, 24 U.S.T. 2389, 961 U.N.T.S. 187 [hereinafter: "LIAB"].
4. Convention on Registration of Objects Launched into Outer Space *entered into force* September 15, 1976, 28 U.S.T. 695, 1023 U.N.T.S. 15 [hereinafter: "REG"].
5. Agreement Governing the Activities of States on the Moon and Other Celestial Bodies *entered into force* July 11, 1984, 1363 UNTS 3 [hereinafter: "MA"].
6. Declaration on the fiftieth anniversary of the Treaty on Principles Governing the Activities of States in the Exploration and Use of Outer Space, including the Moon and Other Celestial Bodies, UN Doc. A/RES/72/78 (December 29, 2017).
7. Commercial Space Launch Competitiveness Act *entered into force* November 25, 2015, H.R.2262, 114th Congress (2015-2016) [hereinafter: "USCLCA"].

Resources Law of 2017[8] *(LUXSRL) and the more recent 2019 UAE Federal Law on the Regulation of the Space Sector (UAEFLRSS) and 2021 Japan Space Resources Act.*[9] *Based on these findings, section 3 assesses the interaction among the international and national governance levels for the regulation of space resource activities, further developing three alternative scenarios for its evolution. Finally, the chapter concludes by presenting the systemic consequences of the current status of the multi-level regulation of space mining on the enforcement options, liaising with the next and final chapter.*

1 INTERNATIONAL SPACE LAW

Any assessment of the multi-level regulation of space mining should naturally begin with the rules of international space law.[10] As mentioned, these norms are laid down in five international treaties—the OST, the ARRA, the LIAB, the REG and the MA—as complemented by a series of resolutions[11] from the United Nations General Assembly (UNGA). Altogether, these sources compose the *Corpus Iuris Spatialis,*[12] which is discussed in this section. The section analyzes first the OST, then moves to the LIAB and the REG, which are considered together in light of their reciprocal connections, and concludes by discussing the role played by the MA. The section does not address the ARRA in light of the fact that space mining operations will likely fall outside the scope of the agreement insofar as they will not involve any humans. The Agreement will likely become relevant in the long term when space mining is complemented by a number of crewed activities to provide a viable legal basis for search and rescue operations. From a methodological standpoint, the analysis of each provision begins with a general overview of its fundamental features and purposes and then presents the relevant implications on space mining activities and regulation.

8. Loi du 20 juillet 2017 sur l'exploration et l'utilisation des ressources de l'espace, *entered into force* July 28, 2017, Lux Recueil de Legislation A674 (2017) [hereinafter: "LUXSRL"].
9. Respectively, for the UAE: Federal Law No. 12 of 2019 on the Regulation of the Space Sector, entered into force January 20, 2020, 669 UAE Official Gazette 111 (2019) [hereinafter: "UAEFL-RSS"]; and for Japan: Space Resources Act, entered into force December 23, 2021, 141 Japan Official Gazette 4 (2022) [hereinafter: "JSRA"].
10. For a historical overview on the creation of international space law, *see* Bin Cheng, *Studies in International Space Law* 150-211 (2004) and also Vladimir Kopal, *United Nations and the Progressive Development of International Space Law,* VII Finnish Yearbook of International Space Law 1-58 (1996).
11. As reported by United Nations Office on Outer Space Affairs (UNOOSA) https://www.unoosa.org/oosa/en/ourwork/spacelaw/resolutions.html (last accessed October 2022).
12. For contemporary assessments on the *Corpus Iuris Spatialis, see:* Mahulena Hofmann & Tanja Masson-Zwaan, *Introduction to Space Law* (2019); Francis Lyall & Paul Larsen, *Space Law: A Treaties* (2nd ed., 2018); Frans Von Der Dunk & Fabio Tronchetti (eds.), *Handbook of Space Law* (2015).

1.1 The Outer Space Treaty

The OST is considered to be the *Magna Carta* of space law.[13] Its universal recognition[14] makes it a crucial reference point for the conduct and regulation of all space activities.[15] The following sections analyze the fundamental rules laid down in Articles I to XII OST (with the exception of Articles V and X OST, in light of their irrelevance in the context of space mining). The importance of these provisions is confirmed by the fact that several commentators consider them as declaratory of customary international law,[16] which would render them applicable to the whole international community of States.[17]

1.1.1 The Freedoms of Space under Article I OST

Fundamental Features and Purposes

The analysis of the OST begins with the cornerstones[18] of the entire system of space law: the freedoms of exploration and use of outer space, including the Moon and other celestial bodies. These fundamental freedoms are enshrined in Article I (2) OST and provide the legal basis for every activity conducted in outer space or celestial bodies.[19] Under Article I (2) OST, space "shall be free for exploration and use by all States without discrimination of any kind, on a basis of equality and in accordance with international law, and there shall be free access to all areas of celestial bodies."[20] The dense formulation of Article I (2) OST has many legal implications. First and foremost, it is important to note that according to this provision, there is a freedom to *explore* and there is a freedom to *use*.[21] Needless to say, the same activity could rely on both freedoms, but not necessarily. Some actors venture into outer space with the sole

13. Peter Haanappel, *The Law and Policy of Air Space and Outer Space: A Comparative Approach* 9 (2003).
14. When this book has been finalized in October 2022, the OST counted 112 Parties. UNOOSA, *Status of International Agreements Relating to Activities in Outer Space as at 1 January 2022*, available https://www.unoosa.org/res/oosadoc/data/documents/2022/aac_105c_22022crp/aac_105c_22022crp_10_0_html/AAC105_C2_2022_CRP10E.pdf (last accessed October 2022).
15. Frans Von der Dunk, *International Space Law*, in *Handbook of Space Law*, *supra* note 12 at 59-60.
16. For a recent re-evaluation of this argument *see* Ram S. Jakhu & Steven Freeland, *The Relationship Between the Outer Space Treaty and Customary International Law*, 2016 (2) Proceedings of the International Institute of Space Law 183-191 (2016); *see also* Valentina Vecchio, *Customary International Law in the Outer Space Treaty: Space Law as Laboratory for the Evolution of Public International Law*, 66 German Journal of Air and Space Law 491 (2017).
17. On the formation and effects of customary international law, *see*, Paola Gaeta, Jorge E. Vinuales & Salvatore Zappalà, *Cassese's International Law* 181-192 (3rd ed., 2020) [hereinafter: "Cassese's IL"].
18. Isabella Diederiks-Verschoor, *An Introduction to Space Law* 24-25 (3rd ed., 2008); Hofmann & Masson-Zwann, *supra* note 12 at 24.
19. Stephen Gorove, *Freedom of Exploration and Use in the Outer Space Treaty: A Textual Analysis and Interpretation*, 1 Journal of International Law and Policy 95 (1971).
20. Article I OST, *supra* note 1.
21. Stephan Hobe, *Article I of the Outer Space Treaty*, in *Cologne Commentary on Space Law: Vol. 1* 34-36 (Stephan Hobe, Bernhard Schmidt-Tedd & Kai-Uwe Schrogl eds., 2009—book hereinafter: "CoCoSL I"); Gorove, *supra* note 19 at 95.

purpose of exploration, like in many cases of scientific missions.[22] Other actors do it with different interests in mind, like in the case of strategic[23] or commercial[24] missions. Being as it may, the formulation of Article I (2) OST serves the purpose of providing an equally legitimate legal basis for both exploratory and use-oriented activities. Importantly, the use of broad terms like "exploration and use" refers to a wide range of activities, including scientific and commercial endeavors.[25] The importance of commercial endeavors has become more and more relevant in practice,[26] as also shown by the impressive figures of the global space economy.[27] At the same time, Article I OST gives particular consideration to the freedom of scientific investigation,[28] which is specifically declared and promoted in the third and last paragraph of the provision.[29] Notably, this should not be interpreted as creating a third *genus* in addition to the freedoms of exploration and use[30] because these broad expressions naturally also include also scientific activities. The reason why Article I (3) OST solemnly declares that "there shall be freedom of scientific investigation" is to emphasize the primary importance of this activity within the system of international space law. Notably, this is further underlined by the related obligation[31] for all States to "facilitate and encourage international cooperation in such investigation."[32]

The analysis of Article I OST continues with the main purpose of shaping the exercise of the freedom to explore and use outer space. To do so, it is necessary to take a step back and look at the very first paragraph of Article I OST. According to this provision, "the exploration and use of outer space, including the Moon and other celestial bodies, shall be carried out for the benefit and in the interests of all countries, irrespective of their degree of economic or scientific development, and shall be the province of all mankind."[33] First of all, from a legal-theory viewpoint, the fact that the declaration of a freedom is preceded by the proclamation of its purposes is certainly noteworthy: ordinary logic would suggest the other way around. According to the drafting history of the OST,[34] this particular order was chosen to emphasize the

22. Like the various missions for the exploration of the solar system https://sci.esa.int/web/home/-/51459-missions of the European Space Agency (ESA) https://esamultimedia.esa.int/docs/corporate/This_is_ESA_EN_LR.pdf (last accessed October 2022).
23. Like the https://www.nasa.gov/directorates/heo/scan/communications/policy/what_is_gps GPS or the https://www.gsa.europa.eu/european-gnss/galileo/galileo-european-global-satellite-based-navigation-system Galileo missions (last accessed October 2022).
24. Like the https://spacenews.com/spacex-marks-anniversary-of-first-launch-with-starlink-mission/ Starlink constellation developed by https://www.spacex.com/ SpaceX (last accessed October 2022).
25. Tanja Masson-Zwaan, *Article VI of the Outer Space Treaty and Private Human Access to Space,* 2008 (9) Proceedings of the International Institute of Space Law 537 (2008). Gorove, *supra* note 19 at 98-99.
26. Hobe, *supra* note 21 at 41-42.
27. Bryce Space Technology, *Global Space Industry Dynamics* 5 (2017).
28. Cheng, *supra* note 10 at 252.
29. Article I (3) OST, *supra* note 1.
30. Hobe, *supra* note 21 at 36.
31. On the legal implications of this obligation *see* Cheng, *supra* note 10 at 252-256.
32. Article I (3) OST, *supra* note 1.
33. Article I OST, *supra* note 1.
34. Hobe, *supra* note 21 at 29-31.

importance of the two principles laid down in that paragraph: the inherent international relevance of space activities and the legal status of space as a global common.[35] Article I (1) OST bounds the exploration and use of outer space to these two fundamental features.[36] Concerning the first feature, States debated whether spacefaring nations are legally obliged to share the benefits of their space activities[37] (and, if so, in which form) for a long time. Ultimately, the question was answered through a dedicated UNGA resolution[38] guiding the implementation of Article I (1) OST. This resolution—also known as the Space Benefit Declaration—makes it very clear that there is no general duty to share the various benefits of space activities.[39] At the same time, the Space Benefit Declaration encourages States to voluntarily do so through cooperation, mutual assistance and inclusiveness.[40] In these respects, the Space Benefit Declaration is essentially a codification of consistent State practice.[41] Since the adoption of the OST, no State felt—or has, in fact, ever been—obliged to share the benefits of its national space activities.[42] At the same time, while State practice shows a flexible interpretation of the principle, the global trend is very much in favor of sharing benefits rather than not.[43] This confirms the inherent international relevance of space activities as one of the two fundamental implications of Article I (1) OST,[44] with the second being the legal status of outer space and celestial bodies as global commons.[45] This fundamental feature results from the solemn declaration that the "exploration and use of outer space shall be the province of all mankind"[46] and is confirmed by a systematic and teleological reading of the treaty.[47] Since the legal status of celestial bodies as global commons is fundamentally connected with the prohibition of national appropriation under Article II OST and the principle of due regard under

35. Von Der Dunk, *supra* note 15 at 55-60.
36. Cheng, *supra* note 10 at 234-236.
37. *Ibid.*
38. Declaration on International Cooperation in the Exploration and Use of Outer Space for the Benefit and in the Interest of All States, Taking into Particular Account the Needs of Developing Countries, UN Doc A/RES/51/122 (December 13, 1996) [hereinafter: "Space Benefit Declaration"].
39. Stephan Hobe & Fabio Tronchetti, *Free Determination of Cooperation*, in *Cologne Commentary on Space Law: Vol. 3* 333-336 (Stephan Hobe, Bernhard Schmidt-Tedd & Kai-Uwe Schrogl eds., 2015—book hereinafter: "CoCoSL Vol. 3").
40. Paragraphs 3 & 5 Space Benefit Declaration, *supra* note 38.
41. Hobe & Tronchetti, *supra* note 39; Hobe, *supra* note 21 at 40-42.
42. Antonino Salmeri, *Developing and Managing Moon and Mars Settlements in Accordance with International Space Law*, 2020 (2) Proceedings of the International Institute of Space Law 107-120 (2020).
43. Jim Brindestine, *Life on Earth Is Better Because of NASA*, September 25, 2020, available https://blogs.nasa.gov/bridenstine/2020/09/25/life-on-earth-is-better-because-of-nasa/ (last accessed October 2022).
44. Ram Jakhu, *Legal Issues Relating to the Global Public Interest in Outer Space*, 32 Journal of Space Law 67 (2006).
45. Cheng, *supra* note 10 at 229-230; Hobe, *supra* note 21 at 30.
46. Article I OST, *supra* note 1.
47. Frans Von Der Dunk, *International Space Law*, in *Handbook of Space Law*, *supra* note 12 at 55-60.

Article IX OST,[48] further considerations will be added when addressing those provisions.

Inherent Limits

Having clarified the fundamental features and purposes of the freedoms of space, it is now possible to consider their relative scope and extent. The literal, systematic and teleological interpretation of Article I OST reveals that the freedoms of exploration and use of outer space are not absolute.[49] Already within Article I OST, it is possible to identify four "limitations" shaping the exercise of these two freedoms.[50] On top of those, each of the subsequent treaty provisions adds further implications to be taken into account depending on the specific features of the activity in question. For structural reasons, this paragraph addresses only the "internal"/"inherent" limits provided within Article I OST. As the section progresses in the analysis of the OST provisions, it will also incrementally consider and account for the additional limitations provided thereby.

To begin with the first two, according to Article I (2), OST space shall be free for exploration and use (1) "without discrimination of any kind" and (2) "on a basis of equality."[51] These two limits serve complementary purposes and can be thus addressed together. In essence, the principle of non-discrimination reinforces the concept of outer space as a global common and further characterizes it as a shared environment whereby all actors should act cooperatively. As such, the main implication of the principle of non-discrimination is that there shall be no active barriers impeding the exploration and use of outer space by a particular country. Along the same line of reasoning stands the principle of equality, according to which all States are entitled to participate on an equal foot in the exploration and use of outer space.[52] Like many others that will be examined later, this principle is based on the legal status of space as a global common.[53] Compared to non-discrimination, the principle of equality has more far-reaching implications[54] as it suggests a constructive engagement between spacefaring and non-spacefaring nations.[55] Ideally, the implementation of this principle should result in the development of a "common level-playing field" whereby all States become capable of conducting their own space activities by learning from, and

48. *Id.*, at 59: Hobe, *supra* note 21 at 40.
49. Hobe, *supra* note 21 at 36-39; Gorove, *supra* note 19 at 100; Jakhu, *supra* note 44 at 31.
50. Salmeri, *supra* note 42.
51. Article I (2) OST, *supra* note 1.
52. Significantly, the Soviet camp insisted on including the principle of equality as a necessary means to foster international cooperation, proposing to adopt it as a "most favored nation" clause. This clause is a legal obligation part of the regime of the World Trade Organization, according to which every WTO member has to extend the same privileges and immunities granted to one country to all WTO members. Hobe, *supra* note 21 at 33.
53. Von der Dunk, *supra* note 15 at 59.
54. Kai-Uwe Schrogl, *The Concept of Space Traffic Management as a Basis for Achieving the Fair and Equitable Use of Outer Space*, in *The Fair and Responsible Use of Space: Studies in Space Policy* 140 (Wolfgang Rathgeber, Kai-Uwe Schrogl & Ray Williamson eds., 2010).
55. Tare Brisibe, *Africa and Common Interests in Outer Space*, in *Innovation in Outer Space: International and African Legal Perspectives* 93-104 (Mahulena Hofmann & P.J. Blount eds., 2018—book hereinafter: "Innovation in Outer Space").

participating in, the activities of the others.[56] The limitations enshrined in the principles of non-discrimination and substantive equality are closely related to the fundamental purposes and features laid down in the first paragraph of Article I OST and reinforce one another. Moving on with the analysis, the third limit provided within Article I OST comes from the applicability of international law,[57] a topic that has been extensively discussed in the previous Chapter.[58] In a nutshell, the main implication of this third limit is that the freedoms of outer space cannot be exercised in any manner or purpose that would be inconsistent with applicable international law.[59]

Fourth and last, Article I OST provides that "there shall be free access to all areas of celestial bodies."[60] The principle of free access is recognized as a fundamental guarantee of the freedom to explore celestial bodies.[61] At the same time, the literal interpretation of this provision needs to be adjusted in light of the systematic and teleological criteria.

If taken literally, the principle of free access might lead to manifestly unreasonable results since it would practically outlaw every stable activity on the surface of celestial bodies[62] and direct jeopardize the application of other OST provisions.[63] Therefore, pursuant to Article 32 of the VCLT,[64] this literal interpretation should be set aside. Rather, the principle of free access has to be interpreted in light of the utilization rights granted by other articles of the treaty[65] and, in particular, Article XII OST.[66] Pursuant to this provision, all stations built on another celestial body shall be open to representatives of other OST Parties "on a basis of reciprocity."[67] Logically, the obligation to allow access to artificial stations built on celestial bodies is based on the right to build such stations in the first place.[68] Systematically, this conclusion is confirmed by Article VIII OST,[69] according to which States shall retain jurisdiction and control over their registered space objects,[70] including those *built* on the surface of another celestial body.[71] At the same time, the very existence of an artificial station de facto impedes "free access" to the territory over which the said station has been built. Thus, we must conclude that the OST drafters conceived the principle of free access in

56. Timiebi Agaba-Jeanty, *Realizing a Regional African Space Program,* in Innovation in Outer Space, *supra* note 55 at 258-259.
57. Article I (2) OST, *supra* note 1.
58. As to which, *see* section 2.1 in Chapter 1.
59. Hofmann & Masson-Zwann, *supra* note 12 at 17.
60. Article I (2) OST, *supra* note 1.
61. Hobe, *supra* note 21 at 36.
62. Philippe De Man, *Exclusive Use in an Inclusive Environment: The Meaning of the Non-appropriation Principle for Space Resource Exploitation* 417 (2016).
63. Most notably, Articles VIII and XII OST. Salmeri, *supra* note 42.
64. Vienna Convention on the Law of Treaties, *entered into force* January 27, 1980, 1155 U.N.T.S. 331 [hereinafter: "VCLT"].
65. Cheng, *supra* note 10 at 401.
66. *Ibid.*
67. Article XII OST, *supra* note 1. For a closer look at the legal implications of Article XII, *see* Cheng, *supra* note 10 at 248-251. Article XII OST is also discussed in section 1.1.8 in Chapter 2.
68. Cheng, *supra* note 10 at 402.
69. *Id.*, at 400.
70. Article VIII OST, *supra* note 1.
71. Cheng, *supra* note 10 at 502-504.

a dynamic way so that its practical implications will have to be assessed pursuant to an ad hoc balance with other applicable OST provisions. In general, the opinion of this author is that the principle of free access forbids States to exclusively "seize control" of natural areas of celestial bodies,[72] essentially translating into a right of free passage.[73]

Consequences of Space Mining Activities and Regulation

Space resource activities are clearly allowed as an application of the freedom to use celestial bodies under Article I OST.[74] Truth be told, they have actually been among the very first applications of this freedom. As soon as the Apollo 11 mission safely landed on the Moon, right after taking pictures and recordings of the landing, the U.S. astronauts started to collect lunar rocks.[75] Ultimately, they brought home around 25 kg of lunar materials.[76] Following, other States joined the U.S. in retrieving and collecting space resources,[77] with a growing frequency in recent times.[78] As these endeavors were happening, no State protested against them. On the contrary, the global community has always reacted with support and great interest.[79] This is not to say that space resource activities should be considered legal at all times. As discussed in this section, the freedoms of space are not absolute. Already from Article I OST, it is clear that space resource activities will have to respect a series of requirements in order to be lawfully conducted. To begin with, space mining will have to be performed in harmony with the international relevance of space activities and the legal status of celestial bodies as global commons.[80] Following the principle of adaptive governance,[81] the practical implications of this "harmonization" will evolve together with the stabilization—some may even say industrialization—of space resource activities.[82] In the early stages of space mining, one way to implement Article I (1) OST could be through the sharing of

72. Especially in connection with Article II OST. P.J. Blount, *Outer Space and International Geography: Article II and the Shape of the Global Order,* 52 (2) New England Law Review 102-103 (2018).
73. Whose exercise will be subjected to the conduct of appropriate international consultations to avoid the causation of potentially harmful interference, pursuant to the tenets of Article IX OST. On the role of consultations, *see* section 1.1.6 in Chapter 2.
74. Mahulena Hofmann, *Space Resources: Regulatory Aspects,* in Innovation in Outer Space, *supra* note 55 at 202-203.
75. As reported by https://www.nasa.gov/mission_pages/apollo/missions/apollo11.html NASA (last accessed October 2022).
76. *Ibid.*
77. Starting with the https://www.nasa.gov/mission_pages/LRO/multimedia/lroimages/lroc-2010 0316-luna.html Luna Missions of the Soviet Union (last accessed October 2022).
78. On which *see* the https://www.ncbi.nlm.nih.gov/books/NBK540827/#sec_3-1 overview provided by the U.S. National Academies of Sciences, Engineering and Medicine (last accessed October 2022).
79. Allan Treiman, *Sample Return from the Earth's Moon,* available https://www.lpi.usra.edu/decadal/leag/AllanTreimanMoon.pdf (last accessed October 2022).
80. Fabio Tronchetti, *Legal Aspects of Space Resource Utilization,* in *Handbook of Space Law, supra* note 12 at 778-782.
81. As to which, *see* section 1.2.1 in Chapter 1.
82. Olavo De Bittencourt Neto, Mahulena Hofmann, Tanja Masson-Zwaan & Dimitra Stefoudi (eds.), *Building Blocks for the Development of an International Framework for the Governance of Space Resource Activities: A Commentary* 2 (2020) [hereinafter: "BB Commentary"].

relevant scientific information discovered during the mining operations.[83] Then, as space resource activities evolve and scale, further mechanisms could be considered depending on these future developments. To be sure, proposals demanding mandatory monetary sharing do not have any grounds not in the history of space activities[84] nor in the system of space law[85] and neither in the economic realities of space mining.[86] To this date, the global space economy is valued at USD 344.5 billion,[87] but not a single cent has ever been "shared" on the basis of Article I (1) OST because no obligation to share revenues can be established under this provision. Further, it will take years, perhaps decades, before space resource activities can recover their costs, let alone become profitable.[88] Therefore, by insisting on monetary sharing, the international community would not get any benefit at all from space mining.[89] There are other ways in which space resource activities could and should be conducted for the benefit and in the interest of all countries.[90]

Moving to the implications related to the legal status of space as a global common, it is important to specify first what this concept means.[91] In law, the term global common is used to identify areas beyond the national jurisdiction of sovereign States.[92] The high seas, outer space, Antarctica and cyberspace are generally considered to be global commons.[93] The legal implications of space being considered a global common are enshrined in the cornerstones of space law: the freedoms of exploration and use under Article I OST and the prohibition of appropriation under Article II OST. Outer space and celestial bodies can be freely explored and used by all States, but none of them can preclude the others from doing so by appropriating these areas. Applying this concept to space resource activities, we can derive some very important implications. In order to respect the legal status of celestial bodies as global commons, at the

83. As suggested in Building Block 13. *Id.*, at 74-75.
84. Salmeri, *supra* note 42.
85. Hobe, *supra* note 21 at 40-42.
86. On which *see* David Kornuta et al., *Commercial Lunar Propellant Architecture: A Collaborative Study of Lunar Propellant Production*, 13 Reach 1-79 (2019).
87. Bryce, *supra* note 27.
88. Kornuta et al., *supra* note 86 at 51.
89. BB Commentary, *supra* note 82 at 79.
90. *Inter alia:* cooperation and contribution in education and training; access to and exchange of information; incentivization of joint ventures—as suggested in Building Block 13. BB Commentary, *supra* note 82 at 74-75.
91. On the legal status of outer space as global common, *see* Manfred Lachs, *The Law of Outer Space: An Experience in Contemporary Law-Making* 11-20 (Tanja Masson-Zwaan & Stephan Hobe eds., reissued on the occasion of the 50th anniversary of the International Institute of Space Law, 2010); Cheng, *supra* note 10 at 434-444.
92. Surabhi Ranganathan, *Global Commons*, 27 (3) European Journal of International Law 693 (2016); Ivaylo Angelov, *Global Commons and Their Strategic Significance for the European Union and NATO*, 2 (2) Security & Future 67-71 (2018).
93. Global Governance and Governance of the Global Commons in the Global Partnership for Development Beyond 2015, available https://www.un.org/en/development/desa/policy/untaskteam_undf/thinkpieces/24_thinkpiece_global_governance.pdf (last accessed October 2022). *See also* Elizabeth Mrema, *Protecting the Global Commons: The Challenge of Collective Action*, 18 (1) Georgetown Journal of International Affairs 3-5 (2017).

very minimum, these activities should be limited in scale and duration.[94] To give a practical example, in a time when global interest in lunar exploration has prominently resurged,[95] no actor should be allowed to mine the entire south pool of the Moon. Likewise, no entity should be allowed to "extract" solar energy from the lunar peaks of eternal light[96] for an indefinite amount of time. To be sure, these kinds of behaviors would be legally questionable and politically problematic. Thus, in order to avoid tensions and conflicts, space resource activities will need to be conducted in a reasonably fair manner. Interestingly, opposite considerations should shape the regulation of asteroid mining.[97] There are millions of asteroids which are no larger than a football stadium,[98] and whoever will mine those objects cannot clearly "share" the site with anybody else due to the simple fact that there is not enough space available. At present, this differentiated approach is impeded by the fact that both the Moon and small asteroids still fall within the definition of celestial bodies, which encompasses all natural objects in outer space.[99] To address this issue, some authors have proposed to establish a physical threshold for the definition of celestial body.[100] Ultimately, the main implication of the legal status of celestial bodies as global commons on space resource activities is that their regulation—especially in the early stages—needs to ensure their fair conduct. Similar considerations can be made on the impact of the first two limitations laid down in Article I (2) OST, the principles of non-discrimination and equality, because of their close connections with the concept of space as a global common. In essence, these principles would be best implemented by undertaking space resource activities as a truly international effort.[101] Obviously, this expression in itself can have different meanings, ranging from globally conducted mining operations to the promotion of ad hoc international partnerships. In accordance with the principle of adaptive governance, it is not possible—nor desirable—to predetermine what form should exactly international cooperation take place within the context of space mining.

One interesting approach in this regard can be found in section 5 of the Artemis Accords (AA),[102] a multilateral document unveiled by (originally) a group of eight

94. Antonino Salmeri, *Houston We Have a Law: A Model for National Regulation of Space Resource Activities*, Proceedings of the 70th International Astronautical Congress 5 (2019).
95. Brycetech, *Projected Exploration Missions (2020-2030)*, (2020).
96. Philippe Gläser et al., *Illumination Conditions at the Lunar South Pole Using High Resolution Digital Terrain Models from Lola*, 243 Icarus 78-90 (2014).
97. On this topic, *see* John Lewis, *Asteroid Mining 101: Wealth for the New Space Economy* (2014).
98. As reported by https://ssd.jpl.nasa.gov/?asteroids#: ~ :text = Asteroids&text = Asteroids %20are %20small %20rocky %20bodies,or %20cross %20the %20Earth's %20orbit NASA (last accessed October 2022).
99. Hobe, *supra* note 21 at 32.
100. Andrea Capurso, *The Non-appropriation Principle: A Roman Interpretation*, 2018 Proceedings of the International Institute of Space Law 111-128 (2019).
101. Tronchetti, *supra* note 80 at 781.
102. The Artemis Accords—Principles for Cooperation in the Civil Exploration and Use of the Moon, Mars, Comets, and Asteroids for Peaceful Purposes, available https://gouvernement.lu/dam-assets/documents/actualites/2020/10-octobre/14-luxembourg-nasa-artemis/Artemis-Accords-signed-13102020.pdf (last accessed October 2022) [hereinafter: "Artemis Accords"]. In October 2022, when this book has been finalized, the total number of Signatories has grown to a total of twenty Signatories. An updated count is kept by NASA on their website (last accessed October 2022).

States at the occasion of the 71st International Astronautical Congress in 2020.[103] This option consists of "the development of interoperable and common exploration infrastructure and standards,"[104] a practice indicated under the name of *interoperability*.[105] According to the signatories of the Accords, interoperability "will enhance space-based exploration, scientific discovery and commercial utilization."[106] Whether these outcomes will be reached through interoperability will mostly depend on how the concept is implemented in practice. For the purposes of the present analysis, interoperability could broaden participation in space mining activities in many ways.[107] First, the deployment of interoperable infrastructure would foster international partnerships by allowing multiple entities to work cooperatively in the same facility. Second, the development of common and open standards for the realization of said infrastructure (but also of software applications) would enable the participation of all interested countries.[108] Third and final, by combining the two previous applications, one could potentially envision space resource activities relying on *shared* interoperable infrastructure developed from common international standards. This approach may seem unrealistic, but it is being increasingly adopted[109] on board the International Space Station[110] (ISS) with encouraging results. From both technical and economical grounds, extending that experience to surface operations would allow for maximizing efficiency and reducing the high costs of deep space missions.[111] The real challenge is mostly legal[112] since the ISS is governed by a complex legal framework that took various decades to be negotiated and is further based on a certain balance among the ISS partners.[113] In order to foster space resource activities as a truly international effort and thus implement Article I (2) OST, it is necessary to come up with more flexible legal

103. As https://www.nasa.gov/press-release/nasa-international-partners-advance-cooperation-with-first-signings-of-artemis-accords/ reported by NASA (last accessed October 2022).
104. Section 5 Artemis Accords, *supra* note 102.
105. In essence, interoperability is the "ability of a system to work with or use the parts or equipment of another system." https://www.merriam-webster.com/dictionary/interoperability Interoperability, Merriam-Webster Dictionary (last accessed October 2022).
106. Section 5 Artemis Accords, *supra* note 102.
107. On the importance of interoperability for the future of space exploration, *see* Antonino Salmeri, *One Size to Fit Them All: Interoperability, the Artemis Accords and the Future of Space Exploration*, available https://spacewatch.global/2020/11/spacewatchgl-opinion-one-size-to-fit-them-all-interoperability-the-artemis-accords-and-the-future-of-space-exploration/ (last accessed October 2022).
108. Adhering to the invite sent by former NASA Administrator Jim Brindestine. Jim Brindestine, *Shared Standards Are a Vital Part of Future Space Exploration*, available https://blogs.nasa.gov/bridenstine/2020/10/12/statement-on-international-exploration/ (last accessed October 2022).
109. Thanks to the https://www.internationaldeepspacestandards.com/ International Deep Space Standards (last accessed October 2022).
110. National Aeronautics and Space Administration, Reference Guide to the International Space Station (2010).
111. Brindestine, *supra* note 108.
112. As underlined in David Lengyel & Steven Newman (eds.), *International Space Station: Lessons Learned for Space Exploration* 6 (2014).
113. For a thorough analysis of this legal regime, *see* Masahiko Fukushima, *Legal Analysis of International Space Station (ISS) Program Using the Concept of "Legalization,"* 24 Space Policy 33-41 (2008).

solutions.[114] Being as it may, at present, it can be concluded that interoperability is emerging not only as a technical and economical enabler but also as a legal tool for implementing the principles of non-discrimination and equality as laid down in Article I (2) OST.

To present analysis continues with the third and fourth limits enshrined in Article I OST. Concerning the applicability of international law (as the third limit), the reader is referred to the sections specifically dedicated to this fundamental principle.[115] The final part of the analysis will thus be dedicated to the implications of the principle of free access (as the fourth and last limit identified in Article I OST). First of all, it is important to recall what has been already clarified earlier within the general analysis of the principle: the principle of free access has to be balanced with other applicable provisions from international space law in light of the specific circumstances at hand. In the case of space mining, the principle of free access has to be balanced with the freedom of use under the same article and the principles of due regard and non-harmful interference under Article IX OST. One example might help to clarify. Let's consider the case of ice mining on the Shackleton crater within the south pole of the Moon.[116] Since most of the valuable ice is located at a certain level of depth, any mining activity thereby will need to operate around a fixed excavation site.[117] For the mining to be successful, it is essential that the relevant machines safely operate without harmful interferences.[118] If a rocket were landing (or taking off) anywhere within a certain range from the mining site, the consequent spreading of lunar dust would pose a critical threat to the safety of these operations.[119] This simple example already raises important legal questions. Does the right to operate without harmful interferences take precedence over the principle of free access? Or vice versa: does the right to access all areas of celestial bodies justify interferences with ongoing space activities in those areas? In this author's view, such questions do not and should not have any binary answer because space activities should never be conducted at the expense of others. It would be very troubling to say that a space mining operator is entitled to forbid any and all actors from accessing its site or the areas nearby. At the same time, it would be equally disturbing to argue that all actors on celestial bodies can go anywhere they like, even at the cost of causing harmful interference. In the absence of international governance mechanisms, potential conflicts between space mining and the principle of free access should be handled through ad hoc coordination within a general set of rules of behaviors guiding the negotiations between the parties. Since similar proposals are mostly based on the principle of due regard and non-harmful interference under Article IX OST, further considerations will be added in the dedicated section.

114. Hofmann & Masson-Zwann, *supra* note 12 at 105-107.
115. As to which, *see* section 2.1 in Chapter 1 and section 1.1.3 earlier in this chapter.
116. Which according to https://www.nasa.gov/feature/moon-s-south-pole-in-nasa-s-landing-sites NASA is one of the most attractive areas of the Moon.
117. Paolo Pino et al., *Waste Management for Lunar Resources Activities: Towards a Circular Lunar Economy*, 9 (4) New Space (2021).
118. *Id.*, at 11-12.
119. Timothy J. Stubbs, Richard R. Vondrak & William M. Farrell, *Impact of Dust on Lunar Exploration* 2 (2005).

To summarize the analysis of the implications of the freedoms to explore and use celestial bodies under Article I OST over space mining activities and regulations, it is possible to argue the following. First, space resource activities represent a legitimate use of celestial bodies under Article I OST. However, in accordance with the principle of benefit sharing and the legal status of space as a global common, space mining needs to be regulated and conducted in a fair and reasonable manner. On the one hand, regulators should not burden space mining operators with excessive demands, like sharing their profits with the international community. On the other hand, regulators must also avoid space resource activities happening in an uncontrolled manner. Guided by the principle of adaptive governance, licensing conditions of space mining should be adjusted to their practical status. At a minimum, space resource activities need to be limited in size, time and manner. Needless to say, finding the right balance will not happen overnight. In the meantime, one way to reduce the tensions currently associated with space resource activities is to promote opportunities for international cooperation and information sharing. Leveraging the concept of interoperability—based on the ISS experience and the AA—may prove to be a crucial step in this process. Ultimately, the safe and sustainable conduct of space resource activities depends on the enactment of adequate regulation. As it will be discussed later, this could be achieved through the development of a middle-level framework enabling and guiding coordination efforts on a case-by-case basis.[120]

In order to understand the purposes and scope of such a framework, it is first necessary to identify the additional implications of the other fundamental principles and norms laid down at the international and national levels.

1.1.2 The Prohibition of National Appropriation under Article II OST

Fundamental Features and Purposes

According to Article II OST, "outer space, including the Moon and other celestial bodies, is not subject to national appropriation by claim of sovereignty, by means of use or occupation, or by any other means."[121] The principle of non-appropriation is a cardinal rule of international space law[122] and forbids States from extending their sovereign influence over outer space and celestial bodies either directly ("by claim of sovereignty") or indirectly ("by means of use or occupation, or by any other means"). Article II OST plays a central role within the system of space law as the natural complement to Article I OST.[123] These norms represent two sides of the same coin: in order to ensure that space remains free for exploration and use by all States, none of them can be allowed to control it. In forbidding States from exerting and exercising their sovereign powers in outer space, Article II OST consecrates its legal status as a

120. *See* more in section 3 of Chapter 2.
121. Article II OST, *supra* note 1.
122. Fabio Tronchetti, *The Non-appropriation Principle under Attack: Using Article II of the Outer Space Treaty in Its Defence*, 2007 (5) Proceedings of the International Institute of Space Law 526-536 (2007).
123. Tronchetti, *supra* note 80 at 779.

global common.[124] The question then becomes: what constitutes "national appropriation" under the terms of Article II OST? To answer this interrogative, one needs to understand the rationale behind the enactment of the provision. As argued by Blount, Article II OST was enacted to "settle questions of international geography, namely the nature of State territory in space."[125] To avoid that space activities would degenerate into an unwanted *neo-colonialist* movement, it was decided that no State should be allowed to extend its territory over outer space and celestial bodies. It is essential to note that "territory" is here intended as one of the fundamental components of Statehood according to the Montevideo Convention.[126] By impeding the territorial annexation of outer space and celestial bodies, Article II OST prevents that any sovereign authority can be extended thereby. This is further made clear by the addition of the general clause "by any other means"[127] to the list of the traditional ways through which States can legally gain new territory.[128] This general clause has been included to cover all legal avenues potentially justifying the exercise of sovereign powers over outer space and celestial bodies. From a systematic viewpoint, it is important to note that what Article II OST forbids is the result—the direct or indirect extension of sovereign influence—but not necessarily all the activities mentioned in the provision.[129] With the obvious exception of "claims of sovereignty,"[130] use or occupation represent a theoretically legitimate exercise of the freedom to use celestial bodies.[131] One example may help to clarify. Pursuant to the combination of Articles I, IV, VIII and XII OST, States may "occupy" the territory of a celestial body for the purpose of building exclusively peaceful stations and installations, where they are entitled to exercise their jurisdiction and control. If the scope of Article II OST was to forbid any use or occupation of celestial bodies, then this provision would have been in open conflict with many other articles under the very same treaty.[132] Applying the systematic criteria, one must therefore reject this option and conclude that within Article II OST, the use or occupation of celestial bodies is not prohibited per se but rather as means to exert sovereign control over them.

The main implication of Article II OST is the consecration of outer space as a global common,[133] i.e., as an environment subtracted from the sovereign influence of all States.[134] Importantly, this does not make space or celestial bodies a lawless area,[135]

124. Von Der Dunk, *supra* note 15 at 55-60.
125. Blount, *supra* note 72 at 96.
126. Convention on the Rights and Duties of States adopted by the Seventh International Conference of American States, *entered into force* December 26, 1934, 165 LNTS 19 (1936).
127. Article II OST, *supra* note 1.
128. On which, *see* Stephen Gorove, *Interpreting Article II of the Outer Space Treaty*, 37 Fordham Law Review 350 (1969).
129. Blount, *supra* note 72 at 102.
130. Article II OST, *supra* note 1.
131. Hofmann & Masson-Zwaan, *supra* note 12 at 99.
132. Blount, *supra* note 72 at 102-103.
133. Von Der Dunk, *supra* note 15 at 55-60.
134. Ranganathan, *supra* note 92.
135. Antonino Salmeri, *No, Mars Is Not a Free Planet, No Matter What SpaceX Says*, November 16, 2020 Space News 25-28, available https://spacenews.com/op-ed-no-mars-is-not-a-free-planet-no-matter-what-spacex-says/ (last accessed October 2022).

thanks to the direct applicability of international law established by Articles I and III OST[136] and the exercise of (limited) jurisdiction and control under Article VIII OST. These provisions have crucial importance because, without the presence of dedicated rules preserving space as a shared environment, the freedoms of outer space, as well as the prohibition of non-appropriation, would be a dead letter. Not by chance, Article II OST, together with Articles I and III OST, lay down the very foundations upon which the entire system of space law is built.[137]

It is important to clarify that the prohibition of Article II OST fully applies also to private actors.[138] In the past, some companies have tried to argue that since individuals and corporations are not directly bound by the OST, they are entitled to claim ownership of outer space.[139] This reasoning is clearly fallacious because, under Article VI OST, private activities in space require the authorization and continuing supervision of a State,[140] which would be internationally responsible for assuring that said activities are carried out in conformity with the OST.[141] Therefore, a State could not validly authorize a private entity to engage in an activity that the State itself could not undertake.[142] Arguing otherwise would lead to the paradoxical result that private entities would enjoy a much broader freedom to explore and use outer space than States. Thus, it can be concluded that the prohibition of non-appropriation laid down in Article II OST also applies to private actors.[143]

Consequences of Space Mining Activities and Regulation

The implications of Article II OST for space resource activities depend on the answer to a fundamental question: does the scope of its prohibition extend to space resources? Based on the analysis conducted in this section, the answer is negative. As discussed, the prohibition of "national appropriation" under Article II OST forbids the direct or indirect extension of sovereign authority over outer space and celestial bodies. In this respect, it is important to note that terrestrial and space mining activities are based upon opposite legal basis. With the relevant exception of the Deep Seabed,[144] mining activities on Earth are always conducted within the territory of a sovereign State.[145] The

136. Hofmann & Masson-Zwaan, *supra* note 12 at 17-18.
137. Tronchetti even argues that Article II OST should be considered as a *structural* norm, one without which the entire normative edifice of space law would collapse. Tronchetti, *supra* note 122 at 535.
138. Statement by the Board of Directors of the International Institute of Space Law (IISL) on Claims to Property Rights Regarding the Moon and Other Celestial Bodies, available http://iislwebo.wwwnlss1.a2hosted.com/wp-content/uploads/2015/03/IISL_Outer_Space_Treaty_Statement.pdf (last accessed October 2022).
139. More information on these claims can be found http://www.geocities.ws/moonsayles/ (last accessed October 2022).
140. On the role of private entities within the system of space law, *see* section 1.1.4 in Chapter 2.
141. Article VI OST, *supra* note 1.
142. IISL Statement, *supra* note 138.
143. As notably confirmed by the U.S. State Department. Blount, *supra* note 72 at 113-114.
144. Due to its status as common heritage of humankind, as to which, *see* section 2.1.1 in Chapter 3.
145. For a very interesting comparison between terrestrial and space mining, *see* Lauren E. Shaw, *Asteroids, the New Western Frontier: Applying Principles of the General Mining Law of 1872 to Incentive Asteroid Mining*, 78 Journal of Air Law & Commerce 121-169 (2013).

legal basis for these activities comes from the sovereign authority that every State exercises over its territory.[146] In space, the situation is reversed because under Article II OST, no State can exercise its sovereign authority over the territories of celestial bodies, and in fact, the legal basis for space mining comes from the freedom to use celestial bodies under Article I OST.[147] As a corollary, establishing a mining site for the purpose of extracting space resources cannot be considered equivalent—and can conversely never lead—to territorial annexation. Therefore, space resource activities do not fall within the scope of Article II OST.

In the past, some authors argued against the legality of space mining by pointing out the existence of a *lacuna* within the system of space law.[148] Even assuming that a lacuna might have existed at the origins of space law, it has been clearly filled by means of subsequent State practice, as per the tenets of Article 31 (3) (b) VCLT.[149] As discussed in the previous section, over the past fifty years, various States have successfully engaged in the recovery and use of space resources without any objections from the international community.[150] The same authors have tried to undermine this conclusion by arguing that those activities were supported only because of their "scientific purposes."[151] Even if that would be true—and there is no evidence in support of such reasoning—a similar objection would be inconsistent from a legal viewpoint. As it has been seen in this section, the prohibition of Article II OST forbids all types of sovereign influence over a celestial body, so that the specific purpose behind this influence is irrelevant. Arguing otherwise would imply that States could appropriate outer space provided that they do it "for scientific purposes," which would be in open violation of Article II OST. Simply put, either space resource activities fall within the scope of the provision, or they do not: *tertium non datur*. Since space mining is not based upon—nor does it entail—the extension of a State's sovereign authority over a given celestial body, this activity is not prohibited under Article II OST.

Having said that, considering space mining a legitimate endeavor under both Articles I and II OST does not automatically make it fully compatible with the OST. This is because the OST is a treaty on principles, and compliance with principles is always a two-step process that needs to be assessed at both the theoretical and practical levels. In theory, based on the analysis laid down above, space mining is not per se prohibited by the OST. However, there is no doubt that certain types of space resource activities may very well violate fundamental principles of space law. While actual violations can only be ascertained based on the practical features of the given activity, the next sections illustrate the additional implications based on the other fundamental rules of space law.

146. Fabio Tronchetti, *Private Property Rights on Asteroid Resources: Assessing the Legality of the Asteroids Act*, 30 Space Policy 194 (2014).
147. Hofmann, *supra* note 74 at 203.
148. Stephen Gorove, *Studies in Space Law: Challenges and Prospects* 69 (1977); Aldo Armando Cocca, *Property Rights on the Moon and Other Celestial Bodies*, 1996 (1) Proceedings of the International Institute of Space Law 9 (1996).
149. Article 31 VCLT, *supra* note 64.
150. In addition to the considerations expressed in the previous section at pp., *see also* Blount *supra* note 72 at 111-112.
151. Tronchetti, *supra* note 80 at 788.

1.1.3 *Respect of International Law and Exclusively Peaceful Purposes under Articles III and IV (2) OST*

Fundamental Features and Purposes

This section jointly considers the applicability of international law under Article III OST and the exclusively peaceful purposes under Article IV (2) OST. The relevance of international law for space activities has already been discussed in this book,[152] and related general remarks on its features and purposes will not be repeated here. Thus, this section focuses on the principle of exclusively peaceful purposes under Article IV (2) OST. According to this provision, "the Moon and other celestial bodies shall be used exclusively for peaceful purposes."[153] Following the general OST approach to definitions,[154] this article does not define the meaning of the term "peaceful." Subsequent State practice and an analysis of the treaty's drafting history reveal that the term "peaceful" could be interpreted either as "non-military" or "non-aggressive."[155] As to the first, interpreting peaceful as "non-military" would outlaw both direct and indirect uses of space within the context of military activities.[156] Conversely, the second interpretation forbids only the use of space for aggressive actions, thus allowing indirect uses for strategic support, defense and even *espionage*.[157] Within Article IV (2) OST, this dilemma is made irrelevant by the use of the adverb "exclusively" before "peaceful purposes."[158] This choice of wording indicates a broad prohibition outlawing the direct or indirect use of celestial bodies for any military purposes.[159] This interpretation has been consistently upheld in State practice[160] and is confirmed by a systematic reading of Article IV OST.

Comparing the two paragraphs in which the provision is divided, it is possible to notice that its drafters were clearly pursuing different objectives. The first paragraph of the provision addresses the so-called weaponization of outer space[161] and has a strong focus on the Earth's orbit. Article IV (1) OST explicitly forbids the placement in Earth's orbit of nuclear weapons or other kinds of weapons of mass destruction[162] and further

152. As to which, *see* section 2.1 in Chapter 1.
153. Article IV OST, *supra* note 1.
154. P.J. Blount, *Innovating the Law: Fifty Years of the Outer Space Treaty*, in *Innovation in Outer Space, supra* note 55 at 34.
155. Stephan Hobe & Niklas Hedman, *Preamble of the Outer Space Treaty*, in *CoCoSL I, supra* note 21 at 22. For a comprehensive analysis on the various interpretations proposed, *see* Cheng, *supra* note at 10 at 513-522.
156. Ivan Vlasic, *Disarmament Decade, Outer Space and International Law*, 6 Annals of Air and Space Law 26 (1981).
157. Paul G. Dembling & Daniel M. Arons, *The Evolution of the Outer Space Treaty*, 33 Journal of Air Law and Commerce 434 (1967).
158. Kai-Uwe Schrogl & Julia Neumann, *Article IV OST*, in *CoCoSL I, supra* note 21 at 82.
159. Fabio Tronchetti, *Legal Aspects of the Military Uses of Space*, in *Handbook of Space Law, supra* note 12 at 338-341.
160. To name the most famous example, when the Apollo 11 astronauts reached the lunar surface in July 1969, they solemnly announced to "come in peace on behalf of all mankind."
161. Jose Monserrat, *Acts of Aggression in Outer Space*, 2001 (4) Proceedings of the International Institute of Space Law 365-375 (2002).
162. Article IV OST, *supra* note 1.

prohibits the stationing of all weapons in any part of outer space.[163] This formulation of Article IV (1) OST is generally considered to be rather "permissive": by forbidding specific behaviors, it implies that everything that is not explicitly prohibited is permitted. Therefore, Article IV (1) OST may appear to be rather lenient toward the military uses of outer space. To a certain extent, this was a specific choice of the OST drafters[164] motivated by the highly strategic value of Earth's orbit for military operations.[165] Having just begun to venture into outer space, States were not ready to renounce the military advantages offered by that environment and thus agreed to forbid only the most dangerous and destructive behaviors.[166] In this regard, it is important to note that even though space can be used for military purposes, it has not become a theatre of conflicts.[167] With the relevant—but also numerically quite insignificant[168]—exception of anti-satellite tests,[169] no weapon has ever been used in outer space or against a space object.[170] There has never been an armed conflict in space, and despite recent rhetoric on the matter, the chances of this actually happening are rather low. Furthermore, some military programs like the U.S. Global Positioning System (GPS)[171] have enabled the development of civilian applications for the benefit of all humankind.[172] To better understand the role of military uses of space, it is important to note that at the outset of the space age, governments funded their own space activities[173] almost entirely for military purposes.[174] If military uses of space had been entirely prohibited, fundamental technologies like the GPS may have never been developed. Thus, Article IV (1) OST has proved to be very useful in keeping outer space free from conflicts[175] while also enabling the development of critical space technologies.

Moving to the second paragraph of Article IV OST, this part of the provision addresses the uses of outer space beyond Earth's orbit and clearly states that "the Moon

163. *Ibid.*
164. Carl Christol, *The Modern International Law of Outer Space* 24 (1982); Christopher Petras, *The Debate over the Weaponization of Space: A Military-Legal Conspectus*, 28 Annals of Air and Space Law 171 (2003).
165. Jonathan Havercroft & Raymond Duvall, *Critical Astropolitics: The Geopolitics of Space Control and the Transformation of State Sovereignty*, in *Securing Outer Space* 43 (Natalie Bormann & Michael Sheehan eds., 2012).
166. *Ibid.*
167. For a comprehensive assessment of State practice on the military uses of space, *see* Schrogl & Neumann, *supra* note 158 at 87-93.
168. Gerry Doyle, *Factbox: Anti-satellite Weapons: Rare, High-Tech, and Risky to Test*, March 27, 2019 Reuters Aerospace and Defence, available https://www.reuters.com/article/us-india-satellite-tests-factbox-idUSKCN1R80UW (last accessed October 2022).
169. Kurt Gottfried & Richard Ned Lebow, *Anti-satellite Weapons: Weighing the Risks*, 114 (2) Daedalus 147-170 (1985).
170. For a recent assessment on the weaponization of space, *see* Dave Webb, *Space Weapons: Dream, Nightmare or Reality?*, in *Securing Outer Space*, *supra* note 165 at 24-41.
171. GPS, *supra* note 23.
172. With countless https://www.gps.gov/applications/ applications worldwide, the GPS is certainly among the most beneficial uses of outer space to date (last accessed October 2022).
173. Mark Sundahl, *Financing Space Ventures*, in *Securing Outer Space*, *supra* note 165 at 876.
174. Isabella H. Diederiks-Verschoor, *The Development of Financing of Spacecraft*, 1997 (3) Proceedings of the International Institute of Space Law 212 (1997).
175. Schrogl & Neumann, *supra* note 158 at 93.

and other celestial bodies shall be used exclusively for peaceful purposes."[176] A comparison with the previous paragraph reveals that the two parts of the provision are perfectly specular to each other. Within Article IV (1) OST, every military activity that is not explicitly prohibited is generally permitted.[177] Conversely, within Article IV (2) OST, every military activity that is not explicitly permitted is strictly prohibited. This conclusion is evident from the adoption of the clearcutting expression "exclusively for peaceful purposes,"[178] which indicates the clear intent to preserve celestial bodies from any conflictual use.[179] This is further confirmed by the fact that the provision further includes a list of allowed military activities: "the use of military personnel for scientific research or for any other peaceful purposes"[180] and "the use of any equipment or facility necessary for the peaceful exploration."[181] These exceptions can be explained by remembering that at the time in which the OST was drafted, civil astronauts were primarily recruited from military corps.[182] Therefore, the OST drafters felt the need to include an exception allowing for their employment on celestial bodies, provided that it remained for exclusively peaceful purposes.[183] Finally, it should be noted that Article IV (2) OST is closely connected with Articles III and IX OST since the complete demilitarization of celestial bodies represents a safeguard of international peace and security on Earth as well as of international cooperation in space exploration.[184]

Consequences of Space Mining Activities and Regulation

The implications of the applicability of international law in space on the regulation of space mining activities are noteworthy. First, in the absence of binding international norms accepted by the global space community, the applicability of general international law provides a fundamental legal basis for the national regulation of space mining.[185] This is because, under general international law, States retain the power to interpret and integrate relevant regulatory gaps through the enactment of domestic legislation.[186] Further, in the absence of any international authority entrusted with the governance of space resource activities, the direct applicability of the UN Charter provides a sound legal basis for the involvement of the UN's principal organs.[187] As such, the UNGA, the UNSG, the UNSC and the ICJ might each play a role in the development, application, enforcement and adjudication of space mining regulations.

176. Article IV (2) OST, *supra* note 1.
177. Without prejudice to further prohibitions laid down in other sources of international law.
178. Article IV (2) OST, *supra* note 1.
179. Tronchetti, *supra* note 159 at 340; Schrogl & Neumann, *supra* note 158 at 82.
180. Article IV (2) OST, *supra* note 1.
181. *Ibid.*
182. Mostly because they were the only ones with the required piloting skills. Patrick Long, *Becoming a NASA Astronaut and Military Service*, June 25, 2019, available https://www.thebalancecareers.com/so-you-want-to-become-an-astronaut-3345123 (last accessed October 2022).
183. Schrogl & Neumann, *supra* note 158 at 85.
184. Tronchetti, *supra* note 159 at 338-341; Schrogl & Neumann, *supra* note 158 at 81-85.
185. Hofmann, *supra* note 74 at 206.
186. Antonino Salmeri, *The Integration Between National and International Regulation of Space Resources Activities under Public International Law*, 43 (1) Journal of Space Law 60-85 (2019).
187. As to which, *see* section 2.2.2 in Chapter 1.

In a time when the multi-level regulatory system of space mining has produced an institutional structure, the possibility to rely on the guidance and powers of the UN's principal organs provides an important backup.

Moving to the principle of exclusive purposes under Article IV (2) OST, also this rule has far-reaching implications on the conduct and regulation of space mining. Insofar as space resource activities make "use" of celestial bodies, they are fully bound by the principle of exclusively peaceful purposes. While the applicability of this principle provides a fundamental safeguard for international cooperation in the exploration and use of celestial bodies, its practical implications on the conduct of space resource activities are virtually unexplored in space law literature (with the relevant exception of The Hague Building Blocks).[188] Two important questions in particular concern whether Article IV (2) OST imposes any limitation on the kind of entities that can conduct space resource activities, as well as on the purposes for the use of space resources.

Concerning the first question, Article IV (2) OST adopts a strict approach concerning the involvement of military entities in the exploration and use of celestial bodies. After providing a non-exhaustive list of specific prohibitions, the provision specifically authorizes (1) the use of military personnel for scientific research (or any other peaceful purposes) and (2) the use of "any equipment or facility" which might be "necessary" for the peaceful exploration of the Moon. In both cases, military involvement seems to be limited to a *supportive* role within the context of another activity in the peaceful exploration and/or use of celestial bodies. Based upon this reading of Article IV (2) OST, it seems that military entities do not have the right to autonomously engage in the exploration and use of celestial bodies, including to conduct space resource activities.[189] In accordance with the exceptions laid down in the provision, they might only provide "in kind" support—i.e., personnel, equipment and facilities—to space mining activities conducted by civilians.

Concerning the second question, whether Article IV (2) OST limits the use of space resources to exclusively peaceful purposes is by no means another complex issue. A literal interpretation of the provision would suggest a negative answer for the simple reason that recovered or extracted space resources possess an autonomous legal standing and do not fall under the definition of "celestial bodies." However, testing this conclusion against the object and purpose of Article IV (2) OST would suggest

188. Building Block 4.3 states that "the international framework should provide that space resources shall be used exclusively for peaceful purposes" to ensure compliance with Article IV OST. BB Commentary, *supra* note 82 at 33.

189. Recently, even the simple interest shown by the U.S. Defense Advanced Research Projects Agency in funding research related to lunar mining raised strong criticism and oppositions, even from U.S. space experts. Theresa Hitchens, *DARPA Space Manufacturing Project Sparks Controversy,* February 12, 2021 Breaking Defense, available https://breakingdefense.com/2021/02/darpa-space-manufacturing-project-sparks-controversy/ (last accessed October 2022). For more information on this project, *see* Sandra Erwin, *DARPA to Survey Private Sector Capabilities to Build Factories on the Moon,* February 7, 2021 Space News, available https://spacenews.com/darpa-to-survey-private-sector-capabilities-to-build-factories-on-the-moon/ (last accessed October 2022).

otherwise. As discussed, the main purpose of this provision is to completely demilitarize celestial bodies to preserve both international cooperation in their exploration and use as well as the maintenance of international peace and security on Earth. Envisioning the use of space resources within military activities or for military purposes—like weapons manufacturing—seems to be in open conflict with these goals. From a systemic viewpoint, such behaviors would defeat the object and purpose not only of Article IV (2) but also of the whole OST. Accordingly, it seems safe to argue that space resources shall be used exclusively for peaceful purposes.

In conclusion, the general prohibition to use celestial bodies for military purposes also covers the extraction and use of space resources. Thus, only civilian entities shall engage in, and benefit from, space mining activities. At the same time, military personnel could theoretically be employed for space resource activities conducted by civilian entities for exclusively peaceful purposes. However, since the early stages of space resource activities will hardly involve any humans, it is difficult to envision the application of this exception anytime soon.

1.1.4 State Responsibility for National Space Activities under Article VI OST

Fundamental Features and Purposes

At the core of the present analysis of the fundamental rules of space law lays the principle of State responsibility for national space activities, as established and shaped within the three sentences of Article VI OST. According to the first sentence of this provision, "States Parties to the Treaty shall bear international responsibility for national activities in outer space, whether such activities carried on by governmental agencies or by non-governmental entities, and for assuring that national activities are carried out in conformity with the provisions set forth in the present Treaty."[190] This first part of Article VI OST reinforces the central role played by States in the conduct and regulation of space activities.[191] In light of the enormous difficulties and potentially catastrophic dangers associated with space activities, the drafters of the OST considered it essential to always link their conduct with the international responsibility of a given State.[192] This principle was perceived to also play a critical role in safeguarding the rule of law in outer space, considering that international obligations are not directly applicable to individuals under many national jurisdictions.[193] Therefore, under Article VI OST, States directly guarantee the lawfulness of their national space activities[194] and are obliged to ensure that they conform to the provisions of the OST. As a consequence,

190. Article VI OST, *supra* note 1.
191. Von Der Dunk, *supra* note 15 at 45-46.
192. Michael Gerhard, *Article VI OST*, in *CoCoSL I*, *supra* note 21 at 105.
193. For a comprehensive analysis on the role of individuals and private entities under modern international law, *see* Cassese's IL, *supra* note 17 at 158-165.
194. Cheng, *supra* note 10 at 632-633.

any national space activity violating the treaty would trigger the international responsibility of the appropriate State under the ARSIWA[195].

To prevent these violations, the central part of Article VI OST establishes that "the activities of non-governmental entities in outer space shall require authorization and continuing supervision by the appropriate State Party to the Treaty."[196] Historically, this part of Article VI OST represents a compromise between the position of the U.S., which wanted to allow private activities in space, and the one of the USSR, which was worried about the low level of reliability of private entities.[197] Ultimately, a compromise was reached through the mandatory requirement of "authorization and continuing supervision" for non-governmental space activities.[198] This part of Article VI OST is of paramount importance within the multi-level system of space law.[199] Through this provision, the gates of outer space have also been opened for private actors.[200] At the same time, through the requirements of authorization and supervision, States made sure to remain the exclusive gatekeepers of that domain.[201] As a consequence, while States can directly engage in space activities without having to ask for permission, private actors will always be subject to prior authorization and continuing supervision. It is important to stress that the central part of Article VI OST establishes two consequently related obligations: first to authorize and then to continuingly supervise. Concerning the material scope of these two obligations, States will have to actively verify that private space activities for which they are responsible comply with international space law,[202] both before authorizing them and for their entire duration. For the above reasons, Article VI OST is considered to establish an obligation of due diligence,[203] which acts as one of the most important safeguards for the peaceful and sustainable uses of space.

Finally, the last part of Article VI OST addresses the space activities of international organizations by providing that the relevant "responsibility for compliance shall be borne by the international organization and by the States Parties to the Treaties participating in such organization."[204] Accordingly, the last part of Article VI OST further reinforces the principle of the State's responsibility by preventing them from

195. Responsibility of States for Internationally Wrongful Acts, [hereinafter: "ARSIWA"]. The consolidated text as adopted by UNGA Resolution 56/83 of December 12, 2001 and corrected by document A/56/49(Vol. I)/Corr.4. is available https://legal.un.org/ilc/texts/instruments/english/draft_articles/9_6_2001.pdf (last accessed October 2022).
196. Article VI OST, *supra* note 1.
197. Frans Von Der Dunk, *The Origins of Authorisation: Article VI of the Outer Space Treaty and International Space Law*, in *National Space Legislation in Europe* 3 (Frans Von Der Dunk ed., 2011). *See also* Gerhard, *supra* note 192.
198. Article VI OST, *supra* note 1.
199. Diederiks-Verschoor, *supra* note 18 at 26.
200. Gorove, *supra* note 19 at 100.
201. Irmgard Marboe, *National Space Law*, in *Handbook of Space Law*, *supra* note 12 at 130-133.
202. *Inter alia*: consistency with State's international obligation; safety of persons and goods; national security and public health; environmental concerns; financial issues. Masson-Zwaan, *supra* note 25.
203. Cheng, *supra* note 10 at 606.
204. Article VI OST, *supra* note 1.

potentially circumventing it by conducting their space activities through intergovernmental organizations.[205]

Consequences on Space Mining Activities and Regulation

The obligation to authorize and continuously supervise private activities in space is the very reason behind the enactment[206] of existing domestic legislation on space mining.[207] Both the United States and Luxembourg have explicitly stated multiple times that their legislations serve the purpose of providing a legal framework for the conduct of space resource activities by private entities.[208]

To better understand these statements, it is important to contextualize the technical and economic realities of space mining. As mentioned earlier, the various States that have already engaged in the extraction and recovery of space resources were primarily guided by scientific purposes. The collected extraterrestrial materials were used as samples and studied in order to understand the chemical composition of a given celestial body and draw the related implications on its future exploration as well as on the origins of the solar system. While these activities played a foundational role and certainly belong to the genus of space resource activities, they represent just a fraction of this domain. The transformative potential of space mining primarily comes from *in-situ* resource utilization (ISRU) practices,[209] which can significantly reduce the costs of operations on a given celestial body and expand their scale to an unprecedented level.[210] However, developing ISRU technologies and deploying the necessary capabilities is in itself a challenging and expensive endeavor.[211] The significant investments required for these efforts could only be recovered after having implemented them in an equally significant number of missions.[212] At present, States do not intend nor can actually afford to pursue the many missions that would be required to make ISRU economical—but commercial companies could.[213] A private corporation dedicated to the extraction and use of space resources would be in a position to recover the high initial costs by industrializing the process and providing its services to multiple entities.[214] In order for this to happen, pursuant to Article VI OST, the said

205. Gerhard, *supra* note 192 at 122-123.
206. Marboe, *supra* note 201 at 122.
207. These laws will be discussed more in details in section 2 later in this chapter.
208. For the United States, *see* the summary written Congressional Research Service, a non-partisan division of the Library of Congress, available https://www.govtrack.us/congress/bills/114/hr2262/summary#libraryofcongress (last accessed October 2022). For Luxembourg, *see* the description of the "spaceresources.lu" initiative, available https://space-agency.public.lu/en/space-resources/commercial-use-space-resources.html (last accessed October 2022).
209. A great overview on the usefulness of ISRU is provided by NASA, available https://www.nasa.gov/isru/overview (last accessed October 2022).
210. According to the Luxembourg Space Agency, this is the rationale behind the "spaceresources.lu" initiative, available https://space-agency.public.lu/en/space-resources/commercial-use-space-resources.html (last accessed October 2022).
211. *See* NASA's overview on ISRU, *supra* note 209.
212. Kornuta et al., *supra* note 86.
213. This is the proposal of the multi-national company *ispace*, available https://ispace-inc.com/project/ (last accessed October 2022).
214. A parallel could be drawn with the development of reusable launchers. It took almost fifteen years to SpaceX to go from start to the first reusable Falcon, and the only way to successfully

company would need the authorization and continuing supervision of a State. In light of the critical role that ISRU can play in accessible and sustainable space exploration,[215] the U.S., Luxembourg, the UAE and Japan decided to be those States.[216] Therefore, they began to develop a domestic legal framework regulating the recovery and use of space resources by commercial entities,[217] with the ultimate goal of promoting ISRU as a commercial effort.

Lastly, while providing a legal basis for the regulation of private space resource activities, Article VI OST also plays a crucial role in ensuring that they will be compliant with the treaty itself. This is why, for instance, the USCLCA explicitly mentions that the right to extract, own and sell space resources is granted "in accordance with the international obligations of the United States and subject to authorization and continuing supervision by the Federal Government."[218] On a similar line of reasoning, the AA clarify that space resources "should be executed in a manner that complies with the Outer Space Treaty"[219] and that "contracts and other legal instruments relating to space resources should be consistent with that Treaty."[220] Therefore, the enactment of national legislation regulating private space resource activities under the auspices of Article VI OST is an essential guarantee of the compatibility of space mining with the rules of space law.[221]

1.1.5 International Liability and Exercise of Jurisdiction and Control under Articles VII & VIII OST

Fundamental Features and Purposes

The principles of State liability and State jurisdiction and control—as respectively laid down in Articles VII and VIII OST—are two essential rules of space law.[222] To begin with the first, according to Article VII OST, "each State Party to the Treaty that launches or procures the launching of an object into outer space, and each State Party to the Treaty from whose territory or facility an object is launched, is internationally liable for damage to another State Party to the Treaty or to its natural or juridical person [caused] by such object or its component parts on Earth, in air space or in outer space, including

recover the related investments is by flying each of the reusable Falcons as many times as possible. Those numbers are more easily reached within the context of a business rather than of a civilian space program. For an interesting outlook on SpaceX's transformation of the launching industry, *see* Eric Berger, *Liftoff: Elon Musk and the Desperate Early Days That Launched Spacex* (2021).

215. Jim Brindestine, *Space Resources Are the Key to Safe and Sustainable Lunar Exploration,* available https://blogs.nasa.gov/bridenstine/2020/09/10/space-resources-are-the-key-to-safe-and-sustainable-lunar-exploration/ (last accessed October 2022).
216. On the role of sustainability as one of the main drivers behind the national regulation of space resource activities, *see* Mahulena Hofmann & Federico Bergamasco, *Space Resources Activities from the Perspective of Sustainability: Legal Aspects,* 3 (4) Global Sustainability 1-7 (2020).
217. For an analysis of these legal frameworks *see* section 2 later in this chapter.
218. USCLCA, *supra* note 7 at §51302.
219. Artemis Accords, *supra* note 102 at section 10.
220. *Ibid.*
221. Hofmann, *supra* note 74 at 206.
222. Hofmann & Masson-Zwaan, *supra* note 12 at 20.

the Moon and other celestial bodies."[223] The purpose of Article VII OST is to make sure that the risks associated with launching activities are fully borne by all States meaningfully involved in their conduct.[224] To this end, the application of Article VII OST is based on two "purely factual" elements: the "launching" of an object into outer space and the causation of a "damage" by said object.[225] It should be emphasized that this provision was intentionally drafted in order to have the broadest possible scope of application.[226] To this end, Article VII OST creates four "types" of launching States: (1) those directly "launching" an object, (2) those "procuring"[227] the said launch and finally, those from whose (3) territory or (4) facilities the launch took place.[228] The result of the broad formulation of Article VII OST is that any State providing its public resources for launching an object into outer space will also bear international liability for any damage directly caused by the latter. Before moving to Article VIII OST, it should be noted that the principle of State liability has been further expanded in the LIAB.[229] Pursuant to the *lex specialis* rule,[230] in case of an accident between two States who are both Parties to the OST and the LIAB, the latter rules would prevail. For structural purposes, the LIAB will be analyzed together with the other treaties composing the *Corpus Iuris Spatialis* in section 2 of this chapter.

The concept of launching State is essential for the purposes of Article VIII OST, which establishes the principle of State jurisdiction and control over objects launched into outer space and any personnel thereof.[231] According to the first part of this provision, "a State Party to the Treaty on whose registry an object launched into outer space is carried shall retain jurisdiction and control over such object, and over any personnel thereof, while in outer space or on a celestial body."[232] The principle of State's jurisdiction and control, as laid down in Article VIII OST, plays a central role in the system of international space law[233] and is intricately connected with many of the other principles examined earlier.[234] In light of outer space's legal status as global common, Article VIII OST provides a legal basis for identifying which State is entitled to—and responsible for—the exercise of a minimum level of jurisdictional control thereby.[235] In this respect, Article VIII OST is considered to be declaratory of a general

223. Article VIII OST, *supra* note 1.
224. Cheng, *supra* note 10 at 613.
225. For this reason, Article VII OST could be considered to codify a principle of absolute liability. Cheng, *id.*, at 238.
226. Armel Kerrest & Lesley Jane Smith, *Article VII OST,* in *CoCoSL I, supra* note 21 at 132-133, 136.
227. The expression "procuring the launch" is generally understood as either paying for it by means of public spending or directly organize it through State channels. Kerrest & Smith, *supra* note 226 at 137.
228. Cheng, *supra* note 10 at 613.
229. LIAB, *supra* note 3.
230. As to which, *see* sections 1.1.1 and 1.3.2. (i) in Chapter 1.
231. Hofmann & Masson-Zwaan, *supra* note 12 at 20.
232. Article VIII OST, *supra* note 1.
233. Cheng, *supra* note 10 at 622-626.
234. Bernhard Schmidt-Tedd & Stephan Mick, *Article VIII OST,* in *CoCoSL I, supra* note 21 at 147.
235. *Id.*, at 158-160.

principle of international law,[236] which is common to all international regimes governing the use of global commons.[237] Under the United Nations Convention on the Law of the Sea[238] (UNCLOS), any ship navigating the high seas is subject to the jurisdiction and control of its flag State.[239] Likewise, under the Antarctic Treaty System[240] (ATS), research stations in Antarctica are under the quasi-territorial jurisdiction of a relevant State.[241] In all these cases, the establishment of a link with the jurisdiction of a given State is a fundamental safeguard in defense of the rule of law.[242] If no State were entitled to exercise any form of jurisdictional control thereby, global commons would quickly descend into chaos. In the absence of supranational authorities entrusted with the management of these common areas, this responsibility is thus diffused within the various States directly or indirectly undertaking activities thereby. Within the system of space law, the power to exercise jurisdiction and control over a space object, including any personnel thereof, is inherently vested in all launching States. This is clear from the use of the term *retain* within Article VIII OST to indicate that national registration is not the source of these powers but rather the formal mechanism through which we identify *which* State is entitled to exercise them.[243]

The analysis of the provision reveals that registration within Article VIII OST is based on two elements. First, in order to register a space object, a State must qualify as launching State.[244] Second, among the various States launching an object into outer space, only the one including it within its (national) *registry* will be entitled to "retain" jurisdiction and control over it.[245] These two conditions are fundamentally important for transparency and liability purposes. By requiring the formal insertion of an object launched into outer space within a national registry, Article VIII OST provides a measure of confidence building.[246] Registration, in fact, helps to keep track of the various space objects as well as to identify at least one State which shall be liable for

236. Article 38 ICJ Statute, *supra* note 226.
237. Cheng, *supra* note 10 at 466-467.
238. United Nations Convention on the Law of the Sea, *entered into force* November 16, 1994, 1833 UNTS 3 [hereinafter: "UNCLOS"].
239. Article 92 UNCLOS, *supra* note 238.
240. The Antarctic Treaty, *entered into force* June 23, 1961, 402 U.N.T.S. 71 [hereinafter: "AT"].
241. Article VII AT, *supra* note 240.
242. On the importance of national jurisdiction in the context of the law of the sea, *see* Stuart Kaye, *Threats from the Global Commons: Problems of Jurisdiction and Enforcement,* in *Global Legal Challenges: Command of the Commons, Strategic Communications and Natural Disasters* 69-82 (Michael Carsten ed., 2007). On the role of national jurisdiction within the ATS, *see* Renè Lefeber, *The Exercise of Jurisdiction in the Antarctic Region and the Changing Structure of International Law: The International Community and Common Interests,* 21 Netherlands Yearbook of International Law 81-137 (1990), as well as Odd Gunnar Skagestad, *Sovereignty, Jurisdiction, and Cooperation: The Antarctic Treaty, Preconditions, Substance and Future Relevance,* 1 New Ground Research Journal 6-20 (2013). On the function played by national jurisdiction and control in the system of international space law, *see* Schmidt-Tedd & Mick, *supra* note 234 at 158, as well as Cheng, *supra* note 10 at 622-632.
243. Specifically, the provision refers to the State Party "on whose registry an object launched into outer space is carried." Article VIII OST, *supra* note 1.
244. Schmidt-Tedd & Mick, *supra* note 234 at 151.
245. Article VIII OST, *supra* note 1.
246. Ram Jakhu, Bhupendra Jasan & Jonathan McDowell, *Critical Issues Related to Registration of Space Objects and Transparency of Space Activities,* 143 Acta Astronautica 407 (2018).

any damage they may cause.[247] Both these purposes play a fundamental role in the peaceful and responsible uses of space, which is why this part of Article VIII OST has been later expanded in a separate international agreement dedicated to the registration of space objects.[248] To conclude our general analysis of Article VIII OST, it is important to briefly address its second sentence, according to which "ownership of objects launched into outer space, including objects landed or constructed on a celestial body, and of their component parts, is not affected by their presence in outer space or on a celestial body or by their return to the Earth."[249] This part of Article VIII OST acts as a notwithstanding clause[250] harmonizing the regimes of space law and property law. On the one hand, the provision reiterates that being the owner of a space object does not trigger any right or obligation under international space law.[251] On the other hand, the provision clarifies that being a space object does not have any effect within the realm of property law.[252] As will be discussed in the next part of this section, this separation between space law and property law may have significant implications for the establishment of "property rights" over objects made from space resources. Finally, the third sentence of Article VIII OST establishes the duty for a State retrieving a registered space object to return it to its State of Registry, subject to an explicit request coupled with minimum identification data.[253]

Consequences on Space Mining Activities and Regulation

The implications of Article VII OST will be further discussed in conjunction with the analysis of the LIAB. Therefore, this section focuses on the consequences of the principle of State jurisdiction and control under Article VIII OST. To begin with, thanks to the link established with both a space object as well as any personnel thereof, the State registering a space object involved in a space resource activity will be able to extend its jurisdiction and control over the entire chain of operations. Notably, this may include both "objects constructed on celestial bodies"[254] as well as any "space-made product"[255] manufactured thereby. In this author's view, this extension is in line with the formulation of the article, which provides for the legal inclusion of "objects constructed on a celestial body" within the category of "objects launched into outer space."[256] This legal equivalence implies that also objects constructed on a celestial body may be included in a State's national registry for the purpose of retaining jurisdiction and control over them.[257] In the absence of a launching event, the link to

247. Kerrest & Smith, *supra* note 226 at 139.
248. *Alias* the REG, *supra* note 4.
249. Article VIII OST, *supra* note 1.
250. On the role of these clauses for the systemic integration of international law, *see* section 1.3.3 (i) in Chapter 1.
251. Schmidt-Tedd & Mick, *supra* note 234 at 164.
252. *Id.*, at 163.
253. Article VIII OST, *supra* note 1. Schmidt-Tedd & Mick, *supra* note 234 at 165.
254. Article VIII OST, *supra* note 1.
255. According to Building Block 1, a "space-made product" can be any object "made, in whole or in part, from space resources in outer space." BB Commentary, *supra* note 82 at 24.
256. "Ownership of objects launched into outer space, *including objects landed or constructed on a celestial body ....*" Article VIII OST, *supra* note 1.
257. Similar considerations can also be found in Cheng, *supra* note 10 at 503-504.

identify the appropriate State of registry would be provided by the jurisdiction exercised over the "personnel"[258] constructing the object or manufacturing the space-made product. *Mutatis mutandis*, the same conclusion can be reached in case the space object or space product would be autonomously developed by a rover sent on a celestial body, provided, of course, that the latter has been duly registered by its launching State. Finally, in case the constructing or manufacturing processes would incorporate previously registered space objects, the extension of jurisdiction and control may be supported by the concept of collective space object.[259] Applying this new notion of international space law, the existing registration of the space objects used in the manufacturing process may be expanded to cover the newly formed collective, thus extending related jurisdiction and control.[260]

For the foregoing reasons, it can be concluded that Article VIII OST is of critical importance for the regulation of space resource activities, as it will provide the necessary legal basis for their concrete oversight.

1.1.6 Due Regard, Non-harmful Contamination and International Consultations under Article IX OST

Fundamental Features and Purposes

Article IX OST is one of the longest and most complex provisions of the OST. This article lays down three important norms of international space law: the principle of due regard, the prohibition of harmful contamination and the obligation of undertaking international consultations to handle potentially harmful interferences.[261]

The Principle of Due Regard

To begin with the first principle, according to Article IX OST, States "shall conduct all their activities in outer space, including the Moon and other celestial bodies, with due regard to the corresponding interests of all other States Parties to the Treaty."[262]

As with many other ambiguous terms, the OST does not define the meaning of "due regard." Following the rules of systemic integration analyzed in Chapter 1,[263] we can look at how the term is used within the broader environment of international law. Historically, the principle of due regard made its first appearance in the foundational

258. According to Article VIII OST, States retain jurisdiction and control over "any personnel" onboard a space object included in its registry. Article VIII OST, *supra* note 1.
259. Which has been advanced for the first time by this author. *See* Antonino Salmeri, *Collective Space Objects as a New Concept of International Space Law*, 46 (2) Air & Space Law 203-222 (2021).
260. Since the space objects used in the process have now become component parts of the newly formed space-made product, the extension of jurisdiction and control would happen pursuant to a simple update of the existing registration information.
261. Sergio Marchisio, *Article IX OST*, in *CoCoSL I*, *supra* note 21 at 170.
262. Article IX OST, *supra* note 1.
263. As to which, *see* section 1.3.3 in Chapter 1.

document of air law, the Chicago Convention.[264] Later on, the principle was also adopted within the law of the sea, specifically in Article 87 (2) UNCLOS.[265] Under both these provisions, the term "due regard" refers to the performance of an act with a certain standard of care, attention or observance.[266] Recently, this expression has been defined in a leading case[267] of the International Tribunal for the Law of the Sea[268] (ITLOS), appearing for the first time in a decision of an international court.[269] Within the M/V Norstar proceedings, the principle of due regard has been defined by one of the parties[270] as a twofold obligation. First, when exercising their freedoms under the UNCLOS, States must consider the interests of other States.[271] Second and related, when exercising said freedoms, States must refrain from "activities that interfere with the exercise by other States of their parallel freedoms to do likewise."[272] Since the ITLOS found that Article 87 (2) UNCLOS was not applicable in the case at hand, it did not address Panama's proposed interpretation of the principle of due regard.[273] However, it is already noteworthy that said interpretation was not contested by Italy,[274] Panama's respondent in the M/V Norstar case. Leveraging this interpretation for the purposes of international space law, one may argue that paying "due regard to the corresponding interests of other States"[275] implies that a State shall not undertake activities that would threaten the exercise of the freedoms of exploration and use by other States.[276] Framed in these terms, the principle of due regard is considered to be an important limit to the freedom of exploration and use of outer space provided for in Article I (2) OST.[277] Within Article IX OST, this principle is implemented in the remaining parts of the provision, which provide two examples of how the principle of due regard limits the freedoms of space.

The Prohibition of Harmful Contamination of Celestial Bodies

The first implementation of the principle of due regard is laid down in the part of Article IX OST which addresses the environmental aspects of space activities. According to this

264. Chicago Convention on International Civil Aviation, *entered into force on* April 4, 1947, 15 U.N.T.S. 295 (1994) [hereinafter: "Chicago Convention"]. The principle of due regard appears in its Article 3 (d), according to which "the contracting States undertake, when issuing regulations for their state aircraft, that they will have due regard for the safety of navigation of civil aircraft."
265. Article 87 UNCLOS, *supra* note 238.
266. Marchisio, *supra* note 261 at 175-176.
267. The M/V "Norstar" case (*Panama v. Italy*), ITLOS case no. 25, (Judgment, April 10, 2019), 58 ILM 673 at para. 199 (2019) [hereinafter: "Norstar case"].
268. Information on the ITLOS can be found https://www.itlos.org/en/main/latest-news/ on its website (last accessed October 2022).
269. BB Commentary, *supra* note 82 at 57.
270. Specifically, the State of Panama—initiator of the proceedings before the ITLOS. Norstar case, *supra* note 267.
271. Norstar case, *supra* note 267.
272. *Ibid.*
273. *Id.*, at para. 231.
274. To be precise, Italy contended the alleged breach of the due regard principle, but did not question the interpretation of the principle in itself. *Id.*, at para. 211.
275. Article IX OST, *supra* note 1.
276. Marchisio, *supra* note 261 at 175.
277. Hobe, *supra* note 21 at 39-40.

provision, "States Parties to the Treaty shall pursue studies of outer space, including the Moon and other celestial bodies, and conduct exploration of them so to avoid their harmful contamination and also adverse changes in the environment of the Earth resulting from the introduction of extraterrestrial material matter and, where necessary shall adopt appropriate measures for this purpose."[278] The interpretation of this central part of Article IX OST reveals a series of incremental obligations related to the environmental protection of outer space.[279] The first two are the non-harmful contamination of outer space and celestial bodies and the protection of Earth's environment, which are both revealed by a textual interpretation of the provision. In order to understand the first obligation, it is important to identify the legal meaning to be attributed to the expression "non-harmful contamination."[280] Pursuant to Article 31 VCLT, the ordinary meaning[281] of the term harmful is "capable of causing harm,"[282] which could be understood as unwanted disturbance producing negative effects. The question then becomes: harmful *for whom*? The drafting history of the OST reveals that the prohibition of harmful contamination was intended to preserve the safe conduct of other space activities.[283] Concerning the interpretation of the term "contamination," its ordinary meaning refers to the insertion of non-autochthonous biological material within the space environment.[284] Based on these initial findings, States should refrain from those forms of biological contamination that, because of their impact on the outer space environment, would negatively affect other space activities conducted by States.

Framed in these terms, the prohibition of forward contamination laid down in Article IX OST has played a crucial role[285] in preserving the pristine conditions of outer space environment for the scientific investigations conducted in the field of astrobiology. This discipline investigates the origins of life in the universe by studying the environmental conditions of natural objects in the solar system.[286] For astrobiologists to conduct their research, it is vital that those conditions are not altered by the introduction of biological material from the Earth's biosphere. Concerning the prohibition of backward contamination, this obligation serves the purpose of protecting our

278. Article IX OST, *supra* note 1.
279. Marchisio, *supra* note 261 at 176.
280. Article IX OST, *supra* note 1.
281. Article 31 VCLT, *supra* note 64.
282. Merriam-Webster Dictionary, *Harmful,* available https://www.merriam-webster.com/dictionary/harmful#:~:text=%3A%20causing%20or%20capable%20of%20causing%20harm%20%3A%20injurious%20Keep,harmful%20substances%20away%20from%20children (last accessed October 2022).
283. Marchisio, *supra* note 261 at 171-174. This interpretation is further reinforced by the last part of Article IX OST, setting up a consultation mechanism for preventing or resolving harmful interferences among States' activities in space.
284. Merriam-Webster Dictionary, *Contamination,* available https://www.merriam-webster.com/dictionary/contamination (last accessed October 2022).
285. Marchisio, *supra* note 261 at 178-179.
286. According to the description provided by NASA in its https://astrobiology.nasa.gov/about/astrobiology website (last accessed October 2022).

planet's delicate biosphere from potentially dangerous extraterrestrial biological materials.[287] Drawing again from the teachings of astrobiology, we know that any form of biological entity able to survive the extremely harsh conditions of outer space could be capable of exponentially prospering on our planet, to the point of potentially wiping out Earth's autochthonous life.[288] Thus, it is essential that any object re-entering the Earth's environment is safely stored and managed in order to avoid the uncontrolled proliferation and distribution of extraterrestrial biological material on our planet.[289] In order to implement these obligations, Article IX OST provides that States "where necessary, shall adopt appropriate measures for this purpose."[290] With regard to the prohibitions of forward and backward contamination, these measures can be found in the "planetary protection policies"[291] developed and updated under the auspices of Article IX OST[292] by the Committee on Space Research[293] (COSPAR). These "policies" are scientific documents discussed bi-annually in dedicated scientific gatherings organized by COSPAR.[294] In themselves, COSPAR's policies are not legally binding. At the same time, due to the credibility of COSPAR and the need to coordinate efforts at the global level,[295] they are universally recognized as a reference document for implementing the obligations laid down in Article IX OST.[296] Accordingly, COSPAR's planetary protection policies are widely implemented by those States who are engaged in the exploration of the solar system.[297] Notwithstanding some unfortunate exceptions,[298] the prohibitions of forward and backward contamination, as laid down in Article IX OST and implemented in COSPAR's planetary protection policies, enjoy a

287. To better understand the dangers of astrobiology it is always useful to look at the https://www.hq.nasa.gov/office/pao/History/SP-4214/ch4-3.html practices developed by NASA to "secure" the return of the Apollo 11 astronauts from their mission to the lunar surface (last accessed October 2022).
288. NASA, *supra* note 286.
289. NASA, *supra* note 287.
290. Article IX OST, *supra* note 1.
291. The globally relevant reference document for planetary protections has been recently updated in June 2020 and is available https://cosparhq.cnes.fr/assets/uploads/2020/07/PPPolicyJune-2020_Final_Web.pdf. Based on this document, space agencies like https://sma.nasa.gov/sma-disciplines/planetary-protection#: ~ :text = It%20covers%20all%20space%20flight,biosphere%20from%20extraterrestrial%20targets%20of NASA or https://www.esa.int/Science_Exploration/Human_and_Robotic_Exploration/Exploration/ExoMars/Planetary_protection ESA develop their own versions (last accessed October 2022).
292. Hofmann & Masson-Zwaan, *supra* note 12 at 124.
293. COSPAR has been established in 1958, even before the enactment of the OST, "to promote at an international level scientific research in space, with emphasis on the exchange of results, information and opinions, and to provide a forum, open to all scientists, for the discussion of problems that may affect scientific space research." More information on its activities and missions are available https://cosparhq.cnes.fr/ (last accessed October 2022).
294. As clarified in COSPAR' strategy, which is available https://cosparhq.cnes.fr/about/cospar-strategy-statement/ (last accessed October 2022).
295. Marchisio, *supra* note 261 at 178.
296. Hofmann & Masson-Zwaan, *supra* note 12 at 129.
297. For a comprehensive assessment of the most prominent cases of national space legislations, *see* Marboe, *supra* note 201 at 139-178.
298. Brilliantly summarized by Keren Shahar & Dov Greenbaum, *Lessons in Space Regulations from the Lunar Tardigrades of the Beresheet Hard Landing*, 4 Nature Astronomy 208-209 (2020).

high degree of compliance.[299] As such, one of the most notable results of Article IX OST is to have preserved the conduct of vital scientific investigations on the origins of life in the universe as well as the delicate balance of Earth's biosphere.

While these achievements are certainly important, Article IX OST has the potential to do much more.[300] For decades, a mere textual interpretation of the provision has limited the environmental protection of outer space to planetary protection policies.[301] However, a systematic reading of the provision reveals another layer of obligations consisting of the duties recently developed in international law for the environmental protection of global commons.[302] As discussed earlier in this chapter, Articles I and II OST provide for the legal status of outer space and celestial bodies as global commons, while Article III OST determines the dynamic integration between space law and international law.[303] Based on these provisions, new norms of international environmental law can come into play both as a limit to the exploration and use of space under Articles I and III OST,[304] as well as a parameter for the interpretation of Article IX OST under Article 31 (3) (c) VCLT.[305] Consequently, a systematic reading of Article IX OST in conjunction with Articles I, II and III OST may result in the integration of the new norms of international environmental law that are also applicable to the space environment. Among those, the prohibition of transboundary harm has emerged as a general obligation of fundamental importance. This rule has been codified in Principle 2 of the 1992 Rio Declaration[306] and subsequently consolidated by the ICJ in the 1996 advisory opinion on the *Legality of the Threat or Use of Nuclear Weapons*[307] and in the 1997 judgment on the *Gabčikovo-Nagymaros* case.[308] In the words of the ICJ, the prohibition of transboundary harm entails "a general obligation of Stats to ensure that activities within their jurisdiction and control respect the environment of other States or areas beyond national jurisdiction."[309] According to the World Court, this obligation is twofold: it entails a duty of both control and of preventive action.[310] The question then becomes what "appropriate measures"[311] shall States take to implement

299. For a thorough analysis of this subject, *see* The International Planetary Protection Handbook (2009), available https://ec.europa.eu/research/participants/documents/downloadPublic?documentIds=080166e5c1c292c4&appId=PPGMS (last accessed October 2022).
300. Isabella Diederiks-Verschoor, *Environmental Protection in Outer Space*, 30 German Yearbook of International Law 144, 147 (1987).
301. Hofmann & Masson-Zwaan, *supra* note 12 at 122-123.
302. Marchisio, *supra* note 261 at 175.
303. As to which, *see* respectively sections 2.1. and 2.2 in Chapter 1, and sections 1.1.1 and 1.1.3 in Chapter 2.
304. Hobe, *supra* note 21 at 35-36.
305. Leveraging the role of Article 31 as the systemic clause holding together the legal order of international law, as discussed in sections 1.1.2 and 1.3.3. (iii) in Chapter 1.
306. Report of the United Nations Conference on Environment and Development, *Rio Declaration on Environment and Development*, UN Doc. A/CONF.151/26 (Vol. I) (August 12, 1992) [hereinafter: "Rio Declaration"].
307. Legality of the Threat or Use of Nuclear Weapons, (Advisory Opinion, July 8, 1996), 1996 ICJ 226 [hereinafter: "Legality Advisory Opinion"].
308. Gabčikovo-Nagymaros Project (*Hungary v. Slovakia*), (Judgment, September 25, 1997), 1997 I.C.J. 7 at para. 88 [hereinafter: "Gabčikovo-Nagymaros"].
309. Legality Advisory Opinion, *supra* note 307 at 241-242.
310. Gabčikovo-Nagymaros, *supra* note 308 at para. 140.
311. Under Article IX OST, *supra* note 1.

the obligation of transboundary harm in their space activities. In this regard, consolidated practice on the matter reveals an increasing attention of States toward the minimization of the impact of their activities on the space environment.[312] At the international level, concrete examples of this new trend are the 2007 UN Space Debris Mitigation Guidelines,[313] endorsed by the UNGA in its Resolution 62/217,[314] and the 2019 Long-Term Sustainability Guidelines for Outer Space Activities,[315] approved by UNCOPUOS and welcomed with appreciation by the UNGA. At the national level, many States have now included within their licensing conditions dedicated clauses ensuring the protection of the space environment.[316] On average, these clauses range from requiring the presentation of appropriate deorbiting and debris mitigation plans to the development of actual "environmental impact assessments" accounting for the broader impact of the mission on the space environment.[317] The proposed systematic and evolutionary interpretation of Article IX OST is supported not only by subsequent State practice but also by a teleological reading of the provision. As revealed by the drafting history of the OST, the purpose of Article IX OST was to preserve the peaceful uses of space by minimizing the potential for conflict among States.[318] The principle of due regard, the prohibition of harmful contamination and the consultation mechanism that will be analyzed in the final part of this section were introduced to oblige States to make sure that their exercise of the freedom to explore and use outer space would neither prevent nor jeopardize the parallel freedoms of others. Since both our consciousness of environmental issues and our technical means to solve them evolve over time, incorporating these developments in Article IX OST would be in line with its object and purpose. As such, it can be concluded that the environmental obligations laid down in Article IX OST should be allowed to evolve over time in order to avoid outer space from becoming another tragedy of the commons.[319]

The Duty to Consult in case of Potentially Harmful Interference

The last part of Article IX OST concretely operationalizes the principle of due regard by requiring States to consult with each other in case of potentially harmful interference. More specifically, "if a State Party to the Treaty has reason to believe that an activity or experiment planned by it or its nationals in outer space, including the Moon and other celestial bodies, would cause potentially harmful interference with activities of other States Parties in the peaceful exploration and use of outer space [...] it shall undertake

312. Lotta Vikari, *Environmental Aspects of Space Activities*, in *Handbook of Space Law, supra* note 12 at 718.
313. Report of the 50th Session of the Committee on the Peaceful Uses of Outer Space, *Space Debris Mitigation Guidelines*, UN Doc. A/62/20 (2008).
314. Resolution adopted by the General Assembly at its 62nd Session on December 22, 2007, *International Cooperation in the Peaceful Uses of Space*, UN Doc. A/62/217 (2008).
315. Report of the 62nd Session of the Committee on the Peaceful Uses of Outer Space, *Guidelines for the Long Term Sustainability of Outer Space Activities*, UN Doc. A/74/20, Annex II (2020) [hereinafter: "LTS Guidelines"].
316. Hofmann & Masson-Zwaan, *supra* note 12 at 129-130; Vikari, *supra* note 312 at 743.
317. Marboe, *supra* note 201 at 139-178.
318. Marchisio, *supra* note 261 at 171-174.
319. Garret Hardin, *The Tragedy of the Commons*, 162 (3859) Science 1243-1248 (1968).

appropriate international consultations before proceeding with any such activity or experiment."[320] As revealed by the drafting history of the OST,[321] the rather complex drafting of this provision is the result of many discussions between the U.S. and the USSR pursuant to the U.S. "West Ford Experiment."[322] In summary, this experiment involved the launch of millions of copper needles into space for the purpose of creating an artificial belt around Earth to reflect radio waves originating from ground stations. Per its part, the USSR denounced these actions before the UN as a "military criminal experiment,"[323] further complaining about the lack of prior consultations with the global scientific community. As a result of the tensions created between the two superpowers, the issue was discussed before UNCOPUOS. There, the U.S. supported the idea of recommending that States undertake careful studies prior to any experiment in space and that they would also consult with relevant international scientific groups—as appropriate—in case any harmful effects would be envisaged.[324] Conversely, the U.S. rejected the idea that similar obligations would be imposed for all space activities and considered them appropriate only within the context of scientific experiments.[325] Ultimately, as seen above, the formulation of Article IX OST refers to both activities and experiments,[326] thus showing a broader scope than originally proposed by the U.S.

Under Article IX OST, the obligation to consult only arises in the presence of two conditions: (1) that a State "has reason to believe"[327] that there would be a potentially harmful interference, and (2) that said interference would occur with "activities of other States in the peaceful exploration and use of outer space."[328] As to the first, it is believed that the broad discretion connected with the expression "reason to believe"[329] may significantly reduce the applicability of Article IX OST and thus undermine its role within the system of space law.[330] Concerning the second, it should be noted that only legitimate, peaceful space activities are protected under Article IX OST, thus triggering the duty to consult.[331] While this requirement may seem obvious, it was explicated to prevent potential abuses by malicious parties. If both conditions are satisfied, the interfering State(s) shall undertake "appropriate international consultations before proceeding with any such activity or experiment."[332] To better understand this process, it is important to clarify three aspects. First, the term "appropriate"[333] is directly

320. Article IX OST, *supra* note 1.
321. Marchisio, *supra* note 261 at 172-174.
322. A factual overview of the West Ford Experiment done by Wired is available https://www.wired.com/2013/08/project-west-ford/ (last accessed October 2022).
323. Letter dated May 24, 1963 from the Permanent Representative of the Union of Soviet Socialist Republics addressed to the Secretary General (May 28, 1963), UN Doc A/AC. 105/13 (1964).
324. Marchisio, *supra* note 261 at 172.
325. *Ibid.*
326. Article IX OST, *supra* note 1.
327. *Ibid.*
328. *Ibid.*
329. *Ibid.*
330. Hofmann & Masson-Zwaan, *supra* note 12 at 123.
331. Marchisio, *supra* note 261 at 180.
332. Article IX OST, *supra* note 1.
333. *Ibid.*

connected with the potential harmful interference in the sense that the consultation undertaken should be appropriate to deal with it. Second, the expression "international consultations"[334] indicates a preference for consultation mechanisms that include the international community unless bilateral consultations would be more "appropriate" to the case at hand. Third, any consultation should be undertaken prior to proceeding with the activity, thus obliging States to adopt a proactive approach to the prevention of potentially harmful interferences.[335]

To counterbalance the discretion given to the "interfering" State in deciding whether it would like to consult or not, the final part of Article IX OST considers the position of States that may suffer from said potentially harmful interferences. Accordingly, "a State Party to the Treaty which has reason to believe that an activity or experiment planned by another State Party in outer space, including the Moon and other celestial bodies, would cause potentially harmful interference with [its] activities in the peaceful exploration and use of outer space [...] may request consultation concerning the activity or experiment."[336] This last part of Article IX OST might seem to mirror the sentence analyzed above. Nevertheless, there are two significant differences between the two consultation mechanisms. First, in this last provision, there are no temporal references: a State may request consultations either before, during or after the concerned activity takes place. Second, the article does not say whether the requested State is actually obliged to engage in consultations. Certainly, a State cannot refuse to enter into consultations at its pleasure because that would deprive the provision of any legal value.[337] Similarly, a State arguing that it did not find "any reason to believe"[338] that a potentially harmful interference might occur will have to support such statements with convincing facts. While not directly enshrined in Article IX OST, these considerations come from the customary rule of international law that treaties must be performed in good faith.[339] A State circumventing the consultation mechanism as established under Article IX OST would actually breach this provision twice: first, it would infringe its own obligation to proactively engage in prior consultations, and second, it would violate its obligations to pay due regard and cooperate with other States.

Article IX: The Systemic Clause of International Space Law

From the above analysis, we can conclude that Article IX OST plays a critical role in the preservation of space as a peaceful environment and the incentivization of its sustainable uses. First, in requiring States to take into account the corresponding interests of others when conducting their space activities, Article IX OST integrates and connects all the various principles of the OST. Further, in obliging States to take appropriate measures to avoid the harmful impact of their activities on the space environment, Article IX OST preserves it as a shared domain free for exploration and use by all actors.

334. *Ibid.*
335. Cheng, *supra* note 10 at 257.
336. Article IX OST, *supra* note 1.
337. Marchisio, *supra* note 261 at 180.
338. *Ibid.*
339. Article 26 VCLT, *supra* note 64.

Finally, in requiring States to undertake appropriate international consultations in case of potentially harmful interferences, Article IX OST is the only provision of the OST concretely bringing its States Parties vis-à-vis to one another. Because of these features, it can be concluded that Article IX OST is *the* provision that turns a set of specialized rules into an actual system: the ultimate *systemic clause* of international space law.

Consequences on Space Mining Activities and Regulation

The implications of Article IX OST on space mining activities and regulation are manifold. Because of the inherently invasive and consumptive nature of space mining, respecting the systemic obligations of Article IX OST becomes extremely important to ensure its actual compatibility with the OST. In this author's view, the implementation of Article IX OST will be among the decisive factors influencing the assessment of the legality of a given space resource activity or regulation under international space law.

To comply with the principle of due regard, States will have to make sure that the space mining activities for which they are responsible are not spoiling the possibility for others to undertake parallel space activities. For instance, a State authorizing a private company to mine all the available ice in the entire south pole of the Moon would be clearly breaching its obligation to pay due regard to the corresponding interests of other States.

Further to the principle of due regard, also the consultation mechanism is going to play a crucial role in ensuring the compatibility of space resource activities with international space law. Because it is in the very nature of space mining to disrupt the environment in which it takes place, most of the time, it will be necessary to find ad hoc solutions through appropriate international consultations. To give another example, a State deploying a number of remotely controlled mining rovers on the far side of the Moon would be breaching its obligation not to harmfully contaminate the lunar environment. This is because the far side of the Moon offers an incomparable site for scientific investigation due to its unique radio-silent environment, which, however, would be compromised every time an actor activates any radio-emitting source thereby. A potential solution to conduct mining activities on the far side without violating Article IX OST would be offered by the consultation mechanism provided by the provision itself. Through that mechanism, the mining State could offer to consult with relevant actors (either planning to or already) conducting scientific radio observations from the far side of the Moon in order to alternate operations or adjust locations so as to minimize reciprocal interferences. Subject to the successful conduct of these consultations, the "contamination" of the lunar far side would not be harmful anymore, thus reducing the potential for conflict with the provision. Ultimately, it seems safe to state that the principles and mechanisms laid down in Article IX OST will play a crucial role in determining a fair and reasonable balance between space resource activities vis-à-vis competing or overlapping endeavors in space.

1.1.7 Information Sharing under Article XI OST

Fundamental Features and Purposes

Article XI OST lays down the obligation to share information about space activities. Pursuant to this provision, States agree to inform the UNSG, as well as the public and the international scientific community, to the greatest extent feasible and practicable, of the nature, conduct, locations and results of their space activities.[340] The principle of information sharing, as laid down in Article XI OST, plays several important roles within the system of space law.[341] First and foremost, sharing information about the nature and conduct of a given space activity functions as a verification mechanism to ensure its compliance with the OST.[342] By being transparent about their space activities, States contribute to developing space as a trustful environment. Second, sharing information about the conduct and locations of a space activity supports their safe conduct by enabling due regard and coordination under Article IX OST.[343] This is because a State can practically pay due regard only to those interests that have been stated in concrete terms by others. Therefore, the availability of proper information about the (potentially corresponding) interests of other States is a critical precondition for the applicability of the obligation of due regard. Likewise, the availability of sufficient information on space activities is essential to ensure their safe coordination among the involved actors.[344] Again with reference to Article IX OST, the availability of appropriate information on the activities planned or conducted by others is a fundamental precondition to evaluate the risk of potentially harmful interference that triggers the obligation to conduct appropriate international consultations. Third and final, sharing information about the results of space activities is instrumental in promoting international cooperation in the peaceful exploration and use of outer space.[345] In this sense, engaging in information sharing enhances compliance with the principle of benefit sharing laid down in Article I OST.[346] This is notably confirmed by the inclusion of both the public and the international scientific community among the beneficiaries of the provision, as well as by existing State practice on benefit sharing.[347] Having said that, it is important to note that pursuant to the formulation of Article XI OST, information sharing should not be intended as an absolute obligation. This is because the provision establishes that States *agree* to—and not shall—inform the UNSG about their space activities only *to the greatest extent feasible and practicable*. This implies that information sharing is based upon the consent of States, which are not

340. Article XI OST, *supra* note 1.
341. For an analysis of the main purposes of Article XI OST, *see* Jean-François Mayence & Thomas Renter, *Article XI OST*, in *CoCoSL I*, *supra* note 21 at 189-206.
342. *Id.*, at 202.
343. Mark Sundahl & Antonino Salmeri, *The Registration of Lunar Activities: Recommendations from the Registration Project*, 2021 (2) Proceedings of the International Institute of Space Law (2021, in press).
344. *Ibid.*
345. Mayence & Renter, *supra* note 341 at 202.
346. Hobe & Tronchetti, *supra* note 39.
347. Hobe, *supra* note 21 at 40-42.

bound to provide it whenever there is a valid justification not to do so, such as in the case of national security or intellectual property interests.[348]

In order to facilitate the distribution of information shared, the final part of Article XI OST provides that the UNSG should be prepared to disseminate it immediately and effectively. This task is discharged by UNOOSA through the compilation of the submissions received in the *Index of Submissions by States Under Article XI of the Outer Space Treaty*.[349] Even though it has existed since 1969, the Article XI Index only counts a handful of submissions. At first look, this might suggest that Article XI OST is not very considered in State practice. However, a systematic analysis reveals that Article XI OST can be implemented in many ways.[350] Several States, for example, comply with their duty to share information through the registration of space objects. As the greatest majority of space activities are conducted in Earth's orbit, furnishing information on space objects under either Resolution 1721 XVI B or the REG would also fulfill the obligation laid down in Article XI OST.[351] Further to that, virtually all spacefaring nations regularly share information on their space activities every year during the UNCOPUOS meetings. Finally, many States also share information about their space activities directly with the public and/or the international community by making them publicly available in their online repositories.[352] In all these cases, the amount of information shared goes way beyond the minimum requested by Article XI OST.

Consequences on Space Mining Activities and Regulation

The principle of information sharing has vital importance for the peaceful, safe and sustainable conduct of space resource activities. As mentioned, we know very little about the characteristics of the environments of celestial bodies, let alone about their reaction to mining operations. In this context, no State is in the position to determine on its own how its space resource activities may impact the corresponding interests of other States, nor whether and to what extent they could cause potentially harmful contamination or interference. These determinations entirely depend on the availability of adequate information about the environment of celestial bodies as well as the activities of others, including a number of technical details needed to ensure safety and prevent interference. Accordingly, sharing information about space resource activities in accordance with Article XI OST will be vital to build trust, enable coordination and foster cooperation.

However, in order to unleash its full potential for transparency and safety, the current mechanism for sharing information under Article XI OST will need to be

348. Mayence & Renter, *supra* note 341 at 197-198.
349. Index of Submissions by States under Article XI of the Outer Space Treaty, available https://www.unoosa.org/oosa/en/treatyimplementation/ost-art-xi/index.html (last accessed October 2022).
350. Mayence & Renter, *supra* note 341 at 196.
351. Sundahl & Salmeri, *supra* note 343.
352. As notably evidenced by the websites of https://www.nasa.gov/ NASA and https://www.esa.int/ ESA (last accessed October 2022).

adjusted to better fit modern needs associated with the exploration and use of celestial bodies.[353]

1.1.8 Open Access to Stations and Installations under Article XII OST

Fundamental Features and Purposes

Article XII OST regulates access to stations, installations, equipment and vehicles on celestial bodies. Pursuant to this provision, all these shall be open to the representatives of other Parties on a basis of reciprocity.[354] With a view to ensuring safety and avoiding interference with nominal operations, Article XII OST establishes that representatives shall give reasonable advance notice of their projected visit so as to hold appropriate consultations and take maximum precautions. The openness of stations, installations, equipment and vehicles located on celestial bodies is meant to ensure their exclusively peaceful uses.[355] In obliging States to give access to their facilities on celestial bodies, Article XII offers an opportunity to verify their compliance with Article IV (2) OST.

The interpretation of the condition of reciprocity will play a critical role in ensuring the practical relevance of this provision. In this regard, some authors have suggested that this clause should be interpreted as establishing that if a State refuses to give access to its facility, the rejected State may, in turn, equally deny access to its own.[356] While literally plausible, this interpretation does not seem to be in line with the object and purpose of the provision. This is because the practical result of this interpretation would likely be a series of cross-vetoes, ultimately resulting in reduced access for everyone. In turn, this would frustrate the principle of transparency which constitutes the *raison d'etre* of the provision in the first place, with potentially serious repercussions on the exclusively peaceful uses of celestial bodies.[357] An alternative interpretation might be suggested by the formulation of an analog mechanism under Article VII of the Antarctic Treaty (AT). Pursuant to this provision, all facilities in Antarctica shall be open for inspections at any time, but the right to conduct such inspections is recognized only to the representatives of those States which demonstrate an interest in the region by conducting activities thereby.[358] Likewise, the condition of reciprocity included in Article XII OST might be interpreted in the sense of giving States the right to refuse access only to the representatives of those States which do not have *any* station, installation, equipment or vehicle of their own that could be accessed as

353. Sundahl & Salmeri, *supra* note 343.
354. Article XII OST, *supra* note 1.
355. For an analysis of the main purposes of Article XII OST, *see* Lesley Jane Smith, *Article XII OST*, in *CoCoSL I*, *supra* note 21 at 207-214.
356. Bin Cheng, *The 1967 Outer Space Treaty*, 95 Journal du Droit International 532, 610 (1968). Some authors have argued an even broader application of the reciprocity clause Christopher M. Petras, *"Space Force Alpha": Military Uses of the International Space Station and the Concept of "Peaceful Purposes,"* 53 Air Force Law Review 135, 145 (2002).
357. Smith, *supra* note 355 at 213.
358. Article VII in conjunction with Article IX AT, *supra* note 240.

well. As a result of this interpretation, the grounds for refusal would be objective in nature, thus reducing the risk of abuse.

Under the same line of reasoning, also the conditions laid down in the second part of the provision should be interpreted in such a way that does not hamper or frustrate the fundamental principle of openness. In this sense, it has been rightly suggested that the nature of the advance notice to be given as well as of the consultations to be held are inherently procedural.[359] This, in turn, means that States cannot rely on these conditions to refuse access tout court but only to (eventually) delay it accordingly. To avoid potential abuses, these conditions have to be applied in good faith and with a view to the object and purpose of the provision.

It is interesting to note that in regulating access to stations and installations on celestial bodies, Article XII OST implicitly recognizes the right to build such facilities in the first place. On the one hand, the existence of this right is confirmed by Article IV (2) OST, which forbids the establishment of *military* bases and installations on celestial bodies,[360] and Article VIII OST, which determines the exercise of jurisdiction and control over objects *built* on the surface of celestial bodies.[361] On the other hand, the exercise of this right is limited by the principle of free access under Article I OST and the prohibition of national appropriation under Article II OST.[362] A combined reading of these provisions suggests keeping stations open for visits and inspections as much as possible to ensure a better balance with the principle of free access under Article I OST and to prevent allegations of potential violations of Articles II and IV (2) OST.

Consequences on Space Mining Activities and Regulation

The implications of Article XII OST on space mining are of a highly delicate nature.

This is because there may well be technical and commercial reasons suggesting a limited application of the principle of open access to space mining facilities. For example, a space mining company might want to access the facilities of its competitor to acquire privileged information on its business activities. Similar abuses should be prevented and addressed by States in accordance with the principle of good faith. For what concerns technical issues, they are recognized by the part of Article XII OST which acknowledges the need to take maximum caution to assure safety and avoid interference with nominal operations. In accordance with the procedure designed in the provision, technical coordination would have to be agreed upon during the consultations preceding the visit.

1.2 The Liability and Registration Conventions

As is well-known, both the LIAB and the REG have been developed to elaborate and expand each on a specific OST provision. For the LIAB, this provision is Article VII

359. Smith, *supra* note 355 at 211-212.
360. Article IV OST, *supra* note 1.
361. Article VIII OST, *supra* note 1.
362. In light of the status of space as a global common, *see* sections 1.1.1, 1.1.2 and 1.1.3 in Chapter 2.

OST,[363] which establishes the liability of launching States for damages caused by space objects.[364] For the REG, this provision is Article VIII OST,[365] according to which a launching State can retain jurisdiction and control over a given space object by including it in a national registry.[366]

1.2.1 The Liability Convention: Fundamental Features and Purposes

The LIAB was adopted in 1972 with the goal to provide "effective international rules and procedures concerning liability for damage caused by space objects."[367] In accordance with its preamble, the twenty-eight articles of the LIAB lay down the fundamental rules governing international liability for space objects and further provide detailed procedures for settling relevant disputes arising thereof.[368] The goal of the LIAB is to provide the highest possible protection for the potential victims of damages caused by space objects.[369] To this end, building upon Article VII OST, the LIAB introduces various significant additions strengthening the relevant obligations already established under the OST and further elaborating on the practical aspects which were not covered thereby.[370]

The very first novelty of the LIAB is a list of definitions clarifying the meaning of the terms "damage," "launching," "launching State," and "space object."[371] While the effort is certainly positive, the definitions laid down in Article I LIAB are not as exhaustive as one would expect in other fields of law.[372] Truth be told, this provision uses the very same words of the OST and just rearranges them as definitions.[373] There are two explanations for this choice. The first is that the LIAB drafters, like the OST ones, did not manage to reconcile their views on definitional aspects.[374] The second, and related to the first, is that the creators of international space law were fundamentally skeptical of definitions.[375] Conscious that space technologies could have evolved

363. Von Der Dunk, *supra* note 15 at 82.
364. Article VII OST, *supra* note 1. For an analysis of Article VII OST, *see* section 1.1.4 in Chapter 2.
365. Von Der Dunk, *supra* note 15 at 94.
366. Article VIII OST, *supra* note 1. For an analysis of Article VIII OST, *see* section 1.1.5 in Chapter 2.
367. Preamble LIAB, *supra* note 3.
368. For a comprehensive assessment of the LIAB, *see* Cheng, *supra* note 10 at 286-355.
369. Lesley Jane Smith & Armel Kerrest, *Article I LIAB (Definitions)*, in *Cologne Commentary on Space Law: Vol. 2* 101-103 (Stephan Hobe, Bernhard Schmidt-Tedd & Kai-Uwe Schrogl eds., 2013; book hereinafter: "CoCoSL II").
370. When this book has been finalized in October 2022, the LIAB counted 98 Parties. UNOOSA, *supra* note 14.
371. Article I LIAB.
372. For an interesting analysis on definitional issues in space law, *see* Cheng, *supra* note 10 at 492-509.
373. The four criteria for the definition of a launching State can for instance be found already within Article VII OST. Similarly, damages compensated under the LIAB were already sanctioned as well under Article VII OST.
374. The negotiations of the LIAB were often conducted "in secret" and suffered through various deadlocks. Cheng, *supra* note 10 at 292-300.
375. Stephan Hobe, *Historical Background of the Outer Space Treaty*, in *CoCoSL I*, *supra* note 21 at 14.

in unforeseeable ways, they did not want to attach the applicability of space law to fixed definitions that were doomed to become outdated or, worse, counterproductive.[376] The definitions laid down in Article I LIAB have no presumption of completeness[377] and are intended to continuingly adapt to the evolution of technology.[378]

The second novelty introduced in the LIAB is the development of different forms of liability based on the target and location of the damage. For "damage caused by a space object on the surface of the Earth or to an aircraft in flight,"[379] Article II LIAB determines the absolute liability of the relevant launching State(s).[380] However, "in the event of damage being caused elsewhere than on the surface of the Earth to a space object [...] or to persons or property onboard [...] by a space object of another launching State,"[381] Article III LIAB provides that "the latter shall be liable only if the damage is due to its fault or the faults of the persons for whom it is responsible."[382] The combination of Articles II and III LIAB achieves two results. On the one hand, Article II LIAB reiterates and clarifies the absolute liability provided by Article VII OST for any damage caused to any person or property on the surface of the Earth.[383] On the other hand, Article III LIAB introduces the element of fault as a decisive criterion to determine the apportion of liability in the event of damage caused by a space object to another. This addition was necessary because, under Article VII OST, this scenario would have had two States absolutely liable toward one another,[384] with the paradoxical result of reducing incentives for responsible behavior in space. By introducing the element of fault, Article III LIAB intends to push States to do everything they can to avoid the collision, with the goal of proving that they are not at fault in case damage ultimately happens.[385]

As to the other provisions, Articles IV and V LIAB regulate the apportion of liability in cases involving different launching States,[386] while Articles VI and VII LIAB provide for causes of exoneration.[387] Finally, the remaining articles lay down a detailed procedure for presenting and handling a liability claim under the Convention, from the initial steps to be taken to the potential establishment of a Claim Commission for disagreements.[388]

In this regard, it should be noted that the procedure provided by the LIAB has never been used, even though there have been some cases potentially justifying its

376. Blount, *supra* note 154 at 34.
377. In the sense of fixing the related terms once and for all. Smith & Kerrest, *supra* note 369 at 115.
378. Mahulena Hofmann & P.J. Blount, *Innovation in Outer Space: International and African Legal Perspectives—Lessons Learned*, in *Innovation in Outer Space*, *supra* note 55 at 14-15.
379. Article II LIAB, *supra* note 3.
380. Through the direct use of the expression "shall be absolutely liable." *Ibid.*
381. Article III LIAB, *supra* note 3.
382. *Ibid.*
383. Cheng, *supra* note 10 at 326.
384. Hofmann & Masson-Zwaan, *supra* note 12 at 28.
385. Smith & Kerrest, *supra* note 369 at 131.
386. On the topic of "joint and several liability," *see* Cheng, *supra* note 10 at 328-332.
387. Lyall & Larsen, *supra* note 12 at 110.
388. Articles X-XX LIAB, *supra* note 3.

application.[389] This is because, in these (few) instances, States preferred to address any issue by means of bilateral diplomatic negotiations.[390] Despite that, it can be concluded that the LIAB represents a useful addition to the fundamental rules provided in the OST on the international liability of States for damage caused by space objects.

1.2.2 The Registration Convention: Fundamental Features and Purposes

Moving to the REG, this treaty was adopted in 1975[391] with the purpose of "making provision for the national registration" of space objects and enhancing their identification through "a central register to be established and maintained, on a mandatory basis, by the Secretary General of the United Nations."[392] The twelve articles of the REG build upon Article VIII OST to expand its scope and provide practical rules for its implementation.[393]

Thanks to this treaty, the registration of space objects has been established as a legal obligation.[394] The first reason behind this decision was to foster transparency and build confidence in the exploration and use of outer space.[395] By obliging States to share minimum identificatory information on their space objects, the REG aims to discourage the conduct of malicious space activities.[396] Even if the obligation to register space objects is substantially unenforceable,[397] the mere fact of being put in the spotlight for not having registered a given space object is already an incentive to minimize their ambiguous uses. Further to that, the mandatory registration of space objects serves the purpose of enhancing the application of the liability rules[398] by ensuring the establishment of a "legal link"[399] between every given space object and at least one launching State. Finally, in centralizing essential information on objects launched into outer space at the international level, the REG also enables better

389. Hofmann & Masson-Zwaan, *supra* note 12 at 30. Another shortcoming of the LIAB is that only covers only damages physically caused by space objects, thus excluding from its scope immaterial damages caused, for instance, by service malfunctioning. Maria Elena De Maestri & Sergio Carbone, *The Rationale for an International Convention on Third Party Liability for Satellite Navigation Signals*, 14 (1-2) Uniform Law Review 35-55 (2009).
390. Like in the famous Cosmos 954 case, available https://www.jaxa.jp/library/space_law/chapter_3/3-2-2-1_e.html, (last accessed October 2022).
391. Forty-seven years later, when this book has been finalized in October 2022, the REG counts seventy-two Parties. UNOOSA, *supra* note 14.
392. Preamble REG, *supra* note 4.
393. For a comprehensive analysis on the REG, *see* Bernhard Schmidt-Tedd, Ulrike Bohlmann, Natalya Malysheva, Olga Stelmakh & Leslie Tennen, *The 1975 Convention on the Registration of Objects Launched into Outer Space*, in *CoCoSL II*, *supra* note 369 at 227-324.
394. Although some authors have argued the existence of an implicit obligation to the national registration of space objects under UNGA Resolution 1721B (XVI). Jakhu et al., *supra* note 246 at 407.
395. Schmidt-Tedd et al., *supra* note 393 at 234-235.
396. Jakhu et al., *supra* note 246 at 413.
397. Von Der Dunk, *supra* note 15 at 98.
398. Either from the OST or the LIAB. Kerrest & Smith, *supra* note 226 at 139.
399. Vladimir Kopal, *The 1975 Convention on Registration of Objects Launched into Outer Space in View of the Growth of Commercial Space Activities*, in *Air and Space Law in the 21st Century: Liber Amicorum Karl-Heinz Bockstiegel* 375 (Marietta Benkoe & Walter Kroll eds., 2001).

coordination among space activities, thus reducing the risks of potentially harmful interferences.[400]

Similar to the LIAB,[401] the REG begins with a list of definitions clarifying the meaning of the terms "launching State," "space object" and "State of Registry."[402] Following, Article II REG provides for the main novelty of the treaty: the obligation for launching States (1) to register their space objects "by means of an entry in an appropriate registry which [they] shall maintain"[403] and (2) to inform the UNSG of the establishment of such a registry.[404] Notably, under paragraph 3 of Article II REG, "the content of each registry and the conditions under which it is maintained shall be determined by the State of Registry concerned."[405] While this decision was perfectly understandable at the time, subsequent practice revealed the need for minimum harmonization of the various registries established all around the world.[406] In light of the difficulties usually implied in amending a treaty, this gap was later filled by the UNGA through its Resolution 62/101 of December 17, 2007,[407] which, *inter alia*, included the development of a model registration form.[408]

In addition to the registration of space objects at the national level, Article III REG requests the UNSG to maintain an international registry for the purpose of recording the information furnished by the States in accordance with the treaty.[409] Notably, Article III REG uses the term "maintain"[410] rather than "establish" because the UN "Registry of Objects Launched into Outer Space"[411] was originally set up[412] pursuant to UNGA Res. 1721B (XVI) of December 20, 1961.[413] Back then, the goal of that Registry was to support both technical and legal discussions in UNCOPUOS with voluntary information shared by States. To this date, the mechanism foreseen in UNGA Res. 1721B is still used by States which are not Parties to the REG to voluntarily share relevant information on their space objects.[414] Therefore, the UN Registry of space

400. On the importance of registration for coordination of space activities *see* Sundahl & Salmeri, *supra* note 343.
401. With the difference that the REG does not include attempted launches within the scope of its application. Cheng, *supra* note 10 at 493.
402. Article I REG, *supra* note 4. Schmidt-Tedd et al., *supra* note 393 at 244-248.
403. Article II REG, *supra* note 4.
404. Which is essential to achieve the objective of transparency of the Convention. Jakhu et al., *supra* note 246 at 413.
405. Article II REG, *supra* note 4.
406. Schmidt-Tedd et al., *supra* note 393 at 259-261.
407. Resolution adopted by the General Assembly at its 62nd Session, Recommendations on enhancing the practice of States and international intergovernmental organizations in Registering Space Objects, UN Doc A/RES/62/101 (December 17, 2007).
408. For an assessment of A/RES/62/201 *see* Tanja Masson-Zwaan, *Registration of Small Satellites and the Case of the Netherlands*, in *Small Satellites: Regulatory Challenges and Chances* 174-194 (Imgard Marboe ed., 2016).
409. Cheng, *supra* note 10 at 421.
410. Article III REG, *supra* note 4.
411. Pursuant to Article III REG, the UN Registry is publicly available https://www.unoosa.org/oosa/en/spaceobjectregister/index.html (last accessed October 2022).
412. Schmidt-Tedd et al., *supra* note 393 at 298-299.
413. Resolution adopted by the General Assembly at its 16th Session, *International Cooperation in the Peaceful Uses of Outer Space*, UN Doc. RES 1721B (XVI) (1961).
414. Jakhu et al., *supra* note 246 at 407.

objects is currently composed of two sections:[415] one for information submitted under UNGA Res. 1721B and other information provided in accordance with the REG. In this regard, Article IV REG obliges the launching State to share a minimum degree of information determined in the article to be furnished to the UNSG "as soon as practicable."[416] Needless to say, this rather vague clause has often been criticized for leaving too much discretion to the launching State, ultimately weakening the mandatory character of registration.[417] Albeit some of these concerns have been addressed in UNGA Res. 62/101,[418] the absence of a clear time limit for the international registration of space objects is the most significant shortcoming of the REG. Notwithstanding this weakness, the REG is a very successful instrument. According to UNOOSA, to date, over 86% of all satellites, probes, landers, crewed spacecraft and space station flight elements launched into Earth orbit or beyond have been registered with the UN.[419] This high level of compliance shows the continuing relevance of the REG in fostering the peaceful and sustainable uses of space.

1.2.3 The Liability and Registration Conventions: Consequences on Space Mining Activities and Regulation

With respect to space mining activities and regulations, the LIAB and the REG each provide a crucial complement to the fundamental principles of the OST. Not by chance, recent developments in policy urge for their timely ratification among States planning to undertake space resource or lunar activities.[420] Enhancing the ratification status of the two Conventions would serve two complementary purposes. First and foremost, it would ensure that all States share the same legal obligations, avoiding regulatory discrepancies that can potentially result in tensions or disputes. Further, sharing the same fundamental set of treaties would allow the involved States to adapt their application for the specific purposes of space resource activities. As seen above, the LIAB and the REG have been originally conceived as complements to the OST.[421] However, almost fifty years later, both Conventions are in need of further regulatory instruments complementing and updating their rules, especially if they are to be successfully applied to space resource activities.

---

415. As it can be noted also from its https://www.unoosa.org/oosa/osoindex/search-ng.jspx?lf_id= searching mechanism (last accessed October 2022).
416. Article IV REG, *supra* note 4.
417. Lyall & Larsen, *supra* note 12 at 93-96; Christol, *supra* note 164 at 235-239; Kopal, *supra* note 399 at 380-381.
418. Hofmann & Masson-Zwaan, *supra* note 12 at 43-45.
419. As reported by UNOOSA itself https://www.unoosa.org/oosa/en/spaceobjectregister/index.html (last accessed October 2022).
420. For instance, section 7 of the Artemis Accords commits its Signatories to register their objects under the REG. Artemis Accords, *supra* note 102. With specific reference to space mining, Building Block 14 calls the international framework to ensure that States "register space objects in accordance with the REG, UNGA Resolution 1721 B (XVI), or Article XI OST, taking into account UNGA Resolution 62/101." BB Commentary, *supra* note 82 at 79-81.
421. Von Der Dunk, *supra* note 15 at 82, 94; Hofmann & Masson-Zwaan, *supra* note 12 at 26, 31.

To begin with the LIAB, the applicability of a fault-based regime for the apportion of liability related to space mining operations is of essential importance. Simply put, the high risks associated with these activities would become economically unbearable if liability were attributed based on absolute criteria. Conversely, a fault-based liability would adhere more to the realities of space mining. Precisely for this reason, it is of the utmost importance to find objective parameters for the concrete application of the fault's criterion foreseen in Article III LIAB.[422] As is well-known, terrestrial mining activities can rely on hundreds of years of practice and are based on widely recognized operational standards.[423] On the contrary, space resource activities are brand new, have no standards and further present additional risks due to the hostile, unexplored environments of celestial bodies.[424] It follows that in order for the LIAB to properly achieve its purpose, we need to develop standards and parameters that could determine what constitutes fault within an accident caused by a space object during a space mining activity.[425]

On a similar line of reasoning, also the applicability of the REG is of fundamental importance for the peaceful and sustainable conduct of space resource activities.

By obliging all States involved in space mining to register the space objects involved in space mining, the REG will contribute to monitoring the respect of international space law as well as to enabling the prevention of potentially harmful interference.[426] At the same time, the specificities of space mining require the development of further regulation integrating the Conventions' shortcomings. Among them, the most significant one is that REG was developed for the registration of objects operating in orbit, not on the surface of celestial bodies. Apart from those related to the identification of the launching State and the general function of the object, the information required under Article IV REG is not applicable to objects involved in surface activities.[427] Furthermore, the dynamic and area-based nature of space mining call for the inclusion of data concerning the location and duration of related activities, which are not required under the REG.[428] These shortcomings could be addressed through a UNGA resolution inviting States to develop new sections of their national registries for space objects involved in space resource activities and then to share the

422. Truth to be told, this task has been attempted without success since the very enactment of the LIAB. Smith & Kerrest, *supra* note 369 at 222-226.
423. The most famous ones being the Australian http://www.jorc.org/ "JORC" and the Canadian https://www.osc.ca/en/securities-law/instruments-rules-policies/4/43-101 "National Instrument (NI) 43-101" (both last accessed October 2022).
424. Fengna Xu, *The Approach to Sustainable Space Mining: Issues, Challenges, and Solutions,* available https://iopscience.iop.org/article/10.1088/1757-899X/738/1/012014/pdf (last accessed October 2022).
425. It is worth noting that in the absence of dedicated parameters for the determination of fault, the position of each State might also be evaluated in accordance with the principle of *no harm* under general international law.
426. On the usefulness of the REG for space resource and lunar activities *see* Sundahl & Salmeri, *supra* note 343.
427. Being explicitly related to "basic orbital parameters." Article IV REG, *supra* note 4.
428. Although States "agree" to share this information under Article XI OST.

information included thereby in the UN Register.[429] In conclusion, if properly enhanced, both the LIAB and the REG could play a key role in promoting the safe and sustainable conduct of space resource activities.

1.3 The Moon Agreement

To conclude the present analysis of the rules of international space law relevant to space mining, this section considers the provisions of the MA.[430] Despite being the space treaty with the lowest number of ratifications,[431] the MA is the only one that has been specifically drafted for the purpose of regulating activities on celestial bodies, including but not limited to space mining.[432] As such, albeit strongly opposed by the U.S.[433] and largely ignored by other spacefaring nations, the MA could still be relevant as a useful source of inspiration for the international regulation of space mining.[434]

1.3.1 The Moon Agreement: Fundamental Features and Purposes

For most parts, the MA simply restates the same principles of the OST.[435] However, the agreement also presents some additions and innovations that are important to consider, especially with regard to space mining.

To begin with, although the primary focus of the treaty is the Moon, Article 1 MA extends its scope of application to all celestial bodies within the solar system, at least until the subsequent enactment of dedicated legal norms superseding it.[436] Following, Article 2 MA restates the applicability of international law to space activities.[437] This article is a combination of Article III OST and the first part of Article IX OST, with an additional mention of the Declaration of Friendly Relations.[438] Likewise, Article 3 MA

429. For more recommendations on how to improve the application of the REG in the context of space resource and lunar activities *see* Sundahl & Salmeri, *supra* note 343.
430. For a comprehensive assessment of the MA, *see* Cheng, *supra* note 10 at 357-380.
431. When this book has been finalized in October 2022, the MA counted eighteen Parties and four Signatories. For comparison, the second-to-last treaty for number of ratifications is the REG with a total of seventy-two. UNOOSA, *supra* note 14.
432. Diederiks-Verschoor, *supra* note 18 at 48.
433. Donald J. Trump, *Executive Order on Encouraging International Support for the Recovery and Use of Space Resources,* enacted on April 6, 2020, available https://trumpwhitehouse.archives.gov/presidential-actions/executive-order-encouraging-international-support-recovery-use-space-resources/ (last accessed October 2022) [hereinafter: "Space Resources EO"].
434. Renè Lefeber, *Relaunching the Moon Agreement,* 1 Air & Space Law 41-48 (2016). While Lefeber's belief that "the MA provides the best available option for Mankind, States and industry to develop space mineral resources in a harmonious way" is maybe too extreme; it is certainly agreeable that the MA should play a role in the global multi-stakeholder dialogue on the international regulation of space resources activities.
435. Von Der Dunk, *supra* note 15 at 99-100.
436. Article 1 MA, *supra* note 5.
437. Article 2 MA, *supra* note 5.
438. Resolution adopted by the General Assembly at its 25th Session, Declaration on Principles of International Law Friendly Relations and Co-operation among States in Accordance with the Charter of the United Nations, UN Doc. A/RES/25/2625 (1970).

on the peaceful uses of the Moon is fundamentally based upon Article IV (2) OST. However, the provision adds a new paragraph prohibiting "any threat or use of force or any other hostile act or threat of hostile act on the Moon,"[439] clearly recalling the language of Article 2 (4) UN Charter.[440] It should be noted that the additions made in both Articles 3 and 4 MA do not bring any real novelty to the substance of international space law.[441] This is because both the Declaration of Friendly Relations as well as Article 2 (4) UN Charter were already applicable to the exploration and use of the Moon under Article III OST.[442] Nevertheless, the MA includes them in order to reaffirm and emphasize the importance of cooperation and peace as guiding principles for the exploration and use of the Moon.[443]

The first element of novelty can be found in Article 4 MA, which expands the province principle laid down in Article 1 OST with two new legal obligations. First, Article 4 MA requires States to pay due regard "to the interests of present and future generations."[444] This addition is noteworthy because it is the first time that the concepts of sustainability and intergenerational balance form the basis of a legal obligation of international space law.[445] In light of the special value that the Moon has for our species, the MA was indeed supposed to be a treaty "not only for our generation but also for future generations."[446] Interestingly, while this solemn declaration by U.S. President Johnson expresses a shared desire for a more proactive international space law, the unfortunate destiny of the MA ultimately produced the opposite result. In addition to the interests of present and future generations, Article 4 MA further requires States to pay due regard to "the need to promote higher standards of living and conditions of economic and social progress and development in accordance with the Charter of the United Nations."[447] Through this ambitious clause, the MA links the exploration and use of the Moon to the promotion of economic and social progress on Earth. In this respect, one could argue that the MA was perhaps too ambitious for the technological possibilities available at the time. Unfortunately, since the adoption of the MA, humans have never returned to the Moon, and even its robotic exploration was abandoned in favor of more "terrestrial" activities.[448] Nevertheless, the idea of connecting the exploration and use of space for the promotion of social and economic

439. Article 3 MA, *supra* note 5.
440. Article 2 (4) UN Charter.
441. Cheng, *supra* note 10 at 367.
442. On the function of Article III OST within the system of space law *see* sections 2.1. and 2.2. in Chapter 1.
443. Stephan Hobe, Peter Stubbe & Fabio Tronchetti, *Historical Background and Context MOON*, in *CoCoSL II*, *supra* note 369 at 343.
444. Article 4 MA, *supra* note 5.
445. Stephan Hobe & Fabio Tronchetti, *Article 4 MOON*, in *CoCoSL II*, *supra* note 369 at 365.
446. Senate Committee on Aeronautical and Space Sciences, Space Treaty Proposals by the United States and U.S.S.R.—Staff Report Prepared for the Use of the Committee on Aeronautical and Space Sciences, 89th Congress, 2nd Session, U.S. Government Printing Office, Washington 1966, p. 1 (reported in *CoCoSL II*, *supra* note 369 at 359).
447. Article 4 MA, *supra* note 5.
448. A comprehensive historical overview of lunar exploration is provided https://www.nationalgeographic.com/science/article/moon-exploration by National Geographic (last accessed October 2022).

progress on Earth remains valid and, since recent times, is at the core of the UN strategy for space.[449]

Article 5 MA builds upon Articles IX and XI OST by obliging States to share a significant amount of information on their lunar activities and leveraging them for the purposes of international coordination.[450] Paragraph 2 of this provision is especially forward-thinking in requiring States to promptly inform each other of the timing and plans for their lunar activities if they become aware that "another State Party plans to operate simultaneously in the same area"[451] or lunar orbits or trajectories. Interestingly, a similar logic can be found behind the modern concept of *safety zone*, an area-based measure calling for close coordination among all States operating therein.[452]

Article 6 MA elaborates on Article I (3) OST to reinforce the importance of the freedom of scientific investigation.[453] The most interesting part of this provision is again the second paragraph, which addresses in great detail the collection of Moon samples and the use of "minerals and other substances"[454] for scientific purposes. According to this article, in the course of scientific investigations, States have the right to "collect on and remove from the Moon samples of its mineral and other substances,"[455] which shall remain at their disposal and "may be used for scientific purposes."[456] Further to collecting samples, Article 6 (2) MA also allows States to "use" them "in the course of scientific investigations" and "in quantities appropriate for the support of their missions."[457]

To better understand the role of Article 6 MA within the Agreement, it is essential to interpret it in light of the systematic and teleological criteria of Article 31 VCLT.[458] Through the use of these criteria, we can notice that Article 6 (2) MA is closely connected with the new version of the non-appropriation principle as enshrined in Article 11 MA.[459] In this respect, it is important to remember that previous State practice had shown that the prohibition of Article II OST did not apply to space resources since both the U.S. and the USSR had already collected and brought back significant kilograms of lunar resources.[460] In light of the declaration of the Moon and

449. UNOOSA, Space Supporting the Sustainable Development Goals, available https://www.unoosa.org/oosa/en/ourwork/space4sdgs/index.html (last accessed October 2022).
450. Stephan Hobe & Fabio Tronchetti, *Article 5 MOON*, in *CoCoSL II*, *supra* note 369 at 368.
451. Article 5 MA, *supra* note 5.
452. The concept of safety zone is one of the contentious issues currently discussed at the international level for the regulation of space resources and lunar activities. Within the context of space resource activities, the concept of safety zones has been advanced for the first time in Building Block 11: BB Commentary, *supra* note 82 at 64-70. More recently, safety zones have been included in the Artemis Accords as a suggested measure for deconfliction of activities. Artemis Accords, *supra* note 102 at section 11.
453. Stephan Hobe & Fabio Tronchetti, *Article 6 MOON*, in *CoCoSL II*, *supra* note 369 at 370.
454. Article 5 MA, *supra* note 5.
455. *Ibid.*
456. *Ibid.*
457. *Ibid.*
458. Article 31 VCLT, *supra* note 64.
459. Hobe & Tronchetti, *supra* note 453.
460. As discussed earlier in sections 1.1.1 and 1.1.2 in Chapter 2.

its natural resources as "the common heritage of mankind," (CHM)[461] Article 11 MA formulates a broader version of the non-appropriation principle, which also includes space resources.[462] At the same time, the drafters of the MA wanted to ensure that this broader scope of the non-appropriation principle would not prevent the utilization of space resources for scientific or operational purposes.[463] Since the object and purpose of Article 6 MA is to promote and reinforce the freedom of scientific investigation on the Moon,[464] its second paragraph exempts the use of lunar resources for scientific purposes from the governing system envisaged in Article 11 MA. This connection is established *expressis verbis* within the latter provision, which in its paragraph 8 specifies that "all the activities with respect to the natural resources of the Moon shall be carried out in a manner compatible with [...] the provisions of Article 6, paragraph 2, of this Agreement."[465] Therefore, Article 6 (2) MA serves the purpose of excluding the application of the legal, administrative and economic barriers posed for the commercial use of lunar resources under Article 11 MA.

Next comes Article 7 MA, which is dedicated to the environmental preservation of the Moon.[466] Article 7 MA significantly expands the scope of Article IX OST[467] by requiring States conducting activities on the Moon to take measures "to prevent the disruption of the existing balance of its environment, whether by introducing adverse changes in that environment, by its harmful contamination through the introduction of extra/environmental matter or otherwise."[468] The fact that Article 7 MA provides for new, stricter legal obligations than Article IX OST is already evident from a textual comparison of the two provisions. This is further confirmed by both the systematic and teleological criteria, again with special reference to Article 11 MA. The declaration of the Moon and its resources as the "common heritage of mankind," in fact, has direct implications also on the necessary level of environmental protection. Consequently, Article 7 MA takes measures to preserve the status quo of the lunar environment as a fundamental precondition for the practical implementation of the CHM regime. In this respect, Article 7 MA certainly goes beyond the prohibition of harmful biologic contamination laid down in Article IX OST, which here is incorporated into a general duty[469] to "prevent the disruption of the existing balance"[470] of the lunar environment whether "by introducing adverse changes [...] by its harmful contamination [...] or otherwise."[471] The use of the clause "otherwise" at the end of the sentence confirms the broad scope of the provision, indicating the non-exhaustiveness of the list of prohibited

461. Article 11 MA, *supra* note 5.
462. As to which, *see* section 1.3.2 in Chapter 2.
463. Hobe & Tronchetti, *supra* note 453 at 370-371. Not by chance, Article 6 MA never mentions the term "appropriation" or "resources": Cheng, *supra* note 10 at 369.
464. *Ibid.*
465. Article 11 MA, *supra* note 5.
466. Cheng, *supra* note 10 at 372.
467. Steven Freeland, *Article 7 MOON*, in *CoCoSL II*, *supra* note 369 at 373-374.
468. Article 7 MA, *supra* note 5.
469. Freeland, *supra* note 467.
470. Article 7 MA, *supra* note 5.
471. *Ibid.*

behaviors formally considered as disrupting the existing balance of the Moon.[472] Accordingly, the prohibitions of "introducing adverse changes"[473] and of "harmful contamination through the introduction of extra-environmental material"[474] should be considered as two mere examples of what could constitute a disruption of the existing balance of the lunar environment.[475] Drawing from these two examples, as well as on the ordinary meaning of the expression "disruption of the existing balance," it seems that Article 7 MA requires lunar activities to be environmentally neutral, i.e., without any prejudice toward the environment around them.[476] The question then becomes what creates prejudice to the lunar environment and what does not. One criterion to make such assessment could be the duration of the changes, in the sense of prohibiting permanent alterations to the lunar environment. However, the low level of active geology on the Moon[477] practically makes *every* change a permanent one, with the result that a similar interpretation of Article 7 MA would outlaw any activity on the Moon. When Buzz Aldrin became the second human to set foot on the Moon on July 24, 1969, making him one of the few humans to bear witness to the lunar surface, he characterized it as "magnificent desolation."[478] There was, according to him, "no place on earth as desolate ... because I realised what I was looking at, towards the horizon and in every direction, had not changed in hundreds, thousands of years."[479] Aldrin's footprints permanently changed that "magnificent desolation," but nobody would argue that they disrupted the existing balance of the lunar environment.[480] Therefore, the permanent duration of the changes cannot be a decisive element in assessing whether or not something creates a disruption to the lunar environment. Looking closely at the terminology used in the examples provided within Article 7 itself, we find that both of them are characterized by the use of two negative terms, "adverse" and

---

472. Freeland, *supra* note 467.
473. *Ibid.*
474. *Ibid.*
475. Freeland, *supra* note 467 at 375.
476. Stephen Gorove, *Pollution and Outer Space: A Legal Analysis and Appraisal*, 5 New York University Journal of International Law & Policy 53-56 (1972).
477. Until few years ago, the Moon was considered to be "tectonically dead." Recent discoveries are partially changing this idea, although the fact remains that "recent" changes to the surface of the Moon have all been externally caused. Adam Mann, *The Moon May Be Tectonically Active, and Geologists Are Shaken*, National Geographic, available https://www.nationalgeographic.com/science/article/moon-may-be-tectonically-active-geologists-shaken-apollo-moonquakes (last accessed October 2022).
478. Steve Gorman, *Buzz Aldrin, Second Man on Moon, Recalls "Magnificent Desolation,"* available https://www.reuters.com/article/us-space-exploration-aldrin-idUSKCN1UC01P (last accessed October 2022).
479. *Ibid.*
480. To the contrary, the U.S. has recently approved the "One Small Step to Protect Human Heritage in Space Act" to protect them during future lunar activities. This bill has been strongly https://www.forallmoonkind.org/wp-content/uploads/2019/05/One-Small-Step-Act-one-pager.pdf advocated by https://www.forallmoonkind.org/ For All Moonkind, a U.S. non-governmental, non-profit organization established with the purpose to protect human heritage in space (last accessed October 2022). One Small Step to Protect Human Heritage in Space Act, *entered into force* December 31, 2020, H.R. 3766, 116th Congress (2019-2020) [hereinafter: "OSSA"].

"harmful."[481] Accordingly, not *all* the changes introduced to the lunar environment are prohibited: only the *adverse* ones.[482] Likewise, only the *harmful* introduction of extraterrestrial material constitutes a prohibited form of contamination. Therefore, we can conclude that Article 7 MA does not prohibit *all* disruptions of the existing balance of the Moon, but *only* those that have a somehow negative effect on it as a whole.[483] As a consequence, our question becomes what a negative effect is—and most importantly, from whose perspective such an assessment should be made. As seen earlier, under Article IX OST, the protection of the space environment served the purpose of preserving the freedom of exploration and use of other States as a specific implementation of the principle of due regard.[484] Under Article 7 MA, this purpose needs to be adjusted in light of the CHM status of the Moon and its natural resources.[485] Accordingly, a disruption of the lunar environment should be considered either legal or illegal, depending on its impact on the CHM regime. As a result, any activity altering the lunar environment in a way that would obstruct the application of the CHM regime should be considered to be prohibited by Article 7 MA.

On a similar line of reasoning, Article 8 MA lists a series of possible uses of the Moon[486] that are not considered to be in conflict with the other provisions of the treaty.[487] Among those, Article 9 MA specifically addresses the establishment of robotic or human stations.[488] To this end, the provision builds upon Article XII OST by formalizing the implicit right of States to develop installations on the territory of the Moon and further subjecting it to a series of significant limitations.[489] First, Article 9 (1) MA limits the use of the lunar territory only to the area "required for the needs of the station."[490] Second, the provision requires the State establishing a station to "immediately inform [the UNSG] of the location and purposes of the station."[491] Third, Article 9 (2) MA explicitly obliges States to establish their lunar stations "in such a manner that they do not impede the free access to all areas of the Moon"[492] as it may be required by other States for the conduct of their legitimate activities thereof. Similar to Articles 7 and 8 MA, also this provision takes a fundamental principle of the OST and adjusts its application in light of the CHM regime.[493] As seen, under Article I (2) OST, the principle of free access had to be balanced with the freedom to use celestial bodies under the same provision as well as with the possibility to establish stations under Article XII

481. Article 7 MA, *supra* note 5.
482. Freeland, *supra* note 467 at 375.
483. *Ibid.*
484. On the interconnection between the principle of due regard the prohibition of harmful contamination *see* section 1.1.6 in Chapter 2.
485. Which is the very *raison d'être* of the Agreement. Cheng, *supra* note 10 at 365.
486. For instance, landing space objects on the Moon as well as launching them from there. Article 8 MA, *supra* note 5.
487. Steven Freeland, *Article 8 MOON*, in *CoCoSL II*, *supra* note 369 at 379-380.
488. In light of the particularly invasive character of this activity. Article 9 MA, *supra* note 5.
489. Steven Freeland, *Article 9 MOON*, in *CoCoSL II*, *supra* note 369 at 383.
490. Article 9 (1) MA, *supra* note 5.
491. *Ibid.*
492. Article 9 (2) MA, *supra* note 5.
493. Cheng, *supra* note 10 at 367.

OST.[494] Under Article 9 MA, because of the CHM status of the Moon, that logic is reversed: the right to build stations is seen as a tolerated exception to the principle of free access and thus is subject to strict limitations.[495]

Another provision of the Agreement significantly expanding the scope of a fundamental rule from the OST is Article 15 MA, which builds upon Articles IX and XII OST to regulate the relations among the States Parties to the Agreement.[496] According to this provision, each State Party "may assure itself that the activities of other States in the exploration and use of the Moon are compatible with the provisions of this Agreement."[497] To this end, Article 15 MA requires all human-made objects on the Moon to be open to other States Parties, which—per their parts—shall give reasonable advance notice of a projected visit.[498] As anticipated, this provision partially builds upon Article XII OST, according to which States could visit each other's facilities on the basis of reciprocity.[499] Article 15 MA removes this latter condition and excludes any ground upon which a State may refuse to give access. In this regard, the provision explicitly links this right to the verification of compliance with the provisions of the Agreement, to whom Article XII OST was only implicitly connected. On this note, the second paragraph of Article 15 MA regulates the procedure to be followed in case a State has reason to believe that another State Party is either not fulfilling its obligations under the Agreement or interfering with the rights of the concerned State.[500] To govern this scenario, Article 15 (2) MA flips the consultation mechanism laid down in Article IX OST. What used to be a largely discretionary process to prevent or resolve harmful interferences becomes a binding confrontation aimed at discussing potential violations of the MA.[501] According to Article 15 (2) MA, a State suspecting violations is entitled to request consultations with the "accused" State, which "shall enter into such consultations without delay."[502] What is more, any other State Party is entitled to take part in these consultations upon presentation of a simple request.[503] Article 15 (2) MA further regulates how the consultations shall be held, including an obligation to communicate their results to the UNSG, which shall then transmit said information to all States Parties concerned.[504] If the consultations would not lead to "a mutually acceptable settlement which has due regard for the rights and interests of all States Parties,"[505] paragraph 3 of Article 15 MA requires States to take all measures necessary to settle their dispute by other peaceful means. Finally, as part of this process, Article 15 (3) MA further provides that any State Party involved may seek the assistance of the UNSG to

494. As to which, *see* sections 1.1.1 and 1.1.8 in Chapter 2.
495. Freeland, *supra* note 489.
496. Steven Freeland, *Article 15 MOON*, in *CoCoSL II*, *supra* note 369 at 408.
497. Article 15 MA, *supra* note 5.
498. *Ibid.*
499. Article XII OST, *supra* note 1.
500. Cheng, *supra* note 10 at 373.
501. Freeland, *supra* note 496 at 409.
502. Article 15 (2) MA, *supra* note 5.
503. *Ibid.*
504. *Ibid.*
505. Article 15 (3) MA, *supra* note 5.

resolve the controversy without having to obtain prior consent from any of the other Parties concerned.[506]

Before moving to the CHM regime established under Article 11 MA, it is worth briefly considering the remaining provisions of the MA. To begin with, Article 10 MA expands on Article V OST to enhance the protection of human life and health on the Moon.[507] Articles 12 and 13 MA substantially reiterate existing rules under Article VIII OST and the ARRA.[508] Finally, Article 14 MA addresses together responsibility and liability, further specifying that "detailed arrangements concerning liability for damage caused on the Moon [...] may become necessary as a result of more extensive activities."[509]

1.3.2 The Moon Agreement: The CHM

To complete the analysis on the fundamental features and purposes of the MA, this section gives special attention to its Article 11. Pursuant to this provision, the Moon and its natural resources are declared to be the "common heritage of mankind, which finds its expression in the provisions of this agreement."[510] It is important to note that the CHM regime made its debut in international space law with Article 11 MA.[511] Before going into the origins and the implications of such expression, it is crucial to distinguish it from the "province of all mankind"[512] mentioned under Article I (1) OST. Within this provision, declaring the exploration and use of outer space as the province of all mankind served the purpose of clarifying the status of space as a global common.[513] Under Article 11 MA, declaring the Moon and its natural resources as CHM is meant to establish a new, stricter status governing the exploration and use of celestial bodies and their natural resources. Article 11 MA restricts the freedom to use celestial bodies established by Article I OST by subjecting it to the terms of the international regime mentioned thereby.

The concept of CHM was not invented by the drafters of the MA. The general notion had, in fact, been first suggested in 1967 as part of a speech delivered at the UN by the Maltese Ambassador Pardo.[514] Thirty years later, the notion was adopted in the UNCLOS to govern the exploitation of the mineral resources located in the deep seabed,

506. *Ibid.*
507. Article 10 MA, *supra* note 5. For an analysis of this provision, *see* Ram Jakhu, *Article 10 MOON,* in *CoCoSL II, supra* note 369 at 385-387.
508. Articles 12 and 13 MA, *supra* note 5. For an analysis of these provisions, *see* respectively Ram Jakhu, *Article 12 MOON,* in *CoCoSL II, supra* note 369 at 400-402, and Ram Jakhu & Peter Stubbe, *Article 13 MOON,* in *CoCoSL II, supra* note 369 at 403-404.
509. Article 14 MA, *supra* note 5. For an analysis of this provision, *see* Stephan Hobe & Fabio Tronchetti, *Article 15 MOON,* in *CoCoSL II, supra* note 369 at 405-406.
510. Article 11 MA, *supra* note 5.
511. Hofmann & Masson-Zwaan, *supra* note 12 at 35.
512. *Ibid.*
513. As to which, *see* section 1.1.1 in Chapter 2.
514. Rudolph P. Arnold, *The Common Heritage of Mankind as a Legal Concept,* 9 International Lawyer 153 (1975).

which were both declared to be "the common heritage of all mankind."[515] As a consequence of this status, the UNCLOS entrusts the management of the deep seabed and its resources to a dedicated intergovernmental organization called the International Seabed Authority[516] (ISA). The ISA acts as a custodian of the deep seabed for present and future generations, governing the use of mineral resources to be prospected or extracted from the deep seabed and ensuring the effective protection of the marine environment.[517] The CHM regime laid down in the UNCLOS is essentially based on two pillars. The first one is the sharing of revenues: according to Article 140 UNCLOS, the ISA is obliged to establish norms and procedures for the sharing of the revenues generated by mining activities.[518] The second pillar is the so-called parallel system of reserved areas.[519] For this purpose, the UNCLOS provides the ISA with a specialized commercial arm—the Enterprise—to undertake its own mining operations, primarily through joint ventures with other entities.[520] Any application to commence exploration within the seabed is required to identify two areas of sufficient size and equal economic value to accommodate two mining operations.[521] Subject to a discretionary decision of the ISA, one of the two sites will become a reserved area retained by the organization itself for conducting mining activities through the Enterprise.[522] Under the UNCLOS, no mining activity can take place in the seabed without the consent of the ISA,[523] which to date has approved a total of twenty-one exploration contracts.[524]

Despite using the same terminology, the CHM regime set forth in the MA is very different from the UNCLOS one. This is made very clear at the very beginning of the provision, according to which the CHM regime of the MA "finds its expression in the provisions of this agreement, in particular in paragraph 5 of this article."[525]

Following the usual drafting technique of the Agreement, Article 11 MA incorporates and expands the scope of the non-appropriation principle established under Article II OST.[526] Consequently, under Article 11 MA, it is prohibited to appropriate not

515. Article 135 UNCLOS, *supra* note 238.
516. Articles 156-185 UNCLOS, *supra* note 238.
517. Information on the ISA can be found https://www.isa.org.jm/index.php/our-work/protection-marine-environment (last accessed October 2022).
518. Article 140 UNCLOS, *supra* note 238. After years of discussions and consultations, the ISA has developed Draft Exploitation Regulations which are now under consideration by its Legal and Technical Commission as well by the Council. Information on the process can be found https://www.isa.org.jm/index.php/mining-code/ongoing-development-regulations-exploitation-mineral-resources-area (last accessed October 2022).
519. More information on this topic as well as the current status of the reserved areas with ISA can be found https://www.isa.org.jm/files/files/documents/statusofreservedareas-01-2019-a.pdf (last accessed October 2022).
520. Article 170 UNCLOS, *supra* note 238.
521. Agreement Relating to the Implementation of Part XI of the Convention (1994), Annex 1 to the UNCLOS, *supra* note 238.
522. Reserved Areas, *supra* note 519.
523. Article 137 UNCLOS, *supra* note 238.
524. Information on the process and signed contracts can be found https://www.isa.org.jm/exploration-contracts in a dedicated section of the ISA website (last accessed October 2022). It is important to note that as exploration already entails significant expenditure, interested entities can meanwhile apply for exclusive rights over the area they are exploring.
525. Article 11 MA, *supra* note 5.
526. Cheng, *supra* note 10 at 368.

only the Moon, "including its surface and sub-surface as well as any part thereof,"[527] but also its "natural resources in place."[528] The use of the term "in place" raises the question of whether the prohibition of Article 11 MA also applies to *extracted* resources.[529] Looking at the drafting history of the Agreement,[530] it seems that the MA does not prohibit ownership of *extracted* resources.[531] In any event, the last sentence of Article 11 (3) MA specifies that "the foregoing provisions are without prejudice to the international regime referred to in paragraph 5 of this article,"[532] thus meaning that the final word is left to the international regime. In contrast to these prohibitions, Article 11 (4) MA reiterates the right to the exploration and use of the Moon under Article I OST while also subjecting its exercise to the provisions of the Agreement.[533]

Article 11 (5) MA solemnly declares that "States Parties to this Agreement hereby undertake to establish an international regime, including appropriate procedures, to govern the exploitation of the natural resources of the Moon as such exploitation is about to become feasible."[534] The idea of committing States Parties to the future establishment of an international agreement—based on the evolution of the circumstances—marks one of the first applications of the principle of adaptive governance within the system of space law. In this respect, Article 11 (5) MA should certainly be appreciated for its pragmatic approach. Moving from the premise that States did not know enough to develop a proper governing regime for the use of lunar resources, Article 11 (5) MA hits "pause" on the normative process to avoid the enactment of inadequate regulation.[535] At the same time, the Agreement does not leave the development of the governing regime entirely to the future.[536] Article 11 (7) MA, in fact, lays down four main purposes to which the Agreement binds the future configuration of the international regime: the "orderly and safe development" of the natural resources of the Moon (a), the "rational management" of those resources (b), "the expansions of opportunities" in their use (c) and finally an "equitable sharing by all States Parties in the benefits derived" therefrom.[537] Looking at these purposes, the common thread uniting them is the desire to ensure the sustainability and accessibility of space resource activities.[538] These principles are also at the core of contemporary discussions

527. Article 11 MA, *supra* note 5.
528. *Ibid.*
529. Frans Von Der Dunk, *The Moon Agreement and the Prospects of Commercial Exploitation of Lunar Resources*, 32 Annals Air and Space Law 103 (2007).
530. Report of the 22nd Session of the Committee on the Peaceful Uses of Outer Space, UN Doc. A/34/20 (Supplement 20), para. 65 (1979). Notably, the dichotomy between resources in place and extracted was present in both U.S. and Soviet drafts of the Agreement.
531. Cheng, *supra* note 10 at 389; Christol, *supra* note 164 at 40; Eilene Galloway, *Status of the Moon Treaty*, Space News 21-22 (August 3-9, 1998); Von Der Dunk, *supra* note 15 at 103.
532. Article 11 (3) MA, *supra* note 5.
533. Article 11 (4) MA, *supra* note 5.
534. Article 11 (5) MA, *supra* note 5.
535. Ram Jakhu, Steven Freeland, Stephan Hobe & Fabio Tronchetti, *Article 11 MOON*, in *CoCoSL II*, *supra* note 369 at 394.
536. Von Der Dunk, *supra* note 15 at 101-102; Hofmann & Masson-Zwaan, *supra* note 12 at 35.
537. Article 11 (7) MA, *supra* note 5.
538. Jonathan S. Koch, *Institutional Framework for the Province of All Mankind: Lessons from the International Seabed Authority for the Governance of Commercial Space Resources Activities*, 16 Astropolitics 15-16 (2018).

on space mining[539] and, with the relevant exception of benefit sharing,[540] will likely find their way to any regime governing the use of space resources.

1.3.3 *The Moon Agreement: Consequences on Space Mining Activities and Regulation*

Since the purpose of the Moon Agreement is precisely to regulate the use of the Moon and its natural resources, its implications on space mining activities and regulations are obviously manifold. Before addressing them, it is worth reminding the reader that with only eighteen ratifications and four signatories, the MA is the least ratified instrument of the *Corpus Iuris Spatialis*.[541] Therefore, there are two kinds of implications determined by the MA: (1) the legal obligations placed upon the Parties and the Signatories to the Agreement and (2) the policy implications on the debate for the governance of space resource activities.

To begin with the first type, it is clear from the analysis conducted above that the MA builds upon fundamental principles of international space law to further develop a whole new series of legal obligations. As noted already, all these elaborations are driven by the fundamental concept, placed at the core of the Agreement, that the Moon and its natural resources are the "common heritage of mankind." Even though this exact terminology has been contested by some of the negotiating parties until the very last minute,[542] a systematic reading reveals the CHM concept as the architrave of the entire Agreement.

Accordingly, if and when the international regime of Article 11 MA is established, it can be assumed that the States Parties to the MA will be able to conduct activities on the Moon exclusively under its terms. This is because the Agreement is characterized by a strong distrust for unilateral initiatives and ultimately aims to bring all lunar activities under international control through the CHM regime. Conversely, the teleological dependence of the norms of the MA on the concept of CHM subordinates their practical application to the establishment of an international regime for its management under Article 11 of the Agreement. Not by chance, the negotiating States of the MA clarified that pending the establishment of the international regime envisaged in Article 11 MA, there is no *moratorium* on the utilization of lunar resources.[543] From a systemic viewpoint, this is justified by the central role played by the CHM within the entire Agreement.

For the above reasons, in this author's view, until the establishment of the international regime foreseen in Article 11, the MA should be considered incomplete and, as such, not fully operational. Without this central piece of the puzzle, the other provisions of the MA are deprived of their legal justification and thus become

539. As showed by Hofmann & Bergamasco, *supra* note 216. The concept of sustainability is also indirectly incorporated within Building Blocks 10 and 12: BB Commentary, *supra* note 82 at 59, 71.
540. Jakhu et al., *supra* note 535 at 398; Von Der Dunk, *supra* note 15 at 102.
541. UNOOSA, *supra* note 14.
542. Most notably the Soviet Union. Jakhu et al., *supra* note 535 at 392.
543. Cheng, *supra* note 10 at 376-379; Jakhu et al., *supra* note 535 at 392.

inapplicable. An example may help to clarify. As discussed earlier, Article 7 MA aims to preserve the natural status quo of the lunar environment in order to support its international management under Article 11 MA. Read in conjunction with this provision, the rather strict environmental obligations of Article 7 MA are justified by the need to impede individual activities threatening the overall balance upon which the CHM regime relies for its application. Therefore, within the systemic architecture of the Agreement, the limitations of Article 7 MA are balanced by the possibilities of the international regime of Article 11 MA. If that regime is not operational, then so is also Article 7 MA, and *mutatis mutandis*, so are the other articles of the Agreement. As a result, until the establishment of the governance regime foreseen in Article 11 MA, States Parties to the MA should not be operatively constrained by its various obligations, except for the one to take good faith efforts toward the establishment of an international regime. In this respect, the drafters of the MA may have been too optimistic in assuming that the complex political process which led to the adoption of the Agreement would have easily restarted as soon as space mining "is about to become feasible."[544] Furthermore, the mechanism foreseen in Article 18 to this end is indeed rather bureaucratic and, as a matter of fact, has never been used to this day. In this regard, it is important to underline that nothing in the MA prevents its States Parties from participating in other multilateral initiatives promoting the development of international governance for lunar resources, even if not formally linked to the Agreement, as demonstrated by the participation of Australia in the Artemis Program.[545] *Mutatis mutandis*, similar findings apply for the States which have only signed but not ratified the MA. Under Article 18 VCLT, these States must refrain from "acts which would defeat the object and purpose of the treaty,"[546] which in the case of the MA is to govern the use of the Moon and its natural resources as the common heritage of all humankind.

The second type of implication from the MA operates at a general policy level. Even though today it is not very popular, the fact remains that the MA has been developed by UNCOPUOS with the consensus of all its members[547] and has been endorsed with the unanimous approval of the UNGA.[548] Furthermore, as mentioned earlier, MA is the only binding document specifically regulating the use of the Moon and its natural resources. For these reasons, it would be myopic and counterproductive to act like the MA never existed. On the contrary, the current global debate on space mining and lunar governance should seriously study the Agreement in order to learn from its mistakes and benefit from its innovations. For example, the MA demonstrated that a fully fledged international regime centralizing the governance of the Moon and

544. Von Der Dunk, *supra* note 15 at 103; Hofmann & Masson-Zwaan, *supra* note 12 at 36.
545. Fabio Tronchetti & Hao Liu, *Australia Between the Moon Agreement and the Artemis Accords*, available https://www.internationalaffairs.org.au/australianoutlook/australia-between-the-moon-agreement-and-the-artemis-accords/#: ~ :text = On%2015%20October%202020%2C% 20Australia,to%20promote%20its%20prosperous%20future. (last accessed October 2022).
546. Article 18 VCLT, *supra* note 64.
547. Jakhu et al., *supra* note 535 at 393.
548. Resolution adopted by the General Assembly at its 34th Session, *Agreement Governing the Activities of States on the Moon and Other Celestial Bodies*, UN Doc A/RES/34/68 (December 5, 1979).

its natural resources is not an appropriate solution to the challenges of our times. Leaving aside the political issues associated with the CHM concept, the reality is that we do not have enough information about the lunar environment to justify the development of a comprehensive international regime governing it.[549] So far, the only activities on the Moon have been limited to a few human missions performing scientific experiments, some orbiters mapping the lunarscape and a handful of rovers operating on the surface.[550] There are no data confirming our estimations on the composition of the lunar soil, and we are rather far from being able to operate permanently in the hostile conditions of the lunar environment.[551] With these premises, any regulation can, at best, guess the types of activities that will be actually conducted on the Moon, let alone determine what rules they should follow. Given the relevant costs associated with the negotiation of treaties, it would be wise to postpone this demanding process to a point in time when it can produce adequate and effective results. This is perhaps the most precious lesson learned from the experience of the MA, a treaty that did too much too early.

This is not to say that there should not be international regulation, but rather that in the early stages, it should focus on providing foundational rules that could ensure the safe and sustainable use of the Moon and its natural resources. In this regard, there are many inputs from the MA that could inspire the development of new regulatory instruments, like the idea that lunar activities should be conducted with due regard to the interests of future generations.[552] Another great source of inspiration might come from Article 5 MA, which invites States to share fundamental information on their lunar activities and provides for the prompt exchange of additional data among States planning to simultaneously operate in the same area or orbits.[553] Article 5 MA is probably the most useful provision of the Agreement at this point in time due to the universally recognized need for enhanced information-sharing mechanisms.[554] Another useful idea for the contemporary regulation of lunar activities comes from Article 7 (3) MA. This provision foresees the international designation of "areas of special scientific interests" as well as the development of "special protective arrangements" for their preservation.[555] Significantly, a similar concept is at the core of a recent statute passed in the United States—the firmest political opposer of the MA—for the protection of "cultural heritage sites" on the Moon.[556]

To conclude, in this author's view, the MA is a useful source of international space law that deserves respect and consideration. Even though its political destiny is

549. *Mutatis mutandis*, the same considerations expressed by The Hague Group on space resource activities should be kept in mind also for the exploration and use of the Moon. BB Commentary, *supra* note 82 at 1-2.
550. National Geographic, *supra* note 448.
551. Pino et al., *supra* note 117.
552. Article 4 MA, *supra* note 5.
553. Article 5 MA, *supra* note 5.
554. As evidenced by sections 4 and 11 of the Artemis Accords and argued by Sundahl & Salmeri, *supra* note 343.
555. Article 7 MA, *supra* note 5.
556. OSSA, *supra* note 480.

compromised, the Agreement could still serve as a useful inspiration.[557] To this end, it is important to approach the MA with an objective approach, so to understand what should be kept and what should be abandoned. In this respect, the analysis conducted in this section reveals two findings. First, the main mistake of the MA was to do too much too early. Accordingly, any national or international regulation of space mining should not repeat this mistake. At the moment, we need rules that could enable the safe and sustainable conduct of groundbreaking missions collecting essential information and developing practical experience. Later, the lessons learned from these missions will form the basis for the enactment of adequate and effective norms. Second, the provisions of the MA on intergenerational balance, sharing of information and international designation of special scientific areas address important topics and deserve to be carefully considered.

2 NATIONAL SPACE LEGISLATION

To complement the assessment of the regulatory configuration of the multi-level system of space mining, this section shifts the focus to the norms available at the national level. The principles laid down in the *Corpus Iuris Spatialis* provide the foundations upon which States build their domestic space legislations.[558] Primarily, these laws are enacted to authorize and continuously supervise private activities in space, for which States are internationally responsible under Article VI OST.[559] The possibility for private entities to participate in the exploration and use of outer space has shaped the development of space law as multi-level regulatory system. At present, thirty-six States all around the world have enacted domestic provisions regulating the conduct of their national activities in space.[560] Among these thirty-six Countries, only four of them have allowed their nationals to undertake space resource activities: the United States,[561] the Grand Duchy of Luxembourg,[562] the United Arab Emirates and Japan.[563] As discussed earlier, the decision to enact favorable legislation for the commercial recovery of space resources is based on the idea that space mining should be primarily pursued by private companies rather than governmental agencies.[564] In short, private actors are considered to be better equipped to develop the necessary technologies as well as more suited to significantly reduce costs and expand applications.[565] For these reasons, in November 2015, the U.S. became the first State to pass

557. Hofmann & Masson-Zwaan, *supra* note 12 at 36.
558. Marboe, *supra* note 201.
559. Article VI OST, *supra* note 1.
560. As reported https://www.unoosa.org/oosa/en/ourwork/spacelaw/nationalspacelaw/index.html by UNOOSA at the time this this was finalized (last accessed October 2022). For a comprehensive assessment of the most prominent national space legislations, *see* Ram Jakhu (ed.), *National Regulation of Space Activities* (2010), and also Marboe, *supra* note 201 at 139-178.
561. USCLCA, *supra* note 7.
562. LUXSRL, *supra* note 8.
563. UAEFLRSS and JSRA, *supra* note 9.
564. As to which, *see* section 1.1.4 in Chapter 2.
565. *Ibid.*

legislation to enable the commercial recovery and use of space resources.[566] Shortly after, in July 2017, the U.S. was joined by the Granduchy of Luxembourg, which became the first European State to support a role for private entities in space mining endeavors.[567] In December 2019, the two States were joined by the UAE,[568] which is getting more and more involved in the exploration of the Moon and Mars. Finally, in June 2021, Japan passed the Japan Space Resources Act (JSRA) to authorize and supervise the conduct of space resource activities by Japanese entities.[569] In addition to these four countries, the U.K. has been considering passing similar legislation for several years now and is likely to do so in the near future.[570] Accordingly, this section presents the laws enacted in the U.S., Luxembourg, the UAE and Japan in order to show their impact on the configuration of space mining as multi-level regulatory system.

2.1 The U.S. Law of 2015

The U.S. is one of the most influential spacefaring nations in the world. Since the dawn of the space era, the U.S. has played a crucial role in the development and flourishing of the entire body of international space law.[571] In parallel to that, the U.S. has also produced an advanced and comprehensive body of domestic space legislation, largely consolidated into Title 51 of the United States Code entitled "National and Commercial Space Programs."[572] With the enactment of the USCLCA,[573] the U.S. became the first nation in the world to allow its nationals to engage in space resource activities.

Fundamental Features and Purposes

The USCLCA has been enacted with the goal to "spur private aerospace competitiveness and entrepreneurship"[574] in a number of domains like human spaceflight, launching capabilities, space situational awareness and space mining. The law is divided into four titles. The first one includes a series of overarching administrative provisions adapting the current regulatory regime to the needs of private entities.[575] The second title gives an update on commercial remote sensing,[576] while the third one

566. USCLCA, *supra* note 7.
567. LUXSRL, *supra* note 8.
568. UAEFLRSS, *supra* note 9.
569. JSRA, *supra* note 9.
570. The Asteroid Mining Corporation, a UK registered mining company, has been advocating for a "UK Space Resources Bill" since 2018. The draft text is available https://asteroidmining corporation.co.uk/uk-space-resources-activities-bill on the AMC website (last accessed October 2022).
571. Haanappel, *supra* note 13 at 7-11.
572. National and Commercial Space Programs, *entered into force* December 18, 2010, H.R. 3237, 111th Congress.
573. USCLCA, *supra* note 7.
574. *Id.*, at section 102.
575. *Id.*, at sections 101-117.
576. *Id.*, at sections 201-202.

rebrands the office of space commerce and assigns it a series of functions in support of aerospace competitiveness and entrepreneurship.[577]

Title IV of the USCLCA, called "Space Resource Exploration and Utilization," is dedicated to space mining.[578] Interestingly, the title begins by separately defining the terms asteroid resource and space resource. According to the USCLCA, "an asteroid resource is a space resource found on or within a single asteroid,"[579] while a space resource is defined as an "abiotic resource in situ in outer space, including water and minerals."[580] It is unclear why the USCLCA includes two separate definitions for asteroid and space resources[581] since, under international space law, all celestial bodies are subject to the same rules.[582]

Being as it may, from a legal viewpoint, the distinction does not seem to have any function even within the USCLCA itself since its provisions apply to both asteroid and space resources. After the initial definitions, the first part of Title IV tasks the U.S. President with a series of actions to promote the commercial exploration and recovery of space resources by U.S. citizens.[583] Specifically, the title directs the President to facilitate these endeavors while also discouraging "governmental barriers to the development in the United States of economically viable, safe and stable industries for the commercial exploration and recovery of space resources in manners consistent with the international obligations of the United States."[584] Finally, this first part of Title IV instructs the executive branch to promote the right for U.S. citizens to engage commercial space resource activities "free from harmful interference, in accordance with the international obligations of the United States and subject to authorization and continuing supervision by the Federal Government."[585] Already this initial part of Title IV deserves some considerations. First, it should be noted that the law carefully promotes the development of space resource industries that are "economically viable, safe and stable" and which operate "in manners consistent with the international obligations of the United States."[586] These requirements are important because they clarify that commercial space resource activities should not be pursued at all costs but only at certain conditions established in the law.[587] Among those conditions, the first part of Title IV references two times the international obligations of the United States and explicitly recalls the need for the authorization and continuing supervision of the

577. *Id.*, at sections 301-302.
578. *Id.*, at sections 401-403.
579. *Id.*, at sections 402, §51301.
580. *Ibid.*
581. It seems that the reason for this distinction comes from the political support given to asteroid mining by the Obama administration. The White House Office of the Press Secretary, *Remarks by the President on Space Exploration in the 21st Century* (2010), available https://www.nasa.gov/news/media/trans/obama_ksc_trans.html (last accessed October 2022).
582. The space treaties always refer to celestial bodies collectively. The only exception is the MA, which however explicitly extends the applicability of the provisions developed for the Moon to all other celestial bodies within the solar system. Article 1 MA, *supra* note 5.
583. USCLCA, *supra* note 7, at section 402, §51302.
584. *Ibid.*
585. *Ibid.*
586. *Ibid.*
587. Consistently with the analysis conducted in sections 1.1.1 and 1.1.5 in Chapter 2.

U.S. Government. These clauses make sure that commercial space resource activities are always aligned with relevant developments in international space law under the international responsibility of the U.S.[588]

On these bases, the second part of Title IV solemnly declares that "a U.S. citizen engaged in commercial recovery of an asteroid resource or a space resource shall be entitled to any asteroid resource or space resource obtained, including to possess, own, transport, use, and sell it according to applicable law, including U.S. international obligations."[589] Finally, Title IV concludes by stating that through the enactment of the USCLCA, "the US does not thereby assert sovereignty or sovereign or exclusive rights or jurisdiction over, or the ownership of, any celestial body."[590] Upon its entry into force, the USCLCA directs the President to submit to the Congress, within 180 days, a report specifying "the authorities necessary to meet the international obligations of the US" as well as "recommendations for the allocation of responsibilities among Federal agencies" for the activities described in the initial part.[591] Pursuant to this provision, the U.S. Congress has been debating "The American Space Commerce Free Enterprise Act" since 2017.[592]

Consequences on Space Mining Activities and Regulation

As the very first piece of national legislation regulating the commercial recovery and use of space resources, the USCLCA is responsible for having initiated the development of space mining as multi-level regulatory system. Notwithstanding some initial resistance,[593] the USCLCA has rapidly become a normative reference within the global debate on space mining. Other three States have already followed the example of the U.S., and shortly after the enactment of the USCLCA, the LSC of UNCOPUOS decided to adopt a permanent agenda item dedicated to the legal aspects of space resources.[594]

Having said that, a thorough assessment of the USCLCA reveals that this law operates at a rather general level. Even though it establishes the right for U.S. citizens to engage in space resource activities under the authorization and continuing supervision of the U.S. Government,[595] the USCLCA does not provide any administrative procedure to this end. Despite being the first country to promote the national regulation of space resource activities, the U.S. still does not have a system in place for licensing them.[596] Therefore, until such a licensing system is established, the impact of the USCLCA on the multi-level regulation of space mining remains rather theoretical. The

588. On the responsibility of States for private space activities, *see* section 1.1.4 in Chapter 2.
589. USCLCA, *supra* note 7, at section 402, §51303.
590. *Id.*, at section 403.
591. *Id.*, at section 402, §51302.
592. For a comprehensive analysis on this process *see* Mark Sundahl, *Regulating Non-traditional Space Activities in the United States in the Wake of the USCLCA*, 42 Air & Space Law 29-42 (2017).
593. Fabio Tronchetti & Liu Hao, *The American Space Commerce Free Enterprise Act of 2017: The Latest Step in Regulating the Space Resources Utilization Industry or Something More?*, 47 Space Policy 1-6 (2019).
594. Resolution adopted by the General Assembly at its 71st Session, *International Cooperation in the Peaceful Uses of Outer Space*, UN Doc. A/RES/71/90 (2016).
595. USCLCA, *supra* note 7, at section 402, §51303.
596. Sundahl, *supra* note 592.

lack of concrete provisions determining how space resource activities should be conducted in practice also prevents any further considerations on its legality. In this respect, the International Institute of Space Law (IISL), a leading institution for space law matters worldwide, has taken position in favor of the compatibility of the USCLCA with international space law.[597] According to the IISL, "in view of the absence of a clear prohibition of the taking of resources in the Outer Space Treaty one can conclude that the use of space resources is permitted. Viewed from this perspective, the new United States Act is a possible interpretation of the Outer Space Treaty."[598]

2.2 The Luxembourgish Law of 2017

While the debate on the international regulation of space mining continues,[599] in 2017, Luxembourg became the second country in the world—and the first in Europe—passing legislation to regulate commercial space resource activities.[600] When it enacted the LUXSRL, Luxembourg did not have any general legislation governing private activities in space except for the 1991 law on electronic media.[601] Four years later, this gap was closed with the enactment of the general space law in 2020.[602] However, this law does not apply to space resource activities and will therefore not be addressed in this book.

Fundamental Features and Purposes

Inspired by the USCLCA and eager to replicate its successful experience in the field of satellite telecommunications, in February 2016, the Luxembourg Ministry of Economy launched the "spaceresources.lu initiative"[603] to transform Luxembourg into the European hub for space resource activities. Following the successful reception of the initiative, a "draft law on the exploration and use of space resources" was presented before the Luxembourgish Chamber of Deputies to ensure that "private operators working in space can be confident about their rights to the resources they extract in outer space."[604]

597. Position Paper on Space Resources Mining, Adopted by Consensus by the IISL Board of Directors on December 20, 2015, available https://www.iislweb.org/docs/SpaceResourceMining.pdf (last accessed October 2022).
598. *Id.*, at 3.
599. As to which, *see* section 3.1.1 in Chapter 2.
600. LUXSRL, *supra* note 8.
601. Loi du 27 juillet 1991 sur les médias électroniques, modifiée par Loi du 2 avril 2001, *entered into force* August 1, 2001, Lux Recueil de Legislation A88 (2001) [hereinafter: "Electronic Media Law"].
602. Loi du 15 décembre 2020 sur les activités spatiales, *entered into force* January 1, 2021, Lux Recueil de Legislation A1086 (2020) [hereinafter: "Space Activities Law"].
603. Available https://space-agency.public.lu/en/space-resources/the-initiative.html (last accessed October 2022).
604. Press Release by the Ministry of Economy of Luxembourg, Luxembourg's New Space Law Guarantees Private Companies the Right to Resources Harvested in Outer Space in Accordance With International Law 2, available http://www.spaceresources.public.lu/content/dam/spaceresources/press-release/2016/2016_11_11PressReleaseNewSpacelaw.pdf (last accessed October 2022).

While the Chamber was debating the law, the Luxembourgish Government signed two memoranda of understanding with foreign space mining companies—Deep Space Industries[605] and iSpace[606]—for the establishment of their European subsidiaries in the Granduchy.[607] Finally, on August 1, 2017, the LUXSRL entered into force, inaugurating the Luxembourgish regulatory framework for space (resource) activities.[608]

Throughout its eighteen articles, the LUXSRL establishes the right to own space resources and lays down the relevant authorization procedure to undertake space mining activities. The most important provision of the law is naturally Article 1, according to which "space resources are capable of being owned."[609] It is interesting to note that the wording of this article was different from the original draft of the law, which also included an express reference to international law. This reference was removed from Article 1 by the Luxembourgish legislator pursuant to the negative opinion expressed by Luxembourg's *Conseil D'Etat* (*Conseil*) on the validity of the LUXSRL.[610] The main concern pointed out by the *Conseil* was whether a State is legally able to grant private property rights to space resources in the uncertainty of their status under international space law.[611] After discussing arguments in favor and against,[612] the *Conseil* decided to issue a negative opinion due to the inability of the law to actually meet its declared purpose, which was the establishment of legal certainty for commercial operators. Ultimately, the *Conseil* held that, pending a decisive resolution at the international level, Luxembourg could not adopt its own legislation on the matter.[613]

605. As reported https://www.businesswire.com/news/home/20160505005655/en/Luxembourg-Government-Deep-Space-Industries-Sign-MoU (last accessed October 2022). It should be noted that Deep Space Industry ceased to be a mining company and was https://spacenews.com/deep-space-industries-acquired-by-bradford-space/ acquired by Bradford Space in 2019 (last accessed October 2022).
606. As reported https://www.businesswire.com/news/home/20170302005800/en/Luxembourg-ispace-Tokyo-Based-Lunar-Robotic-Exploration-Company (last accessed October 2022).
607. Notably, these Memorandum of understandings were concluded on top of a conspicuous https://spacenews.com/luxembourg-government-to-buy-up-to-49-of-planetary-resources-european-business/ financial investment in another space mining company called Planetary Resources, which also ceased its activities after being https://spacenews.com/asteroid-mining-company-planetary-resources-acquired-by-blockchain-firm/ acquired by a blockchain firm (both links last accessed October 2022).
608. For a thorough assessment of the Luxembourgish framework for space activities *see* Mahulena Hofmann, P.J. Blount, Gabrielle Leterre, Antonino Salmeri & Laetitia Zarkan, *The Space Legislation of Luxembourg: A Commentary* (2022).
609. Article 1 LUXSRL, *supra* note 8.
610. Projet de loi sur l'exploration et l'utilisation des ressources de l'espace, Avis du Conseil D'État 51.987, *issued on* April 7, 2017, available http://www.conseil-etat.public.lu/content/dam/conseil_etat/fr/avis/2017/07042017/51987.pdf (last accessed October 2022) [hereinafter: "Avis du Conseil"].
611. *Id.*, at 5. A similar concern was also expressed in literature by Philippe De Man, *Luxembourg Law on Space Resources Rests on Contentious Relationship with International Framework*, 8 Working Paper available https://ghum.kuleuven.be/ggs/publications/working_papers/2017/189deman (last accessed October 2022).
612. Avis du Conseil, *supra* note 610 at 1-8. For a deeper analysis *see* Hofmann et al., *supra* note 608 at pp. 12-16.
613. *Id.*, at 8.

Based on these arguments, the *Conseil* recommended the suppression of Article 1.[614] While certainly respecting the prudence shown by the *Conseil*, it should be noted that fundamental norms of both international space law and general international law would have called for the opposite decision.[615] First, it is incorrect to say that the legal status of space resources is unclear under international space law. On the contrary, space mining is a legitimate manifestation of the freedom to use celestial bodies under Article I OST, while the prohibition to appropriate outer space and celestial bodies laid down in Article II OST does not apply to space resources.[616] Second, even if doubt on the meaning of these provisions exists, States always retain the right to promote their interpretation of international law, pending a definitive resolution from the competent institutions at the international law.[617] Based on a similar line of reasoning, the Luxembourgish legislator decided not to follow the *Conseil's* advice to suppress Article 1 and moved the reference to international to the following article. As a result, Article 2 of the LUXSRL provides the fundamental limits for conducting space resource activities in Luxembourg. Pursuant to this Article, "no person can explore or use space resources without holding a written mission authorization" to be given by the competent minister(s) in charge of space activities.[618] Further, Article 2 specifies that authorized operators have to conduct their space resource activities "in accordance with the conditions of the authorisation and the international obligations of Luxembourg."[619] This provision is further complemented by Article 15, according to which the minister(s) authorizing a space resource mission are also in charge of its "continuous supervision."[620]

Similar to what has been observed for the USCLCA, these requirements have been included to comply with Article VI OST.[621]

From Article 2 onwards, albeit being inspired by the USCLCA, the scope of the LUXSRL expands much further than its American analog to complement the recognition of private property rights on space resources with the establishment of a licensing procedure for the associated activities.[622] Certainly, this inclusion is an important step toward the development of space mining as multi-level regulatory system. However, a closer look at the law reveals that the legislator only dealt with the strictly administrative aspects of the licensing process. To begin with, under Articles 3 and 5 LUXSRL, authorization for space resources activities shall be granted only to corporations

614. *Id.*, at 11.
615. Hofmann et al., *supra* note 608 at pp. 12-16.
616. As to which, *see* sections 1.1.1 and 1.1.2 in Chapter 2.
617. Hofmann, *supra* note 327; Salmeri, *supra* note 186.
618. Article 2 LUXSRL, *supra* note 8. For a deeper analysis on Article 2, *see* Hofmann et al., *supra* note 608 at pp. 17-26.
619. *Ibid.*
620. Article 15 LUXSRL, *supra* note 8. For a closer look at this article, *see* Hofmann et al., *supra* note 608 at pp. 64-65.
621. Article VI OST, *supra* note 1. On the role of Article VI OST, *see* section 1.1.4 in Chapter 2.
622. Gabrielle Leterre, *Providing a Legal Framework for Sustainable Space Mining Activities* 48-51, Master Book available https://wwwen.uni.lu/content/download/102978/1231496/file/Gabrielle%20Leterre%20Providing%20a%20Legal%20Framework%20for%20Sustainable%20Space%20Mining%20Activities.pdf (last accessed October 2022).

incorporated in Luxembourg upon presentation of a written application to the government, and it shall be personal and non-assignable.[623] Complementarily, Article 13 provides that for each application, the minister(s) shall set a fee covering the relevant administrative expenses in the rather wide range between EUR 5,000 and EUR 500,000, "depending on the complexity of the application and the amount of work involved."[624] Under Article 6, the applicant is responsible for providing all the information that may be useful for its assessment.[625] In this respect, Article 7 requires evidence of a number of organizational elements like incorporation in Luxembourg or robust schemes of "financial, technical and statutory procedures and arrangements" for the planning and implementation of the space mining missions.[626] Notably, Article 7 also requires the presence of a "robust internal governance scheme," including "effective procedures to identify, manage, monitor and report the risks" to which the operator may be exposed together with "adequate internal control mechanisms."[627] On top of these requirements, Articles 8, 9 and 11 further impose a series of additional conditions borrowed from the law on the provision of financial services.[628]

At a more operational level, Article 10 requires the inclusion of a risk assessment of the mission, which must specify the coverage of the associated risks either by personal financial means, by insurance policy or by bank guarantee.[629] Based on this information, Article 12 provides that the authorization "shall describe the manner in which the operator fulfills the conditions of articles 6 to 11."[630] Article 12 further allows for the inclusion of additional provisions on four aspects: the practical activities to be carried out either within or outside Luxembourgish territory (a), the limits associated with the mission (b), the modalities for its supervision (c) and finally the conditions for ensuring the operator's compliance with its obligations under the license.[631] Article 14 regulates the modalities for withdrawing authorization in case "the conditions for the granting thereof are no longer met" (1), "the operator does not make use thereof within thirty-six months, renounces it or has ceased to carry out its business" (2), or finally "if it has been obtained through false statements or through any other irregular means."[632] Toward the end of the law, Article 16 provides that operators are "fully responsible for any damage caused at the occasion of the mission, including at the occasion of all preparatory works and duties."[633] It is important to note that this provision has only internal effects since, at the international level, Luxembourg will always remain internationally responsible for the mission[634] as well as internationally liable for any damage caused by any relevant space objects for which it qualifies as launching

623. Articles 3 and 5 LUXSRL, *supra* note 8.
624. Article 13 LUXSRL, *supra* note 8.
625. Article 6 LUXSRL, *supra* note 8.
626. Article 7 LUXSRL, *supra* note 8.
627. *Ibid.*
628. Articles 8, 9 and 11 LUXSRL, *supra* note 8.
629. Article 10 LUXSRL, *supra* note 8.
630. Article 12 LUXSRL, *supra* note 8.
631. *Ibid.*
632. Article 14 LUXSRL, *supra* note 8.
633. Article 16 LUXSRL, *supra* note 8.
634. Under Article VI OST, *supra* note 1.

State.[635] Thus, the main purpose of the provision is to create an obligation upon the operator to compensate the Luxembourgish Government for any expenses anticipated upfront for damage caused at the occasion of the mission.

Article 17 clarifies that "the granting of an authorisation for a mission does not dispense from the need to obtain other approvals or authorisations."[636] Besides the normal authorization required to conduct business in Luxembourg, this provision clearly refers to any other approval needed for collateral space activities. At the time when the LUXSRL was enacted, this clause was mostly included for the purposes of "satellite communications, orbital positions or the use of frequency bands," which under Article 2 (4) of the LUXSRL are explicitly excluded from its application[637] and remain regulated by the Electronic Media Law.[638] Today, it is possible to add to this list also the registration of space objects and tax-related provisions, which are covered by the Space Activities Law.[639]

The last provision of the LUXSRL is Article 18, which is dedicated to sanctions. Pursuant to this article, any person contravening or attempting to contravene the provisions of Article 2 "shall be punished by a term of imprisonment of between eight days and five years and a fine of between 5.000 and 1.250.000 euros."[640] On a relatively lighter note, the violation of "the provisions of articles 5, 9 paragraph 3 subparagraph 1, 11 paragraph 1 or 2" as well as of "the terms and conditions of the authorisation" will be sanctioned with "a term of imprisonment of between eight days and one year and a fine of between 1.250 and 500.000 euros."[641] Without prejudice to these sanctions, Article 18 (3) concludes by clarifying that "the court to which the matter is being referred may declare the discontinuance of an operation contravening the provisions of the present law" under a maximum penalty of EUR 1,000,000 per day of infringement found.[642]

Consequences on Space Mining Activities and Regulation

Building upon the USCLCA, the LUXSRL represents another important step forward in the development of space mining as multi-level regulatory system. In this respect, the inclusion of an administrative procedure for licensing space resource activities should be welcomed as further substantiating the concrete involvement of national regulators.[643]

635. Under Article VII OST, *supra* note 1.
636. Article 17 LUXSRL, *supra* note 8.
637. Article 2 LUXSRL, *supra* note 8.
638. Electronic Media Law, *supra* note 601.
639. As clarified within the https://space-agency.public.lu/en/agency/legal-framework.html Spaceresources.lu framework (last accessed October 2022). Within the general space law, tax provisions are dealt within Article 1 while registration is regulated under Article 7. Law on Space Activities, *supra* note 8. For more considerations on the relationship between these laws, *see* Hofmann et al., *supra* note 608.
640. Article 18 LUXSRL, *supra* note 8.
641. *Ibid.*
642. *Ibid.*
643. Leterre, *supra* 622 at 50.

At the same time, the LUXSRL does not provide any guidance on the substantive conditions that should be imposed by the Government on the practical aspects of space resource activities. While this is certainly understandable from the viewpoint of adaptive governance, it would have been interesting to see at least some minimum requirements addressing compliance with the fundamental limits to the freedom of exploration and use of celestial bodies. This might have been something as simple as requiring the establishment of a maximum duration and extension of the mission within the authorization conditions to ensure compliance with Article II OST.[644] Having said that, considering the infancy of space resource activities, the LUXSRL certainly provides a positive contribution toward the responsible and balanced multi-level regulation of space mining.

2.3 The UAE Law of 2020

Following the examples of the U.S. and Luxembourg, also the UAE decided to address space resource activities within its national space legislation.[645] The starting point for this process has been provided by the Federal Law on the Regulation of the Space Sector (UAEFLRSS), which refers to space mining in three articles.[646] First and foremost, Article 1 defines space resources as "any non-living resources present in outer space, including minerals and water."[647] Following, Article 4 include "space resources exploration or extraction activities" as well as "activities for the exploitation and use of space resources for scientific, commercial or other purposes" among the space activities permitted and regulated in the UAE under the Federal Space Law.[648]

Finally, "subject to the provisions of article 14 of this law," Article 18 defers the actual regulation of all these activities to "a decision issued by the Council of Ministers."[649]

In this respect, under Article 14 (1), it is prohibited to conduct any space activity in the UAE without obtaining a permit from the UAE Space Agency.[650] However, pursuant to the following paragraph 2, the main aspects of the authorization procedure have also been delegated to another decision of the Council of Ministers.[651] Thus, pending the adoption of the implementing acts mandated by Articles 14 and 18 UAEFLRSS, it is not possible to assess the meaning and impact of the national regulation of space resource activities in the UAE. For the time being, it can be noted that the UAEFLRSS seems to provide a sound legal basis for the authorization and supervision of private space resource activities under Article VI OST. From a systemic

644. Further on the impact of Article II OST on the regulation of space mining, *see* section 1.1.2 in Chapter 2.
645. As reported https://spacewatch.global/2020/02/uae-space-law-details-announced-to-facilitate-space-sector-development/ (last accessed October 2022).
646. Articles 1, 4 and 18 UAEFLRSS, *supra* note 9.
647. Article 1 UAEFLRSS, *supra* note 9.
648. Article 4 UAEFLRSS, *supra* note 9.
649. Article 18 UAEFLRSS, *supra* note 9.
650. Article 14 UAEFLRSS, *supra* note 9.
651. *Ibid.*

viewpoint, the lack of substantive provisions regulating the actual conduct of space mining within the UAE Federal Law is a further confirmation of the rather premature status of space mining as multi-level regulatory system.

2.4 The Japanese Law of 2021

Fundamental Features and Purposes

In June 2021, Japan became the fourth State in the world to enact legislation to regulate the conduct of space resource activities by its own nationals.[652] To begin with, it is important to note that Japan has a comprehensive body of national space legislation.[653] The JSRA thus builds upon this pre-existing framework to enable the conduct of space resource activities by Japanese private entities and provide additional conditions for their licensing.[654] Every space resource activity authorized under the JSRA will have to comply also with the basic principles laid down in the foundational space law of Japan.[655] Additionally, as also stated in the USCLCA, the LUXSRL and the UAEFLRSS, private space resource activities will have to be conducted in accordance with the international obligations of Japan, with special reference to those stemming from the OST, ARRA, LIAB and REG.[656]

Article 2 JSRA frames the scope of the Act by providing a definition of both space resources and related activities.[657] Pursuant to this provision, space resource means "water, mineral, or other natural resources present in outer space including those on the Moon and other planets."[658] Building upon this definition, the Act authorizes private entities to (1) research the presence of space resources for the purposes of mining, recovery, (2) mine, recover, process, and store the resources discovered, and (3) conduct other activities or actions as prescribed by Cabinet Office Order.[659] Importantly, space resource activities carried out solely "as scientific research or for the purpose of scientific research are excluded" are explicitly excluded from the scope of the Act.[660]

The core of the JSRA is Article 3, which provides the specific conditions governing the conduct of space resource activities in addition to those already imposed under the 2016 Japanese Space Activities Act. Under Article 3 (1) JSRA, an applicant

652. JSRA, *supra* note 9. At present, no official English translation of the space resources act exists. Thus, the analysis conducted in this section is based upon an unofficial, ad hoc translation kindly provided by Professor Setsuko Aoki from the Keio University Law School, to whom this author is most grateful and obligated.
653. For a comprehensive overview of the Japanese space legislation, *see* Hiroko Yotsumoto, Daiki Ishikawa & Tetsuji Odan, *Mori Hamada & Matsumoto, The Space Law Review: Japan*, available https://thelawreviews.co.uk/title/the-space-law-review/japan#footnote-003 (last accessed October 2022).
654. Article 1 JSRA, *supra* note 9.
655. *Ibid.*
656. *Ibid.*
657. Article 2 JSRA, *supra* note 9.
658. *Ibid.*
659. *Ibid.*
660. *Ibid.* These activities are governed under the 2016 Japanese Space Activities Act.

seeking authorization for a space resource activity has to provide information on its (i) purpose, (ii) duration, (iii) location, (iv) method, (v) conduct, and (vi) related business plan, in addition to other items as requested by the Cabinet Office.[661] Pursuant to Article 3 (2) JSRA, the business plan should respect the provisions of the Basic Space Law and be in line with the international obligations of Japan.[662] The article further includes a public safety exception and requires the applicant to demonstrate its capability of carrying out the business plan presented.[663] Administratively speaking, Article 3 (3) JSRA attributes the competence to authorize the conduct of a space resource activity to the Prime Minister in consultation with the Ministry of Economy, Trade and Industry.[664]

Pursuant to Article 4 JSRA, the Cabinet Office has to publicly disclose the information received about items i-vi under Article 3 (1), with the notable exclusion of the business plan and other information which may unfairly impair the interests of the applicant, as decided by the Cabinet.[665] Article 5 JSRA is another key provision since it provides the conditions for acquiring ownership of space resources. According to this article, the licensee will obtain ownership of a space resource provided that (1) it acquired it through mining or recovery in accordance with the license received and (2) it possesses it with the intention to own it.[666] Notably, the wording of this provision has been determined by Article 239 of the Japanese Civil Code, according to which ownership of movables *without an owner* shall be acquired by possessing it with the intention to own.[667]

Articles 6 and 7 JSRA deal specifically with the international dimension of space resource activities. Under Article 6 JSRA, the Act should be executed in a manner that "is not likely to disrupt" the good faith implementation of the treaties and international agreements concluded by Japan.[668] This clause is similar to analog provisions examined under the other three laws and is included to ensure formal compliance with international law. However, the JSRA goes beyond that: pursuant to Article 6 (2) JSRA, "nothing in the present Act should unreasonably impair the interests of other States to exercise their freedom of exploration and use outer space, including the Moon and other celestial bodies."[669] This clause closely resembles the first part of Article IX OST, according to which in conducting their exploration and use of outer space, States shall pay "due regard to the corresponding interests of all other States Parties to the Treaty."[670]

The systemic approach adopted by the Japanese legislator is notably evident in Article 7 JSRA. Pursuant to this provision, Japan, "jointly with other States," shall

661. Article 3 JSRA, *supra* note 9.
662. Article 3 (2) (i) JSRA, *supra* note 9.
663. Article 3 (2) (i) and (ii) JSRA, *supra* note 9.
664. Article 3 (3) JSRA, *supra* note 9.
665. Article 4 JSRA, *supra* note 9.
666. Article 5 JSRA, *supra* note 9.
667. Article 239 of the Japanese Civil Code, available https://www.moj.go.jp/content/000056024.pdf (last accessed October 2022).
668. Article 6 JSRA, *supra* note 9.
669. Article 6 (2) JSRA, *supra* note 9.
670. Article IX OST, *supra* note 1.

endeavor to establish an internationally consistent regime on the exploration and exploitation of space resources through cooperation with international organizations and other international frameworks.[671] To this end, Article 7 (2) JSRA mandates the Japanese government to take necessary measures to promote internationally available information sharing, as well as ensure measures for international coordination and partnerships with respect to private business activities in the exploration and exploitation of space resources.[672] On a related note, Article 8 JSRA mandates the Japanese government to promote the development of commercial space resource activities by providing space operators with technical advice, information and other assistance.[673]

Finally, Article 4 of the supplementary provisions attached to the JSRA is the first provision in any national space legislation addressing space resource activities to recognize the importance of adaptive governance. Pursuant to this article, the Japanese government has to constantly monitor the application of the law, the progress of science and technology, the status of the regulatory efforts for the development of an international system as mandated under Article 7 (1) JSRA, and the conduct of commercial space resource activities.[674] Based upon the results of this monitoring, the Government shall review the suitability of the Act and, if necessary, suggest the necessary amendments to ensure its improvement.[675]

Consequences on Space Mining Activities and Regulation

The 2021 JSRA is an impressive piece of legislation. In the opinion of this author, this Act is without question the most advanced and forward-thinking example of national regulation of space resource activities currently in force. Different from the other legislation examined, the JSRA acknowledges the importance of fundamental principles such as information sharing and international coordination and takes measures to implement them. Beyond the usual safeguards on the necessary respect of international law, the JSRA creates mechanisms to ensure that its own provisions will be in harmony with future normative developments at the international level. For instance, Article 7 JSRA mandates the Japanese Government to take an active role in the development of an internationally consistent regime for space mining, including through mechanisms for international information sharing and coordination.[676] On a similar line of reasoning, Article 4 of the supplementary provisions welcomes any future development in law and practice as an opportunity to improve the Act and requires the Government to be ready to respond to them positively.[677] The systemic approach behind these provisions is of exceptional importance for the overall stability of the multi-level regulatory system of space mining, and one can only hope that it will be replicated in future legislation. The only "defect" that could be found in the JSRA is

671. Article 7 JSRA, *supra* note 9.
672. Article 7 (2) JSRA, *supra* note 9.
673. Article 8 JSRA, *supra* note 9.
674. Article 4 of the Supplementary Provisions to the JSRA, *supra* note 9. For the translation of this particular provision, this author would like to thank Mr. Kikuchi Koichi from the JAXA.
675. *Ibid.*
676. Article 7 JSRA, *supra* note 9.
677. Article 4 of the Supplementary Provisions to the JSRA, *supra* note 9.

the same already discussed for the other laws, i.e., that it does not take any position concerning the substantive conduct of space mining. In this particular case though, in light of the systemic approach adopted by the JSRA, it seems that the lack of substantive provisions has been the result of an intentional choice aimed at promoting their enactment at the international level.

3 MULTI-LEVEL INTERACTIONS

The analysis conducted in the previous sections reveals a rather complex picture. Primarily, this complexity is generated by the very nature of international space law. Because of the variety and broadness of its principles, its concrete impact on the regulation and conduct of space mining significantly varies based on the combinations promoted by the interpreter. Initially, it was thought that this uncertainty would have been reduced through the involvement of national regulators. As seen above, this was not the case. Surely, the USCLCA, the LUXSRL, the UAEFLRSS and the JSRA all declare the legality of commercial space resource activities. In the case of Luxembourg and Japan, they also provide an administrative procedure for their authorization. Undoubtedly, this is good progress. However, nowhere in these laws is it possible to find any indication as to how a private company under those jurisdictions should conduct its space mining activities. Therefore, from a systemic viewpoint, these laws did not reduce the complexity or uncertainty within the system. If anything, they actually increased it by adding another layer of potential regulatory combinations without, however, promoting any concrete proposal as to how these combinations may look like.

One can easily understand why national regulators did not make specific propositions for the substantive regulation of space resource activities besides simply stating that their commercialization should be allowed and promoted. First, even before the USCLCA, there was a lot of pressure from the international community against the development of national rules for space mining. Most likely, any substantive provision on the concrete conduct of space resource activities would have been perceived as an attempt to hegemonize the debate at the international level, thus significantly backfiring its proponent. Second, and even more decisive, national regulators have neither the knowledge nor the expertise to determine which rules should govern the conduct of space mining. Simply put, none of them knows whether a mining license should extend for 1 or 10 km, last for ten or twenty years or make use of a certain extraction technology over another. Likewise, it is unclear what will be the consequences of permanent mining operations on the surface of celestial bodies, especially because these will change drastically depending on the type of techniques utilized and the celestial body in question.

This is not to say that the current lack of information should lead to regulatory inaction, but rather to acknowledge that making the first move at the substantive governance of space mining is a heavy burden to carry. Even a powerful spacefaring nation like the U.S. could not sustain it alone and explicitly called for international support in the regulation of commercial space resource activities.[678] At the same time, these difficulties could not be solved by a fully fledged international system either.[679] In other words, the system is facing a regulatory *impasse*. In this author's view, a potential solution might come from the development of a middle-level framework operating between the international principles of space law and the various domestic space legislation adopted by States.

The goal of this framework should be to harmonize the interpretation of the fundamental principles of international space law with reference to space resource activities in order to enable the harmonious, adaptive enactment of substantive norms at the domestic level.

Based on the above analysis, this section presents recent policy developments aimed at solving the regulatory *impasse* currently faced by the multi-level system of space mining.

3.1 Policy Developments

Pursuant to the enactment of the USCLCA, space resource activities rapidly gained the attention of the global space community. Over the past five years, the regulation of space mining has been extensively discussed by States, practitioners and academics. Ultimately, these debates produced a series of policy documents and proposals that are discussed in this section. Moving from the diplomatic debate in UNCOPUOS as reference point, this section identifies the baseline laid down in the Hague Building Blocks[680] as the critical starting point for the multi-level regulation of space mining. Accordingly, the section explores complementary efforts promoted by the global space community to confirm the validity of the ideas proposed in the Building Blocks. Specifically, the section looks at the Vancouver Recommendations,[681] the Best Practices for Sustainable Lunar Activities,[682] the Lunar Resources Policies[683] and the EAGLE Lunar Governance Report.[684] Finally, the section concludes by discussing the importance of the AA[685] for the future development of State practice on the matter.

678. Space Resources EO, *supra* note 433.
679. And in particular by the MA, due the political barriers raised against its application—*Ibid.*
680. BB Commentary, *supra* note 82.
681. Vancouver Recommendations on Space Mining, available http://www.outerspaceinstitute.ca/docs/Vancouver_Recommendations_on_Space_Mining.pdf (last accessed October 2022) [hereinafter: "Vancouver Recommendations"].
682. Best Practices for Sustainable Lunar Activities, available https://moonvillageassociation.org/wp-content/uploads/2020/10/MVA-Best-Practices-Issue-1-19.10.2020-FINAL.pdf (last accessed October 2022) [hereinafter: "Best Practices"].
683. Lunar Resources Policy, available https://www.openlunar.org/library/lunar-resources-policy (last accessed October 2022).
684. Space Generation Advisory Council, Effective and Adaptive Governance for a Lunar Ecosystem: Recommendations from the Young Generations at the United Nations. Lunar Governance Report, available https://spacegeneration.org/wp-content/uploads/2021/12/EAGLE-Report.pdf (last accessed October 2022).
685. Artemis Accords, *supra* note 102.

3.1.1 *Policy Developments in UNCOPUOS: The Working Group on Legal Aspects of Space Resource Activities*

Shortly after the enactment of the USCLCA, the LSC of UNCOPUOS introduced an agenda item on "general exchange of views on potential legal model for activities in the exploration, exploitation and utilization of space resources."[686] During the first year of discussions under this new agenda item, some States have expressed their concerns about the involvement of private entities in space mining and the related multi-level framework that was initiated with the enactment of the USCLCA.[687] The main reason behind these concerns was the fear that commercial companies could monopolize and spoil the use of space resources. However, it soon became clear that this fear was purely speculative, as it is actually disproven by the technical and economic realities of space mining. Companies are far from possessing the necessary technology to conduct space resource activities on a scale that would justify fears of monopolist behaviors or catastrophic impacts.[688] Likewise, space mining is far from being a remunerative industry: the very first companies established in the field have already disappeared because of the lack of any foreseeable profit during the initial decades of activities.[689] Therefore, the focus of the debate has moved from the dangers of private mining activities to the risks of national regulation.

Since 2019, the LSC has been divided[690] between those demanding direct regulations at the international level[691] and those favoring a more prominent role, at least in the initial stages, for national legislation.[692] Supporters of international regulation argue that the legal status of celestial bodies as areas subtracted from sovereign control naturally calls for their international governance.[693] While perfectly valid from a theoretical viewpoint, this argument does not take into account either the abovementioned realities of space mining or the history of international regulation of global commons. First and foremost, the lack of information and practice on space mining calls for adaptive regulatory mechanisms, which can hardly be provided by direct international governance. Second, comparable examples like the UNCLOS took decades to be negotiated and were based upon centuries of practice in those areas.[694] Therefore, direct international regulation of space mining should rather follow and not

686. UNGA RES 71/90, *supra* note 594.
687. Report of the Legal Subcommittee on its 56th Session, held in Vienna from March 27 to April 7, 2017, UN Doc A/AC.105/1122 30-33 (2017).
688. Kornuta, et al., *supra* note 86.
689. Planetary Resources was https://spacenews.com/asteroid-mining-company-planetary-resources-acquired-by-blockchain-firm/ acquired by a blockchain firm in 2018, while Deep Space Industries was https://spacenews.com/deep-space-industries-acquired-by-bradford-space/ acquired by Bradford Space in 2019 (both links last accessed October 2022).
690. Report of the Legal Subcommittee on its 57th Session, held in Vienna from April 9 to 20, 2018, UN Doc A/AC.105/1177 29-32 (2018); *see also* Report of the Legal Subcommittee on its 58th Session, held in Vienna from April 1 to 12, 2019, UN Doc A/AC.105/1203 32-36 (2019).
691. Like the Russian Federation.
692. Like the United States.
693. Tronchetti, *supra* note 146.
694. For an analysis of the analogies between these systems *see* section 1.3.2 earlier in this chapter and section 2.1 in Chapter 3.

precede its early developments. At the same time, this is not an argument in favor of exclusive national regulation either. Surely, the latter could provide for more adaptive regulatory mechanisms and can better take into account the technical and economic realities of space resource activities. However, the risk of developing conflicting regimes and consequently undermining the peaceful and sustainable uses of space is real and should not be underestimated.[695]

Acknowledging the need to discuss the topic in greater detail, in 2019, the LSC decided to hold informal consultations on the development of a dedicated working group that could find a compromise drawing from both sides of the debate.[696] Due to the outbreak of the COVID-19 pandemic, these consultations could not take place in 2020 and were rescheduled for the 60th Session in 2021, which took place in an unprecedented hybrid format and operated under a very tight schedule. Despite these challenges, the Moderator and Vice-Moderator managed to hold eight rounds of informal consultations, which successfully led to the development of consensus, at least on the establishment of a new working group under agenda item fourteen.[697] However, due to the lack of available time, further discussions on its mandate and terms of reference (ToR) had to be postponed to the 64th Session of the Plenary Committee.[698] In that instance, the newly established working group held a total of four formal and informal meetings, which allowed the group to finalize its mandate and ToR[699] but not the five-year workplan, whose consideration had been postponed to the 2022 meetings of the LSC.[700]

At the 61st session of the LSC, the working group reconvened to (1) agree on its name, (2) approve its five-year workplan and method of work, (3) consider possible topics and areas of contributions for initial gathering of information by Member States, and (4) provide guidance to the Chair and Co-Chair for the organization, under the auspices of the UN, of an international conference on space resources.[701] The working group considered these tasks during nine formal and informal meetings, held again in a hybrid format. Ultimately, the working group managed to complete three out of the four tasks mentioned above. First, the working group agreed to henceforth be named the "Working Group on Legal Aspects of Space Resource Activities"[702] (within the

695. Hofmann & Masson-Zwaan, *supra* note 8 at 105.
696. Report of the Committee on the Peaceful Uses of Outer Space on its 62nd Session, held in Vienna from June 12 to 21, 2019, UN Doc A/74/20 32-33 (2019).
697. Report of the Legal Subcommittee on its 60th Session, held in Vienna from May 31 to June 11, 2021, UN Doc A/AC.105/1243 30-33 (2021). In that instance, the Moderator and Vice-Moderator of the informal consultations have been appointed respectively as Chair and Co-Chair of the Working Group, to be collectively referred to as "the Bureau."
698. *Ibid.*
699. Report of the Committee on the Peaceful Uses of Outer Space on its 64th Session, held in Vienna from August 25 to September 3, UN Doc A/76/20 53 (2021).
700. As per the relevant proposal developed by the Working Group's Chair and Vice-Chair (available https://www.unoosa.org/documents/pdf/copuos/lsc/space-resources/Attachment_to_WG_SR_Intersessional_2022.pdf, last accessed October 2022).
701. Report of the Chair and Vice-Chair of the working group established under the Legal Subcommittee agenda item entitled "General exchange of views on potential legal models for activities in the exploration, exploitation and utilization of space resources," UN Doc A/AC.105/C.2/2022/SRA/L.1, p. 1 (2022) [hereinafter: "SRWG Report"].
702. *Ibid.*

context of this book: "SRWG"). It is worth mentioning that this renaming is the result of a careful compromise between several options presented by Member States, which ranged from "Working Group on Space Resources" to "Working Group on Legal Aspects of Space Resources." The SRWG also decided that this renaming is without prejudice to the mandate, ToR and workplan and methods of work of the working group.[703] In addition to the title, the SRWG also approved its five-year workplan and method of work.[704] This approval was critical to the continuation of the activities of the SRWG and was achieved right before the end of the very last meeting for the session.[705]

In accordance with the approved workplan, the SRWG decided to discuss the topics and agenda of the international conference at the following LSC session in 2023 in order to hold the event in conjunction with its meetings in 2024.[706] Finally, the SRWG did not achieve consensus on possible topics and areas of contribution for initial information gathering by Member States. In this regard, the working group simply noted that during the intersessional period, the Bureau would circulate a request for "information from States members of the Committee on issues related to and arising from its mandate," including with regard to the international conference. It should be noted that under the newly approved workplan, those are the only tasks that will be executed by the SRWG during the year 2022 and that the information received will be collated and disseminated by the Bureau for discussion at its meetings in 2023.[707]

The establishment of a dedicated working group on legal aspects of space resource activities at the UN level is naturally of great significance for the analysis conducted within this book. In light of this importance, this paragraph analyzes the mandate, ToR, workplan and methods of work of the SRWG to assess the implications on the multi-level regulatory system of space mining. To begin with, the mandate of the SRWG includes six incremental tasks to be performed over the five years term of the working group. Under point (a) of the SRWG mandate, the working group shall collect information related to space resource activities, "including with respect to scientific and technological developments and current practices, taking into account their innovative and evolving nature."[708] Under the newly approved workplan, the SRWG will perform this task for three years, beginning in 2023 and ending in 2025.[709] Pursuant to point (b) of the SRWG mandate, the working group shall "study the legal framework for such activities."[710]

It is worth noting that at its meetings in 2021, the SRWG discussed at length what exactly should be studied as part of the legal framework. In this regard, some Delegations proposed to individually name all the five UN Treaties on outer space, but there was no consensus on the inclusion of the Moon Agreement due to its low

703. *Ibid.*
704. SRWG Report at 2.
705. As witnessed first-hand by this author, attending the session as representative of an observer organization.
706. SRWG Report, *supra* note 701 at 3.
707. *Id.*, at 2.
708. Report of the Committee, *supra* note 699.
709. SRWG Report, *supra* note 701 at 3-4.
710. Report of the Committee, *supra* note 699.

ratification status.[711] Ultimately, the working group agreed to specifically mention the OST and make generic references to "other applicable United Nations treaties, also taking into account other relevant instruments, as appropriate."[712] In accordance with the SRWG workplan, this task will be performed for four years, between 2023 and 2026, beginning with an initial exchange of views and concluding with a summary of the discussions held on the existing legal framework.[713] This task is inherently connected with the one established under point (c) of the SRWG mandate, according to which the working group shall "assess the benefits of further development of a framework for such activities, including by way of additional international governance instruments."[714] Here again, this wording has been carefully chosen to balance the different preferences of the delegations, which ranged from an internationally binding agreement to voluntary guidelines and political commitments. In particular, the use of the term "framework" and "international governance instruments" was considered to be sufficiently neutral to leave open all potential options[715] based on the results of the study conducted under point (b) of the mandate. Under the SRWG workplan, task (c) of the mandate will be performed for three years, between 2024 and 2026, in conjunction with the related discussions on the existing legal framework.[716]

Pursuant to point (d) of the SRWG mandate, the working group shall "develop a set of initial recommended principles for such activities."[717] This task is of key importance as it will hopefully result in the very first international provisions specifically addressing the substantive conduct of space resource activities, "taking into account the need to ensure that they are carried out in accordance with international law and in a safe, sustainable, rational and peaceful manner."[718] This latter clause is already of extreme significance since it provides, for the very first time, foundational international guidance on the goals to be achieved through the multi-level regulation of space mining. Thus, it is worth spending a few words on each of the boundary conditions set forth in point (d) of the SRWG mandate. First, the regulation of space resource activities shall ensure that they are carried out "in accordance with international law." This clause should naturally be read in conjunction with the obligation to conduct all space activities in accordance with international law, including the Charter of the United Nations, under Article III OST.

To complement this fundamental requirement, point (d) of the SRWG further includes the need to ensure that space resource activities are carried out "in a safe, sustainable, rational and peaceful manner."[719] As with every other term employed in this document, these four words have been the result of delicate negotiations. While

711. As witnessed first-hand by this author, attending the session as representative of an observer organization.
712. Report of the Committee, *supra* note 699.
713. SRWG Report, *supra* note 701 at 3-4.
714. Report of the Committee, *supra* note 699.
715. As witnessed first-hand by this author, attending the session as representative of an observer organization.
716. SRWG Report, *supra* note 701 at 3-4.
717. Report of the Committee, *supra* note 699.
718. *Ibid.*
719. *Ibid.*

safety, sustainability and peacefulness are frequently used with respect to the conduct of space activities in general, the same cannot be said about "rational." The inclusion of this term is particularly striking, given that the "rational management" of space resources is one of the main purposes of the international regime mandated under Article 11 (6) of the Moon Agreement.[720] In this regard, several delegations proposed to include references to "inclusive" uses and "benefit sharing," but ultimately, these inclusions did not achieve the necessary consensus.[721] Lastly, pursuant to the final paragraph of point (d) of the SRWG mandate, this set of principles is meant for "consideration of and consensus agreement by the Committee, followed by possible adoption by the General Assembly as a dedicated resolution or other action."[722] Also, in this case, there have been several discussions on the immediate employability of these principles, but ultimately the SRWG was able to find consensus only on the "usual" procedure of endorsement by the Committee and subsequent adoption by the UNGA. Pursuant to the SRWG workplan, the development of the space resources principles mandated under point (d) of the SRWG mandate will be the focus of the last three years of the working group's activities, from 2025 to 2027.[723]

Last but not least, under point (e) of the SRWG mandate, the working group shall also "identify areas for further work of the Committee" and eventually "recommend next steps."[724] This task has been at the center of several discussions concerning the future of the SRWG and was included as a compromise between the position of those delegations committed to a result-oriented approach and the position of those delegations wishing to maintain the working group as a reference point for discussions on space resources under a longer timeframe.[725] With regard to the next steps, point (e) specifically mentions "the development of potential rules and/or norms" for the exploration and use of space resources, "including with respect to related activities and benefit sharing."[726] Notably, the language employed in this clause has also been chosen as a compromise between the positions expressed within the working group on the opportunity to develop binding rules versus voluntary norms of behavior.[727] The inclusion of "related activities" in connection with the development of potential rules and/or norms is particularly significant since it signals the importance of a holistic approach to regulation, taking into account the broader value chain linked to space resources. Finally, the explicit mention of "benefit sharing" has been included at the request of several delegations from developing countries as a compromise with the choice made on the objectives associated with the principles under point (d) of the mandate.[728] In accordance with the SRWG workplan, the identification of the areas for

720. Article 11 MA, *supra* note 5.
721. As witnessed first-hand by this author, attending the session as representative of an observer organization.
722. *Ibid.*
723. SRWG Report, *supra* note 701 at 3-4.
724. *Ibid.*
725. As witnessed first-hand by this author, attending the session as representative of an observer organization.
726. *Ibid.*
727. *Ibid.*
728. *Ibid.*

further work of the Committee mandated under point (e) of the mandate will be discussed in the last two years of activities of the working group between 2026 and 2027.[729] Last but not least, the SRWG workplan also includes, for the year 2025, a presentation to the Scientific and Technical Subcommittee of UNCOPUOS of the activities undertaken thus far by the working group to facilitate appropriate coordination between the Subcommittees.[730]

Concerning the ToR, these essentially identify the boundary conditions delimiting the activities of the working group. According to the ToR, the SRWG shall (1) report to the LSC, (2) operate in accordance with the procedure, methods of work and established practices of the Committee, and (3) be led by a Chair and Co-Chair with the support of UNOOSA.[731] As to its membership, the SRWG shall be open to all States members of the Committee, with particular encouragement to the participation of developing Countries.[732] In line with the intergovernmental nature of UNCOPUOS, States will be the primary contributors to the substantive discussions of the working group. Nonetheless, under point (f) of the ToR, the working group is allowed to "avail itself" of work conducted in the area of space resource activities "submitted by any means as may be determined by the working group,"[733] including through the international conference mentioned above. Point (e) of the ToR further provides that the working group operates "taking into account" the inputs of permanent observers and other stakeholders, so long as they are (1) submitted in accordance with the established practice of the Committee and (2) regarded as relevant to the work of the working group by its Chair and Co-Chair, in consultation with the Member States.[734] In this regard, it should be noted that the workplan does not provide any concrete instruction as to how the contributions of non-governmental actors mentioned under points (e) and (f) should be submitted to the working group. Hopefully, this will be clarified pursuant to the gathering of guiding inputs from Member States that, in accordance with the "initial tasks to be undertaken in 2022" listed in the workplan, will take place later this year.[735]

From the above analysis of the mandate, ToR and methods of work of the SRWG, it is possible to derive the following considerations. First, the very establishment of a UN working group reinforces the configuration of space mining as a multi-level regulatory system by adding a critical reference point for normative development at the international level. Pursuant to its mandate, the SRWG has been established to provide multilateral coordination on the regulation of space resources. However, whether the working group will succeed in neutralizing the current risk of regulatory divergence among national legislations remains to be seen. In this regard, it is important to note that there is a number of private space resource missions planned for the coming years. Under Article VI OST, these missions will need to be authorized and supervised by the

729. SRWG Report, *supra* note 701 at 3-4.
730. *Ibid.*
731. Report of the Committee, *supra* note 699 at 53-54.
732. *Ibid.*
733. *Ibid.*
734. *Ibid.*
735. SRWG Report, *supra* note 701 at 3-4.

appropriate State, which will be internationally responsible for ensuring compliance with the provisions of the Treaty.[736] National decision-makers will thus have to make precise choices on the substantive conduct of space mining in order to fulfill their obligations under Article VI OST. Since the first regulatory "product" of the SRWG will be completed only in 2027,[737] the question is whether the studies, exchange of views and discussions conducted in the meantime will suffice to provide a minimum shared ground for the normative choices that will be made by national regulators. If this is the case, then the SRWG will be able to make a positive impact and enable the flourishing of space mining as multi-level regulatory system. However, if the working group fails to provide such guidance, there is a significant risk that its work might be blocked by political opposition and that the system would descend into the chaos of regulatory conflicts. Which of the two will it be, only time will tell.

3.1.2 Policy Developments in Civil Society: Multi-Stakeholder Contributions

The 2019 Building Blocks for the Development of an International Framework on Space Resource Activities

In 2016, right after the beginning of diplomatic discussions in UNCOPUOS, various stakeholders from the space community convened a global consortium called "The Hague International Space Resources Governance Working Group"[738] (The Hague Group) to exchange views and develop proposals for the regulation of space mining. After four years of work, at the end of 2019, The Hague Group condensed the results of its discussions into twenty "Building Blocks for the Development of an International Framework on Space Resource Activities,"[739] which were released together with an accompanying Commentary.[740] The Building Blocks are the first and so far only attempt at the substantive regulation of space mining, and as such, represent a significant milestone toward its multi-level governance. For this reason, some States in UNCOPUOS initially met The Hague Group with skepticism and hostility, as they saw it as an attempt to circumvent or undermine its guiding role.[741] With time, it became apparent that these concerns were unjustified since the purpose of The Hague Group was rather to support the diplomatic debate in UNCOPUOS.[742] In accordance with this logic, the Governments of the Netherlands and of Luxembourg officially submitted the

736. Article VI OST, *supra* note 1.
737. SRWG Report, *supra* note 701 at 4.
738. Information on the Hague Group can be found https://www.universiteitleiden.nl/en/law/institute-of-public-law/institute-of-air-space-law/the-hague-space-resources-governance-wo rking-group (last accessed October 2022). Further details are also provided within the BB Commentary, *supra* note 82 at 1-4.
739. Building Blocks for the Development of an International Framework for the Governance of Space Resource Activities, available https://www.universiteitleiden.nl/binaries/content/assets/rechtsgeleerdheid/instituut-voor-publiekrecht/lucht--en-ruimterecht/space-resources/bb-thissrwg--cover.pdf (last accessed October 2022).
740. BB Commentary, *supra* note 82.
741. Report of the Legal Subcommittee, *supra* note 687 at 30.
742. BB Commentary, *supra* note 82 at 1-2.

Building Blocks for the consideration of the LSC after their official adoption in November 2019.[743]

Content-wise, the Building Blocks move from the premise that the regulation of space mining should be dealt with in a dedicated international framework to be developed in accordance with the principle of adaptive governance.[744] Even though The Hague Group did not attach any label to the proposed international framework, Building Block 1 immediately clarified its multi-level dimension. Under this provision, the objective of the international framework should be to create "an enabling environment" for the conduct and regulation of space resource activities.[745] To this end, the international framework should clarify the applicability of international space law to space mining and consequently guide States in the development of their domestic regulation.[746] It follows that the international framework proposed by The Hague Group could be placed in between the binding obligations of the *Corpus Iuris Spatialis* and the relevant domestic frameworks of States Parties to those Treaties. Besides the various substantive proposals laid down in the Building Blocks, this methodological suggestion is perhaps the most significant contribution provided by The Hague Group. In identifying the need for guided multi-level regulation and framing a proposal for its development, the Building Blocks literally live up to their name: providing a foundational basis upon which States can begin to build the multi-level regulatory system of space mining.

Complementary contributions from the space community: The Vancouver Recommendations, the Lunar Resources Policy, the EAGLE Lunar Governance Report and the Global Expert Group on Sustainable Lunar Activities

The successful experience of The Hague Group inspired other entities from all over the world to develop similar processes for continuing the discussion on space resources. Shortly after the enactment of the Building Blocks, in March 2020, the Outer Space Institute[747] (OSI) released a document called the "Vancouver Recommendations" with the declared purpose of complementing certain aspects of space mining that were not covered by The Hague Group.[748] The Vancouver Recommendations elaborate on the regulation of space resource activities with a particular focus on scientific investigation and environmental protection. Because of the scientific outlook of the OSI, the primary concern of the Recommendations is the prevention of individual actions that could jeopardize key scientific interests in lunar exploration.[749] For this reason, this document strongly pushes for direct international regulation and oversees space mining. As

743. Working paper submitted by Luxembourg and the Netherlands, Building Blocks for the Development of an International Framework for the Governance of Space Resource Activities, UN Doc A/AC.105/C.2/L.315 (2020).
744. BB Commentary, *supra* note 82 at 1-2.
745. Building Block 1, *supra* note 739.
746. BB Commentary, *supra* note 82 at 17-19.
747. More information on the OSI can be found on its http://outerspaceinstitute.ca/index.html website (last accessed October 2022).
748. Vancouver Recommendations, *supra* note 681 at 2.
749. *Ibid.*

a consequence, albeit intended to augment and complement the Building Blocks, the Vancouver Recommendations rapidly became a much more divisive document.[750]

Some months after, in a somehow opposite direction, the Moon Village Association[751] (MVA) published its proposed "Best Practices for Sustainable Lunar Activities."[752] Notably, also this document is connected to the work of The Hague Group and, in fact, is based upon Building Block 1.2 (d).[753] Contrary to the Vancouver Recommendations, the Best Practices refine the pragmatic approach of The Hague Group by emphasizing the importance of the operational level as a third governance layer. Accordingly, the Best Practices provide a series of recommended practices to be voluntarily implemented by lunar operators. Unfortunately, the Best Practices were not met with the support desired by MVA, which therefore announced their revision through a new multi-stakeholder platform called "Global Expert Group on Sustainable Lunar Activities" (GEGSLA).[754] This platform is composed of thirty-eight members representing all stakeholders interested in lunar activities, and its work is followed by over 100 registered observers from the space community.[755] The purpose of GEGSLA is to develop (1) a proposed recommended framework for the consideration of UNCOPUOS as well as (2) a series of technical guidelines for the consideration of operators.[756] GEGSLA kicked off its activities in January 2021, so far held a total of 16th meetings and aims to finalize its documents by the end of 2022 in order to submit them for the consideration of UNCOPUOS in 2023.[757]

In October 2020, the Open Lunar Foundation[758] (OLF) officially entered the global debate on space resource activities by releasing its "Lunar Resources Policy."[759] Similar to the Building Blocks and the Best Practices, the Lunar Resources Policies acknowledge the need for minimal but effective regulation to be agreed upon at the international level.[760] Accordingly, OLF recommends the adoption of a foundational document composed of guiding principles and shared agreements enabling the enactment of

750. Mostly due to the accompanying letter and its frontal opposition to the U.S. Space Resources EO. Ian Christensen & Christopher Johnson, *Putting the White House Executive Order on Space Resources in an International Context*, available https://www.thespacereview.com/article/3932/1 (last accessed October 2022).
751. More information on MVA can be found on its https://moonvillageassociation.org/ website (last accessed October 2022).
752. Best Practices, *supra* note 682.
753. According to which "promote the identification of best practices by States, international organizations and non-governmental entities." Building Block 1.2 (d), *supra* note 739.
754. As announced on its https://moonvillageassociation.org/press-release-moon-village-association-launches-global-expert-group-for-sustainable-lunar-activities/ website (last accessed October 2022).
755. As reported on GEGSLA's https://moonvillageassociation.org/gegsla/gegsla-team/ webpage (last accessed October 2022).
756. Under GEGSLA's https://moonvillageassociation.org/download/gegsla-methods-of-work-and-plan-05-may-2021/ Methods of Work and Plan (last accessed October 2022).
757. *Ibid.*
758. More information on OLF can be found on its https://www.openlunar.org/ website (last accessed October 2022).
759. Lunar Resources Policy, *supra* note 683.
760. *Id.*, at 1-2.

a minimal set of overarching policies committed to peace, cooperation and accessibility.[761] Since then, the OLF has provided a growing number of excellent contributions to the debate on space resources and lunar governance. The most recent example of these contributions is the "Res Luna" project, which has identified more than twenty different lunar resource systems, each requiring a different regulatory approach for their successful use.[762]

Finally, the last contribution from the space community analyzed in this section is the "Lunar Governance Report" developed by the Action Team on EAGLE[763] of the Space Generation Advisory Council[764] (SGAC). Between the years 2020 and 2021, the EAGLE Team studied the abovementioned policy developments and interviewed relevant stakeholders from the space community on the governance of lunar activities, including space mining. Based on these studies, the EAGLE Team identified the existence of a general consensus on the development of a middle-level framework enabling the enactment of adaptive regulation governing these activities. In its Lunar Governance Report,[765] the EAGLE Team proposes the adoption of a Lunar Governance Charter as a flexible instrument capable of enabling the further development of multi-level regulation.[766] Differently from the various documents examined above, the proposal developed by the EAGLE Team is not a final product.[767] While substantiating it with a list of recommended topics and processes, the EAGLE Team leaves the actual development of the Charter in the hands of States in UNCOPUOS.[768] Among these recommendations, the EAGLE team suggests the LSC address space mining within the context of lunar activities and not as a subject of its own.[769] Similar to the Best Practices and Lunar Resources Policy, the EAGLE Team makes this suggestion because to produce adequate regulation for space resource activities, one needs to take into account their technical and economic realities.[770] Since the early practice of space mining will almost exclusively take place on the Moon, it seems more appropriate to begin with the regulation of lunar resource activities. In conclusion, the complementary efforts described in this section confirm the validity of the proposal laid down in Building Block 1: a shared international framework that could clarify the applicability of international space law and guide the development of domestic legislation.

761. *Id.*, at 3-4.
762. More information on Res Luna can be found on its https://www.openlunar.org/resluna webpage (last accessed October 2022).
763. More information on the EAGLE team can be found on its https://spacegeneration.org/eagle webpage (last accessed October 2022).
764. More information on SGAC can be found on its https://spacegeneration.org/ website (last accessed October 2022).
765. Lunar Governance Report, *supra* note 684.
766. *Id.*, at 39-56.
767. *Id.*, at 40.
768. *Id.*, at 54-56.
769. *Id.*, at 55.
770. *Ibid.*

3.1.3 *Policy Developments in State Practice: Artemis and ILRS*

Over the last two years, States involved in the Artemis Program and the International Lunar Research Station (ILRS)[771] have started to develop guiding principles and policies to govern their planned development of permanent robotic and human bases on the Moon.

On October 13, 2020, at the occasion of the 71st International Astronautical Congress, a coalition of eight Countries, including Australia, Canada, Italy, Japan, Luxembourg, the United Arab Emirates, the United Kingdom and the United States of America, presented a multilateral document known as the "Artemis Accords."[772] Formally, the Accords constitute a political commitment toward certain "Principles for Cooperation in the Civil Exploration and Use of the Moon, Mars, Comets and Asteroids for Peaceful Purposes."[773] Practically, the Accords aim to "operationalize" the norms of the OST for the development and implementation of the Artemis Program.[774] Unsurprisingly, the AA have raised both appreciation and skepticism. Some States praised the document as a testament to international cooperation, while some others criticized it as "too U.S.-centric."[775] Likewise, scholars from the space law community either spoke in their support or called for more cautiousness.[776] Within the scope of the present analysis, the AA are an extremely important document as the first diplomatic attempt at developing the middle framework that is needed at present. One obstacle in this respect comes from the fact that, albeit being open to the signature of any State,[777]

771. The International Lunar Research Station (ILRS) is a joint program of the Chinese National Space Administration and Roscosmos announced in February 2021. Andrew Jones, *Russia, China to Sign Agreement on International Lunar Research Station,* Space News, available https://spacenews.com/russia-china-to-sign-agreement-on-international-lunar-research-station/ (last accessed October 2022).
772. Artemis Accords, *supra* note 102. When this book was finalized in October 2022, the Artemis Accords counted twenty Signatories.
773. *Ibid.*
774. More information on the Accords are available https://2017-2021.state.gov/briefings-foreign-press-centers/artemis-accords-enabling-international-partnerships-for-lunar-exploration/index.html in a briefing from the U.S. State Department (last accessed October 2022).
775. Russia has been the first one expressing these concerns https://spacewatch.global/2020/10/russia-calls-parts-of-nasa-moon-projects-too-american-centric/, further reiterated by some European commentators criticizing https://spacewatch.global/2020/10/eight-nations-signed-artemis-accords-nasas-bridenstine-says/ the "divide and conquer" strategy behind bilateral negotiations with "selected" countries in Europe (both links last accessed October 2022).
776. For the first group, *see* Christopher Johnson, *A First Look at the Artemis Accords,* available https://www.linkedin.com/pulse/first-look-artemis-accords-christopher-johnson?articleId=6722061704605286400#comments-6722061704605286400&trk=public_profile_article_view (last accessed October 2022); for the second, *see* Christopher Newman, *The Artemis Accords and Lunar Exploration: Revolution and Evolution,* available https://spacewatch.global/2020/10/spacewatchgl-opinion-the-artemis-accords-and-lunar-exploration-revolution-and-evolution/ (last accessed October 2022).
777. Artemis Accords, *supra* note 102 at section 13. It should be noted that some States (like Italy) have signed through government representatives, others (like the U.S.) have done so through their space agency, and one (Japan) did both.

the Accords have been presented as a specific regulatory framework for the Artemis program.[778]

As such, this document cannot serve as a *universally shared* reference framework because States which do not wish to participate or be associated with the Artemis program are unlikely to sign the Accords. This obstacle is implicitly acknowledged in—and perhaps already overcome by—the Accords themselves. In section 10, which is dedicated to space resources, the Signatories affirm their intention "to use their experience under the Accords to contribute to multilateral efforts to further develop international practices and rules applicable to the extraction and utilization of space resources, including through ongoing efforts at the COPUOS."[779] Therefore, it seems that the Accords intend to offer a model for the future enactment of a complementary document within UNCOPUOS, providing a significant milestone towards the multilevel regulation of space mining.

More recently, on October 27, 2022, the NASA Office of Technology, Policy, and Strategy released a report detailing a comprehensive and innovative "Lunar Landing and Operations Policy Analysis."[780] This document directly builds on the Accords and addresses key policy and operational issues related to lunar activities with due regard to their global relevance, providing solid foundations for further national and international policy developments.

Per their part, in June 2021 the (so far only) two Partners of the ILRS—China and Russia—have released a "Guide for Partnership" providing technical and policy indications for international participation in the program.[781] The Guide declares equality, openness, and integrity as guiding principles for the program and outlines the planned ILRS missions.[782] When releasing the Guide, China and Russia also announced the negotiation of both an ILRS Declaration and an Intergovernmental Agreement as framework documents for the program, which according to the Parties should be signed by the end of 2022.[783]

3.2 Regulatory Scenarios

Based on the analysis conducted in this chapter, it is possible to identify three scenarios for the regulation of space resource activities: uncoordinated national legislation,

778. As declared in their website https://www.nasa.gov/specials/artemis-accords/index.html by NASA (last accessed October 2022). *See also* U.S. State Department, *supra* note 774.
779. Artemis Accords, *supra* note 102 at section 10.
780. Gabriel Swiney & Amanda Hernandez, *(Nasa Office of Technology Policy and Strategy), Lunar Landing and Operations Policy Analysis* (2022), available https://www.nasa.gov/sites/default/files/atoms/files/nasa-otps-lunar-landing-and-operations-policy-analysis-final-report_2.pdf (last accessed October 2022).
781. China National Space Administration and Roscosmos, International Lunar Research Station (ILRS) Guide For Partnership (2021), available http://www.cnsa.gov.cn/english/n6465652/n6465653/c6812150/content.html (last accessed October 2022).
782. *Id.*, respectively at Preface and section 1.
783. Deng Xiaoci, *Lunar Research Station to Be Inked by China and Russia This Year, Operational by 2035: CNSA*, Global Times China, available https://www.globaltimes.cn/page/202201/1250142.shtml (last accessed October 2022).

integrated multi-level regulation and direct international governance. All scenarios move from the same starting point: States passing laws showing their intention to authorize and supervise commercial space resource activities but without including any substantive provision governing their actual conduct.

3.2.1 Uncoordinated National Legislation

The first scenario sees the enactment of substantive regulation at the domestic level in the absence of any international guidance. This choice has the merit of unlocking the current regulatory impasse, but it also brings an inherent risk of unsustainable systemic divergence. Given the many different ways in which States could interpret and implement the principles of international space law, in the absence of an internationally agreed starting point, it is likely that the various domestic regimes will end up conflicting with each other. A critical contrast in this scenario may arise from the situation in which two States have independently authorized the mining of the same resources in a given area.[784] Legally speaking, the two permits would be equally valid. Under Article IX OST, the two States concerned would be obliged to pay due regard to each other's interests and consult in case they foresee any potentially harmful interferences. Therefore, the first actor reaching the site would be in a much more comfortable position. In turn, this could cause a race to occupy as many mining sites as possible, to benefit from a first-mover advantage. Similar behaviors may then be accused of violating the limits posed to the freedom of using celestial bodies under Article I OST, ultimately threatening the peaceful uses of space as well as the maintenance of international peace and security. Furthermore, an increased level of divergence among national regulations of space mining may have a significant impact on the available enforcement options. If States would begin to openly attack the legitimacy of each other's permits and activities, the probability of recourse to unilateral coercive measures will increase significantly. As such, in the scenario of uncoordinated national legislation, there would be few opportunities for peaceful enforcement.

3.2.2 Integrated Multi-level Regulation

If the domestic enactment of substantive regulation for space mining would be based on a shared starting point agreed upon at the international level, we would instead enter the second scenario: integrated multi-level regulation. As discussed in the previous section, this outcome has been directly or indirectly advocated by various actors from the space community.[785] In this scenario, the constructive potential enshrined in the national regulation of space mining would be channeled within clear boundaries limiting the risk of divergence. In addition, this scenario would reduce the

784. Tronchetti & Hao, *supra* note 593 at 6.
785. From the government of The Netherlands endorsing the Building Blocks to the Signatories of the Artemis Accords.

legitimacy pressure upon national authorities and allow them to build their domestic regulation from a solid basis agreed upon at the international level. In time, States can revisit their domestic legislation based on the lessons learned from the actual conduct of space resource activities. After a number of iterations at the domestic level, States can then convene again to update or upgrade the middle-level framework as may be necessary.

In this author's view, in order for this scenario to produce the abovementioned benefits, the enacted international framework must include appropriate procedures for minimum coordination and amicable resolution of disputes. Minimum coordination mechanisms for space mining activities should be based on three pillars: public notification, bilateral coordination and mutual recognition. First, all States authorizing or planning to authorize space mining activities should timely and publicly inform the UNSG of their nature, purpose, location and duration under Article XI OST. This step is of critical importance for the safe conduct of space mining since public notifications will enable States planning to undertake activities in the same area or in its vicinities to coordinate appropriately.

In light of the central role that will be played by private operators, minimum coordination mechanisms should also include the mutual recognition of mining licenses. As underlined in Chapter 1, mutual recognition is an integration tool which is especially useful within the context of private-based activities.[786] From the perspective of private actors, mutual recognition would guarantee their operations against the risk of conflicting claims being granted under foreign jurisdictions. From the perspective of regulators, mutual recognition could prevent the risk of direct conflicts among national regimes, thus maintaining international peace and security and promoting international cooperation and understanding. Since not even the best coordination mechanisms can eradicate the possibility of disagreements, the international framework should also include agreed procedures for the effective and amicable resolution of disputes. As will be discussed in the next chapter, a suitable option is offered by international arbitration, preferably before the PCA.[787] Framed in these terms, the integrated multi-level regulation of space mining would also reduce the risk of conflictual enforcement. While domestic disputes adjudicated domestically could be enforced according to the rules of the concerned State, transnational disputes settled by means of international arbitration would be enforceable under the 1958 New York Convention (NYC).[788]

786. As to which, *see* section 1.3.2 (ii) in Chapter 1. It is important to recall that mutual recognition depends on shared values and reciprocal trust, which in this scenario would be provided by the agreed international framework.

787. As to which, *see* section 1.1.2 in Chapter 3. On the general benefits of international arbitration, *see also* section 2.2.2 (iv) in Chapter 1.

788. Convention on the Recognition and Enforcement of Foreign Arbitral Awards, *entered into force* June 7, 1959, 330 UNTS 3. On the benefits offered by the New York Convention *see* section 1.1.2 in Chapter 3.

3.2.3 Direct International Governance

The last scenario considered in this section is the direct international governance of space resource activities. In this author's view, the success and usefulness of this regulatory scheme crucially depend on its development and timing. As shown by the analysis of the MA, a fully fledged international system should follow and not anticipate the technical and economic development of space mining.[789] In this regard, it seems likely that integrated multi-level governance would progressively move toward the international level as soon as space mining becomes a more "ordinary" space activity. In accordance with the principle of subsidiarity,[790] the regulation of space resource activities should be transferred at the international level when States would not be able to properly control them anymore through their domestic instruments.[791] It should be noted that any attempt to force the development of direct international governance is likely to undermine and potentially jeopardize the entire regulatory process, as confirmed by the dramatic impact that the failure of the MA had on the development of binding norms within international space law. Lastly, for what concerns the enforcement aspects, direct international governance would naturally call for a centralized enforcement structure established at the global level that could ensure its equal, consistent and effective application.

4 CONCLUSIONS

Building upon the systemic findings developed in the first chapter, this chapter assessed the current status of the multi-level regulation of space mining. To begin with, section 1 considered the applicability of the norms of international space law to the conduct and regulation of space resource activities. In light of its foundational role within the system of space law, section 1 centered the analysis on the OST. One by one, the section discussed all the fundamental principles of international space law as laid down in relevant OST provisions, with the goal to understand their implications within the multi-level system of space mining. From the analysis of Article I OST, section 1.1.1 found that space resource activities are allowed as part of the freedom to use celestial bodies granted by this provision. At the same time, the section also argued that in order to be lawfully conducted, they will have to fulfill a series of requirements established pursuant to the other applicable provisions of the OST. Following the principle of adaptive governance, the section specified that regulatory requirements should evolve hand in hand with the practical developments of space mining. From the legal status of celestial bodies as global commons under Article I OST, section 1.1.1 developed three fundamental findings. First, space resource activities should always be limited in scale

789. As to which, *see* sections 1.3.2 and 1.3.3 in Chapter 2.
790. Subsidiarity is a regulatory principle according to which norms should be developed at the normative level which is closer to the given issues, unless farther regulatory levels can be more effective.
791. Under the same line of reasoning, one day the regulation of space mining will be directly entrusted to the local communities permanently operating on the surface of given celestial bodies.

and duration in order to preserve the exploration and use of celestial bodies as the province of all humankind. Second, a right of innocent passage should always be granted pursuant to appropriate coordination to ensure compliance with the principle of free access. Third and final, international cooperation and capacity building in space resource activities should be extensively promoted to promote non-discrimination and equity in the use of celestial bodies. From the analysis of Article II OST, section 1.1.2 found that its prohibition of national appropriation does not extend to space resources. At the same time, the section also held that certain types of invasive and permanent uses of celestial bodies may very well violate the prohibition of their territorial appropriation. Looking at Article III OST, section 1.1.3 found that the direct applicability of the UN Charter provides a legal basis for the potential involvement of the UN principal organs in either the development, application, adjudication or enforcement of space mining regulations. Concerning Article IV OST, the analysis conducted in section 1.1.3 confirmed that the general prohibition to use celestial bodies for military purposes also covers the extraction and use of space resources. Accordingly, only civilian entities shall engage in and benefit from space resource activities. For what concerns Article VI OST, section 1.1.4 stresses its fundamental importance for the development of space mining as multi-level regulatory system and for assuring the compatibility of commercial space resource activities with applicable international space law. Articles VII and VIII OST are jointly assessed in section 1.1.5. For what concerns Article VII OST, the section found that its concrete relevance will depend on the ratification status of the LIAB. For what concerns Article VIII OST, the section found that this provision will play a key role in ensuring the legitimate conduct of space mining. This article, in fact, provides the legal basis for overseeing mining operations and ensuring respect for applicable normative requirements in an area otherwise subtracted from the influence of sovereign States. Concerning Article IX OST, section 1.1.6 developed three essential implications on space mining activities and regulations. First, to comply with the principle of due regard, States will have to make sure that the space mining activities for which they are responsible would not entirely spoil the possibility of others to undertake parallel activities. Second, to prevent the harmful contamination of celestial bodies, States will have to minimize the environmental impact of their mining activities that could interfere with or jeopardize the exploration and use of celestial bodies by other States. Finally, in order to achieve both goals, States will have to engage in meaningful consultations with the other Parties concerned by their activities in order to find a suitable compromise between their respective competing interests. Concerning Article XI OST, section 1.1.7 found that sharing information about space resource activities in accordance with this provision will be vital to build trust, enable coordination and foster cooperation. To this end, the section recommended improving existing practices for information sharing to better fit the coordination needs posed by the exploration and use of celestial bodies. Finally, section 1.1.8 developed two fundamental considerations with regard to Article XII OST. On the one hand, the openness of stations, installations, equipment and vehicles involved in space mining will play a critical role in ensuring their peaceful and legitimate conduct. On the other hand, the technical and commercial realities of space mining will require a balanced application of this principle to avoid potential abuses and ensure the safety of operations conducted thereby.

Section 1.2 considered the role and relevance of the other treaties composing the *Corpus Iuris Spatialis*, with the exception of the ARRA. Assessing the LIAB and REG altogether, section 1.2.1 found that both treaties represent a crucial complement to the fundamental principles of the OST, also with respect to space mining activities. Therefore, the section recommended their wide ratification to avoid regulatory discrepancies and develop implementing mechanisms to enhance their application to the conduct of space mining. With specific reference to the LIAB, section 1.2.1 underlined the importance of developing objective parameters for the concrete application of the fault's criterion foreseen in its Article III. With specific reference to the REG, the section recommended the inclusion of fundamental information on the location and duration of a given space resource activity within the registration information of related space objects. To enhance this practice, the section further encouraged the development, within both national and international registries for space objects, of dedicated segments listing the space objects involved in space resource activities. Concerning the MA, section 1.3 conducted a thorough assessment of its fundamental provisions, with a special focus on the principle of "Common Heritage of Mankind" under its Article 11. From that analysis, the section found that if and when the international regime mandated in Article 11 MA is established, States Parties to the MA will be able to conduct activities on the Moon only under its terms. Conversely, until that moment, States Parties to the MA are not operatively constrained by its various obligations, except for the one to take good faith efforts toward the negotiation of the said international regime. On a general political level, section 1.3 argued that the global debate on space mining and lunar governance should take the MA into proper consideration in order to learn from its mistakes and build upon its strengths. On the one hand, national or international regulation of space mining should be made mostly of foundational norms enabling the safe and sustainable conduct of groundbreaking missions. On the other one, the provisions of the MA on intergenerational balance, sharing of information and international designation of special scientific areas deserve careful consideration and respect as expressing fundamentally important needs.

Section 2 considered the only existing examples of domestic legislation specifically dedicated to space mining: the USCLCA, the Luxembourg LUXSRL, the UAE UAEFLRSS and the Japanese JSRA. Despite the various concerns raised (especially by academics), the section found that these laws are fully compatible with the *Corpus Iuris Spatialis*. They address an activity which is permitted under Article I OST, and they do so in compliance with their regulatory obligations under Article VI OST. At the same time, this compliance is facilitated by the fact that none of these laws includes substantive provisions governing the practical conduct of space resource activities. From a systemic viewpoint, this normative deficiency is a major obstacle withholding the full potential of the multi-level system of space mining. Nonetheless, in light of the infancy of space resource activities, it is safe to state that these four laws provide a positive starting point toward responsible and balanced multi-level regulation.

Based on these findings, section 3 assessed the multi-level interaction among national and international norms of space mining. In this respect, the section highlighted the difficulty of combining the broadness of international space law with the vagueness of dedicated national space legislation. To move past this *impasse*, the section proposed the development of a middle-level framework between the international principles of space law and the various domestic space legislations. In essence, this framework should enable the incremental enactment of internationally compliant national regimes adapting to the evolution of space resource activities. Moving from this premise, section 3 moved to discuss recent developments in State practice and policy discussions aimed at resolving the current impasse in a very similar direction. To begin with, section 3.1 considered the debate in UNCOPUOS and found that States have developed two positions, one in favor of national regulation and one calling for international governance. In 2019, the LSC decided to hold, at its 2020 meetings, informal consultations for the establishment of a working group on space resources. Due to the outbreak of the COVID-19 pandemic, these consultations have been postponed to 2021, when they have been conducted in a hybrid format. Despite the many challenges related to the persistence of the COVID-19 pandemic, the consultations were successfully concluded with the establishment of a new "Working Group on the Legal Aspects of Space Resource Activities." During the meetings of the LSC in 2022, the SRWG completed the enactment of its foundational documents with the approval of its five-year workplan and is now preparing to conduct substantive discussions in 2023. Following, the section moved to consider additional contributions from multi-stakeholder actors. To begin with, section 3.1 praised the Hague Building Blocks as the very first document proposing a middle-level framework to reproach international space law and national legislation. After the enactment of the Building Blocks, the idea of developing a minimum shared ground at the international level was supported and complemented in further policy documents like the Lunar Resources Policies and the Lunar Governance Report. In parallel, through the AA, the need for a middle-level framework has also been acknowledged in recent State practice.

Based on the conducted analysis, section 3.2 identified three potential scenarios for the further development of space mining as multi-level regulatory system: uncoordinated national legislation, integrated multi-level regulation and direct international governance. All scenarios move from the same starting point: States passing laws showing their intention to authorize and supervise commercial space resource activities but not including any substantive provision governing their actual conduct. The first scenario foresees the enactment of these substantive provisions in the absence of any guidance at the international level. Given the many different ways in which States could interpret the principles of international space law, in this scenario, it is assumed that the various domestic regimes will end up conflicting with each other. In turn, these conflicts would threaten the peaceful and sustainable uses of celestial bodies while also drastically reducing the opportunity for peaceful enforcement. The second scenario foresees the domestic enactment of substantive regulation for space mining based upon a shared starting point agreed upon at the international level. In this hypothesis, the potential enshrined in the national regulation of space mining would be constructively channeled within precise international boundaries limiting the risk of divergence. To properly achieve this objective, this integrated multi-level regulation must include appropriate procedures for minimum coordination and amicable resolution of disputes. Minimum coordination mechanisms for space resource activities should be based on three pillars: public notification, bilateral coordination and mutual recognition. As will be discussed in the next chapter, a viable option in this respect may be offered by international arbitration in order to benefit from the enforcement options provided by the NYC. The section concluded by considering the third and last scenario, i.e., direct international governance of space resource activities. In accordance with the principle of subsidiarity, the section argued that the regulation of space resource activities should be fully transferred at the international level only when States are not able to properly control their development at the domestic one. In a similar situation, there would be valid reasons to support direct international governance, together with a centralized structure of enforcement ensuring the equal, consistent and efficient application of its norms.

From the assessment conducted in this chapter, it is possible to draw the following conclusions. First, there is an evident imbalance within the multi-level regulatory system of space mining. The international level is clearly much more developed than the national one, which so far has only acknowledged the mere legality of commercial space resource activities. Undoubtedly, the substantive solutions to the regulatory challenges posed by space mining will have to be based on the *Corpus Iuris Spatialis*. However, the broadness of international space law does not provide the interpreter with any clear direction among the available regulatory options. In the prolonged absence of international guidance, the responsibility of operationalizing the rules of international space law will inevitably fall on national regulators. Since each of these entities will undertake this task based on its preferences and understandings, there is a serious risk of regulatory divergence within the system. If left uncontrolled, this divergence may very well increase up to the point of becoming intolerable and, as a result, conflictual. In such a case, the opportunity for peaceful, legitimate and effective enforcement would decrease dramatically. Conversely, if diversity were properly managed through appropriate international guidance, this, in turn, would reduce the potential for conflict and, as such, enforcement mechanisms. Based on these premises, the final chapter of the book presents the enforcement options currently available within the multi-level system of space mining and evaluates them in terms of legitimacy and effectiveness. Following this evaluation, the chapter discusses how to reinforce the system through the development of dedicated coordination, consultation and adjudication mechanisms, taking inspiration from the models offered by comparable regimes for the governance of global commons.

CHAPTER 3

Enforcement Options and Proposed Reinforcements

Questions of enforcement have remained largely unexplored in space law literature.[1]

To complete the assessment of the multi-level system of space mining, this chapter considers whether and how to enforce the international and national norms composing the system. For the purposes of the present analysis, enforcement is understood as the process envisaged by a given regulatory system to restore compliance with its norms pursuant to the establishment of a normative violation through dedicated adjudicatory processes. In accordance with this notion of enforcement, the present chapter looks at the options available within the multi-level system of space mining for adjudicating and enforcing compliance with its norms, further assessing their legitimacy and effectiveness. In light of the results of this analysis, the chapter also considers how to reinforce the system through the establishment of tailored coordination, consultation and adjudication processes, learning from comparable legal models for the governance of global commons. Structurally, the chapter is divided into three Sections. Section 1 begins the analysis by considering the enforcement options currently available within the system and evaluating them in light of their legitimacy and effectiveness. Section 2 enriches the assessment by looking at potential models that might help reinforce it from comparable legal regimes: the United Nations Convention on the Law of the Sea, the International Telecommunication Union and the Antarctic Treaty. Finally, section 3 concludes the analysis by discussing the applicability of the identified reinforcements in the short, medium and long term.

1. It is very rare for a space law book or article to discuss questions of enforcement. For one of the few sources attempting an enforcement analysis within the realm of space law, *see* Christina Isnardi, *Problems with Enforcing International Space Law on Private Actors*, 58 (2) Columbia Journal of Transnational Law 491-530 (2020).

1 CURRENT ENFORCEMENT OPTIONS FROM INTERNATIONAL LAW

This section explores the options available within the multi-level system of space mining for the enforcement of its international and national norms. In accordance with the notion of enforcement framed above, the section focuses on enforcement tools whose exercise would be triggered by the establishment of a normative violation as a result of adjudicatory processes. Thus, the section begins its analysis by investigating first how the multi-level system of space mining establishes the existence of normative violations. Based on the discovered findings, the section then moves to consider which enforcement tools would be triggered as a result of the identified adjudicatory processes, further evaluating them in terms of legitimacy and effectiveness.

Overview of International and Domestic Adjudicatory Processes

Due to its infant status, the specialized system of space mining lacks dedicated processes for the interpretation, adjudication and enforcement of its norms. However, thanks to its multi-level configuration, the system can rely on applicable mechanisms available at the international and national levels as relevant and appropriate.

At the international level, it is worth noting that the also broader system of space law lacks dedicated rules for the interpretation, adjudication and enforcement of its norms. Pursuant to the principle of systemic integration, these issues will be resolved through the application of the general mechanisms provided by the legal order of international law. While interpretation will be conducted pursuant to the rules laid down in Articles 31-33 of the VCLT,[2] any potential disagreement will be handled through the mechanisms provided by Chapter VI of the UN Charter for the pacific settlement of disputes.[3] However, not all the mechanisms provided under Article 33 UN Charter can justify the exercise of enforcement powers as understood in this book. Accordingly, among the mechanisms listed in Article 33 UN Charter, this section focuses on arbitration and judicial settlement.

As is well-known, the legal order of international law does not have a globally unified system for the adjudication of its normative violations. Under Article 92 of the UN Charter, the ICJ is established as the principal judicial organ of the United Nations, i.e., neither the exclusive nor the supreme one. As discussed in Chapter 1, the past twenty years have actually seen the development of a plethora of international courts and arbitration tribunals, each "competing" with the ICJ for the adjudication of international disputes.[4] Although this proliferation has not ultimately undermined the

2. Vienna Convention on the Law of Treaties, *entered into force* January 27, 1980, 1155 U.N.T.S. 331 [hereinafter: "VCLT"].
3. Charter of the United Nations, *entered into force* October 24, 1945, 1 UNTS 16 [hereinafter: "UN Charter"].
4. *The Proliferation of International Judicial Bodies: The Outlook for the International Legal Order*—Speech by His Excellency Judge Gilbert Guillaume, President of the International Court of Justice, to the Sixth Committee of the General Assembly of the United Nations, available https://ghum.kuleuven.be/ggs/events/2013/springlectures2013/documents-1/guillaume-proliferation-intnat-judicial.pdf (accessed February 2021) [hereinafter: "Fragmentation Speech"]. For the analysis of the fragmentation debate, *see* section 1.1.1 in Chapter 1.

unity of the international legal order, it has certainly complicated the process of ascertaining its normative violations. As a consequence, States seeking the adjudication of an international dispute related to space mining might theoretically have recourse to a number of courts and arbitration tribunals, depending on several elements, such as the subject matter or the geographical scope of the dispute. For example, States alleging violations in the area of international trade law might have recourse to the judicial system of the WTO[5] due to its competence in trade matters. States belonging to the EU might bring their space mining disputes before the CJEU,[6] provided that there is a violation of the EU principles on the internal market or its competition rules. In both cases, the involvement of these institutions would be based on the terrestrial trading and circulation of space resources pursuant to their import from space. Since the space mining industry is quite far from reaching these capabilities, there are no reasonable grounds to justify the involvement of the WTO or EU institutions within the context of the present analysis. Consistently with the findings developed in Chapter 1, the question of which international courts or tribunals might get to adjudicate a space mining dispute is currently answered through Article III OST.[7] In this regard, there are reasonable grounds to argue the involvement of the ICJ due to its status as the principal judicial organ of the United Nations and the PCA due to its reputation as a recognized international tribunal and its adoption of a dedicated set of rules for space disputes.[8] The question then becomes which mechanisms exist under international law for enforcing an ICJ judgment or a PCA award and how legitimate and effective they are.

At the national level, issues related to the interpretation, adjudication and enforcement of domestic legislation regulating space mining will be resolved in accordance with the procedures foreseen in the relevant jurisdiction. Since these processes primarily deal with questions of domestic law, they are not examined here. For the purposes of the present analysis, it is sufficient to state that in all four States that enacted domestic space mining laws—the U.S., Luxembourg, UAE and Japan—their enforcement would be triggered by the establishment of a normative violation by either the administrative regulator or domestic courts. The question then becomes to what extent the result of this adjudication can be legitimately and effectively enforced by competent national enforcers.

Based upon these considerations, sections 1.1 and 1.2 present the enforcement options available for enforcing international and national violations within the multilevel regulatory system of space mining.

5. Marrakesh Agreement Establishing the World Trade Organization, April 15, 1994, 1867 U.N.T.S. 154; General Agreement on Tariffs and Trade 1994, April 15, 1994, Marrakesh Agreement Establishing the World Trade Organization, Annex 1A, 1867 U.N.T.S. 187.
6. Consolidated versions of the Treaty on European Union (TEU) and the Treaty on the Functioning of the European Union (TFEU) [2016] Official Journal of the European Union C202/1.
7. Based on the legal and political links established by this article with general international law and the UN Charter. *See* section 2.2 in Chapter 1.
8. Fausto Pocar, *An Introduction to the PCA's Optional Rules for Arbitration of Disputes Relating to Outer Space Activities*, 38 Journal of Space Law 171 et seq. (2011).

1.1 International Enforcement Options

As mentioned, the ICJ and the PCA are two international bodies that might get to ascertain the violation of international space law within a hypothetical space mining dispute. Due to the fundamental institutional differences between these two institutions, choosing one over the other would consequently trigger the exercise of different enforcement powers. Thus, the following sections separately discuss the various options available for the enforcement of ICJ judgments and PCA arbitral awards.

1.1.1 Enforcing ICJ Judgments

Under Article 92 of the UN Charter, the ICJ is established as the principal judicial organ of the United Nations.[9] This, in turn, determines the primary competence of the ICJ to ascertain normative violations of the UN Charter, as well as its general competence to adjudicate legal disputes among States in all areas of international law.[10] This role of the ICJ is further amplified in the system of international space law, given the particular emphasis that Article III OST places on the respect of international law, "including the Charter of the United Nations."[11] Pursuant to Article 94 (1) UN Charter, the decisions of the ICJ are binding upon UN Member States for all cases to which they are Parties.[12] The question then becomes: who is entrusted with enforcing ICJ decisions?

i Enforcement under Article 94 (2) UN Charter

The first answer to this question is laid down in the subsequent paragraph of the very same article: "if any party to a case fails to perform the obligations incumbent upon it under a judgment rendered by the Court, the other party may have recourse to the Security Council, which may, if it deems necessary, make recommendations or decide upon measures to be taken to give effect to the judgment."[13] When compared to how domestic judgments are enforced within national jurisdictions, the mechanism foreseen in this provision looks quite atypical. This is because Article 94 (2) UN Charter subjects the enforcement of international law violations adjudicated by the ICJ to a double layer of discretion, first from the creditor State and then from the UNSC.

Under the mechanism foreseen in Article 94 (2) UN Charter, the UNSC cannot autonomously intervene to enforce an ICJ judgment unless requested by the relevant creditor State or otherwise justified on other legal grounds. In other words, the UNSC is prevented from intervening just for the sake of ensuring respect for international

---

9. Article 92 UN Charter, *supra* note 3.
10. Fragmentation Speech, *supra* note 4.
11. Treaty on Principles Governing the Activities of States in the Exploration and Use of Outer Space, Including the Moon and Other Celestial Bodies, *entered into force* October 10, 1967, 18 U.S.T. 2410, 610 U.N.T.S. 205 [hereinafter: "OST"].
12. Article 94 (1) UN Charter, *supra* note 3.
13. Article 94 (2) UN Charter, *supra* note 3.

law.[14] In principle, this limitation might significantly undermine the credibility of the enforcement system because the legitimate enforcer is not entitled to act ex officio. However, a systemic reading of the Charter shows that its practical impact is not that relevant in light of the other powers already attributed to the UNSC under Chapters VI and VII.[15] Should the open defiance of an ICJ judgment constitute a threat to international peace and security or even result in a dispute "whose continuance is likely to endanger the maintenance of international peace and security," the UNSC would be entitled to intervene respectively under Article 34 or Article 39 of the Charter.[16] Providing the UNSC with the power to sanction *any* situation of non-compliance with international law, regardless of its impact on international peace and security, would have expanded its competence way beyond its institutional mandate under the Charter.[17]

For similar reasons, if a creditor State seeks the intervention of the UNSC, the latter is not obliged to take any action. Whether or not to intervene, and eventually how, is a discretionary decision of the UNSC "which may, if it deems necessary, make recommendations or decide upon measures to be taken to give effect to the judgment."[18] This additional layer of discretion is meant to preserve the autonomy of the Council and avoid diminishing its role in the UN legal order from the guardian of international peace and security to *on-demand* police at the service of Member States. To be sure, this discretionality might undermine the theoretical credibility of the enforcement system laid down in Article 94 (2) UN Charter due to the inherent arbitrariness connected with the discretion granted to the UNSC.[19] Despite this valid criticism, a supportive role of the UNSC in enforcing ICJ judgments seems to be consistent with its "primary responsibility for the maintenance of international peace and security."[20]

It is interesting to note that Article 94 (2) UN Charter explicitly refers to "the obligations incumbent upon the Parties under a judgment rendered by the Court."[21] This raises the question of whether the mechanism foreseen in the article might be applied to enforce provisional measures decided by the Court in its orders.[22] In

14. Shabtai Rosenne & Yael Ronen, *The Law and Practice of the International Court*, 1920-2005 (4th ed., 2006).
15. Edgardo Sobenes Obregon, *Recourse to the Security Council under Article 94 (2) of the United Nations Charter*, in *Max Planck Encyclopedia of International Procedural Law* 14-16 (2017) [book hereinafter: "MPEiPro"].
16. Articles 34 and 39 UN Charter, *supra* note 3.
17. Rosenne & Ronen, *supra* note 14. Jean D'Aspremont, *The Collective Security System and the Enforcement of International Law*, in *The Oxford Handbook of the Use of Force in International Law* 129-156 (Marc Weller ed., 2015).
18. Article 94 (2) UN Charter, *supra* note 3.
19. Fajri Matahati Muhammadin, *Can International Law Be Enforced Towards Its Subjects Within the International Legal Order?*, 2 Ius Quia Iustum Law Journal of Islamic University of Indonesia 182 (2014).
20. Article 24 UN Charter, *supra* note 3.
21. Article 94 (2) UN Charter, *supra* note 3.
22. Under Articles 41 and 48 of the Statute of the International Court of Justice, *entered into force* August 31, 1965, 33 UNTS 993 [hereinafter: "ICJ Statute"], and in accordance with Articles 73, 74 and 75 of the Rules of the Court, *entered into force* July 1, 1978, available https://www.icj-cij.org/en/rules (last accessed October 2022).

principle, since *orders* are technically not *judgments,* the answer to this question should be negative. In practice, as discussed below, the UNSC has intervened to ensure respect of ICJ provisional measures, such as those ordered by the Court in the case of *Bosnia v. Yugoslavia,*[23] through its Resolution 819/1993.[24] However, it is not technically possible to consider such intervention as resolutive since UNSC Resolution 819/1993 was enacted under Chapter VII of the Charter and did not make any reference to Article 94 (2) UN Charter.[25]

Practice under Article 94 (2) UN Charter

The practice under Article 94 (2) UN Charter naturally depends on the rate of compliance enjoyed by ICJ Judgments. According to Schulte,[26] over almost sixty years of activity, the ICJ rendered twenty-seven judgments on the merits of a case, generally enjoying a "satisfactory record of compliance,"[27] especially after *Nicaragua.*[28] However, Paulson's study of the Court's cases between 1987 and 2003[29] found a decrease in the compliance rate enjoyed by ICJ judgments from 80% to 60%.[30] More recently, Obregon conducted a review of the only five cases in which Article 94 (2) UN Charter has been at least invoked to solve a situation of non-compliance.[31] Among those five cases, two arouse from judgments on the merits of a case, two from an order for provisional measures, and one from judgments of admissibility.

The two final judgments in which a creditor State requested the UNSC to enforce compliance with the obligations identified by the ICJ are *Nicaragua v. United States*[32] and *El Salvador/Honduras: Nicaragua intervening.*[33] In the first instance, the Permanent Representative of Nicaragua to the United Nations explicitly invoked Article 94 (2) UN Charter to request the UNSC to sanction the open defiance of the judgment by the U.S.[34] Even though eleven members of the Council voted in favor of a draft resolution condemning the behavior of the United States, the UNSC was unable to intervene due

23. Application of the Convention on the Prevention and Punishment of the Crime of Genocide, (*Order,* April 8, 1993), 1993 ICJ Reports 3; and Application of the Convention on the Prevention and Punishment of the Crime of Genocide, (*Order,* September 13, 1993) 1993 ICJ Reports 325 [hereinafter both referred to as "Bosnia cases"].
24. Resolution 819/1993 adopted by the Security Council at its 3199th meeting, UN Doc S/RES/819 (April 16, 1993).
25. Even though it took note of the ICJ order of April 8, 1993. *Id.*, at 1.
26. Constanze Schulte, *Compliance with Decisions of the International Court of Justice* (2004).
27. *Id.*, at 89.
28. *Id.*, at 91.
29. Colter Paulson, *Compliance with Final Judgments of the International Court of Justice Since 1987,* 98 American Journal of International Law 434-461 (2003).
30. *Id.*, at 460.
31. Obregon, *supra* note 15 at paras. 31-49.
32. Military and Paramilitary Activities in and Against Nicaragua (*Nicaragua v. United States of America*), (Judgment, June 27, 1986), 1986 ICJ Reports 14.
33. Application for Revision of the Judgment of September 11, 1992 in the case concerning the Land, Island and Maritime Frontier Dispute (El Salvador/Honduras: Nicaragua intervening), (Judgment, December 18, 2003) 2003 ICJ Rep 392.
34. Letter dated October 17, 1986 from the Permanent Representative of Nicaragua to the United Nations addressed to the President of the Security Council, UN Doc S/18415, available https://digitallibrary.un.org/record/122272#record-files-collapse-header (last accessed October 2022).

to the veto exercised by the U.S. itself as a permanent member.[35] In the second instance, the President of Honduras asked the UNSC to intervene under Article 94 (2) UN Charter to assist with the execution of the ICJ judgment.[36] This action alone was enough to convince the debtor State, El Salvador, to find an agreement with Honduras for the voluntary implementation of the judgment, so the UNSC did not need to intervene.[37] Each in its own way, these two cases confirm the more political rather than legal nature of the enforcement power attributed to the UNSC under Article 94 (2) UN Charter. In the case of Nicaragua, the U.S. has been able to escape its obligation to comply with ICJ decisions under Article 94 (1) UN Charter by manipulating the enforcement mechanism designed by the article.

As strongly criticized by Obregon, the U.S. bent the rules of procedure of the Council to consider an intervention of the Council under Article 94 (2) UN Charter a substantive rather than procedural matter and thus be able to exercise its veto power.[38] However, enforcement action should always be of procedural and not substantive nature because the final word on the substance of a violation has already been said in the judgment.[39] While theoretically correct, this is unfortunately not the case with the mechanism designed under Article 94 (2) UN Charter, which grants a significant margin of political discretion to the UNSC. The political rather than legal character of the enforcement powers attributed to the UNSC is further confirmed by the case of El Salvador/Honduras, whereby the potential implications linked with the UNSC intervention convinced the debtor State to cooperate for the execution of the judgment.

The other three cases evaluated by Obregon concern two ICJ orders for provisional measures and one judgment of admissibility.[40] As discussed above, it is unclear whether the UNSC would be justified to act under Article 94 (2) UN Charter to enforce these kinds of ICJ decisions. This very point was raised in the *Anglo-Iranian Oil Case*,[41] whereby the UK requested the Council to consider potential action for ensuring compliance with the provisional measures ordered by the ICJ against Iran.[42] Per its part, Iran contested the binding nature of the order under Article 94 (1) UN Charter, which should not be considered a *decision*, as well as the possibility of UNSC's action under the subsequent paragraph since an order was definitely not comparable to a

35. Repertoire of Practice of the Security Council (1985-1988), available https://www.un.org/securitycouncil/sites/www.un.org.securitycouncil/files/en/sc/repertoire/85-88/Chapter%208/85-88_08-30-Letter%20dated%2017%20October%201986%20from%20the%20Permanent%20Representative%20of%20Nicaragua.pdf (last accessed October 2022).
36. Letter dated January 22, 2002 from the Chargé d'affaires a.i. of the Permanent Mission of Honduras to the United Nations addressed to the President of the Security Council, UN Doc S/2002/108, available https://digitallibrary.un.org/record/457145?ln=en#record-files-collapse-header (last accessed October 2022).
37. Repertoire of Practice of the Security Council (2001-2002), available https://www.securitycouncilreport.org/atf/cf/%7B65BFCF9B-6D27-4E9C-8CD3-CF6E4FF96FF9%7D/a_57_2.pdf (last accessed October 2022).
38. Obregon, *supra* note 15 at para. 28.
39. *Id.*, at 26.
40. *Id.*, at paras. 41-49.
41. Anglo-Iranian Oil Company Case (*United Kingdom v. Iran*), Request for the indication of interim measures of protection, (Order, July 5, 1951) 1951 ICJ Rep 89.
42. Repertoire of Practice of the Security Council (1946-1951), available https://digitallibrary.un.org/record/240012/files/Repertoire_1946-1951.pdf (last accessed October 2022).

judgment.[43] Because the Court had not yet pronounced its own competence on the case, the Council decided to postpone a decision on its intervention only after the Court had confirmed its jurisdiction on the matter.[44] Ultimately, the ICJ found that it did not have the competence to adjudicate the case, and thus the UNSC did not resume consideration of the issue.[45] Forty-two years later, the UNSC had the opportunity to consider this question again when Bosnia and Herzegovina asked it to enforce the order for provisional measures[46] rendered by the ICJ in their case against Yugoslavia. In this instance, the UNSC first urged Yugoslavia to comply with the order through resolution nr. 819,[47] and then decided to sanction its prolonged non-compliance through resolution nr. 820.[48] Despite the enactment of two resolutions, also, in this case, the UNSC did not solve the question of applicability of Article 94 (2) UN Charter because its intervention was justified under Chapter VII of the Charter.[49] The matter was discussed again in 1998, when the Libyan Arab Jamahiriya asked the UNSC to take action[50] under Article 94 (2) UN Charter to ensure respect of two ICJ judgments on the admissibility of the cases concerning *Questions of Interpretation and Application of the 1971 Montreal Convention arising from the Aerial Incident at Lockerbie, 1998.*[51] The letter sent by the Libyan Arab Jamahiriya is particularly interesting for the purposes of the present analysis because of the considerations expressed on the political impact of UNSC intervention under Article 94 (2) UN Charter. According to the letter, a decision of the Council to intervene in support of the judgments "would reflect respect for the rule of law, an enhancement of the principles of the United Nations and a response to international public opinion expressed through the international organization."[52] Against these considerations of principle, the U.K. and the U.S. sent a joint letter contesting the applicability of Article 94 (2) UN Charter to judgments of admissibility, arguing that the two judgments rendered by the Court "did not constitute a final 'judgment' of the kind referred to in Article 94, paragraph 2, of the Charter of the United Nations."[53] On these grounds, the UNSC decided not to uphold Libya's request for intervention.[54] The three cases discussed above further confirm the uncertain nature of

43. *Ibid.*
44. *Ibid.*
45. Obregon, *supra* note 15 at para. 44.
46. ICJ Order of April 8, 1993, *supra* note 23.
47. UNSC Resolution 819/1993, *supra* note 24.
48. Resolution 820/1993 adopted by the Security Council at its 3200th meeting, UN Doc S/RES/820 (April 17, 1993), available https://digitallibrary.un.org/record/165323#record-files-collapse-header (last accessed October 2022).
49. *Ibid.*
50. Letter dated March 4, 1998 from the Permanent Representative of the Libyan Arab Jamahiriya to the United Nations addressed to the President of the Security Council, UN Doc S/1998/192, available https://digitallibrary.un.org/record/251057 (last accessed October 2022).
51. Questions of Interpretation and Application of the 1971 Montreal Convention arising from the Aerial Incident at Lockerbie, (*Libya v. United Kingdom*), Preliminary Objections, (Judgment, February 27, 1998) 1998 ICJ Rep 115.
52. Letter by Libyan Arab Jamahiriya, *supra* note 50.
53. Repertory of Practice of the United Nations Organs (1995-1999) Vol. VI, supplement 9, para. 4, available https://legal.un.org/repertory/art94/english/rep_supp9_vol6_art94.pdf (last accessed October 2022).
54. *Id.*, at para. 6.

the enforcement powers attributed to the UNSC under Article 94 (2) UN Charter.[55] In the one instance where non-compliance with an ICJ decision was endangering international peace and security, the Council took prompt action. In the other two cases, the Council tactically deferred its intervention on procedural grounds. In all cases, the UNSC always refrained from discussing its alleged role as an enforcer of international law as ascertained in relevant ICJ decisions.

Overall, an analysis of the practice under Article 94 (2) UN Charter reveals that this provision is *tamquam non esset*. Over the past seventy years, this article has been invoked only in five instances and has never been used to justify any concrete action. Accordingly, even though theoretically possible, it is highly unlikely that this provision will play any role in the future enforcement of potential space mining disputes adjudicated by the ICJ.

ii *Enforcement under the ARSIWA*

Institutional enforcement through the UNSC under Article 94 (2) UNSC is not the only available option for enforcing ICJ judgments.[56] Under Article VI OST, States are internationally responsible for ensuring compliance of their national space activities with the provisions of the Treaty.[57] Thus, an ICJ judgment ascertaining a violation of the OST would *ipso facto* trigger the international responsibility of the relevant State[58] under the ARSIWA,[59] which in turn would enable the legitimate exercise of the enforcement options provided thereby.

As discussed in Chapter 1,[60] the ARSIWA have been drafted by the ILC to codify the general rules of international law sanctioning the violation of an international obligation and are considered to be declaratory of customary international law.[61] Under Article 2 ARSIWA, an internationally wrongful act arises whenever an action or omission attributable to a State under international law constitutes a breach of an international obligation of that State.[62] According to Article 30 ARSIWA, the State responsible for such violation is under the obligation to cease its conduct and, if the

55. Schulte, *supra* note 26 at 33.
56. Due to the binding nature of ICJ judgments under Article 94 (1) UN Charter, States remain entitled to exercise certain types of *diffused* enforcement powers to ensure their compliance. Muhammadin, *supra* note 19 at 183, D'Aspremont, *supra* note 17.
57. Article VI OST, *supra* note 11.
58. Bin Cheng, *Studies in International Space Law* 632-633 (2004).
59. Responsibility of States for Internationally Wrongful Acts, [hereinafter: "ARSIWA"]. The consolidated text as adopted by UNGA Resolution 56/83 of December 12, 2001 and corrected by document A/56/49(Vol. I)/Corr.4. is available https://legal.un.org/ilc/texts/instruments/english/draft_articles/9_6_2001.pdf (last accessed October 2022).
60. And specifically in section 1.1.1 in Chapter 1.
61. Paola Gaeta, Jorge E. Vinuales & Salvatore Zappalà, *Cassese's International Law* 246 (3rd ed., 2020) [hereinafter: "Cassese's IL"]; James Crawford, *Articles on Responsibility of States for Internationally Wrongful Acts* 3 (2012), available https://legal.un.org/avl/pdf/ha/rsiwa/rsiwa_e.pdf (last accessed October 2022). Simon Olleson, *Internationally Wrongful Acts in the Domestic Courts: The Contribution of Domestic Courts to the Development of Customary International Law Relating to the Engagement of International Responsibility*, 26 (3) Leiden Journal of International Law 615-642 (2013).
62. Article 2 ARSIWA, *supra* note 59.

circumstances so require, even to offer appropriate assurances and guarantees of non-repetition.[63] Beyond the interests of States that might eventually be injured, Article 30 ARSIWA protects the fundamental interest of the international community as a whole in the preservation of, and reliance on, the rule of law.[64] This is confirmed by Article 48 ARSIWA, which allows for the invocation of responsibility by a State other than an injured one when the act violates collective obligations toward a group of States or obligations owed to the international community as a whole.[65] According to the ICJ, examples of such obligations are the prohibition of acts of aggression and of genocide, as well as basic human rights of the individual and the people's right to self-determination.[66]

Pursuant to Articles 49-51 ARSIWA, a State refusing to cease its internationally wrongful act is exposed to countermeasures.[67] Countermeasures are recognized both by governments and international tribunals as a tool of public international law by which injured States may seek to vindicate their rights and restore the international legality ruptured by an internationally wrongful act.[68] According to Article 49 ARSIWA, countermeasures can be taken by any injured State against a State responsible for an internationally wrongful act to induce its cessation and reparation.[69] It should be noted that countermeasures are not intended as a form of punishment but as an instrument for achieving compliance with international law.[70] Accordingly, Article 49 ARSIWA primarily limits countermeasures to the non-performance of international obligations of the State taking the measures toward the responsible one.[71] Articles 50 and 51 ARSIWA, respectively, provide that countermeasures (1) can never infringe on certain types of obligations and (2) that they must always be proportionate to the breach.[72] Even though under Article 48 ARSIWA, responsibility for an internationally wrongful act can be invoked by injured States and non-injured States alike, pursuant to Article 54 ARSIWA, the latter group can only take "lawful measures" to ensure "cessation" and "reparation."[73] While the wording of Article 54 ARSIWA seems to exclude the legality

63. Article 30 ARSIWA, *supra* note 59.
64. Commentary to Article 30 ARSIWA, *supra* note 59 at 89.
65. This "essential distinction" between obligations owed to specific States and those owed "towards the international community as a whole," was drawn by the ICJ in Barcelona Traction, Light and Power Company Limited (*Belgium v. Spain*), (Judgment, February 5, 1970) 1970 ICJ Rep. 32, at para. 33. *See also* Daniel Elias, *Erga Omnes and Countermeasures: Countermeasures by Non-injured States in Response to Mass Atrocities* (2014).
66. Barcelona Traction case, *supra* note 65, at para. 34; *see also* East Timor (*Portugal v. Australia*), (Judgment, June 30, 1995) 1995 ICJ Rep. 90 at para. 29.
67. Articles 49-51 ARSIWA, *supra* note 59.
68. Cassese's IL, *supra* note 61 at 299-303. For specialized literature on countermeasures, *see* Elizabeth Zoller, *Peacetime Unilateral Remedies: An Analysis of Countermeasures* 179-189 (1984); Omer Yousif Elagab, *The Legality of Non-forcible Counter-Measures in International Law* 227-241 (1988); Linos Alexandre Sicilianos, *Les Reactions Decentralises a L'illicte: Des Contre-Mesures a La Legitime Defense* 501-525 (1990). *See also* the considerations of the ICJ in the Nicaragua case, *supra* note 32 at paras. 201, 210.
69. Article 49 ARSIWA, *supra* note 59.
70. Commentary to Article 30 ARSIWA, *supra* note 59 at 130.
71. Article 49 ARSIWA, *supra* note 59.
72. Articles 50-51 ARSIWA, *supra* note 59.
73. Article 54 ARSIWA, *supra* note 59.

of countermeasures taken in the general or collective interest,[74] there have been instances in which non-injured States have enacted countermeasures in the form of economic sanctions[75] or to provide assistance and support to injured State(s).[76]

Countermeasures have been extensively discussed in international law,[77] and it would be beyond the scope of this section to account for such a complex debate. For the purposes of the present analysis, and in light of Article VI OST, Article 94 (1) UN Charter and Article 49 ARSIWA, it is sufficient to mention that they provide a potential option for the enforcement of ICJ judgments adjudicating a space mining dispute.

1.1.2 Enforcing PCA Arbitral Awards

An attractive alternative to judicial adjudication is offered by international arbitration before the PCA, a well-respected international arbitration body established by the 1899 Arbitration Convention.[78] At present, 122 States are Parties to this Convention,[79] including all major spacefaring nations. As discussed in Chapter 1, there are several reasons why a space mining dispute might be submitted for adjudication before the PCA.[80] First, the PCA is currently the only Court provided with both a set of dedicated rules for the arbitration of disputes relating to outer space activities[81] and a specialized panel of expert arbitrators.[82] Second, international arbitration before the PCA is considered by States signatories to the Arbitration Convention as the most effective

74. Commentary to Article 54 ARSIWA, *supra* note 59 at 139. *Contra* this restrictive interpretation of countermeasures, *see* Elias, *supra* note 65 at 37-46, and Muhammadin, *supra* note 19 at 187-189.
75. Such as in the case of *United States v. Uganda* (1978) and Collective measures against the Federal Republic of Yugoslavia (1998). For an overview of these examples, *see* Commentary to Article 54 ARSIWA, *supra* note 59 at 137-138. More recently, the enactment of economic sanctions against the Russian Federation pursuant to the illegitimate invasion of Ukraine can also be justified under a similar logic in connection with the order for provisional measures recently enacted by the ICJ in Allegations of Genocide under the Convention on the Prevention and Punishment of the Crime of Genocide (*Ukraine v. Russian Federation*), (Order, March 16, 2022), available https://www.icj-cij.org/public/files/case-related/182/182-20220316-ORD-01-00-EN.pdf (last accessed October 2022).
76. For some interesting examples of this kind, *see* Muhammadin, *supra* note 19 at 188. Needless to say, the assistance provided by several European States to Ukraine can again be considered as the most recent application of Article 54 ARSIWA.
77. For an overview of the most relevant sources, *see supra* note 68.
78. Convention for the Pacific Settlement of International Disputes *entered into force* September 4, 1900, 32 Stat. 1799 (1900).
79. As clarified on the website https://pca-cpa.org/en/about/introduction/contracting-parties/ of the PCA (last accessed October 2022).
80. Maureen Williams, *Dispute Resolution Regarding Space Activities*, in *Handbook of Space Law* 1031 (Frans Von Der Dunk & Fabio Tronchetti eds., 2015); Pocar, *supra* note 8. *See also* section 2.2.2 (iv) in Chapter 1.
81. Optional Rules for Arbitration of Disputes Relating to Outer Space Activities, Permanent Court of Arbitration, Effective December 6, 2011, available https://docs.pca-cpa.org/2016/01/Permanent-Court-of-Arbitration-Optional-Rules-for-Arbitration-of-Disputes-Relating-to-Outer-Space-Activities.pdf (last accessed October 2022).
82. Specialized Panel of Arbitrators Established Pursuant to the Optional Rules for Arbitration of Disputes Relating to Outer Space Activities, available https://docs.pca-cpa.org/2022/01/2022/01/a42fa03c-pca-184031-v15-current_list_annex_4_sp_outer_space_arb.pdf (last accessed October 2022).

means to resolve those legal disputes which diplomacy has failed to settle.[83] Third, the PCA can adjudicate disputes between States and private companies, as will likely be the case in the area of space mining.[84] This combination of expertise, recognition and flexibility makes the PCA particularly suited to adjudicate space law disputes, especially in the field of space resource activities.

In terms of enforcement, under Article 18 of the Arbitration Convention, States Parties to the PCA agree "to submit loyally" to its awards.[85] Pursuant to this provision, any unjustified resistance to the execution of PCA awards would be in clear breach of the Convention.[86] Further, a PCA award determining a violation of international space law would also trigger the international responsibility of the relevant State under Article VI OST. *Mutatis mutandis,* the same considerations on the enactment of countermeasures under the ARSIWA are also applicable to the enforcement of PCA arbitral awards.

i *Enforcement under the NYC on the Recognition and Enforcement of Foreign Arbitral Awards*

Arbitral awards of the PCA may also be enforced under the NYC.[87] The NYC was concluded in 1958 to replace the previous Geneva Convention[88] to maximize the circulation of foreign arbitral awards by removing unnecessary obstacles to their recognition and enforcement.[89] The NYC has been ratified by 157 States and is universally considered the cornerstone of the international arbitration system.[90] In view of its great success, it is worth analyzing the scope, conditions and limits of application of the NYC[91] in order to better evaluate its suitability as enforcement option for the multi-level system of space mining.

---

83. Williams, *supra* note 80.
84. As to which, *see* section 1.1.4 in Chapter 2.
85. Article 18 Arbitration Convention, *supra* note 78.
86. For instance, States might wish to invoke sovereign immunity to escape the consequences of an arbitral award ruling against their interest. There are examples of domestic legislations preventing these kinds of behaviors by limiting the exercise of sovereign immunity. For instance, section 9 of the 1978 State Immunity Act of the United Kingdom provides that a State agreeing in writing to submit a given dispute to arbitration is considered to have waived its immunity from related proceedings.
87. Convention on the Recognition and Enforcement of Foreign Arbitral Awards, *entered into force* June 7, 1959, 330 UNTS 3 [hereinafter: "NYC"].
88. Convention on the Execution of Foreign Arbitral Awards *entered into force* September 26, 1927, 92 LNTS 301 [hereinafter: "Geneva Convention"].
89. Philippe Fouchard, *Suggestions to Improve the International Efficacy of Arbitral Awards,* in *Improving the Efficiency of Arbitration Agreements and Awards: 40 Years of Application of the New York Convention* 602 (Albert Jan Van den Berg ed., 2009).
90. Message from the Secretary of United Nations Commission on International Trade Law (UNCITRAL), available https://newyorkconvention1958.org/index.php?lvl = cmspage&pageid = 7&id_news = 959&opac_view = -1 (last accessed October 2022).
91. A guiding source in this process has been the Guide on the Convention on the Recognition and Enforcement of Foreign Arbitral Awards of 1958 developed by the UNCITRAL with the assistance of Professor Emmanuel Gaillard and Professor George Bermann. The Guide aims to promote the uniform and effective interpretation and application of the New York Convention

Pursuant to Article I (1) NYC, the Convention applies to "the recognition and enforcement of arbitral awards made in the territory of a State other than the State where the recognition and enforcement of such awards are sought, and arising out of differences between persons, whether physical or legal."[92] In comparison with the 1927 Geneva Convention, the NYC has been provided with a broader scope of application by removing the mandatory reciprocity requirement as well as any reference to the residence or nationalities of the involved parties.[93] However, under paragraph 3 of the same article, States ratifying the NYC might limit its scope of application to "awards made *only in the territory of another Contracting State*" as well as to "differences arising out of *legal* relationships, whether contractual or not, which are considered as *commercial* under the national law of the State making such declaration" (emphasis added).[94] Even though several States Parties to the Convention have made use of the option provided in Article I (3) NYC,[95] the broad ratification status of the Convention, as well as its primary use for commercial disputes, have not negatively impacted its application status.[96] Further to that, the final sentence of Article I (1) NYC ensures the applicability of the Convention also to all arbitral awards which are "not considered as domestic awards in the State where their recognition and enforcement are sought,"[97] thus further expanding the potential applicability of the Convention. Under Article I (2) NYC, "the term 'arbitral awards' shall include not only awards made by arbitrators appointed for each case but also those made by permanent arbitral bodies to which the parties have submitted."[98] This clause is particularly relevant for the purposes of the present analysis as it brings awards rendered by permanent international institutions like the PCA under the scope of the Convention.[99] Moving from this institutional requirement, national courts are free to determine whether a certain decision constitutes an arbitral award by looking at its nature and content.[100]

In general, courts tend to apply the recognition and enforcement mechanisms foreseen under the NYC only to decisions made by arbitrators, which are both binding and final,[101] meaning that awards currently undergoing further review mechanisms of any kind cannot be enforced under the Convention. In this respect, it is important to

---

and is available https://newyorkconvention1958.org/index.php?lvl=cmspage&pageid=10&menu=729&opac_view=-1 (last accessed October 2022) [hereinafter: "NYC Guide"].

92. Article I NYC, *supra* note 87.
93. NYC Guide, *supra* note 91 at Article I, para. 3.
94. Article I NYC, *supra* note 87.
95. Declarations and Reservations to the NYC, available https://www.newyorkconvention.org/list+of+contracting+states (last accessed October 2022).
96. NYC Guide, *supra* note 91 at Article I, para. 75.
97. Article I NYC, *supra* note 87.
98. *Ibid.*
99. From the moment they have appointed arbitrators to adjudicate the dispute. NYC Guide, *supra* note 91 at Article 1, para. 22.
100. Emmanuel Gaillard & Benjamin Siino, *Enforcement under the New York Convention*, in *The Guide to Challenging and Enforcing Arbitration Awards* 88 (J William Rowley, Emmanuel Gaillard & Gordon E. Kaiser eds., 2019).
101. NYC Guide, *supra* note 91 at Article I, paras. 23-25.

state that pursuant to Article IV NYC, the party seeking recognition and enforcement of an arbitral award does not have to prove either of these requirements.[102]

According to Article II (3) NYC, a national court invested in a dispute for which the parties had concluded an arbitration agreement under the meaning of the Convention "shall, at the request of one of the parties, refer the parties to arbitration, unless it finds that the arbitration agreement is null and void, inoperative or incapable of being performed."[103] Pursuant to this provision, States Parties to the Convention are obliged to recognize and give effect also to arbitration clauses and agreements. This extension is important because it prevents abusive behaviors from one of the parties aimed at escaping the application of an arbitral agreement through unilateral recourse to the court.[104] Under Article II (1) and (2) NYC, in order to be recognized and enforced under the Convention, arbitral agreements or clauses must have been concluded in writing, duly signed by the relevant parties and deal with "a subject matter capable of settlement by arbitration."[105] Notably, this latter requirement will appear again under Article V (II) (a) NYC, according to which a court may refuse to recognize and enforce an award which has been given on a subject matter not capable of settlement by arbitration.[106]

The core provision of the Convention is its Article III, which deals with the recognition and enforcement of arbitral awards. According to this article, "each Contracting State shall recognize arbitral awards as binding and enforce them in accordance with the rules of procedure of the territory where the award is relied upon, under the conditions laid down in the following articles."[107] Pursuant to this provision, absent a valid impediment under the other provisions of the Convention—and in particular Articles IV, V, VI and VII—international and foreign arbitral awards must always be recognized and enforced in accordance with relevant domestic rules of procedure. Several national courts consider that Article III NYC expresses a "pro-enforcement bias" that constitutes the object and purpose of the Convention[108] and have been consistently interpreting it as such.[109]

This broad interpretation by national courts has played a critical role in ensuring the effective recognition and enforcement of foreign and international arbitral awards under the Convention. As mentioned, pursuant to Article III NYC, this recognition and enforcement shall be in accordance with the "rules of procedure of the territory where the award is relied upon."[110] This connection with relevant domestic rules of procedure provides Article III NYC with a high degree of flexibility, facilitating its smooth

102. Article IV NYC, *supra* note 87. As we will see when discussing Article IV NYC, national courts limit the verification of these conditions only to a prima facie assessment, and it will be the responsibility of the resisting party to prove that the award cannot be enforced because it has not yet become final.
103. Article II NYC, *supra* note 87.
104. NYC Guide, *supra* note 91 at Article II, para. 59.
105. Article II NYC, *supra* note 87.
106. Article V NYC, *supra* note 87.
107. Article III NYC, *supra* note 87.
108. Gaillard & Siino, *supra* note 100 at 89-90.
109. NYC Guide, *supra* note 91 at Article III, paras. 8-10.
110. Article III NYC, *supra* note 87.

application within the different jurisdictions of the various States Parties to the Convention. In this regard, Article III NYC further specifies that these rules shall not impose "substantially more onerous conditions or higher fees or charges on the recognition or enforcement of arbitral awards to which this Convention applies"[111] compared to those foreseen for the recognition or enforcement of domestic arbitral awards. As a result, even though States Parties to the NYC are entitled to apply their own rules of procedure for the recognition and enforcement of arbitral awards, they cannot discriminate between domestic and foreign awards.[112] In this way, Article III NYC manages to respect the various domestic approaches to the recognition and enforcement of arbitral awards while also ensuring their equal treatment.

Under Article IV NYC, the party seeking recognition and enforcement of an arbitral award shall supply, at the time of the application, (a) "the duly authenticated original award" and (b) "the original agreement referred to in article II," with the possibility of alternatively providing duly certified copies thereof.[113] Additionally, if these documents are made in a language other than the official one of the country in which the award is relied upon, the party shall also have them translated by either an official or sworn translator or by a diplomatic or consular agent.[114] Article IV NYC provides the fundamental requirements for seeking recognition and enforcement of an arbitral award and should, as such, be read in conjunction with Articles III and V of the Convention. If compared to the analog provision under the Geneva Convention, Article IV NYC is much more favorable to the party seeking recognition and enforcement of arbitral awards.[115] Under the previous regime, such party had to provide evidence that the award was binding and had become final under the jurisdiction that produced it.[116] In practice, this placed a significant burden on the part of the applicant and constituted an important obstacle for the applicability of the Geneva Convention. In recognition of these issues, the Dutch delegation to the NYC proposed to remove these conditions from the text of Article IV NYC and place the burden to prove their eventual absence on the resisting party.[117] As a consequence, the current version of Article IV NYC requires the applicant to simply provide the original versions, or official copies thereof, of the documents for which it seeks recognition and enforcement. In connection with the general rule provided under Article III NYC, several national courts have held that the production of such documents triggers a presumption of enforceability of the award.[118] Accordingly, if the resisting party does not prove the existence of a condition justifying refusal of recognition and enforcement under the subsequent Article V NYC, then the court shall grant it.

Pursuant to Article V NYC, there are seven conditions justifying refusal of recognition and enforcement of a foreign or international arbitral award under the

111. Article III NYC, *supra* note 87.
112. NYC Guide, *supra* note 91 at Article III, para. 33.
113. Article IV NYC, *supra* note 87.
114. *Ibid.*
115. NYC Guide, *supra* note 91 at Article IV, paras. 3-6.
116. Article 4 (3) Geneva Convention, *supra* note 88.
117. NYC Guide, *supra* note 91 at Article IV, para. 4.
118. *Id.*, at paras. 7-8.

Convention.[119] Similarly to what we have already observed for Article IV NYC, also this provision determines a much more favorable set of conditions on the part of the applicant.[120] Under the corresponding provisions of the 1927 Geneva Convention, the burden to prove the absence of obstacles for the recognition and enforcement of an arbitral award was placed on the party seeking relief to the Court.[121] Additionally, the resisting party was entitled to raise any additional grounds for refusal available under the law governing the arbitration.[122] Under Article V (1) NYC, the burden of proof has been reversed, and now awards have to be recognized and enforced unless the respondent proves the existence of one of the five conditions laid down in the Article.[123] What is more, in order to further increase the enforceability of the award, the respondent's right to raise additional grounds has been removed. To compensate for that, Article V (2) NYC provides the national court with the power to refuse recognition and enforcement of the award on two grounds of public order.[124] Accordingly, the seven conditions laid down in Article V NYC can be divided into two groups: obstacles that have to be invoked and proven by the resisting party and barriers that can be identified at the discretion of the national courts.

The first group of conditions justifying refusal of recognition and enforcement of a foreign or international arbitral award is laid down in Article V (1) NYC and includes the five hypotheses listed in letters from (a) to (d).[125] Before briefly discussing them, it is worth noticing that even if the resisting party would prove the existence of one of these conditions, national courts are not per se obliged to refuse recognition and enforcement. This is clear from the language used in the article, which states that recognition and enforcement of the award "may" be refused if one of the conditions listed in the article is proven.[126] This is another confirmation of the "pro-enforcement" bias expressed in Article III NYC and influencing the structure and application of the entire Convention.[127]

Under Article V (1) (a) NYC, the resisting party may oppose recognition and enforcement of the award by proving either that the parties to the arbitral agreement were under some incapacity under the law applicable to them at the time or alternatively that the agreement is not valid under either the law to which the parties have subjected or the law of the country where the award was made.[128] The practical relevance of Article V (1) (a) NYC is rather low. On the one hand, the incapacity defense has been rarely invoked by resisting parties,[129] whereas, in the majority of

119. Article V NYC, *supra* note 87.
120. NYC Guide, *supra* note 91 at Article V, paras. 2-4.
121. Articles 1-2 Geneva Convention, *supra* note 88.
122. Article 3 Geneva Convention, *supra* note 88.
123. Article V NYC, *supra* note 87.
124. Article V (2) NYC, *supra* note 87.
125. Article V (1) NYC, *supra* note 87.
126. *Ibid.*
127. NYC Guide, *supra* note 91 at Article V, paras. 5-7.
128. Article V (1) (a) NYC, *supra* note 87.
129. Stefan Kröll, *Recognition and Enforcement of Awards*, in *Arbitration in Germany: The Model Law in Practice* 506, 530 (Karl-Heinz Böckstiegel, Stefan Kröll & Patricia Nacimiento eds., 2007).

reported cases, courts have rejected challenges to recognition and enforcement of an arbitral award based on its alleged invalidity.[130]

Article V (1) (b) NYC allows the resisting party to object recognition and enforcement of the award on grounds related to due process in arbitration, and in particular, either the lack of proper notice of the appointment of the arbitrator or of the arbitration proceedings or to the inability to present their case.[131] In accordance with the logic behind due process, courts tend to examine claims under Article 5 (1) (b) based on the actual facts and conduct of the parties and not the formal respect of the notice times.[132] Interestingly, this has led to a restrictive application of the provision, with the result that the vast majority of respondents are unsuccessful in proving a breach of this provision.[133]

Under Article V (1) (c), a resisting party may object to recognition and enforcement of arbitral awards exceeding the scope of the arbitration agreement,[134] which may be the case for those "dealing with a difference not contemplated by or not falling within the terms of the submission to arbitration"[135] or those "containing decisions on matters beyond the scope of the submission to arbitration."[136] The purpose of this provision is to preserve the free determination of the parties to submit their differences for arbitration as made in the relevant agreement among them. Therefore, courts have excluded the applicability of this provision to awards exceeding the pleas of the parties but still remaining within the scope of the arbitration agreement.[137] In accordance with the pro-enforcement bias of the Convention, the final part of Article V (1) (c) foresees the possibility of partial recognition and enforcement "provided that the decisions on matters submitted to arbitration can be separated from those not so submitted."[138] Notably, this power has been extensively used by national courts way beyond the original intention of the NYC drafters.[139] Based on the limited discussions held during the drafting of this clause, the possibility of partial enforcement was included to prevent potential secondary decisions on matters beyond the scope of arbitration would compromise those taken within the scope of the arbitration agreement.[140] In practice, courts have used this power to split awards into as many parts as possible for the purpose of ensuring their broadest possible recognition and enforcement[141] in accordance with the pro-enforcement bias of the Convention. Further to that, it is worth noting that courts have relied on the possibility of partial recognition and

130. NYC Guide, *supra* note 91 at Article V (1) (a), para. 6.
131. Article V (1) (b) NYC, *supra* note 87.
132. NYC Guide, *supra* note 91 at Article V (1) (b) para. 9.
133. *Id.*, at paras. 5-6.
134. NYC Guide, *supra* note 91 at Article V (1) (c) para. 1.
135. Article V (1) (c) NYC, *supra* note 87.
136. *Ibid.*
137. NYC Guide, *supra* note 91 at Article V (1) (c) para. 8.
138. Article V (1) (c) NYC, *supra* note 87.
139. NYC Guide, *supra* note 91 at Article V (1) (c) para. 30.
140. *Ibid.*
141. Mercédeh Azeredo da Silveira & Laurent Levy, *Transgression of the Arbitrators' Authority: Article V (1)(c) of the New York Convention*, in *Enforcement of Arbitration Agreements and International Arbitral Awards: The New York Convention in Practice* 639, 676 (Emmanuel Gaillard & Domenico di Pietro eds., 2008).

enforcement also in connection with challenges brought under other provisions of the Convention,[142] even though this power is explicitly granted only with respect to those brought under Article V (1) (c) NYC.[143]

Pursuant to Article V (1) (d) NYC, a party may demand refusal of the recognition or enforcement of an award if either "the composition of the arbitral authority" or "the arbitral procedure" were not in accordance with the arbitration agreement or, absent any choice from the parties on these matters, with the law of the country where the arbitration took place.[144] It is important to note that under this provision, the primary reference term for evaluating potential irregularities is constituted by the agreement of the parties. Only if the parties did not express any preference, then it becomes possible to apply, on a residual basis, the relevant provision of the national law governing the arbitration procedure. As we have seen already with potential violations related to due process, courts look at these clauses from a substantive viewpoint and tend to apply them in a restrictive manner, with the result that respondents are usually unsuccessful in proving the grounds for non-enforcement under Article V (1) (d).[145] Truth be told, it rarely occurs that the composition of a tribunal deviates from the parties' agreement or the applicable rules, so the practical relevance of this defense is rather low.[146]

Finally, Article V (1) (e) NYC allows respondent parties to ask refusal of recognition and enforcement of an award that "has not yet become binding on the parties" or that it "has been set aside or suspended by a competent authority" from either the country where the award was made or the country of its applicable law.[147] As discussed above, the situation was reversed under the 1927 Geneva Convention, which required the applicant to prove the existence of both these requirements in order to obtain recognition and enforcement in the first place.[148] In accordance with the pro-enforcement bias of the NYC, Article V (1) (e) turned these elements into potential obstacles and placed the burden to prove their existence on the resisting party. Interestingly, Article V (1) (e) does not define when an award has become "binding," thus leaving it to national courts to decide the conditions under which it should be considered as such. In this regard, courts have generally followed three approaches. A first group determines the binding character of the award based on the law of the country where it has been made.[149] A second group of courts prefers to rely on their own assessment, under the general understanding that an award has become binding where it is no longer subject to *ordinary* means of recourse.[150] Finally, a third group combines these two approaches and evaluates the binding character of an award by looking at the availability of ordinary means of recourse under the law of the country

142. NYC Guide, *supra* note 91 at Article V (1) (c) para. 37.
143. Article V (1) (c) NYC, *supra* note 87.
144. Article V (1) (d) NYC, *supra* note 87.
145. NYC Guide, *supra* note 91 at Article V (1) (d) paras. 6-7.
146. Albert Jan Van Den Berg, *The New York Arbitration Convention of 1958: Towards a Uniform Judicial Interpretation* 323 (1994).
147. Article V (1) (d) NYC, *supra* note 87.
148. Article 1 Geneva Convention, *supra* note 88.
149. NYC Guide, *supra* note 91 at Article V (1) (e) para. 6.
150. *Id.*, at 7.

where the award was made.[151] Related to the hypothesis of an award being set aside or suspended by a competent authority, it should be noted that Article VI NYC allows an enforcing court "if it considers it proper, to adjourn the decision on the enforcement of the award" whenever "an application for the setting aside or suspension of the award has been made to a competent authority referred to in article V (1) (e)."[152] In such case, Article VI NYC also allows the applicant to request the enforcing court to order the other party to give "suitable security" for protecting its legitimate rights under the award during the application time.[153]

The second group of conditions justifying refusal of recognition and enforcement of a foreign or international arbitral award is laid down in Article V (2) NYC and includes two hypotheses based on the grounds of public policy. Also, in this case, national courts *may* refuse recognition and enforcement of the award based upon a discretionary decision as to the application of the two clauses laid down in letters (a) and (b).[154] Under the first of these clauses, recognition and enforcement of an award may be refused "if the subject matter of the dispute is not capable of settlement by arbitration" under the law of the country where they are sought.[155] Notably, Article II (1) NYC uses the same expression when providing the conditions for the recognition and execution of an arbitration agreement.[156] In both cases, the Convention does not identify the types of subject matters that are capable or incapable of settlement by arbitration. However, while Article V (2) (a) NYC provides that this assessment should be done under the law of the country where recognition is sought, Article II NYC leaves it to the discretion of national courts.[157] Accordingly, commentators have pointed out the need to interpret the term in the same manner throughout the Convention.[158] In practice, respondent parties rarely raise the question of whether the subject matter of their dispute is capable of settlement by arbitration.[159] Besides, national courts have exercised their discretion to refuse recognition and enforcement pursuant to Article V (2) (a) in only a handful of instances,[160] almost all of which dealt with non-commercial disputes such as succession.[161]

Finally, under Article V (2) (b), an enforcing court may refuse to recognize or enforce a given award if that would be contrary to the public policy of their country.[162] Exceptions of public policy are very common in private international law and constitute a fundamental defense of the core values of the domestic legal order. Even though the NYC is no exception to this tendency, Article V (2) (b) of the Convention constructs

151. *Id.*, at 8.
152. Article VI NYC, *supra* note 87.
153. *Ibid.*
154. Article V (2) NYC, *supra* note 87.
155. Article V (2) (a) NYC, *supra* note 87.
156. Article II NYC, *supra* note 87.
157. For a summary of the main approaches followed by national courts under Article II NYC, *see* NYC Guide, *supra* note 91 at Article II, paras. 30-35.
158. NYC Guide, *supra* note 91 at Article V (2) (a) para. 3.
159. *Id.*, at 5.
160. *Id.*, at 18.
161. *Id.*, at 29.
162. Article V (2) (b) NYC, *supra* note 87.

this defense in much softer terms than the 1927 Geneva Convention.[163] As with many other instances, the NYC turned what used to be a requirement that the applicant had to prove for recognition into a potential justification for its refusal at the discretion of the court.[164] Further to that, the NYC removed the reference to "principles of law" that was present in the corresponding provision under the 1927 Geneva Convention,[165] again confirming the pro-enforcement bias that constitutes its *raison d'etre*. Even though Article V (2) (b) does not provide any concrete parameter for the application of the public policy exception, courts have been rather consistent in limiting it to rather exceptional cases.[166] This is consistent both with the intent of the drafters of the Convention and the general tendency of private international law to consider the public policy exception as a measure of *extrema ratio*. As held in the *Parsons* case, enforcement of foreign arbitral awards may be refused under the public policy exception only where it would "violate the forum state's most basic notions of morality and justice."[167] Overall, the majority of national courts follow a narrow interpretation of public policy and applications to refuse recognition and enforcement of a foreign arbitral award under Article V (2) (b) NYC have rarely been successful.[168] In over fifty years of practice under the Convention, courts have invoked the public policy exception to refuse recognition and enforcement of awards if that would go against the interests of the State,[169] threaten national security,[170] undermine the sovereignty of the country,[171] violate fundamental constitutional values,[172] conflict with a previous res judicata from the enforcing forum,[173] or finally contravene mandatory rules of the forum in key areas such as competition law, consumer protection, foreign exchange regulation or bans on exports.[174]

Before concluding, it is worth underlining that the conditions laid down in Article V NYC for refusing recognition and enforcement of arbitral awards are regarded as exhaustive.[175] In comparison with the Geneva Convention, this is a significant pro-enforcement twist. In this respect, some might be struck by the fact that the grounds listed under Article V NYC do not include an erroneous decision in law or, in fact, by

163. Article 1 (e) Geneva Convention, *supra* note 88.
164. NYC Guide, *supra* note 91 at Article V (2) (b) para. 3.
165. Article 1 (e) Geneva Convention, *supra* note 88.
166. NYC Guide, *supra* note 91 at Article V (2) (b) para. 4.
167. *Parsons & Whittemore Overseas v. Société Générale de L'Industrie du Papier (RAKTA)*, Court of Appeals, Second Circuit, United States of America, 508 F.2d 969, 974 (1974).
168. NYC Guide, *supra* note 91 at Article V (2) (b) para. 21.
169. *Renusagar Power Co. Ltd. v. General Electric Company & anor.*, Supreme Court, India, October 7, 1993, 1994 AIR 860 (1994).
170. *Ansell S.A. v. OOO MedBusinessService-2000*, Highest Arbitrazh Court, Russian Federation, Ruling No. VAS-8786/10, August 3, 2010 (2010).
171. *Grain Partners S.p.A. v. Cooperativa dos Produtores Trabalhadores Rurais de Sorriso Ltda.*, Superior Court of Justice, Brazil, October 18, 2006 (2006).
172. *CB Holdings Limited and The Belize Bank Limited v. The Attorney General of Belize*, Caribbean Court of Justice, Appellate Jurisdiction, July 26, 2013, (2013).
173. *Hemofarm DD, MAG International Trade Holding DD, Suram Media Ltd. v. Jinan Yongning Pharmaceutical Co. Ltd.*, Supreme People's Court, China, June 2, 2008 (2008).
174. *Eco Swiss China Time Ltd. v. Benetton International NV*, Court of Justice of the European Union, June 1, 1999, Case C-126/97, ECR I-3055, paras. 37-39 (1999).
175. NYC Guide, *supra* note 91 at Article V paras. 8-12.

the arbitral tribunal. However, this is perfectly in line with the nature of enforcement processes, which should never be abused as additional means of recourse on the merits of a case, and yet another important confirmation of the pro-enforcement bias of the Convention.[176]

The last provision examined in this section is Article VII NYC. The first part of Article VII (1) NYC regulates the relationship of the NYC with other bilateral or multilateral instruments in the area of international arbitration: "the provisions of the present Convention shall not affect the validity of multilateral or bilateral agreements concerning the recognition and enforcement of arbitral awards entered into by the Contracting States."[177] The second part of Article VII (1) NYC specifically safeguards the rights of "any interested party" to avail themselves of an arbitral award "in the manner and to the extent allowed by the law or the treaties of the country where such award is sought to be relied upon."[178] Finally, Article VII (2) NYC determines the superseding effect of the Convention between its State Parties with respect to both the Geneva Protocol on Arbitration Clauses of 1923 and the Geneva Convention on the Execution of Foreign Arbitral Awards of 1927.[179] Article VII NYC is considered to be one of the cornerstones of the Convention, and it certainly embodies one of its most forward-thinking provisions.[180] The main merit of this Article is to allow for the application of the norm which is most favorable to enforcement, regardless of whether that might be provided under the NYC, another treaty or domestic law.[181] Through the mechanism laid down in Article VII (1) NYC, the Convention sets out a "ceiling" for the maximum level of control that can be legitimately exerted by courts for the recognition and enforcement of foreign and international arbitral awards.[182] While States Parties to the NYC can never go beyond the level set forth in the Convention, they are free to apply more recent provisions, which would lead to a better result in terms of recognition and enforcement. Thanks to this clause, the NYC has managed to pass the testing of time and maintain its relevance despite the profound transformations that have affected the field of international arbitration over the past sixty-five years.[183]

1.2 Enforcing National Violations

Due to the role attributed to national space legislation under Article VI OST,[184] within the multi-level regulatory system of space mining, national provisions are entrusted

176. *Id.*, at 9.
177. Article VII (1) NYC, *supra* note 87.
178. *Ibid.*
179. Article VII (2) NYC, *supra* note 87.
180. NYC Guide, *supra* note 91 at Article VII para. 1.
181. As seen in section 1.3.3 in Chapter 1, Article VII (1) NYC paved the way as one of the first kinds of non-binary mechanism for the solution of normative conflicts among overlapping sources of international law.
182. NYC Guide, *supra* note 91 at Article VII para. 2.
183. Emmanuel Gaillard, *The Urgency of Not Revising the New York Convention*, in *50 Years of the New York Convention: ICCA International Arbitration Conference* 689 (Albert Jan Van Den Berg ed., 2009).
184. Article VI OST, *supra* note 11.

with the regulation of space resource activities conducted by domestic actors. As discussed in Chapter 2,[185] at present, only four States have enacted national legislation regulating the domestic conduct of space mining: the U.S., Luxembourg, the UAE and Japan. In all these States, space mining disputes might be adjudicated either through domestic administrative decisions, courts' judgments or arbitral awards as rendered by the competent authorities, courts and arbitrators operating thereby.[186]

1.2.1 National or Transnational Disputes?

In terms of enforcement processes, it is important to distinguish between domestic disputes involving only domestic actors as opposed to cross-border disputes involving international entities. Depending on the national or transnational character of the dispute, adjudicating and subsequently enforcing the violation of domestic norms might be relatively easy or extremely problematic. For the purposes of the present analysis, a dispute is considered to be national when it involves domestic actors, and its results can be fully enforced with the use of domestic powers. By exclusion, all disputes involving international actors or requiring the cross-border exercise of enforcement powers are considered to be transnational.

Purely domestic disputes do not raise any particular concern in terms of both adjudication and enforcement. These disputes will be adjudicated by national courts or arbitrators and will be enforced by the domestic authorities of the relevant jurisdiction in accordance with applicable rules and requirements of domestic law.

Cross-border disputes are another story. First, it is important to draw a distinction between those adjudicated by means of arbitration and those resolved through administrative/judicial decisions. This is because domestic arbitral awards falling under the scope of the NYC would be easily enforceable in all its States Parties.[187] For what concerns administrative or judicial decisions, enforcing the results of these domestic adjudicatory processes against international actors operating across several jurisdictions will likely face several issues of extraterritoriality.[188] The general understanding is that the extraterritorial application and enforcement of domestic rules and

185. *See* section 2 in Chapter 2.
186. Recently, the UAE has launched an initiative called "courts of space" aimed at evaluating the benefits of establishing a dedicated court for national and international space disputes. Information on this initiative can be found https://www.thenationalnews.com/uae/courts/dubai-launches-space-court-to-support-thriving-global-sector-1.1157474 (last accessed October 2022).
187. Provided that they respect the conditions of the NYC.
188. For a traditional analysis on extraterritoriality, *see* Malcolm N. Shaw, *International Law* 168 (8th ed., 2017); Cassese's IL, *supra* note 61 at 52-53; Ingrid Detter, *The International Legal Order* 44 (1944). Contemporary issues of extraterritoriality have been extensively discussed in specialized international law such as human rights and economic sanctions. Some interesting readings include Lea Raible, *Extraterritoriality Between a Rock and a Hard Place,* 82 Questions of International Law 7-29 (2021) and Troy Layers, *Law as a Smart Bomb or Just a Limited Tool of Coercion: Considering Extra-Territorial Economic Sanctions,* 146 (5) Royal United Services Institute 17-23 (2001).

acts is in violation of a pivotal norm of international law, the principle of State sovereignty.[189] Traditionally, sovereignty is intended to have both internal and external aspects.[190] As Jean Bodin wrote as early as 1577 in his *Six Livres de la République*, the principle of State sovereignty implies the right of absolute power above national territory but also the obligation of not interfering with those of other States.[191] Nowadays, these principles have been codified in Article 2 of the UN Charter, which lays down the principle of sovereign equality as the very basis of the current system of public international law.[192] Precisely because States are equally sovereign, the extent of their sovereign powers is limited by the sovereignty of other States.[193] In accordance with this principle, a State cannot, on its own, oblige another one to recognize its domestic norms or give effect to its national decisions.[194] However, in some cases, States recognize the value of setting aside this principle in the name of other interests. The powers attributed to the UNSC under Chapter VII of the UN Charter are perhaps the most evident application of this reasoning.[195] The 1958 NYC examined in the previous section is a less visible but arguably much more effective example. Further examples include specialized regimes of international law like the WTO agreements[196] as well as regional agreements like the EU Treaties.[197] In addition to consenting to the extraterritorial recognition and enforcement of foreign administrative decisions and judgments through international agreements, States might also give them effect at the conditions laid down in their domestic rules of private international law. Ultimately, absent the explicit consent of the relevant State through an international treaty or a provision of national law, there are no legitimate options for the extraterritorial recognition and enforcement of domestic administrative decisions or judgments.

Since space resource activities will primarily be conducted by private entities, national disputes involving these entities at the domestic level are likely to be of civil or commercial nature. In the near future, domestic judgments adjudicating these disputes might be recognized and enforced under the Judgment Convention[198] (JC). This recent Convention establishes new mechanisms to facilitate the circulation of domestic foreign judgments in civil or commercial matters. Therefore, this section concludes the analysis of the enforcement options available at the national level with an overview of the solutions offered by the JC.

189. Samantha Besson, *Sovereignty*, in *Max Planck Encyclopedia of Public International Law* (2011).
190. Detter, *supra* note 188.
191. Jean Bodin, *Six Livres De La Republique* 125-154 (1577).
192. Article 2 UN Charter, *supra* note 3.
193. Shaw, *supra* note 188.
194. Cassese's IL, *supra* note 61 at 52-53.
195. Articles 39-51 UN Charter, *supra* note 3.
196. WTO Agreements, *supra* note 6.
197. EU Treaties, *supra* note 7.
198. Convention on the Recognition and Enforcement of Judgments in Civil or Commercial Matters, concluded in The Hague on July 2, 2019, *not yet in force* [hereinafter: Judgment Convention, "JC"].

i Enforcement under the JC

The JC was drafted during the 22nd Session of the Hague Conference on Private International Law to complement the 2005 Convention on Choice of Court Agreements[199] (Choice of Court Convention, CCC), which provides for the recognition and enforcement of judgments arising from an exclusive choice of court among the parties to a dispute.[200] The need for a sister instrument complementing the CCC came from the acknowledgment that oftentimes, the parties to a dispute prefer not to make an exclusive choice of court.[201] Accordingly, the JC addresses this issue by extending the possibility of recognition and enforcement to a much broader range of domestic judgments, with the goal to promote access to justice globally through enhanced judicial cooperation.[202] In furtherance of this goal, the Convention facilitates the circulation of domestic judgments adjudicating civil or commercial matters by providing rules and procedures for their extraterritorial recognition and enforcement.[203] At present, the Convention only counts six States Signatories and no ratification, and as such, it has not yet entered into force.[204]

Under Article 1 JC, the Convention shall apply to the recognition and enforcement of judgments "in civil or commercial matters," excluding "revenue, customs or administrative matters."[205] From a geographical viewpoint, the Convention applies only if both the court of origin and the court of recognition are from a State Party to the Convention.[206] From a personal viewpoint, the Convention applies to cases involving all physical and legal persons alike, including States.[207] Finally, from a substantive viewpoint, Article 2 JC explicitly excludes from the scope of the Convention fifteen selected areas within civil and commercial law.[208] Under Article 4 JC, "a judgment given by a court of a Contracting State (State of origin) shall be recognized and enforced in another Contracting State (requested State)" in accordance with the provisions of the Convention.[209] To complement this general rule, Article 4 (2) JC provides that the merits of a judgment cannot be reviewed beyond what is "necessary for the application of this Convention."[210] Pursuant to Article 4 (3) JC, "a judgment shall be recognized only if it has effect in the State of origin, and shall be enforced only if it is enforceable

199. Convention on Choice of Court Agreements, *entered into force* October 1, 2015 44 ILM 1294 [Choice of Court Convention, CCC].
200. Overview of the Choice of Court Convention, available https://www.hcch.net/en/instruments/conventions/specialised-sections/choice-of-court (last accessed October 2022).
201. Francisco Garcimartín & Geneviève Saumier, *Explanatory Report on the Convention of 2 July 2019 on the Recognition and Enforcement of Foreign Judgments in Civil or Commercial Matters* 3 (2020) [JC Explanatory Report].
202. *Ibid.*
203. Overview of the Judgment Convention, available https://www.hcch.net/en/instruments/conventions/specialised-sections/judgments (last accessed October 2022).
204. Status of the Judgment Convention, available https://www.hcch.net/en/instruments/conventions/status-table/?cid = 137 (last accessed October 2022).
205. Article 1 JC, *supra* note 198.
206. Article 1 (2) JC, *supra* note 198.
207. Article 2 (4) JC, *supra* note 198.
208. Article 2 (1) JC, *supra* note 198.
209. Article 4 JC, *supra* note 198.
210. Article 4 (2) JC, *supra* note 198.

in the State of origin."[211] Complementarily, recognition and enforcement may be postponed or denied if the judgment in question has not yet become final.[212] Notably, these provisions should be read in conjunction with Article 12 (c) JC, according to which the party seeking recognition or applying for enforcement shall produce "any documents necessary to establish that the judgment has effect or, where applicable, is enforceable in the State of origin."[213] As discussed with reference to the 1958 NYC, these provisions essentially create a requirement of *double exequatur* and are likely to impose a significant bureaucratic burden on the part of the applicant.

Article 5 JC provides that a judgment is eligible for recognition and enforcement if any of the thirteen requirements listed in the provision is met.[214] Together with Article 7, which determines grounds for refusal, this provision constitutes the core of the Convention.[215] Article 5 is divided into three paragraphs. Paragraph 1 lists the links with the State of origin that justify recognition and enforcement of the judgment in the requested State.[216] This list includes traditional criteria such as habitual residency, the presence of a principal place of business or the existence of a choice of court agreement, as well as very specific criteria governing selected hypotheses of commercial transactions.[217] Paragraph 2 modifies or excludes the application of certain connections listed in the first paragraph in the case of judgments given against consumers or employees.[218] Finally, the third paragraph provides specific exclusive grounds for the recognition and enforcement of judgment adjudicating tenancy issues or registration of immovable property.[219] Importantly, the following Article 6 provides that a judgment ruling on "rights in rem in immovable property shall be recognized and enforced if and only if the property is situated in the State of origin," notwithstanding the potential applicability of Article 5.[220] Article 7 JC lists the possible grounds on which the requested court might refuse recognition or enforcement of the judgment.[221] Under Article 7 (1) JC, refusal is possible based on five kinds of grounds. First, the requested court might refuse recognition if there has been a violation of the fundamental rules of due process concerning timely notification of the proceedings.[222] Second, courts may refuse to recognize and enforce judgments obtained by fraud.[223] Third, recognition and enforcement may be refused based on fundamental grounds of public

211. Article 4 (3) JC, *supra* note 198.
212. Article 4 (4) JC, *supra* note 198.
213. Article 12 (c) JC, *supra* note 198.
214. Article 5 JC, *supra* note 198.
215. JC Explanatory Report, *supra* note 201 at para. 134.
216. Article 5 (1) JC, *supra* note 198.
217. For a detailed analysis of these links, *see* JC Explanatory Report, *supra* note 201 at paras. 139-220.
218. Article 5 (2) JC, *supra* note 198. For more information, *see* JC Explanatory Report, *supra* note 201 at paras. 221-226.
219. Article 5 (3) JC, *supra* note 198. For further analysis, *see* JC Explanatory Report, *supra* note 201 at paras. 227-230.
220. Article 6 JC, *supra* note 198. For a conjunct reading of the two provisions, *see* JC Explanatory Report, *supra* note 201 at paras. 231-243.
221. Article 7 JC, *supra* note 198.
222. Article 7 (1) (a) JC, *supra* note 198. For an elaboration on the formalistic versus substantive approach to timely notification, *see* JC Explanatory Report, *supra* note 201 at paras. 247-254.
223. Article 7 (1) (b) JC, *supra* note 198.

policy.[224] Fourth, the requested court might deny recognition if the judgment was given in violation of a valid choice of court agreement among the parties.[225] Fifth and final, recognition may be refused in case of inconsistency with other judgments rendered between the same parties, given either (1) by a court of the requested State or (2) by a court of another State, provided that (2.1) the subject matter is the same, (2.2) the judgment was given earlier and (2.3) fulfills the conditions for recognition in the requested State.[226] Notably, the list of grounds provided under Article 7 is of exhaustive nature, meaning that outside these hypotheses, the requested court shall grant recognition and enforcement,[227] provided that at least one of the requirements mentioned by Article 5 is met. Pursuant to Article 7 (2), the requested court might refuse recognition and enforcement also if there is a pending dispute between the same parties on the same subject matter before another court of the requested State, at the double condition that the court of the requested State has been seized before the court of origin and that there is a close connection between the dispute and the requested State.[228]

1.3 (Re)evaluation

The previous sections provided a foundational overview of the adjudicatory avenues and enforcement options that could be "borrowed" by the multi-level regulatory system of space mining in the absence of dedicated processes set up within the system itself. Methodologically speaking, the analysis moved from the premise that legitimate enforcement can only be triggered by the formal adjudication of normative violations. Accordingly, the focus was placed first on the identification of relevant adjudicatory mechanisms within both the legal order of international law as well as applicable national jurisdictions. Consequently, the analysis then presented which options might be available for enforcing the results of such adjudicatory processes. Due to the infant status of the multi-level system of space mining, the overview focused on those options that have more chances of being involved based upon a prima facie assessment of formal legitimacy and perceived effectiveness. Building upon those findings, the present section scrutinizes that assessment by reevaluating the suitability of the identified enforcement options in light of their formal legitimacy and practical effectiveness. Mirroring the structure adopted so far, this section individually considers the various options available at the international and national levels.

224. Article 7 (1) (c) JC, *supra* note 198. For an assessment of the scope of the public policy exception, *see* JC Explanatory Report, *supra* note 201 at paras. 258-266.
225. Article 7 (1) (d) JC, *supra* note 198.
226. Article 7 (1) (e) and (f) JC, *supra* note 198. For a differentiated analysis of the two hypotheses, *see* JC Explanatory Report, *supra* note 201 at paras. 270-272.
227. JC Explanatory Report, *supra* note 201 at para. 244.
228. Article 7 (1) (e) and (f) JC, *supra* note 198. For a specific assessment of the two hypotheses, *see* JC Explanatory Report, *supra* note 201 at paras. 273-276.

1.3.1 Evaluating International Enforcement Options

The analysis conducted in section 1.1 identified international enforcement options based upon the involvement, in the adjudicatory phase, of either the ICJ or the PCA, on account of their mandate, reputation and expertise.

i Legitimacy and Effectiveness of Enforcement Options for ICJ Judgments

As seen, ICJ judgments may be enforced by (1) the UNSC at the conditions laid down in Article 94 (2) UN Charter or (2) through the use of countermeasures by injured and non-injured States at the conditions laid down in Articles 49-54 ARSIWA. The question then becomes: how legitimate and effective are these options for the enforcement of international norms of space mining?

Legitimacy and Effectiveness of UNSC Enforcement Under Article 94 (2) UN Charter

Due to the substantial lack of practice under Article 94 (2) UN Charter, the mechanism designed in this provision has not been discussed much in the literature. Nonetheless, the findings developed from the available sources have been sufficient for this section to provide a targeted assessment in connection with the multi-level regulatory system of space mining.

Let's begin with assessing the general legitimacy of this mechanism. Systemically speaking, entrusting the UNSC with the enforcement of ICJ judgments would be consistent with the legal order designed by the UN Charter, provided that certain conditions are met. As the guardian of international peace and security, the UNSC is certainly well suited to assume a leading role in the restoration of compliance with international law. Especially at the time when the Charter was drafted, the Council was the most logical choice for the exercise of this competence.[229] The problem lies in how this competence has been designed under Article 94 (2) UN Charter. As discussed, the provision foresees an optional and discretionary involvement of the UNSC in the enforcement of ICJ judgments. However, from a legal theory standpoint, law enforcement cannot be optional nor discretionary.[230] Subjecting the exercise of enforcement powers to the exclusive request of the parties is in contradiction with the institutional purpose of enforcement itself. Enabling the executive branch to discretionarily ignore or second guess the final decisions legitimately taken by the competent judicial authorities is inherently inconsistent with the rule of law. Based upon these premises, one can argue whether it is even technically correct to ascribe the mechanism designed under Article 94 (2) UN Charter to the enforcement genus. On top of these concerns, the lack of representativeness of the Council and the unbalanced distribution of power

229. Karin Oellers-Frahm, *Article 94* in *The Statute of the International Court of Justice: A Commentary* 159-176 (Andreas Zimmermann, Christian Tomuschat, Karin Oellers-Frahm & Christian J Tams eds., 2006).
230. Cassese's IL, *supra* note 61.

between its members further raise evident issues of substantive legitimacy.[231] Therefore, the general legitimacy evaluation of Article 94 (2) UN Charter is rather negative. Within the legal order of international law, this finding is notably confirmed by the lack of practice under the provision, especially on the part of the UNSC. It is highly significant that even when the Council had factually intervened to ensure compliance with an ICJ decision, such as in the case of Bosnia Herzegovina,[232] it purposely avoided making any reference to Article 94 UN Charter.[233] Having said that, it should be noted that under Article III OST, States shall conduct their space activities "in accordance with international law, including the Charter of the United Nations, in the interest of maintaining international peace and security and promoting international cooperation and understanding."[234] As a result, the exercise of enforcement powers by the UNSC to ensure compliance with an ICJ judgment under Article 94 (2) UN Charter would rest on direct grounds of normative legitimacy.

Mutatis mutandis, these considerations can be useful also for evaluating the general effectiveness of the mechanism designed under Article 94 (2) UN Charter. Logically, an enforcement mechanism which is both optional and discretional can hardly be effective. The discretional element is particularly problematic in connection with the veto power attributed to the permanent members of the Council.[235] The practical impact of this critical weakness has become apparent in the Nicaragua case, where the United States vetoed a UNSC draft resolution meant to condemn its own defiance of the ICJ judgment.[236] Therefore, also the general evaluation of effectiveness of Article 94 (2) UN Charter is rather negative. Notably, this finding is also confirmed with regard to the system of space law. Considering that the five permanent members of the Council are all active—one might even say rival—spacefaring nations, it is hard to imagine the UNSC being able to agree on the exercise of enforcement powers without at least one permanent member using its veto. This is especially true in the field of space mining, in light of the fact that the U.S. and Russia defend opposite positions as to its legitimate conduct and regulation.[237] Consequently, also the effectiveness evaluation of Article 94 (2) UN Charter as enforcement option for the system of space mining is negative.

It is worth underscoring that the result of both evaluations would have been different had Article 94 (2) UN Charter foreseen an automatic and mandatory involvement of the UNSC for the enforcement of ICJ judgments. In this scenario, the known issues related to the composition and power imbalance within the UNSC would not have impacted its legitimacy as enforcer authority because of the automatic and mandatory character of its powers. Likewise, the concerns discussed in terms of effectiveness were related to the optional and discretional nature of the mechanism designed under Article 94 (2) UN Charter. In the opposite scenario, the UNSC would

231. Muhammadin, *supra* note 19 at 181-183.
232. Bosnia cases, *supra* note 23.
233. As to which, *see* section 1.1.1 in Chapter 3.
234. Article III OST, *supra* note 11.
235. Obregon, *supra* note 15 at paras. 50-52.
236. As to which, *see* section 1.1.1 (i) in Chapter 3.
237. As to which, *see* section 3.1.1 in Chapter 2.

have the potential to be quite an effective enforcer due to the various powers attributed to the Council under the Charter.

Legitimacy and Effectiveness of Self-Enforcement Under Articles 49-54 ARSIWA

The legitimacy and effectiveness of countermeasures have been extensively discussed in public international law literature.[238] Building upon these studies, the present section focuses specifically on evaluating the suitability of countermeasures as enforcement options within the specific multi-level regulatory system of space mining.

As seen in Chapter 1, international space law does not have authorities of its own.[239]

The main goal of one of the two dedicated institutions of international space law, the UN Office for Outer Space Affairs (UNOOSA), is to be the Secretariat of the UN Committee on the Peaceful Uses of Outer Space (UNCOPUOS).[240] Even UNCOPUOS itself is not really autonomous as it reports to the Fourth Committee of the UN General Assembly.[241] This lack of dedicated authorities implies that legitimacy to take action within the system of international space law has been retained by States. Ordinarily, this requires them to collectively agree on measures to be taken through consensus deliberation in UNCOPUOS. However, an ICJ judgment ascertaining that a State is conducting its space activities in violation of international law would likely provide a valid substitute for this collective deliberation. In particular, such adjudication would imply that the concerned State would not be validly exercising its freedom to explore and use outer space under Articles I and III OST.[242] Due to the foundational importance and universal relevance of these provisions, one might even argue that their obligations are owed *erga omnes*.[243]

As a consequence, both injured and non-injured States would be legitimized to intervene to enforce compliance with the judgment through the use of countermeasures.[244]

Assessing the effectiveness of countermeasures as a tool to enforce compliance with ICJ judgments in the field of international space law is particularly complex. On the one hand, States heavily rely on international cooperation for the conduct of their space activities.[245] Therefore, actions directed at preventing or suspending cooperation with wrongful States might prove to be very effective. For the very same reason, countermeasures could conversely trigger a dangerous escalation that might end up

238. For the most relevant sources debating this issue, *see supra* note 68.
239. As to which, *see* section 2.2. in Chapter 1.
240. Information on the role and responsibilities of UNOOSA can be found on its website https://www.unoosa.org/oosa/en/aboutus/roles-responsibilities.html (last accessed October 2022).
241. As also clarified https://www.unoosa.org/oosa/en/ourwork/copuos/index.html by UNOOSA (last accessed October 2022).
242. On the limits affecting the valid exercise of the freedoms of space, *see* section 1.1.1 in Chapter 2.
243. On the concept of *erga omnes* obligations, *see* Elias, *supra* note 65.
244. *Ibid.*
245. Kai-Uwe Schrogl, *Space Law and Diplomacy*, 2016 Proceedings of the International Institute of Space Law 3-4 (2017).

undermining the stability of the outer space environment.[246] Depending on the importance of the target, enacting countermeasures in the space domain might even be counterproductive. An example might help to clarify. In reaction to the unlawful invasion of Ukraine, several western States have decided to enact economic sanctions against the Russian Federation.[247]

In response to these sanctions, Russia has unilaterally suspended its space cooperation with said States[248] and even threatened to stop propelling the ISS[249] in an attempt to use the negative effects of such decisions as a deterrent against the sanctions. As a result, the European Space Agency (ESA) had to suspend ExoMars,[250] an important scientific mission that was supposed to be launched from the Baikonur Cosmodrome at the end of 2022.[251] Likewise, the British consortium OneWeb suspended all launches from Baikonur[252] after Roscosmos refused to launch and actually seized its last batch of satellites.[253] In all these examples, the important role played by Russia in several international space programs shows how difficult it is to enact countermeasures in this field. While this might not be the case with less powerful States, the risk of catastrophic escalation would still remain. Needless to say, the situation would be even more difficult in the case of space mining, given the high political sensitivity of this topic.

ii *Legitimacy and Effectiveness of Enforcement Options for PCA Arbitral Awards*

States Parties to the PCA Convention "agree to submit loyally" to its awards.[254]

As discussed earlier, these awards might be enforced by the individual States concerned through the use of countermeasures under Articles 49-54 ARSIWA or,

246. As clearly demonstrated by the recent developments following the Russian invasion of Ukraine.
247. An overview of the sanctions undertaken so far is available https://www.consilium.europa.eu/it/infographics/eu-sanctions-against-russia-over-ukraine/ (last accessed October 2022).
248. Elizabeth Gamillo, *How Sanctions on Russia Affect International Space Programs*, available https://www.smithsonianmag.com/smart-news/sanctions-on-russia-reach-outer-space-180979679/ (last accessed October 2022).
249. As declared https://www.france24.com/en/europe/20220312-russia-warns-sanctions-could-cause-international-space-station-to-crash by the director of Roscosmos itself (last accessed October 2022).
250. As announced https://www.esa.int/Newsroom/Press_Releases/ExoMars_suspended by the director general of the European Space Agency (last accessed October 2022).
251. Information on ExoMars can be found on its dedicated https://www.esa.int/Science_Exploration/Human_and_Robotic_Exploration/Exploration/ExoMars webpage (last accessed October 2022).
252. As announced https://twitter.com/OneWeb/status/1499317405029437447?ref_src=twsrc%5Etfw%7Ctwcamp%5Etweetembed%7Ctwterm%5E1499317405029437447%7Ctwgr%5E%7Ctwcon%5Es1_&ref_url=https%3A%2F%2Fspacenews.com%2Foneweb-leaves-baikonur-cosmodrome-after-roscosmos-ultimatum%2F by the board of the company (last accessed October 2022).
253. As declared https://www.space.com/russia-refuses-launch-oneweb-satellites-demands by Roscosmos (last accessed October 2022).
254. Article 18 Arbitration Convention, *supra* note 78.

alternatively, pursuant to the 1958 NYC, at the conditions laid down in these provisions.[255]

Legitimacy and Effectiveness of Self-Enforcement Under Articles 49-54 ARSIWA

Mutatis mutandis, the considerations expressed previously on the legitimacy and effectiveness of self-enforcement under Articles 49-54 ARSIWA remain valid also when referred to PCA awards. One additional comment concerns the potential involvement of private parties in disputes before the PCA. In this scenario, countermeasures might still be used as an enforcement tool among the States internationally responsible for the private entities involved, but not directly by or against non-governmental entities.[256]

Legitimacy and Effectiveness of Enforcement Under the NYC

As discussed earlier, the NYC is an international agreement concluded in 1958 with the goal of maximizing the international circulation of arbitral awards by removing unnecessary obstacles to their recognition and enforcement.[257] Currently, the Convention counts 158 Parties and is one of the most successful treaties in the world.[258] As such, it is easy to evaluate the legitimacy and effectiveness of the NYC for the enforcement of PCA arbitral awards. In view of its status as binding international agreement, enforcement options granted under the Convention meet the highest standards of legitimacy. Thanks to its strong pro-enforcement bias and the direct involvement of national courts, the remedies offered under the NYC have proved to be extremely effective.[259] This positive evaluation of the NYC as enforcement tool can also be confirmed with respect to the multi-level system of space mining. Thanks to the wide ratification status of the PCA and NYC Conventions[260] and the direct involvement of domestic courts through the mechanisms of the NYC, enforcing the adjudication of international space law as laid down in a PCA arbitral award will meet high standards of legitimacy and is also likely to guarantee a high degree of effectiveness.

1.3.2 Evaluating National Enforcement Options

As discussed earlier, enforcement options available at the national level vary according to the national or international character of the relevant dispute.[261]

Any potential violation of national space mining legislation will be adjudicated in accordance with the domestic rules of the concerned State, which at present may be either the U.S., Luxembourg, the UAE or Japan.[262] In all these Countries, enforcement powers are exercised by the executive branch pursuant to the adjudication of a

255. As to which, *see* section 1.1.2 in Chapter 3.
256. Since the use of countermeasures is exclusively reserved to States. *See* section 1.1.1 (ii) in Chapter 3.
257. NYC, *supra* note 87.
258. Status of the NYC, *supra* note 91.
259. *Ibid.*
260. As to which, *see* respectively *supra* notes 90 and 79.
261. And specifically at section 1.2 in Chapter 3.
262. For an analysis of these laws *see* section 2 in Chapter 2.

normative violation either in an administrative decision, a judgment or an award.[263] If the dispute were to involve only domestic actors, the would be no legitimacy issues and a high probability of effectiveness. Transnational disputes involving international players or foreign entities are, of course, a very different story. Except for arbitral awards falling under the scope of the NYC, the possibility of legitimate and effective enforcement is conditional on the consent and cooperation of the other States that might be involved. For what concerns administrative decisions, there is no general mechanism in place under international law to promote their cross-border recognition and enforcement. There are, however, examples of bilateral or regional arrangements providing for the mutual recognition of administrative decisions in certain matters, like those done in the WTO and the EU regimes.[264] Concerning domestic judgments, consent to their cross-border recognition and enforcement would be given by national authorities and courts at the conditions laid down either in relevant domestic provisions or applicable international agreements in the area of private international law.[265] As a result, this type of enforcement continues to be managed by national authorities and courts on a case-by-case basis. Attempting the cross-border enforcement of administrative or judicial decisions without the consent of the receiving State would likely be held as illegitimate under international law and thus hardly achieve any effective result. Therefore, for the time being, it would be advisable to solve transnational disputes concerning national space mining legislation by means of arbitration in order to benefit from the applicability of the NYC.[266]

1.3.3 Preliminary Conclusions

The purpose of this section was to present and evaluate the main enforcement options available within the multi-level regulatory system of space mining. To this end, the section focused the analysis on enforcement mechanisms capable of being actioned in the current legal framework, should the need eventually arise.

Based on the above assessment, it can be concluded that *both national and international norms* of space mining can be legitimately and effectively enforced only to the extent that their violation is adjudicated by means of arbitration. Further, *national* provisions regulating space mining can be legitimately and effectively enforced pursuant to domestic administrative or judicial adjudication, provided that only domestic actors are involved.

This minimum set of adjudicatory and enforcement options leaves the system of space mining particularly exposed to potential tensions and conflicts. Since the majority of space mining disputes will likely have a transnational character, the very

263. *Ibid.*
264. As to which, *see* respectively *supra* notes 6 and 7.
265. Such as the Judgment Convention, *supra* note 198. As discussed earlier at pp. 221-225, the many exceptions to the applicability of the JC as well as the current lack of ratifications demand prudence in evaluating its suitability for enforcement purposes.
266. NYC, *supra* note 87.

possibility of enforcement critically depends on the pursuit of national or international arbitration.

This dependence becomes a critical vulnerability in light of the fact that, at present, there is no guarantee that States will agree to resolve their space mining disputes through arbitration. As a result, the system needs to be reinforced through the formalization of dedicated adjudicatory processes, as well as the development of proactive coordination mechanisms that can reduce the need for *ex post* enforcement. With a view to forming a better understanding of how to construct said reinforcements, the next section looks at the solutions adopted in comparable legal regimes governing other global commons.

2 PROPOSED REINFORCEMENTS FROM COMPARABLE MODELS

In the quest for legal and policy tools to reinforce the multi-level system of space mining, this section looks at potential models offered by the UNCLOS,[267] the ITU[268] and the AT.[269] Specifically, the section focuses on the adjudicatory, coordination and consultation tools employed respectively in the UNCLOS, ITU and AT to support the development of analog tools within the multi-level system of space mining. In order to contextualize the analysis, each section starts with a concise summary of the substantive and institutional features of the regime discussed.

2.1 The United Nations Convention on the Law of the Sea

The UNCLOS is one of the most important international agreements in the world.[270]

It was concluded in 1982 after decades of negotiations, and it entered into force twelve years later in 1994.[271] The purpose of the UNCLOS is to "settle all issues related to the law of the sea,"[272] unifying under one instrument all the norms developed in this critical area through centuries of practices and international agreements. At present, the UNCLOS counts 168 States Parties[273] and is the reference instrument concerning issues related to the law of the sea for the entire international community, including those States who are not Party to it (like the United States).[274] In this sense, the

267. United Nations Convention on the Law of the Sea, *entered into force* November 16, 1994, 1833 UNTS 3 [hereinafter: "UNCLOS"].
268. Constitution and Convention of the International Telecommunication Union *entered into force* July 1, 1994, 1825 UNTS 1 [hereinafter: "ITU Constitution and Convention"].
269. The Antarctic Treaty, *entered into force* June 23, 1961, 402 U.N.T.S. 71 [hereinafter: "AT"].
270. Cassese's IL, *supra* note 61 at 104.
271. For an historical overview of the UNCLOS, *see* Tullio Treves, *Historical Development of the Law of the Sea*, in *The Oxford Handbook of the Law of the Sea* 1 (Donald R. Rothwell, Alex G. Oude Elferink, Karen N. Scott & Tim Stephens eds., 2015).
272. UNCLOS Preamble, *supra* note 267.
273. As reported https://treaties.un.org/Pages/ViewDetailsIII.aspx?src=IND&mtdsg_no=XXI-6&chapter=21&Temp=mtdsg3&clang=_en on the Convention page (last accessed October 2022).
274. Prominent commentators have rightly called it "a constitution of the oceans." Cassese's IL, *supra* note 61 at 104.

UNCLOS can be compared to the OST as both treaties provide a codification of foundational rules whose value transcends individual ratification.[275] This book has previously addressed the UNCLOS when discussing the meaning of due regard under international law[276] and when examining the "common heritage of mankind" regime under Article 11 of the Moon Agreement.[277] In accordance with the purpose of this section, the present analysis focuses on the adjudicatory system designed in Part XI UNCLOS for disputes related to activities in the Deep Seabed.

2.1.1 Legal Principles for Activities in the Deep Seabed

The UNCLOS regime for the exploration and exploitation of the mineral resources located in the Deep Seabed is laid down in Part XI of the Convention,[278] as amended by the 1994 New York Agreement.[279] First, it is important to note that within the context of the Convention, "the seabed and ocean floor and subsoil thereof, beyond the limits of national jurisdiction" are collectively referred to as "the Area."[280] Pursuant to Article 136 UNCLOS, the Area and the resources located therein are established as "the common heritage of mankind."[281] This establishment determines a series of significant legal implications laid down in the subsequent provisions of the Convention. To begin with, the Area is subtracted from the sovereign influence of any Country,[282] and all rights in the resources located therein are vested "in mankind as a whole."[283] Consequently, States shall orient their general conduct thereby "in accordance with the provisions of this Part, the principles embodied in the Charter of the United Nations and other rules of international law in the interests of maintaining peace and security and promoting international cooperation and mutual understanding."[284] This general duty is further complemented by the obligation of States to ensure, under their international responsibility, that activities in the Area, "whether carried out by States Parties, or state enterprises or natural or juridical persons which possess the nationality of States Parties or are effectively controlled by them or their nationals," are conducted

275. Peter Haanappel, *The Law and Policy of Air Space and Outer Space: A Comparative Approach* 9 (2003). At the same time, it is important to underline that, unlike the OST, the UNCLOS is a massive treaty composed by hundreds of articles and complemented by nine annexes.
276. As to which, *see* section 1.1.6 in Chapter 2.
277. As to which, *see* section 1.3.2 in Chapter 2.
278. Articles 136-184 UNCLOS, *supra* note 267.
279. Agreement Relating to the Implementation of Part XI of the United Nations Convention on the Law of the Sea of December 10, 1982, *entered into force* July 28, 1996, 1836 UNTS 3.
280. Article 1 UNCLOS, *supra* note 267.
281. Article 136 UNCLOS, *supra* note 267. This declaration is similar to the one made for the Moon and its natural resources under Article 11 of the Agreement Governing the Activities of States on the Moon and Other Celestial Bodies entered into force July 11, 1984, 1363 U.N.T.S. 3 [hereinafter: "MA"].
282. Article 137 UNCLOS, *supra* note 267. In this case the language is similar to Article II OST, *supra* note 11.
283. Article 137 UNCLOS, *supra* note 267. In this case the language resembles again Article 11 MA, *supra* note 281.
284. Article 138 UNCLOS, *supra* note 267. The final part of this provision is almost identical to the concluding sentence of Article III OST, *supra* note 11.

in conformity with the provisions of the UNCLOS.[285] This supervision is further complemented by the additional obligations laid down in paragraphs 2 (b) and 4 of Article 153 UNCLOS.[286] According to this provision, private entities might carry out activities in the Area only through the sponsorship of a State, and the latter is obliged to take all measures necessary to ensure compliance with the provisions of the Convention.[287] It is important to mention that the responsibility of the sponsorship State is limited only to the activities specifically mentioned under Article 145 UNCLOS.[288] Failure to carry out these responsibilities will trigger the international liability of the State(s) concerned,[289] which can however exonerate itself by proving that it has taken "all necessary and appropriate measures to secure effective compliance" with the Convention.[290] From a substantive viewpoint, activities in the Area shall be carried out "for the benefit of mankind as a whole,"[291] and related financial and other economic benefits shall be "equitably shared through any appropriate mechanism, on a non-discriminatory basis."[292] Finally, pursuant to Article 141 UNCLOS, "the Area shall be open to use exclusively for peaceful purposes by all States."[293] As underlined in notes 289-293, there are many similarities between the principles governing activities in the Area and those shaping the conduct of space activities.

2.1.2 The International Seabed Authority

To organize and control "activities in the Area,"[294] Article 156 UNCLOS establishes an intergovernmental organization called the ISA.[295]

The ISA acts as a custodian of the deep seabed for present and future generations, governing the use of mineral resources to be prospected or extracted from the deep seabed and ensuring the effective protection of the marine environment.[296] To fulfill this mission, Part XI of the UNCLOS entrusts the ISA with significant normative,

285. Article 139 UNCLOS, *supra* note 267.
286. Article 153 UNCLOS, *supra* note 267.
287. Pursuant to paragraphs (2) (b) and (4) of Article 153 UNCLOS, *supra* note 267.
288. Responsibilities and obligations of States sponsoring persons and entities with respect to activities in the Area (Advisory Opinion, February 1 2011), ITLOS Reports 2011 10 (2011).
289. Article 139 (2) UNCLOS, *supra* note 267. This mechanism is similar to the one established, albeit in more general terms, under the Convention on International Liability for Damage Caused by Space Objects *entered into force* October 9, 1973, 24 U.S.T. 2389, 961 U.N.T.S. 187 [hereinafter: "LIAB"].
290. With particular regard to those stemming from Article 153 (4) of the Convention and Article 4 (4) of Annex III. *See* Article 139 (2) UNCLOS, *supra* note 267.
291. Article 140 UNCLOS, *supra* note 267. Similar language can be found in Article I OST, *supra* note 11.
292. *Ibid.* In this case, similarly to what is provided under Article 11 MA.
293. Article 141 UNCLOS, *supra* note 267. This provision is similar to Article IV (2) OST and Article 3 (1) MA, which limit the use of celestial bodies for exclusively peaceful purposes.
294. Pursuant to Article 1 (1) (3) UNCLOS, this term includes "all activities of exploration for, and exploitation of, the resources of the Area," *supra* note 267.
295. Article 156 UNCLOS, *supra* note 267.
296. Information on the ISA can be found https://www.isa.org.jm/index.php/our-work/protection-marine-environment (last accessed October 2022).

administrative and enforcement powers.[297] From a normative perspective, the ISA is empowered to enact the rules, regulations and procedures governing the conduct of activities in the Area.[298]

It is important to note, as further discussed in the next paragraph, that the exercise of these normative powers is subject to the sole discretion of the Authority itself.[299] The ISA is also attributed with the power to administer the applicability of said rules, regulations and procedures, including through the issuance of licenses and even the conclusion of mining contracts.[300] Finally, the Convention provides the ISA with a wide range of enforcement powers to ensure compliance with the provisions of the Convention, the rules, regulations and procedures developed by the Authority, as well as the licenses issued to operators and the contracts concluded among them.[301] The concrete exercise of the Authority's normative, administrative and enforcement powers is distributed among its four organs: the Assembly, the Council, the Secretariat and the Enterprise.[302] The Assembly is composed of all States Parties to the UNCLOS and is the supreme organ of the Authority.[303] In accordance with this status, the Assembly determines the composition of all the other organs and is entrusted with the normative powers of the Authority.[304] The Council is composed of thirty-six members elected by the Assembly and is the executive organ of the authority.[305] As such, the Council is entrusted with significant secondary normative powers and exercises the enforcement powers attributed to the Authority.[306] The Secretariat shall comprise a Secretary General and "such stuff as the Authority may require."[307] The Secretary General is the chief administrative officer of the Authority and, as such, is entrusted with all its administrative powers and responsibilities to be fulfilled with the support of its administrative staff.[308] Finally, the Enterprise is the organ of the Authority entrusted with the conduct of activities in the Area directly, including transporting, processing and marketing of minerals recovered from the Area.[309]

Even though the Enterprise is provided with its own legal capacity, it operates under the directives and control of the Council in accordance with the Convention, the rules, regulations and procedures of the Authority, as well as the policies of the Assembly.[310]

297. An excellent synbook of the powers attributed to the ISA has been written by his current Secretary General Michael W. Lodge, *International Seabed Authority*, in *Max Planck Encyclopedia of Public International Law* 26-27 (2020) [book hereinafter: "MPEPIL"].
298. Articles 150-153 UNCLOS, *supra* note 267.
299. Article 189 UNCLOS, *supra* note 267.
300. Articles 160 and 162 UNCLOS, *supra* note 267.
301. *Ibidem.*
302. Article 158 UNCLOS, *supra* note 267.
303. Article 159 UNCLOS, *supra* note 267.
304. Article 160 UNCLOS, *supra* note 267.
305. Article 161 UNCLOS, *supra* note 267.
306. Article 162 UNCLOS, *supra* note 267.
307. Article 166 UNCLOS, *supra* note 267.
308. *Ibid.*
309. Article 170 UNCLOS, *supra* note 267.
310. *Ibid.*

2.1.3 *The Seabed Disputes Chamber*

As mentioned, the institutional framework laid down in Part XI UNCLOS is notably complemented by the establishment of a dedicated Seabed Disputes Chamber[311] (Seabed Chamber or Chamber) within the ITLOS.[312] It is important to underline that the Chamber is established as a specialized section of the ITLOS and not as a separate entity.[313] Nonetheless, the Chamber is provided with relative autonomy in terms of composition, access, procedures and jurisdiction.[314] For example, a distinctive feature of the Chamber compared to the ITLOS is that the former shall be open also to non-governmental entities, so long as they are mentioned under Part XI.[315] Another important difference is that the Chamber is also provided with advisory jurisdiction on legal questions arising within the scope of the activities of the Assembly or the Council.[316]

The exact scope and limits of the Chamber's adjudicatory jurisdiction are laid down under Articles 187-189 UNCLOS. To begin with, Article 187 UNCLOS establishes that the Chamber can adjudicate six kinds of disputes, in many cases on an exclusive basis. First, the Chamber shall have jurisdiction on issues of interpretation or application of Part XI and its related annexes among States Parties to the Convention.[317] Second, the Chamber shall have (exclusive) jurisdiction over disputes between a State Party and the Authority concerning the latter's acts or omissions.[318] Third, the Chamber shall have jurisdiction to adjudicate certain disputes[319] between the parties to a contract[320] for Deep Seabed mining. Fourth and fifth, the Chamber is further provided with (exclusive) jurisdiction over liability disputes under Annex III of the Convention. Finally, the Chamber shall also have (exclusive) jurisdiction over "any other disputes

311. Article 186 UNCLOS, *supra* note 267.
312. Established under Annex VI to the UNCLOS, *supra* note 267.
313. Interestingly, there was more support for a dedicated adjudicatory body for seabed disputes rather than for the ITLOS in itself. Mark W. Janis, *The Law of the Sea Tribunal and the ICJ: Some Notions about Utility*, 16 (2) Marine Policy 103 (1992).
314. On the relationship between the ITLOS and the Chamber *see* Patibandla Chandrasekhara Rao, *International Tribunal for the Law of the Sea*, in MPEPIL, *supra* note 297 at paras. 13-16.
315. Article 37 Annex VI UNCLOS, *supra* note 267.
316. To be precise, under Article 138 of the Rules of the ITLOS, the Tribunal may also give an advisory opinion on a legal question if this is provided for by "an international agreement related to the purposes of the Convention." ITLOS, Rules of the Tribunal, adopted on October 28, 1997, amended on March 15 and September 21, 2001 and on March 17, 2009, available https://www.itlos.org/fileadmin/itlos/documents/basic_texts/Itlos_8_E_17_03_09.pdf (accessed October 2022). For what concerns the Chamber, pursuant to Article 191 UNCLOS, requests for advisory opinion may only be submitted by the Assembly or the Council, and shall be given by the Chamber as a matter of urgency. An interesting analysis of the Chamber's advisory jurisdiction has been conducted by Tim Poisel, *Deep Seabed Mining: Implications of Seabed Disputes Chamber's Advisory Opinion*, 19 Australian International Law Journal 213-233 (2012).
317. Article 187 (a) UNCLOS, *supra* note 267.
318. Article 187 (b) UNCLOS, *supra* note 267.
319. And specifically, disputes concerning either the contract's interpretation and application or the acts and omissions of one party against the other(s), or anyways affecting the legitimate interests of the other parties.
320. Including States Parties, the Authority or the Enterprise, State enterprises and natural or juridical persons. Article 187 (c) UNCLOS, *supra* note 267.

for which the jurisdiction of the Chamber is specifically provided in this Convention."[321]

It is important to note that for cases involving "sponsored entities,"[322] the Convention provides that the relevant States shall be given notice of disputes brought against the private entities for which they are responsible and shall have the right to participate in the proceedings by submitting written or oral statements.[323] Conversely, States cited by a private entity may request the relevant sponsoring State to appear in the proceedings on behalf of that entity and, in case of negative response, may then also arrange to be represented by a juridical person of their nationality.[324]

As mentioned, some of these disputes have been explicitly excluded from the exclusive jurisdiction of the Chamber.[325] First, disputes concerning the interpretation and application of Part XI[326] *may* also be referred to a special chamber of the ITLOS[327] or to an ad hoc chamber within the Seabed Disputes Chamber.[328] Second, commercial disputes related to the interpretation or application of a contract for Deep Seabed mining[329] *shall* be submitted to *binding* commercial arbitration at the request of any party.[330] To preserve the consistent interpretation of the Convention, arbitrators resolving these disputes "shall have no jurisdiction to decide any question of interpretation of this Convention."[331] Should such questions of interpretation arise during the dispute, they shall be referred to the Chamber for a ruling.[332] If a decision of the arbitral tribunal would depend on such a ruling, then the tribunal shall first refer to its questions and then proceed to render its award in conformity with the ruling received.[333] By exclusion, all other disputes are attributed to the Chamber on an exclusive basis.

The jurisdiction of the Chamber has two fundamental limits. First, since the enactment of the New York Agreement,[334] all potential disputes related to matters falling within the scope of the WTO agreements have been excluded from the jurisdiction of the Chamber. Second, to protect the autonomy of the ISA, the Chamber shall have no jurisdiction over the exercise of its discretionary[335] and

321. Article 187 (f) UNCLOS, *supra* note 267.
322. Under Article 153 (2) (b) UNCLOS, private entities can only conduct activities in the Area through the sponsorship of a State. UNCLOS, *supra* note 267.
323. Article 190 (1) UNCLOS, *supra* note 267.
324. Article 190 (2) UNCLOS, *supra* note 267.
325. Article 188 UNCLOS, *supra* note 267.
326. And specifically those mentioned under Article 187 (a) UNCLOS, *supra* note 267.
327. Pursuant to the agreement of all involved parties. Article 188 (1) (a) UNCLOS, *supra* note 267.
328. At the request of any party. Article 188 (1) (b) UNCLOS, *supra* note 267.
329. And specifically those mentioned under Article 187 (c) UNCLOS, *supra* note 267.
330. Unless of course a different agreement would be reached. Article 188 (2) (a) UNCLOS, *supra* note 267. Interestingly, letter (c) of the same article determines the residual applicability of UNCITRAL Arbitration Rules to said arbitration proceedings, unless otherwise agreed by the parties.
331. Article 188 (2) (a) UNCLOS, *supra* note 267.
332. *Ibid.*
333. Article 188 (2) (b) UNCLOS, *supra* note 267.
334. Section VI New York Agreement, *supra* note 279.
335. Specifically, in no case the Chamber shall substitute its discretion for that of the Authority. Article 189 UNCLOS, *supra* note 267.

normative[336] powers. In these areas, the Chamber's jurisdiction shall be confined to adjudicate, in individual cases, whether the *application* of such rules, regulations and procedures would be in conflict either with relevant obligations under either the contract or the Convention.[337]

In terms of enforcement, the decisions of the Chamber shall be enforceable in the territories of the States Parties in the same manner as judgments or orders of the highest court of the State Party in whose territory the enforcement is sought.[338] In this regard, Draft Regulation 106 of the ISA establishes that any final decision relating to the rights and obligations of the Authority and of the Contractor rendered by a court or tribunal having jurisdiction under the Convention shall be enforceable in the territory of any State party to the Convention affected thereby.[339]

2.1.4 The Suitability of the UNCLOS for the Governance of Space Resource Activities: New Insights to an Old Debate

This is not the first time that the UNCLOS regime for Deep Seabed mining has been considered a potential model for the regulation of space resource activities. Distinguished authors have written both in favor and against it,[340] while States continue to either propose or oppose it during their interventions in UNCOPUOS.[341] In this regard, it seems that these discussions within the space law community have reached an *impasse* caused by the ontological differences between the arguments promoted by the two sides of the debate. While supporters of the UNCLOS model primarily rely on strictly legal arguments, their opponents put forward purely political objections. Accordingly, the next paragraph discusses the legal suitability of the UNCLOS model vis-à-vis its political incompatibility with current trends in international space policy.

336. In particular, the Chamber shall not pronounce itself on the question of whether any rules, regulations and procedures of the Authority are in conformity with the Convention and shall not declare invalid any such rules, regulations and procedures. Article 189 UNCLOS, *supra* note 267.
337. In addition, the Chamber may also adjudicate claims concerning excess of jurisdiction or misuse of power, as well as claims requesting damages or other remedies in case of failure to comply with relevant obligations under the contract or the Convention. Article 189 UNCLOS, *supra* note 267.
338. Article 39 Annex VI UNCLOS, *supra* note 267.
339. If confirmed, this regulation might further reinforce the adjudicatory system laid down in Part XI UNCLOS by providing it with effective and capillary enforcement. International Seabed Authority, *Draft Regulations on Exploitation of Mineral Resources in the Area*, available https://isa.org.jm/files/files/documents/isba_25_c_wp1-e_0.pdf (last accessed October 2022).
340. *Pro:* Fabio Tronchetti, *Legal Aspects of Space Resource Utilization*, in *Handbook of Space Law* 796-798 (Frans Von Der Dunk & Fabio Tronchetti eds., 2015); *contra:* Mahulena Hofmann & Tanja Masson-Zwaan, *Introduction to Space Law* 105 (2019).
341. Draft Report of the Legal Subcommittee on its 61st Session, held in Vienna from the 28 of March to the 8 of April 2022, UN Doc A/AC.105/C.2/L.321/Add.1 3-6 (2022).

i *Supporting Legal Arguments*

From a purely legal standpoint, providing a regime with dedicated institutions for developing, applying, adjudicating and enforcing norms is what the law normally does. In terms of legitimacy, the establishment of competent institutions increases the predictability and consistency of the system for the benefit of its subjects. In terms of effectiveness, a clear distribution of competencies ensures that the system can perform its functions in a timely and justiciable manner, again for the benefit of its subjects.

In addition to these systemic reasons, the suitability of the UNCLOS institutional model for the governance of space resource activities is also supported by the several legal similarities between celestial bodies and the Deep Seabed. Both domains are legally subtracted from the national jurisdiction and sovereign influence of States.[342] Both areas shall be explored and used for the benefit and in the interest of all Countries,[343] and all activities thereby shall be for exclusively peaceful purposes.[344] In both domains, States are internationally responsible and liable for private activities[345] and shall ensure compliance with international law, including the UN Charter, in the interests of maintaining international peace and security and promoting international cooperation and understanding.[346] The only legal difference between the Deep Seabed and celestial bodies lies in the former status as the "common heritage of mankind."[347] However, *in itself*, this expression does not mean anything in particular from a legal standpoint. The CHM concept did not exist in legal terms until it was suggested for the first time by Ambassador Pardo[348] and can be implemented through different legal implications.[349] The Deep Seabed and its mineral resources were not the common heritage of humankind until the drafters of UNCLOS decided to make them so,[350] and the related implications on their use are the result of a *political* choice realized with legal tools. Truth be told, the space community has previously made exactly the same choice with the Moon Agreement.[351]

The *political* failure of that choice is precisely the reason why the UNCLOS model is not favorably considered in current discussions.[352]

342. Respectively under Article II OST (*supra* note 11) and Article 137 UNCLOS (*supra* note 267).
343. Respectively under Article I OST (*supra* note 11) and Article 140 UNCLOS (*supra* note 267).
344. Respectively under Article IV (2) OST (*supra* note 11) and Article 141 UNCLOS (*supra* note 267).
345. Respectively under Articles VI-VII OST (*supra* note 11) and Article 139 UNCLOS (*supra* note 267).
346. Respectively under Article III OST (*supra* note 11) and Article 138 UNCLOS (*supra* note 267).
347. Except for the Parties to the Moon Agreement of course.
348. Rudolph P. Arnold, *The Common Heritage of Mankind as a Legal Concept*, 9 International Lawyer 153 (1975).
349. As demonstrated by the different regimes set out under the MA and the UNCLOS.
350. Treves, *supra* note 271.
351. For an analysis of the CHM principle under the Moon Agreement, *see* section 1.3.2 in Chapter 2.
352. Nonetheless, the fact remains that the institutional deficiencies of the multi-level regulatory system of space mining can benefit from the development of tools based on the UNCLOS legal model.

ii *Resisting Political Objections*

It is thus by adopting a *political* perspective that one can understand the reasons why the UNCLOS model is not suitable for the governance of space resource activities. The first objection, usually moved against the applicability of the UNCLOS model, concerns the time that would be required to set up a similar international regime with reference to space mining. As seen in the previous paragraph, it took about thirty years to develop the governance system laid down in the UNCLOS.[353] Several conferences and instruments have been negotiated for decades so that the Convention, and especially its Part XI, could reach its current status. Even though the negotiations of an international regime for the governance of space resource activities would likely have a much narrower scope than the UNCLOS, it can be safely assumed that no concrete result would be achieved before at least ten to fifteen years. This determination is notably based upon the workplan agreed upon by the Working Group on Legal Aspects of Space Resource Activities (SRWG) at the 61st Session of the LSC of UNCOPUOS.[354] Under the recently approved workplan, it will take at least five years before the SRWG can finalize *just* "a set of initial recommended principles for such activities for the consideration of and consensus agreement by the Committee."[355] Accordingly, it is safe to estimate that the establishment of a fully fledged institutional regime like the one laid down in the UNCLOS would take at least double the time.

The second political objection raised against the suitability of the UNCLOS model for the governance of space resource activities concerns its excessive bureaucratization. As seen, the ISA is composed of four organs, each with different competencies and procedures.[356] The licensing process designed by the ISA for the approval of an exploitation permit is also rather complex.[357] Further, under Article 8 of Annex III to the Convention, any application from a developed State for the exploration of the Deep Seabed is required to identify two areas of sufficient size and equal economic value to accommodate two mining operations.[358] Upon a discretionary decision of the ISA, one of the two sites will later become a "reserved area"[359] for the exclusive conduct of mining activities by the Enterprise. The applicant might then get a permit for exploiting

353. Treves, *supra* note 271.
354. Report of the Chair and Vice-Chair of the working group established under the Legal Subcommittee agenda item entitled "General exchange of views on potential legal models for activities in the exploration, exploitation and utilization of space resources," UN Doc A/AC.105/C.2/2022/SRA/L.1, p. 1 (2022) [hereinafter: "SRWG Report"].
355. *Ibid.* It should be noted that the five years refer only to the finalization of a set of principles. This number therefore does not include the time required first "for consideration and consensus agreement by the Committee," and then for "possible adoption by the United Nations General Assembly as a dedicated resolution."
356. Article 158 UNCLOS, *supra* note 267.
357. Under Article 153 (3) UNCLOS, "activities in the Area shall be carried out in accordance with a formal written plan of work drawn up in accordance with Annex III and approved by the Council after review by the Legal and Technical Commission." *Supra* note 267.
358. Article 8 Annex III to the UNCLOS, *supra* note 267.
359. Updates and information on the status of reserved areas are provided https://www.isa.org.jm/files/files/documents/statusofreservedareas-01-2019-a.pdf by the ISA (last accessed October 2022).

the other site under an additional regulatory framework that the ISA aims to finalize by the year 2023.[360] Further, this upcoming regulatory framework will also have to include provisions for sharing the revenues generated by commercial activities in the Deep Seabed.[361]

The third and final objection against the suitability of the UNCLOS as potential model for the regulation of space mining rests on considerations of *adaptive governance*. Supporters of this position argue that it is not feasible to design a fully fledged international regime for the conduct of space mining activities in the early stages of these activities.[362] It is better to wait first for these activities to happen, learn from the initial years of operations, develop best practices, and only at that point consider the potential development of international norms governing their conduct. For supporters of this position, their objection is further validated by the low level of interest in Deep Seabed mining demonstrated by operators worldwide.[363] While this is all technically correct, it is important to recall the reason why the UNCLOS regime was set up in the first place. As seen, the rationale behind Part XI UNCLOS is to ensure that Deep Seabed mining is conducted for the benefit of humankind and without prejudice to the marine environment.[364] This prioritization very well implies the possibility that commercial players might decide not to engage in Deep Seabed mining because the conditions imposed under the UNCLOS make their business not (sufficiently) profitable. If due to the strict requirements imposed under the Convention, no entity would ever mine the Deep Seabed, the regime of Part XI UNCLOS would have still met its institutional goal of ensuring that the Deep Seabed is exploited *only at certain conditions*. In accordance with this logic, a number of scientific institutions and marine activists are strongly criticizing the decision of the ISA to finalize its "Draft Regulations on Exploitation of Mineral Resources in the Area"[365] by 2023 because they consider this timeline insufficient to ensure proper protection of marine biodiversity.[366] Therefore, the adaptive governance argument could be convincing only to the extent that the priority is for space resource activities to happen even at the risk of unfair practices or environmental damage. Generally speaking, if the logic behind the development of regulation for space mining is to enable its *experimental* conduct as soon as possible, then all the objections mentioned above are certainly well founded. However, even

360. ISA Draft Exploitation Regulations, *supra* note 339.
361. Article 140 UNCLOS, *supra* note 267. Not by chance, several companies have protested against this system as unfair to pioneering operators, and many space businesses have already declared multiple times that they will not engage in space mining if an UNCLOS-like system would be put in place.
362. Especially due to the current lack of knowledge concerning the operational constraints and challenges posed by the extreme environments of celestial bodies.
363. Hofmann & Masson-Zwaan, *supra* note 340.
364. Article 137 UNCLOS, *supra* note 267.
365. ISA Draft Exploitation Regulations, *supra* note 339.
366. Jan Mellmann, *Deep Sea Mining: Why Now and How?*, available https://www.wfw.com/articles/deep-sea-mining-why-now-and-how/ (last accessed October 2022). In this regard, commentators are also questioning the ability of the ISA to continuously adjust its regulations to the latest environmental standards. Aline Jaeckel, *Deep Seabed Mining and Adaptive Management: The Procedural Challenges for the International Seabed Authority*, 70 Marine Policy 205-211 (2016).

though there is general consensus on the idea that regulation should proceed in an incremental manner, one should be careful in assuming that this experimental logic is universally shared. On the contrary, several Countries are worried about the potential negative effects of space mining on the environment of celestial bodies per se, not to mention its potential impact on the future conduct of scientific studies.[367] From this perspective, the UNCLOS remains an attractive model to be kept in mind. Therefore, there is margin to consider at least the partial relevance of this regime for reinforcing the multi-level system of space mining.

iii *A Legal Argument with Political Support?*

As seen from the debate reported above, discussions around the suitability of the UNCLOS model have so far been centered on regulatory and administrative processes.[368]

The present section aims to enrich this debate by offering a different approach focused on the relevance of adjudicatory mechanisms, with a specific focus on the Seabed Disputes Chamber model laid down at the end of Part XI UNCLOS.[369]

In light of the *impasse* described above, this author searched the Convention for useful legal tools that could also be accepted under the current political climate. Due to the underlined controversies regarding the UNCLOS' normative and enforcement mechanisms,[370] it seemed useful to switch the focus to the Convention's adjudicatory processes. Few contest that the system of space mining needs an agreed mechanism for solving the disputes that might arise due to the application of the OST principles to the space mining activities conducted in the early stages of regulatory development.[371] In the design of such mechanisms,[372] the polycentric adjudicatory system established by Part XI UNCLOS might prove to be particularly insightful. As seen earlier, disputes related to activities in the Area might be adjudicated by either the Seabed Chamber or by international arbitrators, with direct enforceability throughout national jurisdictions and without prejudice to the exclusive jurisdiction of other judicial bodies recognized

367. LSC Draft Report, *supra* note 341.
368. *Ibid*. Tronchetti, *supra* note 340; Hofmann & Masson-Zwaan, *supra* note 340.
369. As analyzed in section 2.1.3 in Chapter 3.
370. Regarding the first, States have agreed to draft an initial set of principles shaping the development of secondary rules at the national level. Concerning the second, there is no consensus in UNCOPUOS for the establishment of an international authority similar to the ISA. *See* LSC Draft Report, *supra* note 341.
371. For an overview of these planned missions, *see* Kaitlyn Johnson, *Fly Me to the Moon: Worldwide Cislunar and Lunar Missions* (2022), available https://csis-website-prod.s3.amazonaws.com/s3fs-public/publication/220215_Johnson_FlyMe_Moon.pdf?eBOSyAKB1ite5cort60IluuBQWvYyADa (last accessed October 2022). Without these mechanisms, the level of legal uncertainty within the system will soon become intolerable for investments and commitments by private operators.
372. Which might lead to either establish a new institution or temporarily attribute such competence to an existing one. For example, the United Arab Emirates are currently considering the development of a dedicated court for space law disputes under their "Courts of Space" initiative. *Supra* note 186.

under the Convention. Taking inspiration from this regime and building upon the observations made at the end of section 1 on the critical role of arbitration in enforcement procedures, it would be possible to design the development of similar mechanisms for solving space mining disputes. As will be discussed in section 2.4 of this chapter, these mechanisms could be crafted to leverage the strengths of international courts and arbitrators, reconnect with domestic systems, ensure prompt enforcement and even integrate potentially competing jurisdictions from relevant overlapping regimes.[373]

2.2 The International Telecommunication Union

Originally founded in 1865 and currently counting 193 Member States,[374] the ITU[375] is the oldest universal international organization and one of the most influential regulatory bodies in the world. The purpose of the ITU is to administer the allocation of bands in the radio-frequency spectrum, as well as the allotment of radio frequencies and registration of related assignments.[376] Within the space domain, the ITU is entrusted with the allotment and registration of orbital positions associated with radio frequencies. Through the exercise of these competencies, the ITU complements the legal regime laid down within the *Corpus Iuris Spatialis* by preventing harmful interference in the use of radio frequencies and associated orbital positions for space activities.[377] To complement the previous analysis of the adjudicatory mechanisms offered by the UNCLOS, this section considers the suitability of the coordination procedures laid down in the ITU regime as a way to reduce the need for *ex post* adjudication and enforcement. In this regard, particular attention is thus dedicated to the norms and mechanisms governing the allocation, allotment and assignment of radio frequencies and associated orbital positions under the ITU Radio Regulations.

2.2.1 Evolution and Composition of the ITU

Today the ITU is a specialized agency of the United Nations,[378] but its history is older than the UN.[379] The foundational agreement at the roots of the current ITU was originally concluded in 1865, bringing life to the former International Telegraph

373. As to which, *see* section 2.4.2 in Chapter 3.
374. As reported on the ITU website https://www.itu.int/en/about/Pages/default.aspx (last accessed October 2022).
375. ITU Constitution and Convention, *supra* note 268.
376. Article 1 ITU Constitution, *supra* note 268.
377. The ITU regime has successfully guaranteed safe and reliable use of the frequency spectrum and associated orbital positions over the last fifty years. Accordingly, its procedures to prevent and resolve situations of harmful interference might provide a potentially useful model for the development of enforcement mechanisms within the multi-level regulatory system of space mining. Hofmann & Masson-Zwaan, *supra* note 340 at 133.
378. The list of the Specialized Agencies of the United Nations is available https://www.un.org/en/about-us/specialized-agencies (last accessed October 2022).
379. *Supra* note 374.

Union.[380] Throughout the centuries, the scope of the ITU was constantly adapted to the evolution of new communication technologies. In 1932, the International Telegraph Convention was merged with the 1906 International Radiotelegraph Convention, producing the very first edition of the International Telecommunication Convention and changing the name of the related organization into the current one. When the first satellite was launched in 1957, States all over the world immediately agreed on the importance of expanding ITU competencies to deal with space communications.[381] Two years later, at the 1959 World Administrative Radio Conference, the ITU laid down the foundations of current regulations of satellite communications, introducing the concepts of earth and space "station" as well as of space and earth "service" and allocating the very first frequencies for space research.[382] As space communications expanded and became increasingly important, the ITU devoted more and more of its attention and resources to its coordination. Few of the last major developments within the ITU framework are the 1994 reorganization of the ITU Membership and Sectors and the 1998 adoption of the Allotment Plan for geostationary satellites.[383] Since then, further changes have focused on amending the secondary framework developed by the ITU, the Radio Regulations, to ensure their adaptation to the evolution of satellite communication technologies.[384]

The ITU is one of the few intergovernmental organizations welcoming the participation of non-governmental entities composed of States and Sectors Members.

In accordance with the intergovernmental nature of the Union, only Member States are provided with voting rights, whereas Sectors Members can express their views and participate in the work of ITU's technical bodies.[385] Due to this peculiar composition, the institutional structure of the ITU features three governing bodies and three Sectors.[386]

The governing bodies of the Union are the Plenipotentiary Conference, the Council and the World Radio Conferences (WRCs), whereas the three Sectors are Radiocommunication, Telecommunication Standardization and Telecommunication Development.[387] These governing bodies and Sectors are assisted and coordinated by a General Secretariat.[388] As mentioned, the difference between bodies and organs is not only functional but also structural. Governing bodies are open only to State Members,

380. A more detailed overview of the ITU's history is available https://www.itu.int/en/history/Pages/DiscoverITUsHistory.aspx on its dedicated portal (last accessed October 2022).
381. Hofmann & Masson-Zwaan, *supra* note 340 at 134.
382. *Ibid.*
383. Francis Lyall, *International Communications: The International Telecommunication Union and the Universal Postal Union* 125 (2016).
384. An interesting overview of the goals driving the updating processes of the Radio Regulations can be found in Mitsuhiro Sakamoto, *WRC's Challenge to Meet Technology Development*, in *Innovation in Outer Space: International and African Legal Perspectives* 56-62 (Mahulena Hofmann & P.J. Blount eds., 2018) [book hereinafter: "Innovatio in Outer Space"].
385. Pursuant to Articles 2-3 ITU Constitution, *supra* note 268.
386. Article 7 ITU Constitution, *supra* note 268.
387. *Ibid.*
388. *Ibid.*

whereas the Sectors also welcome the participation of Sector Members, even though without voting rights.[389]

To begin with the governing bodies, the Plenipotentiary Conference is the supreme organ of the ITU and is composed of all its Member States.[390] The Plenipotentiary Conference has the exclusive power to amend the foundational framework of the ITU, i.e., the Constitution and the Convention, and decides the composition of all other organs.[391]

The Council is the governing body of the Union and is composed of 25% of its Member States,[392] elected by the Plenipotentiary Conferences in accordance with predetermined geographic criteria ensuring a balanced representation of all the regions of the world.[393] The Council acts on behalf of the Plenipotentiary Conference and exercises the fundamental executive powers attributed to the ITU.[394] The WRCs are regular gatherings of both ITU States and Sector Members entrusted with the power to amend the most important normative product of the ITU, the Radio Regulations.[395] The General Secretariat is the administrative organ of the ITU, and it is composed of a Secretary General, its Deputy, and their staff.[396] The Secretary General is elected by the Plenipotentiary Conference and exercises the most important administrative functions within the Union.[397]

Per their part, the Sectors are the technical organs of the ITU and are organized into three branches: Radiocommunication,[398] Telecommunication Standardization[399] and finally, Telecommunication Development.[400] These organs are entrusted with the operational functions of the ITU, are all headed by a Bureau and concretely work through several working and study groups, world and regional conferences and assemblies.[401] Among the three sectors, Radiocommunication is the most relevant for the purposes of the present analysis. The Radiocommunication Sector is headed by a Bureau[402] and works in close cooperation with the national authorities of ITU Member States in charge of frequency management, which in the language of the Union are called *administrations*.[403] The goal of this Sector is to ensure "the rational, equitable,

389. Hofmann & Masson-Zwaan, *supra* note 340 at 136-137.
390. Article 8 ITU Constitution, *supra* note 268.
391. *Ibid.*
392. Article 10 ITU Constitution, *supra* note 268.
393. Article 9 ITU Constitution, *supra* note 268.
394. Article 10 ITU Constitution, *supra* note 268.
395. Article 7 ITU Constitution, *supra* note 268. For more information on this process *see* Sakamoto, *supra* note 384.
396. Article 11 ITU Constitution, *supra* note 268.
397. *Ibid.*
398. Articles 12-16 ITU Constitution, *supra* note 268.
399. Articles 17-20 ITU Constitution, *supra* note 268.
400. Articles 21-24 ITU Constitution, *supra* note 268.
401. Lyall, *supra* note 383 at 155. As mentioned, non-governmental entities can participate in the activities of the Sectors, even though without voting rights.
402. Article 16 ITU Constitution, *supra* note 268.
403. For an overview of the Radiocommunication Sector, *see* Federico Bergamasco, *The ITU and ICAO Regulating Aeronautical Safety Services and Related Radio Spectrum* 60-67 (2021).

efficient and economical use of the radiofrequency spectrum by all radiocommunication services, including those using the geostationary-satellite or other satellite orbits."[404] The Radiocommunication Sector achieves this goal by managing the application and ensuring respect[405] for the ITU Radio Regulations (RR),[406] which in turn govern the allocation, allotment, assignment and registration of radio frequencies and associated orbits, including the technical parameters to be followed by operators.[407]

2.2.2 The ITU Regime for the Allocation, Allotment and Assignment of Radio Frequencies and Associated Orbital Positions

As mentioned, the ITU performs several different functions. In accordance with the scope of the present chapter, this section focuses its attention on the provisions of the Radio Regulations for the allocation, allotment, assignment and recording of radio frequencies and associated orbital positions, as well as on the binding procedures for the resolution of harmful interference. The following paragraphs present an overview of this framework and then evaluate how it can contribute to the reinforcement of the multi-level regulatory system of space mining by introducing norms and procedures able to reduce the need for *ex post* adjudication and enforcement.

i Definitions

First of all, it is important to note that under Article 1 of the Radio Regulation, *allocation* means the distribution of frequencies to a *service* (i.e., to a specific activity, like broadcasting);[408] *allotment* means the distribution of allocated frequencies to *areas or countries* (i.e., to national administrations managing the spectrum at the national level, either grouped on a regional basis or individually);[409] *assignment* means the distribution of allotted frequencies to *stations* (i.e., the concrete infrastructure used by operators);[410] *recording* means the inclusion, with a favorable determination, of a given assignment within ITU's Master International Frequency Register.[411] As a result of this process, recorded frequency assignments shall have the right to international recognition, "which means that other administrations shall take it into account when making their own assignments, in order to avoid harmful interference."[412] The regime laid down in the Radio Regulations is based upon the special legal status of frequencies and associated orbits as limited natural resources, as established by Article 44 of the ITU

404. Article 12 ITU Constitution, *supra* note 268.
405. Article 14 ITU Constitution, *supra* note 268.
406. International Telecommunication Union's Radio Regulations, adopted by the 2019 World Radiocommunication Conference (WRC-19), available https://www.itu.int/pub/R-REG-RR (last accessed October 2022) [hereinafter: "ITU RR"].
407. Hofmann & Masson-Zwaan, *supra* note 340 at 141.
408. Article 1.16 ITU RR, *supra* note 406.
409. Article 1.17 ITU RR, *supra* note 406.
410. Article 1.18 ITU RR, *supra* note 406.
411. At the conditions and pursuant to the procedure laid down in Article 11 ITU RR, *supra* note 406.
412. Article 8 ITU RR, *supra* note 406.

Constitution. Pursuant to this provision, "radio frequencies and any associated orbits, including the geostationary-satellite orbit" are "limited natural resources" which must be used "rationally, efficiently and economically" to ensure their equitable access by all States, "taking into account the special needs of the developing countries and the geographical situation of particular countries."[413] It is the legal status of radio frequencies and associated orbits as limited natural resources under Article 44 of the ITU Constitution that justifies the limitations and procedures imposed through the Radio Regulations for their rational, efficient and economic use, with the goal of guaranteeing their equitable access to all States.[414]

ii Reserved Slots (Planned Services)

Depending on the orbital plane and radio frequency involved, the RR distinguish between "non-planned" and "planned" services.[415] Planned services concern selected geostationary orbital positions and associated frequencies, which are considered of particular importance due to their scarcity and strategic relevance.[416] In accordance with their status, the RR subject the use of these orbits and associated frequencies to special *a priori* planning procedures guaranteeing equitable access in view of their future use.[417] These procedures are laid down in Appendices 30, 30A and 30B to the Radio Regulations, which respectively govern the allocation and allotment of broadcasting-satellite services (BSS) and fixed-satellite services (FSS) from geostationary and geosynchronous positions.[418] The core mechanism governing these procedures is the allocation of these resources to specific services and their subsequent allotment to ITU Member States, either on a regional or global scale, regardless of their technological capability to bring them into use.[419] BSS plans are laid down at the level of the three ITU Regions and are based on the previous allotment of selected orbital positions to ITU Member States in light of their geographical location.[420] In accordance with the BSS plans, each ITU Member State has the right to transmit on certain frequencies from the orbital position assigned to it over a certain period of time.[421] FSS plans are laid down at the global ITU level and provide each ITU Member State with

413. Article 44 ITU Constitution, *supra* note 268.
414. Hofmann & Masson-Zwaan, *supra* note 340 at 133-135. In this regard, it is important to underline that within the ITU regime orbital positions are always considered in association with radio frequencies.
415. Following the guidance provided by the ITU itself, available https://www.itu.int/en/ITU-R/space/elearning/Pages/elearningFAQ.aspx (last accessed October 2022).
416. Hofmann & Masson-Zwaan, *supra* note 340 at 146. Specifically, these refer to geosynchronous orbital slots as well as particularly convenient geostationary slots for broadcasting purposes.
417. *Ibid.*
418. Appendices 30, 30A and 30B, ITU RR *supra* note 406.
419. ITU Radio Regulatory Framework for Space Services 3-4, available https://www.itu.int/en/ITU-R/space/snl/Documents/ITU-Space_reg.pdf (last accessed October 2022) [hereinafter: "ITU Framework Assessment"].
420. Articles 1-3 Appendix 30, ITU RR *supra* note 406.
421. For example, under the first BSS Regional Plan for the Americas adopted in 1983, each ITU Member State within that region got four BSS satellite allotments per time zone, within its borders, for twenty years. Hofmann & Masson-Zwaan, *supra* note 340 at 146.

one geosynchronous orbital slot together with the associated frequencies for one national satellite providing domestic FSS.[422] In accordance with these allotment plans, frequency assignments will be notified under special procedures laid down in the relevant Appendix. However, differently than in the case of non-planned services, international recognition of these assignments is guaranteed solely by the relevant allotment Plan and only to the extent that it conforms to that.[423]

iii First Come First Served (Non-planned Services)

All other frequencies and associated orbits are considered "non-planned" and are allocated, allotted and assigned through coordination procedures aiming at their efficient use and interference-free operations.[424] These radio frequencies are allocated to primary and secondary services within each of the three ITU Regions through a dedicated frequencies table.[425] Based upon the determinations made in the table, radio frequencies are then assigned to specific stations in accordance with the procedures laid down in Article 9 and Article 11 of the Radio Regulations.[426] Pursuant to these provisions, before notifying a frequency assignment in view of its recording in the Master Record, the concerned administration shall first exhaust either the advance public information or coordination procedures, depending on the use of certain orbital positions and/or specific frequency bands.[427]

The advance public information procedure is the simplest one and essentially concerns all non-geostationary (non-GSO) satellite systems,[428] except those operating in certain frequency bands[429]—all other systems are subject to the coordination procedure. Any administration planning the assignment of frequencies and associated orbital positions to a satellite system which is not subject to the coordination procedure shall send to the Radiocommunication Bureau (the Bureau or BR) a general description of the network or system for advance publication in the Radiocommunication Bureau International Frequency Information Circular (BR IFIC).[430] After having verified the completeness and accuracy of the information received, the Bureau shall publish it in a Special Section of its BR IFIC within two months.[431] Upon publication of the BR IFIC containing information on the announced system, national administrations have four months to assess whether it may cause unacceptable interference to their existing or

422. Articles 1-4 Appendix 30B, ITU RR *supra* note 406.
423. Hofmann & Masson-Zwaan, *supra* note 340 at 147.
424. ITU Framework Assessment, *supra* note 419 at 4.
425. Article 5 ITU RR *supra* note 406. For the purposes of allocation and allotment, section I of Article 5 divides the world in three Regions, section II distinguishes between primary and secondary services, whereas sections III and IV distribute them in the frequencies table.
426. Determining a process in two steps: first, advance public information or coordination, and then, notification and recording.
427. ITU Framework Assessment, *supra* note 419 at 4.
428. Defined under section VIII of Article 1 ITU RR, *supra* note 406.
429. Article 9 ITU RR, *supra* note 406.
430. Section 1, Article 9 ITU RR, *supra* note 406. Interestingly, such description shall be sent "not earlier than seven years and preferably not later than two years before the planned date of bringing into use of the network or system."
431. Article 9.2B ITU RR, *supra* note 406.

planned systems and eventually send their comments to both the concerned administration and the Bureau.[432] If no comments are received within four months, it may be assumed that there are no objections to the announced system, and the publishing administration may start the notification procedure under Article 11 RR.[433] In case of comments manifesting potential harmful interference, both administrations shall endeavor to cooperate in joint efforts to resolve any difficulties, with the possible assistance of the Bureau (at the request of either party).[434] Meanwhile, the Bureau shall inform all administrations of the list of administrations which have sent comments and provide a summary of the comments received.[435] In case of difficulties, the publishing administration has the onus of exploring all possible means to resolve them from its side, i.e., without expecting any adjustment from the concerned administrations.[436] If these efforts are unsuccessful, the ball passes to the concerned administrations, which shall also make every possible effort to resolve the difficulties by means of mutually acceptable adjustments to their networks.[437] Continuing disagreements may be decided by the Radio Regulations Board, with the possibility of appeal at the upcoming WRC.[438]

The coordination procedure is mandatory for frequency assignments concerning GSO systems, non-GSO systems in specific frequency bands, or other stations falling under the scope of Article 9.7-9.21.[439] The main difference with the advance public information procedure is that, in this case, the publishing administration shall identify in advance, to the extent possible, the administrations with which coordination is to be effected.[440] Once that determination has been made, the request for coordination shall be sent either directly to the identified administrations or the Bureau, depending on the systems involved. In cases where the Bureau has to be involved, it shall revise the information received and, after having added any other administration with which coordination may be necessary, it shall publish it in a special section of the BR IFIC and inform the concerned administrations.[441] An administration receiving a *direct request* for coordination from another administration shall promptly acknowledge it.[442] Failure to acknowledge a request for coordination will result in a series of notices at the end of which it shall be deemed that (1) the silent administration will make no complaints in case of harmful interference to its assignments by the system for which coordination was requested and (2) that the use of said assignments by the silent administration will not cause harmful interference to the system for which coordination was requested.[443]

432. Article 9.3 ITU RR, *supra* note 406.
433. *Ibid.*
434. *Ibid.*
435. Article 9.5 ITU RR, *supra* note 406.
436. Article 9.4 ITU RR, *supra* note 406.
437. *Ibid.*
438. Article 10 (2) ITU Convention, *supra* note 268.
439. ITU Framework Assessment, *supra* note 419 at 4-8.
440. Article 9.28 ITU RR, *supra* note 406. This determination has to be done through a series of calculation methods and criteria laid down in Appendix 5 to the ITU RR.
441. Article 9.34-9.38 ITU RR, *supra* note 406.
442. Article 9.45 ITU RR, *supra* note 406.
443. Article 9.47-9.49 ITU RR, *supra* note 406.

An administration receiving a request for coordination *from the Bureau* shall promptly examine the matter.[444] Over the following four months, it shall either inform the Bureau and the requesting administration of its agreement[445] or, alternatively, motivate its disagreement with circumstanced information on its own assignments, including punctual suggestions for a satisfactory resolution of the matter.[446] Both the requesting and responding administrations shall make every possible mutual effort to overcome the difficulties in a manner acceptable to the parties concerned.[447] In case of continuing disagreement, the Bureau will get involved as a mediator among the administrations.[448] If disagreement persists, the requesting administration may still proceed with the assignment and notification under Article 11 but shall defer these tasks for six months from the starting date of the coordination procedure.[449] Also, in this case, continuing disagreements may be decided by the Radio Regulations Board, with the possibility of appeal at the upcoming WRC.[450]

The second step of the procedure deals with the notification and recording of frequency assignments within ITU's Master International Frequency Register[451] for obtaining international recognition.[452] To ensure proper coordination, the notification of frequency assignments related to space services, systems or networks shall reach the Bureau at least three years before their planned brought into use.[453] All notifications shall contain the information mandated for the specific assignment in accordance with Appendix 4 to the RR.[454] Upon receipt of complete notices, the Bureau shall publish them in the BR IFIC within no more than two months.[455] Each notice for frequency assignments shall be examined by the Bureau in light of its conformity with (1) the Table of Frequency Allocations,[456] (2) the coordination procedure,[457] (3) the probability of harmful interference that may be caused to or by assignments recorded with a favorable finding under a number of different circumstances,[458] and finally (4) the relevant world or regional allotment or assignment plan,[459] as relevant and appropriate. The examination of a frequency notice may lead to either a favorable or unfavorable finding.[460] A favorable finding leads to recording the assignment in the Master

444. Article 9.50 ITU RR, *supra* note 406.
445. Article 9.51 ITU RR, *supra* note 406.
446. Article 9.52 ITU RR, *supra* note 406.
447. Article 9.53 ITU RR, *supra* note 406.
448. Article 9.63 ITU RR, *supra* note 406.
449. Article 9.64 ITU RR, *supra* note 406.
450. Article 10 (2) ITU Convention, *supra* note 268.
451. Article 11 ITU RR, *supra* note 406.
452. As seen, international recognition of a frequency assignment means that other administrations shall take it into account when making their own assignments, in order to avoid harmful interference. Article 8 ITU RR, *supra* note 406.
453. Article 11.25 ITU RR, *supra* note 406.
454. Article 11.27 ITU RR, *supra* note 406.
455. Article 11.28 ITU RR, *supra* note 406.
456. Article 11.31 ITU RR, *supra* note 406.
457. Article 11.32 ITU RR, *supra* note 406.
458. Article 11.32A and 11.33 ITU RR, *supra* note 406.
459. Article 11.34 ITU RR, *supra* note 406.
460. Article 11.36-11.39 ITU RR, *supra* note 406.

Registry, which in turn creates the right to international recognition.[461] Conversely, all unfavorable findings lead to returning the notice to the concerned administration, with an indication of appropriate action to be undertaken.[462] In some cases, the assignment may also be recorded for information purposes (i.e., without international recognition) if the administration accepts to assume certain obligations.[463] Finally, recorded frequency assignments have to be brought into use no later than seven years following the date of receipt by the Bureau of the complete information[464] at the start of the relevant procedure applicable under Article 9 RR. This rule is of critical importance because any frequency assignment which is not brought into use within the required period shall be canceled by the Bureau.[465]

iv *The Resolution of Harmful Interference*

The golden rule of the ITU is that all stations, whatever their purpose, must be established and operated in such a manner as not to cause harmful interference to the radio services or communications of other Member States in accordance with the provisions of the Radio Regulations.[466] The detailed procedures summarized above implement this rule through a combination of proactive coordination and *ex post* recognition.[467] In addition to following the Radio Regulations, ITU Member States are further required to take "all practicable steps" to prevent the operation of "electrical apparatus and installations of all kinds" from causing harmful interference with the radio services and communications of others.[468] Despite all these rules and efforts, harmful interference might, of course, still occur. In this regard, it is important to note that interference is considered to be *harmful* when it endangers the functioning of a radio navigation service or of other safety services or seriously degrades, obstructs, or repeatedly interrupts a radiocommunication service operating in accordance with Radio Regulations.[469] Situations of harmful interference are addressed by section VI of Article 15 of the Radio Regulations. As a general rule of thumb, ITU Member States have to settle problems of harmful interference in a spirit of utmost goodwill and mutual assistance.[470] In furtherance of this principle, national administrations shall closely cooperate in the detection and elimination of harmful interference.[471] The first step consists in determining the source and characteristics of the harmful interference

461. Article 8 ITU RR, *supra* note 406. This recording may also include notes depending on the details of the procedure followed.
462. Article 11.36-11.39 ITU RR, *supra* note 406.
463. Article 11.36 ITU RR, *supra* note 406.
464. Article 11.44 ITU RR, *supra* note 406.
465. *Ibid.*
466. Article 45 ITU Constitution, *supra* note 268. The prevention of harmful interference has been defined as the very *raison d'etre* of the entire ITU legal system. Francis Lyall, *Law and Space Telecommunications* 351 (1989).
467. Hofmann & Masson-Zwaan, *supra* note 340 at 144-145.
468. Article 45 ITU Constitution, *supra* note 268.
469. Article 1.169 ITU RR, *supra* note 406.
470. Article 15.22 ITU RR, *supra* note 406.
471. Article 15.25 ITU RR, *supra* note 406.

if needed, also with the assistance of the Bureau[472] as well as of other administrations.[473] Once that determination is done, the administration having jurisdiction over the station suffering from the interference shall inform the administration having jurisdiction over the interfering station, providing it with all useful information that it has at its disposal.[474] On receiving the said information, the informed administration shall, as soon as possible, acknowledge receipt.[475] Thereafter, the two administrations shall work together to resolve the issue. If the interference persists, the concerned administration may address a "report of irregularity or infraction" to the administration having jurisdiction over the source of the harmful interference.[476] In such case, the informed administration shall ascertain the facts and take the necessary actions to (eventually) remove the harmful interference.[477] If the harmful interference continues to persist, the concerned administration may inform the Bureau and request its assistance in resolving the situation.[478] Upon such request, the Bureau shall immediately collect all relevant information from the involved administrations[479] and then forward them its conclusions and recommendations, including a request from prompt action addressed to the administration believed to be responsible for the source of harmful interference.[480]

If despite all these efforts the harmful interference continues to persist, at the request of any administration involved, the Bureau shall prepare a report completed of all necessary information and documentation for consideration at the next meeting of the Radio Regulation Board.[481] At this point, the Board may take any required action, including the possible cancellation of the assignment causing the harmful interference.[482] Should that be decided, the Board's decision would then be enforced by the Bureau, whereas the affected administration may present an appeal at the upcoming WRC.[483]

2.2.3 *Suitability of the ITU Regime*

Similar to the UNCLOS, this is also not the first time that the ITU regime has been considered a potential model for the governance of space resource activities.[484] Different from the UNCLOS, opinions on the suitability of the ITU regime are generally

472. Article 15.34 ITU RR, *supra* note 406.
473. Article 15.32 ITU RR, *supra* note 406.
474. Article 15.34 ITU RR, *supra* note 406.
475. Article 15.35 ITU RR, *supra* note 406. In order to encourage administrations to respond timely, this provision clarifies that such acknowledgement "shall not constitute an acceptance of responsibility."
476. Article 15.39 ITU RR, *supra* note 406.
477. Article 15.21 ITU RR, *supra* note 406.
478. Article 15.41-15.42 ITU RR, *supra* note 406.
479. Article 15.44 ITU RR, *supra* note 406.
480. Article 15.46 ITU RR, *supra* note 406.
481. Article 11.42A ITU RR, *supra* note 406.
482. *Ibid.*
483. Article 7 ITU Convention, *supra* note 268.
484. Hofmann & Masson-Zwaan, *supra* note 340 at 105; Tronchetti, *supra* note 340 at 798-803.

much more favorable.[485] This is for several reasons. First, it is a fact that the ITU has successfully ensured the smooth operation of both radio and telecommunication services over the last two centuries. Second, the balance between efficiency and equitability achieved under the ITU regime is particularly appealing to the regulation of space mining. The development of a binary regime featuring both (1) a coordinated *first-come-first-served* mechanism ensuring efficient uses together with (2) a predetermined allotment system ensuring equitable access seems like the perfect compromise for the governance of space resource activities.[486] Third, the ITU's incentivization of self-compliance offers a highly practical solution to the enforcement challenges of space mining. Most of the success of the ITU relies on a regulatory regime that incentivizes operators to follow the rules rather than try to circumvent them.[487] Minimizing the need for *ex post* action through proactive coordination would be ideal also for space mining in light of the practical difficulties impeding the material exercise of enforcement powers on celestial bodies. Fourth and final, the diffused nature of the ITU administrative system is quite compatible with the configuration of space law as multi-level system under Article VI OST.

Having said that, it is important to note that the successful results of the ITU have not been achieved overnight and that its impressive accomplishments crucially depend on a massive administrative apparatus. As such, to fairly evaluate the suitability of the ITU regime as a model for the governance of space resource activities, it is important to underscore that the Union currently counts around 700 employees[488] under a budget of EUR 165 million per annum,[489] in addition to the dedicated personnel working in 193 national administrations all over the world. As shown in the previous paragraphs, the heart of the ITU system beats in its coordination and planning activities. The vast majority of potentially harmful interferences are prevented at these stages, and a significant portion of ITU's financial and human resources is invested in the planning, coordination and notification procedures. Nothing alike currently exists for space mining, nor is there any intention to establish it. The question then becomes: is it possible to successfully apply the ITU model *in the absence of an ITU-like organization?* To properly answer this question, it is crucial to also remember that the means employed by the ITU are proportionate to the number of tasks assigned to the Union. Every year the ITU oversees thousands of filings, whereas the number of planned space resource activities is significantly lower and will stay as such for many years to come.[490] As such, the number of required resources should be reduced proportionally. With this *caveat* in mind, it is possible to favorably determine the suitability of the ITU

485. Not only among authors, but also within the framework of UNCOPUOS. LSC Draft Report, *supra* note 341.
486. Hofmann & Masson-Zwaan, *supra* note 340 at 105.
487. Mitsushiro Sakamoto, *Radio Regulations and Procedures in Cases of Harmful Interference*, in *Harmful Interference in Regulatory Perspective: Legal Rules for Interference-Free Radio Communication* 33 (Mahulena Hofmann ed., 2016).
488. About ITU, available https://www.itu.int/en/careers/Pages/default.aspx (last accessed October 2022).
489. Based upon the budget approved in 2019, available https://www.itu.int/md/S19-CL-C-0122/en (last accessed October 2022).
490. Johnson, *supra* note 371.

regime as a model even in the absence of an ITU-sized organization, provided that there is a minimum level of institutionalization.[491] In conclusion, learning from the successful experience of the ITU, it would be possible to reinforce the multi-level regulatory system of space mining through the introduction of enhanced coordination practices reducing the need for *ex post* adjudication and enforcement, with the twofold objective of preventing harmful interference while also promoting equitable uses.[492]

2.3 The Antarctic Treaty

The last regime that remains to be considered within this section is the 1959 Treaty, or AT.[493] As is well-known, this Treaty is part of a broader legal regime called ATS, which includes five international agreements governing the conduct of activities in Antarctica: the AT, the 1972 Convention on the Conservation of Antarctic Seals[494] (CCAS), the 1980 Convention on the Conservation of Antarctic Marine Living Resources[495] (CCAMLR), the 1988 Convention on the Regulation of Antarctic Mineral Resources[496] (the Wellington Convention) and finally the 1991 Protocol on Environmental Protection[497] (the Environmental Protocol or the Protocol). To complement the previous analysis on the suitability of the UNCLOS and ITU models for dedicated adjudication and enhanced coordination, this section focuses on the mechanisms laid down in Articles VIII and IX AT for confidence building and institutional consultation. Since the CCAS and CCAMLR deal with very specific issues which are not relevant for the purpose of the present analysis, whereas the Wellington Convention never entered into force, this section limits its considerations to the provisions of the AT and its Protocol.

2.3.1 Evolution and Membership of the AT

The AT was concluded during the 1957 International Geophysical Year, which at the time prompted scientific research and international cooperation[498] as means to foster the peaceful and successful use of the Antarctic region.[499] The international regime laid down in the AT has managed to promote compromise instead of conflict, ensuring the

491. This is because the key components of the ITU model—a balanced approach between efficient uses and equitable access achieved through a self-enforcing regime relying on information sharing and proactive coordination—are applicable regardless the number of activities or the size of the entities involved, so long as they are proportionate to the tasks of course.
492. As to which, *see* section 2.4.1 (i) in Chapter 3.
493. AT, *supra* note 269.
494. Convention on the Conservation of Antarctic Seals, London, *entered into force* March 11, 1978, ATS 1987 No. 11; 11 ILM 251 (1972) [hereinafter: "CCAS"].
495. Convention on the Conservation of Antarctic Marine Living Resources, *entered into force* April 7, 1982, ATS 1982 No. 9; 19 ILM 841 (1980) [hereinafter: "CCAMLR"].
496. Convention on the Regulation of Antarctic Mineral Resources, *not yet entered into force*, 27 ILM 868 (1988) [hereinafter: "Wellington Convention"].
497. Protocol on Environmental Protection to the Antarctic Treaty, *entered into force* January 14, 1998, ATS 1998 No. 6; 30 ILM 1455 (1991) [hereinafter: "PEPAT"].
498. It is interesting to underline that the International Geophysical Year also played an enabling role also for the beginning of activities and cooperation in space.
499. Arthur Watts, *International Law and the Antarctic Treaty System* 1-8 (1992).

protection of the continent's natural resources and preservation of its environment over the past fifty years.[500] This result is even more remarkable in light of the relatively limited participation in the Treaty, which currently counts fifty-four States Parties.[501] It is important to clarify that this limited participation is due to historical and practical reasons.[502] The AT was originally concluded among twelve States conducting exploration and scientific missions in Antarctica.[503] Prior to the conclusion of the Treaty, seven of them[504] had declared sovereignty over the portion of territory respectively explored by their nationals,[505] with other States considering the possibility of similar endeavors,[506] even though none of these claims was well recognized by the international community.[507] Prompted by the 1957 International Geophysical Year, the twelve original States recognized that it was "in the interest of all mankind that Antarctica shall continue for ever to be used exclusively for peaceful purposes and shall not become the scene or object of international discord."[508] As a result, they negotiated and concluded the AT "as a firm foundation for the continuation and development" of international cooperation in Antarctica on the basis of scientific investigation, also in furtherance of the "purposes and principles embodied in the Charter of the United Nations."[509] In time, additional States have joined the AT, some due to their activities in Antarctica and some out of a general interest in its preservation.[510] However, not all States Parties to the AT have the same rights. Based upon the governance system designed in Article IX of the Treaty, it is possible to distinguish between three categories of States: the original Signatories, the additional acceding States which prove their interest in Antarctica, and all remaining States.[511] Only States belonging to

500. Donald Rothwell, *The Antarctic Treaty Is Turning 60: In a Changed World, Is It Still Fit for Purpose?,* available https://www.downtoearth.org.in/blog/climate-change/the-antarctic-treaty-is-turning-60-in-a-changed-world-is-it-still-fit-for-purpose--77606 (last accessed October 2022).
501. As reported online on the Treaty's website https://www.ats.aq/devAS/Parties?lang=e (last accessed October 2022). The limited participation to the AT has been frequently criticized by non-State Parties as an argument to bring the governance of Antarctica under the UN. Neil Gilbert, *A Continent for Science and Peace: Governance in Antarctica*, in *Exploring the Last Continent: An Introduction to Antarctica* 329 (Daniela Liggett, Bryan Storey, Yvonne Cook & Veronika Meduna eds., 2015).
502. For a thorough analysis of States' participation to the AT, *see* Erik J. Molenaar, *Participation in the Antarctic Treaty,* 11 (2) The Polar Journal 360-380 (2021).
503. The original Parties to the AT are Argentina, Australia, Belgium, Chile, the French Republic, Japan, New Zealand, Norway, the Union of South Africa, the Union of Soviet Socialist Republics, the United Kingdom of Great Britain and Northern Ireland, and the United States of America.
504. Australia, New Zealand, Argentina, Chile, France, Norway and the United Kingdom. The claims advanced by the UK, Argentina and Chile were overlapping with each other.
505. Ruth Davis, *Enforcing Australian Law in Antarctica: The HSI Litigation,* 8 Melbourne Journal of International Law 148 (2007).
506. Watts, *supra* note 499 at 120.
507. *Ibid.*
508. AT Preamble, *supra* note 269.
509. *Ibid.*
510. Molenaar, *supra* note 502 at 366-376.
511. Silja Vöneky & Sange Addison-Agyei, *Antarctica,* in MPEPIL (book cited *supra* at note 297) 27-31 (2011).

the first two groups enjoy the status of Consultative Party to the AT,[512] which provides them with the right to vote on substantive issues of interpretation and application of the Treaty.[513]

2.3.2 Foundational Principles of the AT

To begin with, it is important to note that the AT applies to "the area south of 60° South Latitude" and that its norms are without prejudice to the rights of any State under international law "with regard to the high seas within that area."[514] The fundamental principle governing activities in Antarctica is that the latter shall be used for peaceful purposes only.[515] This essential rule is laid down in Article I of the Treaty, which also provides a non-exhaustive list of prohibited military activities, such as the establishment of military bases, while also allowing for the use of military personnel or equipment for scientific research or for other peaceful purposes.[516] Notably, the formulation of this article has later inspired the language and structure of Article IV (2) OST, which similarly establishes the exclusively peaceful purposes of activities in the exploration and use of celestial bodies.[517]

Within the legal regime of Antarctica, the principle of peaceful uses guarantees the freedom of scientific investigation and provides the foundations for enhanced international cooperation.[518] To this end, Article II AT declares the continuation of both the freedom of scientific investigation and related cooperation "as applied during the International Geophysical Year" and under the provisions of the Treaty.[519] The very wording of Article II emphasizes the importance of the 1959 International Geophysical Year as a turning point in the history of Antarctica. As we have seen, during that year, the twelve States involved in its exploration and use decided for the first time to set aside jurisdictional disputes in favor of enhanced cooperation, motivated by the desire to stabilize and support everyone's scientific activities in the continent.[520] The main aspects of this enhanced cooperation are determined under Article III AT, according to which States Parties to the AT agree, "to the greatest extent feasible and practicable," to three kinds of mutual exchanges.[521] First, in the interest of maximizing economy and

512. As reported on the Treaty's website, https://www.ats.aq/devAS/Parties?lang=e only twenty -nine out of the fifty-four State Parties to Antarctic Treaty currently enjoy this status (last accessed October 2022).
513. Davis, *supra* note 505 at 150. Vöneky & Addison-Agyei, *supra* note 511.
514. Article VI AT, *supra* note 269.
515. Article I AT, *supra* note 269.
516. *Ibid.*
517. Article IV OST, *supra* note 11. For a comparison between the two principles *see* Armel Kerrest, *Outer Space as International Space: Lessons from Antarctica*, in *Science Diplomacy: Antarctica, Science and the Governance of International Spaces* 136-137 (Paul A. Berkman, Michael Lang, David Walton & Oran R. Young eds., 2011) [book hereinafter: "Science Diplomacy"].
518. Thomas Lord, *The Antarctic Treaty System and the Peaceful Governance of Antarctica: The Role of the ATS in Promoting Peace at the Margins of the World*, 10 (1) Polar Journal 7-12 (2020).
519. Article II AT, *supra* note 269.
520. Watts, *supra* note 499 at 120.
521. Article III AT, *supra* note 269. It is worth underlining that all the exchanges provided in Article III AT serve both confidence-building and operational purposes.

efficiency, States agree to exchange "information regarding plans for scientific programs in Antarctica."[522] This first kind of exchange is of fundamental importance because it allows States operating in Antarctica to identify synergies across their respective operations. Building upon this foundational knowledge of each other's programs, States further agree to also exchange "scientific personnel between expeditions and stations"[523] as well as related "scientific observations and results."[524] In order to maximize the practical relevance of these exchanges of information, the Treaty emphasizes the importance of cooperation and alignment with external entities.[525] Pursuant to Article III (2) AT, the Parties to the Treaty shall give "every encouragement" to the establishment of "cooperative working relations" with any international organization bearing a technical or scientific interest in the exploration and use of Antarctica, especially with UN specialized agencies.[526] Article III AT is particularly important from a systemic viewpoint, as it ensures both the internal and external convergence of the Treaty.[527]

The cooperation architecture designed in the first three provisions of the Treaty finds its keystone in Article IV AT, which had the difficult task of settling the existing jurisdictional disputes among the original twelve Parties.[528] Instead of deciding which claim was right and which wrong, Article IV AT froze them all while also placing a ban on the enactment of future ones.[529] As a result, the establishment of the AT has been without prejudice to (a) previous sovereignty claims, (b) any basis of further sovereignty claims, as well as (c) any position in relation to the recognition or non-recognition of said claims among the original Parties to the Treaty.[530] The mechanism designed in Article IV AT is generally praised as simple but clever: none of the AT Parties was willing to renounce its position in a definite manner, but all of them agreed to put their claims "in standby" to enable the peaceful and cooperative uses of Antarctica.[531] The solution designed in Article IV AT is complemented by the distribution of jurisdictional competencies designed in Article VIII AT. Due to its connections with sovereignty claims, the exercise of territorial jurisdiction over Antarctica was a sensitive topic.[532] Also, in this case, the Treaty strikes another compromise between theory and practice by providing States Parties with exclusive *personal* jurisdiction

522. Article III (1) (a) AT, *supra* note 269.
523. Article III (1) (b) AT, *supra* note 269.
524. Which shall also be made freely available. Article III (1) (c) AT, *supra* note 269.
525. Harlan K. Cohen (ed.), *Handbook of the Antarctic Treaty System* 1-2 (9th ed., 2002).
526. Article III (2) AT, *supra* note 269.
527. In this regard, Article III AT should also be read in conjunction with Article VII (5), which provides for both the immediate and future sharing of certain information concerning the operational situation in Antarctica, with specific reference to (a) all expeditions to and within Antarctica, (b) all stations developed thereby and (c) any military personnel or equipment employed.
528. Davis, *supra* note 505 at 149.
529. Lord, *supra* note 518 at 8.
530. Article IV (1) AT, *supra* note 269.
531. Davis, *supra* note 505 at 150; Watts, *supra* note 499 at 120; Lord, *supra* note 518 at 8.
532. Watts, *supra* note 499 at 166.

over both the observers designated under Article VII and the scientific personnel exchanged under Article III AT.[533]

Since this attribution is without prejudice to the respective positions of the Contracting Parties relating to jurisdiction over all other persons in Antarctica,[534] Article VIII AT further provides that any related dispute shall be promptly addressed through consultations aimed at negotiating a mutually acceptable solution in good faith.[535]

The peaceful, cooperative and scientific uses of Antarctica are further complemented by a ban on nuclear explosions and a prohibition of disposal of radioactive material in the Antarctic region.[536] This principle is of critical importance for the environmental protection of Antarctica, especially in light of the unique marine and biological environment inhabiting the continent.[537] Notably, the prohibition of nuclear activities in Antarctica is "tempered" by a safeguard clause which provides for the applicability of future international agreements on the use of nuclear energy, provided that all the Consultative Parties to the Treaty have joined them.[538]

2.3.3 Institutional Mechanisms for Inspection and Consultation

The fundamental principles of the AT are complemented by innovative institutional mechanisms supporting their concrete application through inspection and consultation procedures. Pursuant to Article VI AT, the Consultative Parties to the AT have the right to carry out inspections "in all areas of Antarctica, including all stations, installations and equipment within those areas" through designated observers.[539] These observers must be nationals of the States appointing them, and their names shall be communicated to all Consultative Parties to the AT, which shall also be informed in advance of termination of their appointment.[540] Each observer designated in accordance with the requirements laid down in Article VII AT shall have complete freedom of access at any time to any or all areas of Antarctica.[541] Pursuant to the inspection mechanism, activities conducted in the Antarctic region are subject to a full (albeit not technically

533. Vöneky & Addison-Agyei, *supra* note 511 at 36. It is important to note that this personal jurisdiction is limited to acts or omissions occurring while they are in Antarctica for the purpose of exercising their functions.
534. Article VIII (1) AT, *supra* note 269.
535. Article VIII (2) AT, *supra* note 269.
536. Article V AT, *supra* note 269. On the importance of this nuclear ban for the peaceful exploration of Antarctica, *see* Lord, *supra* note 518 at 9-10.
537. As further confirmed by the subsequent enactment of the CCAS and CCAMLR, *supra* notes 494 and 495.
538. Article V (2) AT, *supra* note 269.
539. Article VII (1) AT, *supra* note 269.
540. *Ibid.*
541. Article VII (2) AT, *supra* note 269.

public) transparency regime, with the twofold objective of promoting the objectives[542] and ensuring observance of the provisions of the Treaty.[543]

The consultative mechanism is laid down in Article IX AT, which provides the States Parties to the Treaty with the institutionalized opportunity to hold regular exchanges about its status and application.[544] It is important to note while all States Parties to the Treaty can participate in the consultative meetings, only the representatives of the twelve States mentioned in the Preamble, as well as of the additional Parties that have demonstrated their interest in Antarctica, are provided with the right to influence decisions.[545] Accordingly, these States are altogether referred to as Consultative Parties due to their right of active participation in the consultations organized pursuant to Article IX AT. It is worth noting that according to the formulation of Article IX AT, the twelve original States hold the status of Consultative Parties on a permanent basis, whereas all acceding States might acquire it depending on their ability to prove their interest in Antarctica.[546] Even though this mechanism has not gone exempt from criticism, it remains one of the most forward-thinking provisions of the AT[547] and certainly one of the most interesting ones for the governance of space mining. In terms of timeline, the consultative meetings shall happen "at suitable intervals and places" with three main goals: (1) exchange information, (2) consult on matters of common interest, and (3) formulate recommendations for the enactment of additional measures in furtherance of the principles and objectives of the Treaty.[548] Since 1959, the Consultative Parties to the AT have managed to fruitfully meet at regular intervals of two or one year, with the next one being planned in Helsinki for May 2023[549] The meetings organized under Article IX AT are the very reason why the AT evolved into the ATS, thanks to the negotiation of additional instruments facilitated by these regular gatherings.[550] As such, the consultative mechanism designed in Article IX AT is an excellent example of adaptive governance.

Finally, the inspection and consultative mechanisms are complemented by the provisions on external relations and resolution of disputes under Articles X and XI

542. Insofar as free access to all areas of Antarctica plays an instrumental role in promoting international cooperation and furthering the freedom of scientific investigation.
543. Insofar as the possibility of "surprise" inspections provides a strong incentive to the Consultative Parties for voluntary compliance with the Treaty, reducing the need for *ex post* mechanisms. Notably, this mechanism will serve as inspiration for the subsequent drafting of Article XII OST, which provides a softer right to visit and inspect stations and installations on celestial bodies, as well as Article 15 MA, which closely resembles the spirit and structure of Article VII AT.
544. Molenaar, *supra* note 502 at 364-367.
545. Vöneky & Addison-Agyei, *supra* note 511 at 27-35. Article IX AT, *supra* note 269.
546. Article IX (1) AT, *supra* note 269.
547. Vöneky & Addison-Agyei, *supra* note 511 at 97.
548. Article IX (1) AT, *supra* note 269. It is important to note that decisions at the consultative meetings of the AT are taken by unanimity.
549. The list of meetings is available on the Treaty's website https://www.ats.aq/devAS/Meetings?lang=e (last accessed October 2022).
550. On the importance of the consultative mechanism for the success of the AT, *see* Lord, *supra* note 518 at 10-11; Watts, *supra* note 499 at 12-38.

AT.[551] Pursuant to Article X AT, States Parties to the Treaty have to undertake "appropriate efforts, consistent with the Charter of the United Nations" to prevent and eventually neutralize the conduct of any activity in Antarctica which would be contrary to the principles and purposes of the AT.[552] Under Article XI AT, States Parties to the AT shall consult among themselves about any dispute concerning the application or interpretation of the Treaty, with a view to resolving the matter by negotiation, inquiry, mediation, conciliation, arbitration, judicial settlement or other peaceful means of their own choice.[553] If those means would not be helpful, paragraph 2 of Article XI AT provides that any unresolved dispute shall, with the consent of all involved Parties, "be referred to the International Court of Justice for settlement."[554] In light of the (already well-known) potential difficulties in getting the consent of all Parties to submit the dispute to the ICJ, the final part of Article XI (2) AT clarifies that "failure to reach agreement on reference to the International Court shall not absolve parties to the dispute from the responsibility of continuing to seek to resolve it" through the other avenues listed in the first paragraph of the provision.[555] It is worth noting that even though some of the AT Parties have engaged in disputes concerning issues arising in the Antarctic area, the dispute settlement mechanism designed in Article XI AT has never been used.[556]

Recent Achievements of the Consultative Mechanism: the Environmental Protocol and the Secretariat

To conclude the present analysis of the AT, the following paragraphs briefly address first its Environmental Protocol[557] and then its Secretariat.[558] The Environmental Protocol was concluded in 1998 and, as such, is the latest addition to the ATS.[559] Building upon the established success of the AT, the Protocol expands its scope with strict rules and procedures for the environmental protection of Antarctica.[560] The most important novelty of the Protocol is the designation of Antarctica as a "natural reserve, devoted to peace and science."[561] Pursuant to this, the Parties to the Protocol

551. For a thorough analysis of the mechanism laid down in Article XI AT, *see* Donald Rothwell, *Dispute Settlement under the Antarctic Treaty System*, in *MPEiPro*, book cited *supra* at note 15 (2018).
552. This provision completes the legal regime laid down in the Treaty by addressing its (inherently) limited participation and acknowledging the need to act upon it accordingly.
553. Article XI (1) AT, *supra* note 269. Interestingly, this Article reports *verbatim* the measures listed under Article 33 UN Charter for the pacific settlement of disputes, with the obvious exclusion of "regional agencies or arrangements," those being already provided by the Treaty itself.
554. Article XI (2) AT, *supra* note 269.
555. *Ibid.*
556. According to Rothwell, this was done to avoid disruptions to the harmony of the ATS. Rothwell, *supra* note 551 at 28-30.
557. PEPAT, *supra* note 497.
558. Information on the Secretariat of the Antarctic Treaty is available https://www.ats.aq/e/secretariat.html on its webpage (last accessed October 2022).
559. PEPAT, *supra* note 497.
560. Davor Vidas, *The Protocol on Environmental Protection to the Antarctic Treaty: A Ten-Year Review*, in *Yearbook of International Co-operation on Environment and Development* 51 (Olav Schram Stokke & Øystein B. Thommessen eds., 2002).
561. Article 2 PEPAT, *supra* note 497.

committed themselves to the environmental protection of Antarctica, which the Protocol realizes through (1) the enactment of guiding environmental principles,[562] (2) the prohibition of commercial mining of mineral resources,[563] (3) the obligation to conduct an environmental impact assessment for all activities in Antarctica,[564] (4) the creation of a Committee for Environmental Protection (CEP),[565] (5) the development of an emergency response action procedure,[566] and (6) the enactment of additional provisions for dispute settlement.[567] Thanks to the combination of these measures, the Protocol lays down a comprehensive multi-level regime that has successfully ensured the environmental protection of Antarctica to this day.[568] The critical role of the Environmental Protocol within the governance system of Antarctica is underscored by the fact that new States wishing to acquire the status of Consultative Parties will have to become a Party to it.[569]

For almost fifty years, the AT operated without any dedicated administrative institution. At the Antarctic Treaty Consultative Meeting (ATCM) XXIV, held in St. Petersburg in 2001, the Consultative Parties decided to establish a permanent Secretariat in the city of Buenos Aires.[570] The core purpose of this Secretariat is to assist the ATCM and the CEP in performing their respective functions through a series of administrative tasks.[571] To perform these tasks, the AT Secretariat is provided with a simple structure composed of an Executive Secretary and any essential staff member that the latter may decide to appoint.[572] By acting as a reference institution for Antarctic matters, over the last twenty years, the AT Secretariat has strengthened the overall system and helped to ensure that all activities in Antarctica are consistent with the purposes and principles of the AT and its Environmental Protocol.[573] The establishment of the Secretariat is an important demonstration of the ability of the AT to evolve

562. Article 3 PEPAT, *supra* note 497.
563. Article 7 PEPAT, *supra* note 497.
564. Article 8 PEPAT, *supra* note 497.
565. Article 11 PEPAT, *supra* note 497.
566. Article 15 PEPAT, *supra* note 497.
567. Which are laid down in Articles 18-20 of the Protocol and further expanded in a dedicated Arbitration Annex.
568. Vidas, *supra* note 560. The ability to maintain this successful result is one of the most critical challenges lying ahead for the AT. Marcus Haward, *Contemporary Challenges to the Antarctic Treaty and Antarctic Treaty System: Australian Interests, Interplay and the Evolution of a Regime Complex*, 9 (1) Australian Journal of Maritime and Ocean Affairs 21-24 (2017).
569. Article 22 (4) PEPAT, *supra* note 497.
570. This decision was executed two years later at ATCM XXVI, held in Madrid in 2003, with the adoption of the Headquarters Agreement between the ATCM and the Government of the Argentine Republic. Compilation of Key Documents of the Antarctic Treaty System, Measure 1 (2003), available https://documents.ats.aq/atcm43/ww/ATCM43_ww008_e.pdf (last accessed October 2022).
571. Article II Measure 1 (2003), *supra* note 570.
572. Article III Measure 1 (2003), *supra* note 570. So far, the staff of the AT Secretariat includes a deputy secretary and seven specialized officers, as listed on the Secretariat's webpage, *supra* note 552. In light of its institutional link with the ATCM, Article IV Measure 1 (2003) provides that the Secretariat is funded by the Consultative Parties and that it shall operate in a cost effective manner.
573. Secretariat of the Antarctic Treaty, *supra* note 558.

over time in harmony with the principle of adaptive governance.[574] For almost fifty years, the Treaty and its related instruments were managed without the need for a dedicated institution.

As the scope of the system grew, so did also the institutional structure.

2.3.4 Suitability of the AT Regime

The legal regime designed in the AT (and its associated instruments) has been generally praised by commentators, even though the Treaty has not gone exempt from criticisms. As seen above, one of the most appreciated provisions of the Treaty is its Article IV. Thanks to the mechanism laid down in this article, the Parties to the AT have been able to begin cooperation for the peaceful exploration of Antarctica instead of continuing to argue about territorial disputes thereby.[575] The flexible approach adopted in Article IV AT might prove to be useful also in the context of space mining, shifting the attention from theoretical discussions, such as those on safety zones or priority rights, to concrete opportunities for cooperation. Another recognized success of the AT is the maintenance of peace in the region, which has been preserved even in times of military conflicts among its State Parties.[576] Mixed feelings have been expressed by States and commentators about the consultative mechanism designed in Article IX of the Treaty.

To be sure, the mechanism clearly suffers from *input* legitimacy issues since only a handful of States are able to actively influence the concrete governance of Antarctica.[577] Hemmings even calls it "an attempt by a privileged group of nation states to create a system of governance informed by their interests and wishes."[578] The inequality of the governance system has been criticized from day one by many States[579] and currently represents one of the most contested aspects of the Treaty.[580] Having said that, the differentiated system laid down in Article IX AT also has its reasons and merits.[581]

The extreme environmental conditions of Antarctica make it quite difficult and expensive to operate thereby. In light of the challenges and costs involved, it seems justified to attribute a primary role to the States which are practically active in the region. These States possess the necessary knowledge to make informed decisions and will also be directly impacted by their positive or negative consequences. At the same time, this influential role also entails the responsibility of ensuring the preservation and

574. Vöneky & Addison-Agyei, *supra* note 511 at 39-45.
575. Lord, *supra* note 518 at 8; Rothwell, *supra* note 551 at 4 and 28.
576. Such as during the Falkland War between the UK and Argentina. Peter Beck, *The International Politics of Antarctica* 84 (2015).
577. Vöneky & Addison-Agyei, *supra* note 511 at 97-98.
578. Alan D. Hemmings, *Antarctic Politics in a Transforming Global Geopolitics*, in *Handbook on the Politics of Antarctica* 507-522 (Klaus Dodds, Alan D. Hemmings & Peter Roberts eds., 2017).
579. For instance, Gilbert reports that between the 1980s and 1990s, Malaysia had tried to dissolve the Antarctic Treaty and bring the governance of Antarctica under the auspices of the UN. Gilbert, *supra* note 501 at 329-330.
580. *Reform the Antarctic Treaty*, 558 Nature 161 (editorial article, 2018).
581. Vöneky & Addison-Agyei, *supra* note 511 at 97.

use of Antarctica for the benefit of humankind, in light of the critical importance of the region for the environment of the whole planet. So far, the Treaty has managed to achieve this goal through the promotion of peace and science in the region.

Several commentators question the ability of the ATS to maintain its high standards of protection in the face of new challenges, such as the constant increase of tourism activities and the preoccupying spreading of illegal fisheries practices.[582] In the past, the Consultative Parties to the AT have been able to successfully address these challenges at the consultative meetings through the development of new governance instruments.

In this regard, the fact that the last normative fruit of these meetings dates back to 1991[583] might be interpreted as an alarming signal of the ability of the ATCM to keep the Treaty system up to date.[584]

On balance, the AT is generally considered a successful Treaty and various commentators have considered its suitability as a governance model,[585] including, of course, for space resource activities.[586] In this regard, it is important to note that the positive reputation enjoyed by the AT does not automatically imply its necessary suitability as a governance model.[587] Within the context of space mining, the viability of the AT norms and mechanisms is especially supported by (1) the factual similarities between activities in Antarctica and missions on celestial bodies and (2) the legal analogies between the AT and the system of international space law.[588] First, the extreme environmental conditions of Antarctica resemble, *mutatis mutandis*, those of celestial bodies. In both cases, there are significant economic and technical barriers preventing access to the exploration and use of these areas. Second, and related to that, only a handful of States have explored Antarctica so far, in the same way as only a few States have managed to visit other celestial bodies. Third and perhaps most importantly, our knowledge of both environments is rather limited and requires further investigation, which is why the main driver for activities in both realms is science.[589]

In harmony with these factual similarities, it is possible to identify a number of legal analogies between the Antarctica and space law regimes. As we have seen, several key provisions of the OST have been inspired or modeled upon those of the AT. The emphasis on scientific investigation and international cooperation under Article I OST, the non-appropriation principle under Article II OST, the prohibition of nuclear activities and the principle of exclusively peaceful purposes under Article IV (2) OST,

582. Hemmings, *supra* note 578 at 513; Haward, *supra* note 568 at 22-23.
583. PEPAT, *supra* note 497.
584. Lord, *supra* note 518 at 18.
585. Gillian Triggs, *The Antarctic Treaty System: A Model of Legal Creativity and Cooperation*, in *Science Diplomacy supra* note 517 at 39-51.
586. Tronchetti, *supra* note 340 at 803-809. Rosanna Sattler, *Transporting a Legal System for Property Rights from the Earth to the Stars*, 6 Chicago Journal of International Law 32 (2005).
587. An example of this reasoning can be found in literature discussing the suitability of the AT to the governance of the Arctic Ocean. Oran R. Young, *Building and International Regime Complex for the Arctic: Current Status and Next Steps*, 2 (1) Polar Journal 392-394 (2012).
588. Kerrest, *supra* note 517 at 133.
589. Notwithstanding, the insurgence of the *New Space Economy*, past, present and future missions to celestial bodies are primarily driven by scientific objectives. Johnson, *supra* note 371.

and the inspection mechanism designed in Article XII OST, they all resemble relevant corresponding provisions from the AT.[590] From this perspective, the suitability of the AT mechanisms for reinforcing the multi-level system of space mining is suggested by its historical influence on the development of international space law.

It is especially striking that the AT did not initially provide Antarctica with a special legal status or a particular institutional framework. Unlike the OST, UNCLOS or the ITU, the Treaty did not declare the exploration and use of Antarctica as "the province of all mankind,"[591] nor it established the Continent as "the common heritage of mankind"[592] or acknowledged it as a "limited natural resource."[593] As seen above, this was formally done only *forty years later* with the 1998 Environmental Protocol.[594] Nonetheless, thanks to the legal regime designed in the AT, Antarctica substantially benefited from a special treatment.[595] This is particularly significant in the context of the present assessment of the AT to inspire the reinforcement of the multi-level system of space mining. During the early stages of activities in the region, the foundational norms laid down in the Treaty managed to enable international cooperation and ensure the successful conduct of scientific investigations without the need for particular labels or institutions. As the frequency and scope of activities in Antarctica increased, the States Parties to the AT expanded its governance system through additional international instruments, leveraging the knowledge and experience acquired in the meantime.[596] Ultimately, this progression led to the formal designation of Antarctica "as a natural reserve, devoted to peace and science,"[597] as well as to the establishment of a dedicated Secretariat helping with its preservation.[598] As seen, a crucial role in this incremental development has been played by both the inspection and consultative mechanisms laid down in Articles VIII and IX AT.[599] Without these institutionalized opportunities for cross-checks, reviews and updates, the AT would have never evolved into a regulatory system, and the peaceful exploration of Antarctica would have likely been jeopardized by misunderstandings, tensions and distrust.

In light of its general success and due to the underlined similarities between Antarctica and celestial bodies, it can be concluded that the AT norms and procedures for inspection and consultation might serve well the system of space mining. Learning from the successful experience of the AT, the system could be reinforced with the introduction of institutional mechanisms for open access and normative consultation among the States practically involved in space resource activities.[600] In combination with the initial substantive principles that will be developed by the SRWG, these

590. And in particular Articles I, II, V and VI AT.
591. Article I OST, *supra* note 11.
592. Article 136 UNCLOS, *supra* note 267.
593. Article 44 ITU Constitution, *supra* note 268.
594. Article 2 PEPAP, *supra* note 497.
595. Despite the lack of a formal declaration to this end. Watts, *supra* note 499; Davis, *supra* note 505.
596. Vidas, *supra* note 560.
597. Article 2 PEPAP, *supra* note 497.
598. Article I Measure 1 (2003), *supra* note 570.
599. Lord, *supra* note 518 at 7-12.
600. On the model of Articles VI-XI AT, *supra* note 269.

institutional tools might contribute to reducing the risk of tensions and conflicts in the early stages of space mining while also paving the way for its incremental regulation and further institutional development.[601] This combination of foundational substantive regulation with institutionalized mechanisms for periodic normative review would also minimize the need for adjudication and enforcement by offering an institutionalized procedure for internalizing potential conflicts before they become of an adversary nature.

2.4 Reinforcing the System by Combining the Models

As seen in section 1, one of the critical weaknesses of the system of space law, and especially of the portion dedicated to space mining, is the lack of mechanisms and institutions for adjudication and enforcement. From the conducted analysis, it is apparent that the three examined regimes can help address these weaknesses by inspiring the introduction of institutional reinforcements. From each of these regimes, there are certain features and elements that seem to be particularly compatible with the needs and goals of the multi-level system of space mining, in particular from an institutional perspective. Learning from the successful experiences of the UNCLOS, ITU and AT, the system of space mining might be reinforced with the introduction of norms and mechanisms ensuring dedicated adjudication, enhanced coordination and institutional consultation. For what concerns adjudication, the analysis of the UNCLOS regime revealed the usefulness of a dedicated adjudicatory body for the resolution of highly specialized disputes on the model of the Seabed Disputes Chamber. At the same time, the analysis of the UNCLOS regime also revealed the benefits of a flexible regime welcoming recourse to commercial arbitration, albeit only for certain types of disputes and within precise jurisdictional boundaries. The combination of these two elements would serve well the multi-level system of space mining, especially in light of the findings developed in section 1 on the high level of enforceability of arbitral awards. For what concerns coordination, the assessment of the ITU regime showed the importance of balanced norms and procedures enabling both efficiency and equitability. The development of similar coordination mechanisms for the conduct of space resource activities would clearly be beneficial to the stability of the system of space mining, as it would significantly reduce the risk of *ex post* interference and conflict. Finally, with regard to consultation and review, the analysis of the AT regime displayed the benefits of institutionalization and proceduralization for effective and adaptive governance. The introduction of inspection and consultative mechanisms similar to those designed in the AT would allow for the incremental development of the system of space mining while also providing internalized, non-adversary processes for addressing potential normative conflicts. Building upon these considerations, the next

601. In accordance with the strategy outlined in the mandate and workplan of the UNCOPUOS Working Group on Legal Aspects of Space Resource Activities. SRWG Report, *supra* note 354.

paragraphs discuss how to operationalize the development of the proposed adjudication, coordination and consultation mechanisms in a short, medium and long-term perspective.

2.4.1 Short-Term Reinforcements

The previous sections showed that the multi-level system of space mining needs to be reinforced with the introduction of adjudicatory, coordination and consultative tools. Since international space law has become particularly resistant to the development of new binding rules at the international level,[602] reinforcements in the short term will have to be based on the creative use of the existing legal framework for the development of enhanced practices. The hope is that these provisional correctives might stabilize the system during the necessary time to incubate more significant changes at the substantive and institutional levels. Based on these constraints, it seems realistic to begin with enhanced coordination and consultation practices that can help reduce the need for adjudication and enforcement processes in the short term. As the system of space mining evolves, these coordination and consultation practices would need to be complemented with the establishment of a harmonized set of substantive rules and the entrustment of a dedicated body to adjudicate related disputes. Finally, in the long term, all these correctives might be solidified in a fully fledged international regime providing a comprehensive governance system for the safe and sustainable conduct of space resource activities.

i Coordination Correctives

As mentioned, the successful experience of the ITU with coordination procedures might be particularly enlightening for the development of analog tools within the system of space mining. Learning from the mechanisms designed in the Radio Regulations, the goal would be to establish practical tools for the international coordination of space resource activities, with the twofold objective of preventing harmful interference and promoting equitable uses. In the opinion of this author, these tools could be developed by combining the principles of due regard and international consultations under Article IX OST with the information-sharing mechanism established under Article XI OST.

A key element for the success of this operation lies in the operationalization of the obligation to conduct space activities with "due regard to the corresponding interests of other States Parties to the Treaty."[603] As seen in Chapter 2, to be in compliance with this obligation, a space activity should not be conducted at the expense of both existing

602. P.J. Blount, *Innovating the Law: Fifty Years of the Outer Space Treaty*, in *Innovation in Outer Space*, *supra* note 384 at 41-42. Peter Jankowitsch, *The Background and History of Space Law*, in *Handbook of Space Law*, *supra* note 340 at 26-28. Not by chance, the last internationally binding instrument is the Moon Agreement, which has been concluded in 1979.

603. Article IX OST, *supra* note 11.

activities and clearly identified interests of other States.[604] This interpretation is further confirmed by the obligation to undertake appropriate international consultations *prior* to the commencement of a space activity that could cause potentially harmful interferences to those conducted by others.[605] The question then becomes: how far should a State go in assessing the risk of potentially harmful interference? In principle, Article IX OST provides a rather low threshold since it leaves this assessment to the individual discretion of the State in question.[606] However, in accordance with the obligation to perform Treaties in good faith under Article 26 VCLT,[607] it is possible to identify certain limits to the discretionality of this assessment.[608] One of those limits might be derived in connection with the official dissemination of information about ongoing and/or planned space activities by the United Nations Office for Outer Space Affairs (UNOOSA) under Article XI OST. Pursuant to this provision, UNOOSA is tasked to disseminate information on the nature, conduct, location and results of a given space activity "immediately and effectively."[609] Combining the application of these provisions, a State sharing information on its planned and/or ongoing space activities would be entitled to expect other States to pay due regard, i.e., to take them into account when planning or executing their own.

With specific respect to harmful interference, sharing information through Article XI OST would have the effect of triggering the threshold for conducting consultations under Article IX OST. In practice, a State sharing information on its space activities through Article XI OST can assume that it can conduct them *free* from harmful interference, unless informed of the contrary by another State through appropriate international consultations under Article IX OST. As anticipated, this mechanism is inspired by the advanced public information and coordination procedures provided under Article 9 ITU RR—albeit with a fundamental difference. In the system designed by the RR, the BR plays a critical role in verifying the transmitted information and mediating among the involved administrations in case of disagreements. In the mechanism resulting from the combination of Articles IX and XI OST, there would be no such filter or mediator.

On the one hand, under Article XI OST, UNOOSA does not have the competence to verify the information submitted by the States, which the Office shall disseminate in the way it has received it. On the other hand, the international consultations triggered by Article IX OST do not foresee any mediating role for the Office and leave States free to organize them in the way they consider the most appropriate.

604. For an analysis of the principle of due regard *see* section 1.1.6 in Chapter 2.
605. Article IX OST, *supra* note 11.
606. "If a State has reasons to believe that ..." Article IX OST, *supra* note 11.
607. Article 26 VCLT, *supra* note 2.
608. Sergio Marchisio, *Article IX OST*, in *Cologne Commentary on Space Law: Vol. 1* 170 (Stephan Hobe, Bernhard Schmidt-Tedd & Kai-Uwe Schrogl eds., 2009) [book hereinafter: "CoCoSL I"].
609. Upon its submission by the relevant State. Article XI OST, *supra* note 11.

ii Consultation Correctives

The lack of an institution overseeing information sharing and coordination among States creates a structural risk for potential abuses and mistrust. These externalities could be addressed through additional mechanisms for inspection and consultation similar to those laid down in Articles VII and IX of the AT. These correctives could be developed under the existing legal framework by leveraging the principles laid down in Article I OST[610] and Article XII OST[611] to enable the trustful and cooperative exploration and use of celestial bodies.

To this end, it is suggested to interpret Articles I and XII OST as providing each State *operating on a given celestial body* with the right to inspect all space mining facilities located, thereby *through pre-appointed representatives*. This right is inspired by the logic behind Article VII AT and is based on a "negative" interpretation of the reciprocity clause provided under Article XII OST.[612] Under the proposed argument, a State would be able to refuse access to its facilities only to those who are both (1) not conducting operations on the given celestial body and (2) not providing access to their own facilities. This, in turn, would strike a fair compromise between the importance of transparency as a confidence-building mechanism and the practical need to keep external access within a reasonable margin, preventing potential abuses on both ends.

To further reduce the potential for conflicts and misunderstandings, this enhanced right to inspect other facilities should also be complemented by appropriate institutionalized opportunities for consultation and review. For practical reasons, it would be advisable to leverage existing opportunities offered by the annual UNCOPUOS meetings for the specific revision of space mining operations and regulations. Notably, a similar process has already been put in motion pursuant to the newly approved workplan of the SRWG, according to which the Working Group will spend the next three years exchanging views on the suitability of the existing legal framework for the governance of space resource activities.[613] Due to the critical importance of timely discussions for conflict mitigation, it would be ideal if States would also be able to call for extraordinary intersessional meetings of the SRWG as the need may arise. This would be in line with the current practice of the Working Group, which so far seemed inclined to leverage intersessional meetings to ensure the timely advancement of its planned work.

2.4.2 Medium-Term Reinforcements

In the medium term, the above suggestions could be complemented by the development of a dedicated adjudicatory system for the resolution of space mining disputes.

610. According to which there should be "free access to all areas of celestial bodies." Article I OST, *supra* note 11.
611. Pursuant to which stations, installations, equipment and space vehicles "shall be open to representatives of other States on a basis of reciprocity." Article XII OST, *supra* note 11.
612. Lesley Jane Smith, *Article XII OST,* in *CoCoSL I, supra* note 608 at 211.
613. SRWG Report, *supra* note 354.

Applying the lessons learned from the UNCLOS model, an adjudicatory mechanism for space resource activities should leverage the strengths of international courts and arbitrators, reconnect with domestic systems, ensure prompt enforcement and finally make sure to integrate with potentially competing jurisdictions from relevant overlapping regulatory regimes. Bearing in mind the observations made at the end of section 1 of this chapter, the proposed mechanism should foresee a primary role for the PCA so as to benefit from the application of the NYC.[614] Applying the model provided under Article 188 (2) UNCLOS,[615] it would also be possible to foresee the partial involvement of the ICJ in ruling on fundamental interpretation issues that might arise during these disputes. Following the example of the 1994 New York Agreement, an adjudication mechanism for space mining disputes should also include a safeguard clause preventing jurisdictional conflicts with any competing adjudication system.[616] Finally, learning from Draft ISA Regulation 106, this mechanism should provide for the direct enforceability of any final decision rendered by said courts in the territory of any affected State.[617] From a practical viewpoint, since all institutions mentioned in the previous paragraph exist already, the design of the proposed polycentric adjudicatory system could be done by means of a dedicated UNGA Resolution. In accordance with the previous considerations, the text of this Resolution might read as follows:

(1) In order to ensure the peaceful, efficient and effective resolution of international disputes related to the exploration, exploitation and utilization of space resources, States Parties to the OST agree to settle them in accordance with the Optional Rules for Arbitration of Disputes Relating to Outer Space Activities of the PCA. This clause shall not apply to purely domestic disputes concerning the validity or respect of domestic licensing conditions for the authorization and continuing supervision of national space resource activities.

(2) To safeguard the uniform interpretation and coherent application of international space law, States involved in space mining disputes agree to submit related questions of interpretations on the fundamental principles of the five UN Space Treaties to the ICJ.

(3) If, either at the commencement or in the course of arbitration proceedings before the PCA, the latter determines, either at the request of a party to the dispute or *motu proprio*, that its decision depends upon the resolution of a question of interpretation on the fundamental principles of the five UN Space Treaties, States agree to stay the arbitration proceedings until the ICJ has ruled on the matter and record the results of such ruling in the form of an arbitral award on agreed terms before the PCA.

614. NYC, *supra* note 87.
615. On the connection between the Seabed Disputes Chambers and commercial arbitration. Article 188 (2) UNCLOS, *supra* note 267.
616. As the New York Agreement does with the WTO regime. Section VI New York Agreement, *supra* note 279.
617. ISA Draft Regulation 106, *supra* note 338.

(4) To ensure the prompt execution of the decisions taken by the PCA and ICJ under the terms of this resolution, States agree to undertake the necessary actions to enable the domestic enforcement of such decisions in their respective territories.

2.4.3 Perspectives on Long-Term Reinforcements

The full potential of the correctives inspired by the UNCLOS, ITU and AT regimes would be unleashed by the development of an international regime for the governance of space resource activities. In such a scenario, the findings developed on these regimes would be used to inform the optimal design of new mechanisms for coordination, consultation and adjudication. Learning from ITU's advance notice and coordination procedures, a new system could be provided with similar notification mechanism for the recording of space resource activities in an international registry. Following the model of Article 45 of the ITU Constitution and Article 15 of the Radio Regulations, this registry would be managed by an international body similar to the Radio Regulations Board to mediate the coordination among national regulators and help them to resolve situations of harmful interference. Leveraging the successful experience of the ATCM, these coordination procedures could be coupled with the establishment of dedicated, institutionalized opportunities for periodic consultation and review of the existing rules. Finally, bearing in mind the adjudicatory regime of the UNCLOS, the system could be completed with the creation of a dedicated international tribunal entrusted with the interpretation of international norms of space mining and with the adjudication of related disputes.

3 CONCLUSIONS

Building upon the regulatory analysis of the multi-level system of space mining, this chapter set to identify and evaluate present options and proposed correctives for its adjudication and enforcement. To begin with, the chapter framed the concept of enforcement with reference to the proceduralized execution of a (final) judicial or administrative decision ascertaining a normative violation and providing instructions on how to remediate non-compliance. Based on this definition, section 1 considered which options are currently available within the multi-level regulatory system of space mining for adjudicating and enforcing potential violations of its international and national provisions, specifically looking at the remedies provided by each regulatory level.

At the international level, the section found that current norms of international space law are not sufficiently precise to be directly enforced within the context of space mining. Even though the general principles of international space law laid down in the OST are certainly applicable to the conduct of space mining, their broadness prevents the clear identification of a precise normative solution that could be enforced accordingly.

For example, even though it seems obvious that the principle of free access under Article I OST applies to the conduct of space resource activities, it is still very much unclear how this will affect the daily operations of a mining operator, especially when weighed against the rights conferred by potentially contradictory provisions such as Article IX or XII OST. In this regard, the section argued that there are no dedicated processes or institutions formally entrusted with the adjudication and enforcement of international disputes related to space law. Notwithstanding these substantive and institutional deficiencies, the section still found that the system might still be able to exercise adjudicatory and enforcement functions. This is because, in light of the systemic connections between the system of international space law and the legal order of international law (as identified in Chapter 1), the system can borrow adjudicatory and enforcement mechanisms available thereby. Concerning adjudication, the section discovered that international disputes related to space mining would likely be addressed by either the ICJ or the PCA. Therefore, the section moved to identify which options would be available for the enforcement of ICJ decisions and PCA awards. With regards to ICJ decisions, the section found two mechanisms: enforcement by the UNSC under Article 94 (2) UN Charter and self-help under Articles 49-54 ARSIWA. From the conducted analysis, the section discovered that enforcing ICJ judgments through either the powers of the UNSC under Article 94 (2) UN Charter or the individual/collective enactment of countermeasures under Articles 49-54 ARSIWA would raise several issues of legitimacy and effectiveness. Concerning PCA awards, also, in this case, the section identified two mechanisms: self-help under Articles 49-54 ARSIWA and domestic enforcement under the NYC. From its analysis, the section found that the combination of international adjudication before the PCA and domestic enforcement under the NYC provides a balanced solution that meets the highest standards of legitimacy and effectiveness and recommended its adoption.

At the national level, the section identified the same lack of substantive norms previously identified at the international level. Concerning the applicability of domestic institutional mechanisms for adjudication and enforcement, the section distinguished between "purely domestic" and "transnational" disputes, depending on the involvement of domestic and/or foreign entities. With regards to domestic disputes, the section found that they could be adjudicated and enforced through the relevant domestic mechanisms available in the given jurisdiction without raising any particular issue of legitimacy and effectiveness. Concerning transnational disputes, the section discovered that their adjudication and enforcement vary on a case-by-case basis in connection with the types of foreign entities involved, with strong potential for serious issues of legitimacy and effectiveness. In this regard, the section argued that this situation might improve in the future thanks to the recent adoption of the 2019 JC, a new instrument for the global recognition and enforcement of domestic judgments. However, the JC is currently not in force and will require several years before reaching the level of acceptance needed to provide a legitimate and effective solution.

Based on the above, it is possible to formulate the following conclusions with regard to the analysis conducted in section 1. First, international norms applicable to space resource activities can be legitimately and effectively enforced only to the extent that their violation has been adjudicated by international arbitration. This is because normative violations adjudicated by international courts like the ICJ do not trigger particularly legitimate or effective enforcement options, except if the involved Court is part of a supranational regime like the EU or the WTO. Second, national norms regulating private space mining activities can be enforced in a legitimate and effective manner only against actors subject to the same jurisdiction that has adjudicated the related dispute. This is because normative violations adjudicated by domestic authorities or courts cannot be legitimately enforced against actors located outside their national jurisdiction, except if the involved State has provided its consent by means of appropriate arrangements.

In light of these limited options, section 2 looked at comparable legal regimes to inspire the development of adjudication, coordination and consultation correctives that can reinforce the multi-level system of space mining. To this end, the section considered the examples provided by three comparable regimes dealing with the governance of global commons: the UNCLOS, the ITU and the AT. With regards to the UNCLOS, the section focused its attention on the suitability of the adjudication model laid down in the final provisions of Part XI UNCLOS, which governs the conduct of activities in the Deep Seabed. At the end of the analysis, the section found that the system centered on the Deep Seabed Disputes Chamber would be particularly insightful for the development of an adjudicatory mechanism for space mining disputes. With regard to the ITU, the section focused its attention on the coordination rules governing the allocation, allotment and assignment of radio frequencies and related orbits laid down in the Radio Regulations, including mechanisms for resolving harmful interference. At the end of the analysis, the section found that the approach adopted within the ITU model would be particularly suitable for the coordination of space mining activities due to its ability to reduce the need for *ex post* mechanisms through a balanced pursuit of efficiency and equitability. Finally, with regard to the AT, the section focused on the institutional mechanisms provided under Articles VIII and XI AT for inspection and consultation. At the end of its analysis, the section found that these mechanisms would be particularly suitable for both preventing and internalizing potential conflicts related to space mining by promoting transparency and offering an institutionalized opportunity for normative and operational consultations.

Based on the above, the section found that the examined regimes might very well support the reinforcement of the multi-level system of space mining. Learning from the successful experiences of the UNCLOS, ITU and AT, its institutional gaps might be closed with the introduction of correctives ensuring dedicated adjudication, enhanced coordination and institutional consultation. In this regard, the section also found that the opportunity to implement these corrective changes, depending on the temporal horizon adopted. Thus, the section concluded by considering how the proposed correctives could be integrated within the system of space mining from a short, medium and long-term perspective.

In the short term, due to the lack of support for significant normative or institutional changes, the lessons learned from the ITU and AT regimes could be used to leverage the development of enhanced practices for coordination and consultation under Articles I, IX, XI and XII OST. In the medium term, learning from the jurisdictional model designed in Part XI of the UNCLOS, it would be possible to enact a UNGA resolution distributing the competence to adjudicate space mining disputes among the PCA and the ICJ. Finally, in the long term, the proposed mechanisms could be incorporated as foundational elements of an international regime for the governance of space resource activities.

At the end of this chapter, it seems safe to argue that the multi-level regulatory system of space mining is neither practically ready nor legally suited for enforcement. As discussed, the system does not have any substantive norm that could be enforced in the first place.

At the international level, the *Corpus Iuris Spatialis* provides a set of foundational principles that are too general to *directly* regulate the conduct of space resource activities. Even though theoretically possible, the direct application of these principles would not lead to normatively significant results for the simple reason that these principles can be and are, in fact, being interpreted in several different ways. As such, their direct application to the conduct of space resource activities requires precise balancing choices over which there is no international agreement. Since no State has the authority to impose a particular interpretation or balancing choice over another, the result of this direct application would be, at best, the proliferation of *ephemeral* norms and, at worst, a regulatory chaos of conflicting domestic rules. Therefore, the main result that can be derived from these principles is a series of implications to be taken into account in the development of substantive regulation at the national or international level. Probably for this very reason, the only four existing pieces of national space legislation dealing with space resource activities have not yet made a single normative choice on their substantive regulation.

As anticipated, the result of these normative deficiencies is that, at present, there are no substantive norms ready to be enforced. There are two ways in which this situation could be remediated. One option would be the enactment of international principles that could provide agreed foundations for further normative development at the national level. Notably, this is the route currently pursued by the SRWG, even though it remains unclear whether or not the Working Group will be able to pursue it successfully. The alternative option would be the issuance of a judgment from an international adjudicatory body that finally chooses, among the many available interpretative options, which one to uphold for the regulation of space resource activities. Different from the previous option, in this scenario, it is not yet clear *which* adjudicatory body will get to decide on a space mining dispute. As seen, this uncertainty comes from the lack of dedicated institutions tasked with the interpretation, application and enforcement of space law rules, both at the national and international levels. After conducting a thorough systemic analysis of the options available, this chapter narrowed them down to a few possibilities. However, whether this selection will be confirmed in practice remains to be seen. Furthermore, in both scenarios, the vague character of the principles of international space law does not allow to anticipate the concrete normative choices that will be made by either the SRWG or an international court/tribunal.

The consequence of this assessment is that the system of space mining is not equipped to provide predictable and reliable enforcement processes. This is the reason why the ITU and AT models, which both reduce the need for adjudication and enforcement respectively through *ex ante* coordination among operators and *ongoing* review among regulators, are particularly suitable to provide the urgent correctives needed in the short term.

Conclusion

The purpose of this book was to identify and evaluate the regulatory aspects and enforcement options of the multi-level system of space mining. This assessment has been distributed throughout three chapters respectively dedicated to (1) the relationship between space law and international law, (2) the regulatory configuration of the multi-level system of space mining, and (3) the enforceability of the international and national norms composing it.

1 OVERVIEW OF THE MAIN FINDINGS

The following overview provides a snapshot of the main findings developed throughout the book. As such, the paragraphs below are meant as a reference guide to the book to identify the main subjects discussed in each chapter, highlight the fundamental findings developed and how they relate to the main research question of the book. Interested readers are invited to consult the relevant chapter(s) for an in-depth analysis of the topics and issues recalled in this overview.

1.1 The Relationship Between Space Law and International Law

The first chapter of this book assesses the relationship between the system of international space law and the legal order of international law. In order to contextualize this relationship, the chapter begins by first analyzing the configuration of international law as a legal order. Building upon this analysis, the chapter moves to illustrate the substantive and institutional integration between space law and international law.

Within the overall context of the book, the findings developed in this chapter provide the theoretical foundations framing the subsequent analysis of the regulatory aspects and enforcement options that are specific to the system of space mining.

1.1.1 *The Status of International Law as a Legal Order*

The status of international law as a legal order has been at the center of a complex debate prompted by a famous speech rendered by the President of the ICJ Gilbert Guillaume before the UN General Assembly (UNGA) in October 2000. In his speech, President Guillaume condemns the proliferation of multilateral regimes and related judicial bodies as a threat to the unity of international law. Following up on the concerns expressed by the President of the ICJ, the UNGA tasked the ILC to evaluate the extent of the problem. In accordance with the instructions received by the General Assembly, the ILC produced a thorough study finalized by Koskenniemi and a synthetic report presented to the GA. These two documents provide a clear picture of the debate on the status of international law. Based upon the analysis conducted by the ILC, it is possible to disassemble the concept of "fragmentation" proposed by President Guillaume in two complementary phenomena: substantive diversification and functional differentiation.

Substantive diversification is defined by ILC as the "splitting up" of international law in "specialized boxes," claiming autonomy from each other as well as from the general law, whereas functional differentiation refers to the institutional component of this process. Through these two phenomena, the configuration of international law as a legal order changed from a series of special *rules* to a series of special *systems* and *institutions*. President Guillaume unified these trends under the general concept of "fragmentation" and interpreted them as a "rebellion" threatening the unity of the legal order of international law. Per its part, the ILC demystified this narrative and concluded that the unity of the legal order of international law had not been compromised by substantive diversification. In its analysis, the ILC argues that this outcome has been avoided thanks to the unifying function of the principle of systemic integration, which is embodied in Article 31 (c) of the VCLT. According to the ILC, this provision preserves and fosters the unity of international law as a legal order by requiring the interpreters and adjudicators of international law to take into account the systemic relations of a given norm with other applicable and relevant rules of international law. Article 31 (3) (c) VCLT preserves the unity of international law by ensuring that existing connections among rules of international law are duly taken into account in their application. Further, the article fosters this unity by clarifying and strengthening the implicit relations among international norms as a result of their systemic interpretation. The principle behind Article 31 (3) (c) VCLT is of great importance for the purposes of the analysis conducted in Chapter 1 because integration with international law is one of the cornerstones of the system of space law.

Since the ILC focused on substantive diversification, eminent scholars moved to analyze the impact of functional differentiation. This term refers to the distribution of tasks within the global society, which finds its basis in Chapters X and XI of the UN Charter. Based on the UN Charter, *functional differentiation* indicates the development of separate and independent bodies tasked to administrate the application and adjudication of specialized regimes. In modern international law, the creation of these bodies serves the purpose of incrementing its efficiency and effectiveness by allocating the *primary* responsibility to deal with a certain matter to a specific institution that is best equipped and/or legitimized for it. Needless to say, this *functional* division of competence should never be brought to the point of creating *silos* within the legal order itself. On the contrary, institutions should be encouraged and empowered to dynamically interact with each other in the exercise of their functions. In this regard, Peters conducts a critical overview of the techniques adopted by various institutions across several specialized systems to channel fragmentation and preserve the unity of international law. Further elaborating on Peters' findings, these techniques can be divided into three categories: binary criteria, integration mechanisms and political discourses. Binary criteria include interpretation practices for normative conflict resolution, ranging from traditional conflict rules like *lex specialis, lex posterior* and *lex superior* to modern techniques like the margin of appreciation and mutual recognition. The theoretical premise for the use of these techniques comes from the establishment of a normative conflict, which then gets resolved through the use of binary criteria that identifies which norm should be applied in the case at hand. Taking a step forward, the second category includes various integration mechanisms developed and used by lawmakers, law appliers and law adjudicators, such as notwithstanding clauses, cross-references, balancing clauses, regime interaction, presumption of law-abiding intentions, systemic integration and judicial dialogue. The theoretical premise for the use of these tools comes from the systemic nature of international law, which gets concretized through the use of creative harmonization and integration techniques. These techniques are of great importance for the purposes of the present book because of their influence over the substantive and institutional dynamics shaping the relationship between international law and space law. Finally, the third type of instrument includes political discourses publicly contesting a certain regime before the global community. The theoretical premise for the use of this technique comes from a legitimacy argument according to which certain foundational conflicts should only be resolved through the global political discourse. An assessment of the development and use of these techniques shows how lawmakers, law appliers and law adjudicators have all done their part in maintaining the unity of international law by promoting its systemic integration. Based on these studies, Chapter 1 concludes its analysis of the configuration of international law by praising its status as an ordered plurality and welcoming its flexible diversity as a manifestation of its capacity to address global problems.

1.1.2 The Relationship Between International Law and Space Law

The findings developed on the configuration of international law provide the foundational basis for assessing its relationship with the specialized system of space law. To provide a complete picture, the chapter considers this relationship from both substantive and institutional perspectives. Within the overall structure of the book, this assessment is helpful for framing the regulatory analysis of the multi-level system of space mining.

Both the substantive and institutional integration between international law and space law are governed by Article III of the OST. According to this article, space activities shall be conducted "in accordance with international law, including the Charter of the United Nations, in the interest of maintaining international peace and security and promoting international cooperation and understanding." On the one hand, Article III OST ensures the substantive integration between space law and international law by providing for the direct and dynamic applicability of international law to the conduct of space activities. On the other one, Article III OST provides for the institutional integration between the two realms by virtue of the links established with the UN Charter. Consequently, until the system of space law formalizes its own independent institutional structure, the fundamental tasks needed by the system are currently fulfilled by the principal organs of the UN. To begin with, the normative development of international space law is entrusted to the General Assembly of the United Nations (UNGA), which formally enacts all the legal instruments produced at the international level. Even though the UNGA has established the UNCOPUOS as the permanent body tasked with the international regulation of space activities, UNCOPUOS formally reports to the General Assembly and depends on its approval to enact any legal instrument. Not by chance, every year since its establishment, UNCOPUOS has been reporting its progress to the Assembly, which regularly endorses its annual report in a dedicated resolution. Second, the application of international space law formally relies on the UNSG. Also, in this case, even though the UNSG has created a dedicated Office for Outer Space Affairs (UNOOSA) for discharging its duties in the space domain, the fact remains that all primary sources of international space law mention the UNSG and not UNOOSA. For example, the Registration Conventions mandate the UNSG, and not UNOOSA, to maintain a Registry for objects launched into outer space. Moving to the other principal organs of the UN, Article III OST provides a solid legal basis for the involvement of the UNSC in space affairs in light of the connection established between the conduct of space activities and the maintenance of international peace and security. Notably, this interpretation has been confirmed by the UNSC itself in its Resolution 2087/2013 with regard to the enactment of sanctions against the space program of North Korea. Finally, for what concerns the ICJ, its status as the principal organ of the UN would certainly justify its competence to adjudicate a space law dispute, even though this has never happened so far.

From the above assessment, the chapter concludes that the system of space law is well integrated within the legal order of international law both from a substantive and institutional viewpoint.

1.2 The Multi-level Regulation of Space Mining

The second chapter of the book investigates the configuration of the multi-level regulatory system of space mining. Mirroring the multi-level configuration of space law, the chapter conducts a thorough assessment of relevant sources at the international and national regulatory levels. Based upon that assessment, the chapter then looks at how the two levels interact with each other for the multi-level regulation of space mining, identifying normative gaps as well as potential ways for addressing them. To this end, the chapter dedicates particular attention to the discussions annually held at the LSC of UNCOPUOS, with special reference to the activities of the recently established working group on legal aspects of space resource activities. To complement this analysis, the chapter also looks at the policy contributions provided both by coalitions of national governments as well as multi-stakeholder groups. Based on the findings developed, the chapter concludes by envisioning potential scenarios for the evolution of the regulatory system and reflecting on their implications for its overall tenure.

1.2.1 International Space Law

The rules of international space law are laid down in the so-called *Corpus Iuris Spatialis*. This expression encompasses five international treaties—the Outer Space Treaty (OST), the Rescue and Return Agreement (ARRA), the Registration Convention (REG), the Liability Convention (LIAB) and the Moon Agreement (MA)—and a variety of UNGA Resolutions interpreting, clarifying and expanding them. Beginning with the OST (and with the exception of the ARRA), the chapter examines the fundamental provisions of these treaties to identify their implications for the conduct and regulation of space mining.

i The Outer Space Treaty

The core norms of international space law are laid down in the OST, which is also referred to as the *Magna Carta* of space law. The universal recognition enjoyed by the OST makes it *the reference point* of the analysis conducted throughout Chapter 2.

Article I OST is the cornerstone of the system of space law and has many regulatory layers. First, under Article I (2) OST, space "shall be free for exploration and use by all States without discrimination of any kind, on a basis of equality and in accordance with international law." This provision establishes the freedom of exploration and use of outer space and celestial bodies. The broad formulation of these freedoms refers to a wide range of activities, including commercial and private endeavors, and is often interpreted as implying that every activity which is not prohibited is permitted.

At the same time, Article I (2) OST commits the exercise of the freedom to explore and use outer space to three fundamental conditions: non-discrimination, equality and respect for international law. The implications of these principles are (1) that there shall be no active barriers impeding the exploration and use of outer space by a particular country, (2) that spacefaring and non-spacefaring nations shall constructively engage to create a common level playing field, and (3) that all space activities have to be conducted in a consistent manner with applicable international law.

Notably, the article also includes a fourth limit with specific reference to the exploration and use of celestial bodies, establishing that there shall be free access to all their areas. The principle of free access is particularly relevant for the conduct of space resource activities. While the debate on its legal implications is still ongoing, the main finding developed as a result of the analysis conducted in Chapter 2 is that this principle forbids States to exclusively "seize control" of natural areas of celestial bodies, thus translating into a right of free passage.

On top of these four limits, Article I (1) OST further bounds the exploration and use of outer space to the benefit and interests of all Countries and solemnly declares these two activities as the province of all humankind. As is well-known, whether spacefaring nations are legally obliged to share the benefits of their space activities (and, if so, in which form) has been debated for a long time. Ultimately, the question was partially answered in the Space Benefit Declaration, according to which, while there is no legal obligation to share the benefits of space activities, States are encouraged to voluntarily do so through cooperation, mutual assistance and inclusiveness. As revealed in State practice, the benefits of many space activities are generally shared. For what concerns the province principle, its main legal implication is the establishment of outer space and celestial bodies as global commons.

From the analysis of the various regulatory layers condensed in Article I OST, it seems safe to establish space resource activities are allowed as part of the freedom to use celestial bodies. At the same time, since the freedom to use celestial bodies is not absolute, space resource activities will have to respect a series of conditions in order to be lawfully conducted. From the limits and purposes laid down in Article I OST, it is possible to derive the following main implications. First, space resource activities should always be limited in scale and duration in order to preserve the exploration and use of celestial bodies as the province of all humankind. Second, a right of innocent passage should always be granted pursuant to appropriate coordination to ensure compliance with the principle of free access. Third and final, international cooperation and capacity building in space resource activities should be extensively promoted to promote non-discrimination and equity in the use of celestial bodies.

Article II OST is often referred to as a cardinal provision of space law. Pursuant to this article, "outer space, including the Moon and other celestial bodies, is not subject to national appropriation by claim of sovereignty, by means of use or occupation, or by any other means." The non-appropriation principle established under Article II OST has a central role within the system of space law as the natural complement of the freedoms laid down in Article I OST. By forbidding States to exert and exercise their sovereign powers over outer space and celestial bodies, this provision preserves their legal status as global commons. In this regard, it is important to note that the goal of Article II OST is to avoid the *territorial* extension of States' influence over outer space and celestial bodies. At the same time, this does not make space or celestial bodies a lawless area, thanks to the direct applicability of international law as established by Articles I and III OST and the exercise of limited jurisdiction and control under Article VIII OST. In the past, Article II OST was interpreted by some authors as prohibiting the conduct of space resource activities. Even though today it is clear that the scope of this provision does not cover space resources, it is also understood that certain types of invasive and permanent uses of celestial bodies may very well be in violation of its prohibition of territorial appropriation.

Articles III and IV OST are two other key provisions of international space law.

Pursuant to Article III OST, space activities have to be conducted "in accordance with international law, including the Charter of the United Nations, in the interest of maintaining international peace and security and promoting international cooperation and understanding." As discussed in Chapter 1, Article III OST determines the substantive and institutional integration between space law and international law. With specific regard to space resource activities, Article III OST prohibits their conduct in any manner that would be inconsistent with applicable legal obligations of international law or hinder the maintenance of international peace and security.

Article IV (2) lays down another fundamental rule of space law. Pursuant to this provision, "the Moon and other celestial bodies shall be used exclusively for peaceful purposes." The clear-cut formulation of Article IV (2) outlaws the direct or indirect use of celestial bodies for any military purposes, even though the provision allows for the controlled involvement of military personnel or equipment necessary for their peaceful exploration. Insofar as space resource activities make "use" of celestial bodies, the prohibition laid down in Article IV (2) fully applies to their conduct. As a result, Article IV (2) OST determines an important limitation on the kind of entities that can conduct space resource activities, as well as on the purposes justifying the use of space resources. First, military entities do not have the right to autonomously engage in space mining. In accordance with the exceptions laid down in Article IV (2), they might only provide "in kind" support, i.e., personnel, equipment and facilities, to space resource activities conducted by civilians. Second, the use of space resources within military activities or for military purposes would defeat the object and purpose not only of Article IV (2) but also of the whole OST.

As such, space resources shall be used for exclusively peaceful purposes.

Article V OST addresses the legal status and the protection of astronauts. Since space mining does not plan to involve any humans, this article is excluded from the analysis.

Article VI OST is a key provision of international space law. This article establishes the international responsibility of States for national activities in outer space while also enabling the conduct of private space activities under the prior authorization and continuing supervision of a State Party to the Treaty. Pursuant to this provision, States directly guarantee the lawfulness of their national space activities and are obliged to ensure that they conform to the provisions of the OST. As a consequence, any national space activity conducted in violation of the Treaty would trigger the international responsibility of the appropriate State under the ARSIWA. In light of the mechanism designed under Article VI OST, the freedom to explore and use outer space is granted to private actors only through the intermediation of a State providing authorization and continuing supervision. As such, Article VI OST reinforces the central role played by States in the conduct and regulation of space activities and further safeguards the rule of law in outer space, considering that international obligations are not directly applicable to individuals under many national jurisdictions.

Similar to Article III OST, the main impact of Article VI OST is better appreciated on a systemic level, as this provision has shaped the very nature of space law as multi-level regulatory system. With specific reference to space mining, the obligation to authorize and continuously supervise private activities in space under Article VI OST is the very reason behind the enactment of the four existing domestic legislations on space mining. As such, the implications of this provision on space mining are twofold:

on the one hand, it obliges States to ensure the compatibility of private space resource activities with applicable international space law; on the other hand, it provides the legal basis justifying the enactment of national space legislation meant for that goal.

Articles VII and VIII OST are assessed together in light of their common reliance on the concept of launching State. To begin with, Article VII OST establishes the international liability of launching States for damage caused by space objects. The purpose of this provision is to allocate the risks associated with space-launching activities to all the States involved. To this end, Article VII OST creates four "types" of launching States: (1) those directly "launching" an object, (2) those "procuring" said launch and finally, those from whose (3) territory or (4) facilities the launch took place. The result of this broad formulation is that any State providing its material or financial resources for launching an object into outer space will also bear international liability for any damage that it may cause. As is well-known, the principle of State liability has been further expanded in the LIAB. Pursuant to the *lex specialis* rule, liability for an accident involving two States which are both Parties to the OST and the LIAB, would be settled under the rules of the latter. Accordingly, the implications of Article VII OST on space mining will be discussed together with those of the LIAB.

Article VIII OST lays down the fundamental principle of jurisdiction and control over space objects. According to this provision, "a State Party to the Treaty on whose registry an object launched into outer space is carried shall retain jurisdiction and control over such object, and over any personnel thereof, while in outer space or on a celestial body." This principle plays a crucial role in the system of international space law and is closely linked to many of the other principles examined earlier. In light of outer space' status as a global common, Article VIII OST provides a legal basis for identifying which State is entitled to, and responsible for, the exercise of a minimum level of jurisdictional control thereby. The establishment of a link with the jurisdiction of a given State is a fundamental safeguard in defense of the rule of law in outer space. Pursuant to the formulation of Article VIII OST, the right to exercise jurisdiction and control over a space object is inherently vested in all its launching States. This is clear from the use of the term retain within Article VIII OST, which indicates that national registration is not the source of these powers but rather the formal mechanism through which we identify the State that is entitled to exercise them. Similar to Article VII OST; also, this article has been expanded into a separate international agreement dedicated to the registration of space objects, the REG. However, differently from the case of Article VII OST, the rules laid down in Article VIII OST and the REG are not mutually exclusive but rather complementary. As such, Article VIII OST continues to provide the legal basis governing the principle of jurisdiction and control, whereas the REG establishes the registration of space objects as a legal obligation and governs its concrete application.

Article VIII OST has crucial implications for the conduct of space mining. Pursuant to this provision, the State registering a space object involved in a space resource activity will be able to retain the exercise of jurisdiction and control over both of them. The possibility that space mining might result in the assembly of new space objects or the manufacturing of "space-made products" begs the question of whether or not Article VIII OST is applicable to them as well. Since Article VIII OST includes "objects constructed on a celestial body" within the category of "objects launched into outer space," it seems reasonable to argue that the former may be included in a State's national registry for the purpose of retaining jurisdiction and control. In the absence of a launching event, the link to identify the appropriate State of Registry would be provided by the jurisdiction exercised over the "personnel" constructing the object or manufacturing the space-made product. If the constructing or manufacturing processes would incorporate previously registered space objects, the existing registration of the space objects used in the manufacturing process may also be expanded to cover the newly formed collective, thus extending related jurisdiction and control.

Article IX is, by all means, the most complex provision of international space law. This article establishes three essentials obligations: (1) to conduct space activities with due regard, (2) to prevent the harmful contamination of both Earth and celestial bodies and (3) to undertake appropriate international consultations prior to commencing a space activity that may generate potentially harmful interference with others.

To begin with, the interpretation of the principle of due regard is likely one of the most important challenges faced by contemporary international space law due to its impact on the sustainability of space. Pursuant to the systemic integration between international law and space law, a potential solution might be offered by the interpretation and use of this term under international law. In this regard, the principle of due regard is laid down in Article 3 (d) of the Chicago Convention as well as Article 87 of the UNCLOS. Under both these provisions, the expression refers to the performance of an act with a certain standard of care, attention or observance. Recently, the term due regard has been discussed in the proceedings of the M/V Norstar case, a leading case of the ITLOS, where it appeared for the first time in a decision of an international court. Under the interpretation proposed by Panama, one of the parties to the case, the principle of due regard as laid down in Article 87 UNCLOS requires States exercising their freedoms of the high seas to refrain from "activities that interfere with the exercise by other States of their parallel freedoms to do likewise." Even though the ITLOS did not comment on Panama's interpretation, since it found that Article 87 (2) UNCLOS was not applicable in the case at hand, it is noteworthy that said interpretation was not contested by the respondent, Italy. *Mutatis mutandis*, it could be argued that paying "due regard to the corresponding interests of other States" under Article IX OST implies that a State shall not undertake activities that would threaten the exercise of the freedoms of exploration and use by other States. Framed in these terms, the principle of due regard would act as an important limit to the freedom of exploration and use of outer space provided for in Article I (2) OST.

From this perspective, the other two obligations laid down under Article IX OST might be seen as providing two examples of how the principle of due regard limits the freedoms of space. Concerning the first one, States should refrain from conducting activities that would harmfully contaminate the outer space environment. Concerning the second one, States are either obliged or entitled to undertake or request (depending on the perspective) appropriate international consultations if they have reasons to believe that there might be a potentially harmful interference between two activities in the peaceful exploration and use of outer space. The principle of due regard, the prohibition of harmful contamination and the obligation of consultation have a fundamental role to play in preserving space as a peaceful environment and fostering its sustainable uses. For this reason, the importance of Article IX OST is comparable to Articles I and II OST. In requiring States to take into account the corresponding interests of others when conducting their space activities, Article IX OST integrates and connects all the various principles of the OST. Further, in obliging States to take appropriate measures to avoid the harmful impact of their activities on the space environment, Article IX OST preserves it as a shared domain free for exploration and use by all actors. Finally, in obliging States to undertake appropriate international consultations in case of potentially harmful interferences, Article IX OST is the only OST provision concretely bringing its States Parties vis-à-vis to one another. Because of these features, Article IX OST should be considered as the systemic clause of international space law.

The implications of Article IX OST on space mining activities and regulation are manifold. Because of the inherently invasive and consumptive nature of space mining, respecting the systemic obligations of Article IX OST becomes extremely important to ensure its actual compatibility with the OST. First, to comply with the principle of due regard, States will have to make sure that the space resource activities for which they are responsible would not jeopardize the freedom of others to undertake parallel activities. For instance, a State authorizing a private company to mine all the available ice in the entire south pole of the Moon would be clearly breaching its obligation to pay due regard under Article IX OST. Second, to prevent the harmful contamination of celestial bodies, States will have to minimize the generation of environmental impact that could interfere with or jeopardize their exploration and use by other States. Finally, to comply with the obligation of consultation, States foreseeing the potential causation of harmful interference will have to engage in meaningful negotiations with the other States concerned in order to find a suitable compromise between their respective interests.

Article X OST deals with the right to witness space launches. This article does not have any relevance in the context of space mining, and as such, it is excluded from the analysis.

Article XI OST lays down the obligation to share information about space activities. Pursuant to this provision, States agree to inform the UNSG, as well as the public and the international scientific community, to the greatest extent feasible and practicable, of the nature, conduct, locations and results of their space activities. The principle of information sharing, as laid down in Article XI OST, plays several important roles within the system of space law. First and foremost, sharing information about the nature and conduct of a given space activity functions as a verification mechanism to ensure its compliance with the OST. Second, sharing information about the conduct and locations of a space activity supports their safe conduct by enabling due regard and coordination under Article IX OST. Third and final, sharing information about the results of space activities is instrumental in promoting international cooperation in the peaceful exploration and use of outer space. Having said that, it is important to note that pursuant to the formulation of Article XI OST, information sharing should not be intended as an absolute obligation. This is because the provision establishes that States *agree to* (and not that they shall) inform the UNSG about their space activities only to the greatest extent feasible and practicable. This implies that States are not bound to share information whenever there is a valid justification not to do so, such as in the case of national security or intellectual property interests. In order to facilitate the distribution of the information shared, the final part of Article XI OST determines that the UNSG should be prepared to disseminate it immediately and effectively. This task is discharged by UNOOSA through the compilation of the submissions received within the Index of Submissions by States Under Article XI of the OST.

The principle of information sharing has vital importance for the peaceful, safe and sustainable conduct of space resource activities. At present, no State is in the position to determine on its own how its space resource activities may impact the corresponding interests of other States, nor whether and to what extent they could cause potentially harmful contamination or interference. These determinations entirely depend on the availability of proper information about the environment of celestial bodies as well as the activities of other States, including a certain level of technical details as necessary to ensure safety and prevent interference. Accordingly, sharing information about space resource activities under Article XI OST will be vital to build trust, enable coordination and foster cooperation. To this end, the current mechanism for sharing information under Article XI OST will need to be adjusted to better fit the coordination needs linked with the exploration and use of celestial bodies.

Article XII OST regulates access to stations, installations, equipment and vehicles on celestial bodies. Pursuant to this provision, all these shall be open to the representatives of other Parties on a basis of reciprocity. To ensure safety and avoid interference with nominal operations, Article XII OST establishes that representatives shall give reasonable advance notice of their projected visit so as to hold appropriate consultations and take maximum precautions. The openness of stations, installations, equipment and vehicles located on celestial bodies is meant to ensure their exclusively peaceful uses. In obliging States to give access to their facilities on celestial bodies, Article XII offers an opportunity to verify their compliance with Article IV (2) OST. In this regard, the condition of reciprocity included in Article XII OST should be interpreted in the sense of giving States the right to refuse access only to the representatives of those States which do not have any station, installation, equipment or vehicle of their own that could be accessed as well. Under the same line of reasoning, also the conditions laid down in the second part of the provision should be interpreted in such a way that does not hamper or frustrate the fundamental principle of openness. This, in turn, means that States cannot rely on these conditions to refuse access *tout court* but only to (eventually) delay it accordingly.

It is interesting to note that in regulating access to stations and installations on celestial bodies, Article XII OST implicitly recognizes the right to build such facilities in the first place. This right to establish stations and installations on celestial bodies has to be read in conjunction with the principle of free access under Article I OST and the prohibition of national appropriation under Article II OST. A combined reading of these provisions further reinforces the key importance of the principle of openness in order to reduce as much as possible the negative impact on the principles of free access and to prevent allegations of indirect appropriation of the territory over which the facility is built.

The implications of Article XII OST on space mining are quite delicate. This is because the application of this principle will have to be balanced against technical and commercial risks for damages and abuses. For example, a space mining company might want to access the facilities of its competitor to acquire privileged information on its business activities. Similar abuses should be prevented and addressed by States in accordance with the principle of good faith. For what concerns technical sensibilities, these issues would be best addressed during consultations preceding the visit.

ii *The Liability and Registration Conventions*

After analyzing the implications of the OST, Chapter 2 moves to consider the relevance of the LIAB and REG. As mentioned, the ARRA has been excluded from the analysis due to its irrelevance in space mining.

The LIAB was adopted in 1972 with the goal to provide "effective international rules and procedures concerning liability for damage caused by space objects." Throughout its twenty-eight articles, the LIAB lays down the fundamental rules governing international liability for space objects and further provides a dedicated process for settling any disputes arising therefrom. The very first novelty of the LIAB is a list of definitions clarifying the meaning of the term "damage," "launching," "launching State" and "space object." It is important to note that these definitions have no presumption of completeness and are intended to continuingly adapt to the evolution of technology. The second novelty introduced in the LIAB is the development of different forms of liability based on the location of the accident. For damage caused by a space object on the surface of the Earth or to an aircraft in flight, Article II LIAB determines the absolute liability of the relevant launching State(s). In case of damages caused in outer space, Article III LIAB provides that the launching State shall be liable only if the damage is due to its fault or the faults of the persons for whom it is responsible. By introducing the element of fault, Article III LIAB intends to push States to do everything they can to avoid the collision, with the goal to prove that they were not at fault in case damage ultimately happens. In this regard, it will be critical to develop practical criteria guiding the application of the concept of fault so as to increase the practical relevance of the convention.

Moving to the REG, it was adopted in 1975 to expand on Article VIII OST and oblige States to the national and international registration of space objects. From a systemic viewpoint, the mandatory registration of space objects serves the purpose of fostering the principle of transparency under Article XI OST and enhances the application of the liability rules by providing a legal link between space objects and at least one launching State. Similar to the LIAB, the REG also begins with a list of generic definitions of the terms "launching State," "space object" and "State of Registry." The obligation to register objects launched into outer space into a national registry is laid down in Article II REG. Complementarily, Articles III and IV address the duty to register space objects in the UN Registry that had been created pursuant to UNGA Res. 1721B

(XVI) of December 20, 1961. Article IV REG obliges the launching State to share a minimum set of information identified in the article, to be furnished to the UNSG "as soon as practicable." In this regard, the absence of a clear time limit for internationally registered space objects is certainly the most significant shortcoming of the REG. Notwithstanding this weakness, the REG is a very successful instrument: according to UNOOSA, to date, over 86% of all satellites, probes, landers, crewed spacecraft and space station flight elements launched into Earth orbit or beyond have been registered with the UN Registry.

There is no doubt that both Conventions provide complementary contributions of key importance. To ensure regulatory uniformity, all States engaged in the regulation and conduct of space resource activities should become Parties to both Conventions. With specific reference to the LIAB, its fault regime is much more suited to apportion liability for damages caused in the course of space resource activities compared to the absolute regime laid down in Article VII OST. From a practical perspective, it would be useful to complement this regime with the development of objective parameters to help determine the notion of fault in the context of space mining. Concerning the REG, its fundamental role in transparency and confidence building will be extremely important for the successful conduct of space resource activities. From a practical viewpoint, it would be useful to create dedicated sections within the national and international registries for space objects to separately list those involved in space mining. In these sections, States should also provide additional information on the location and duration of space resource activities related to the object(s) in question.

iii *The Moon Agreement*

To complete the analysis of the international layer of the multi-level regulatory system of space mining, Chapter 2 considers the relevance of the MA. In light of its status as the only existing instrument specifically dedicated to governing activities on celestial bodies, the chapter conducts a thorough assessment of the fundamental provisions of the MA, with special consideration to the principle of "Common Heritage of Mankind" established by its Article 11.

For most parts, the MA simply restates rules and provisions of the OST. However, the agreement also presents significant additions and innovations that are worth considering for their implications on space mining activities and regulations.

To begin with, Article 4 expands the province principle laid down in Article 1 OST by requiring States to pay due regard to the interests of present and future generations, as well as to the need to promote higher standards of living and conditions of economic and social progress and development on Earth. These additions are noteworthy because it is the first time that the concepts of sustainability and intergenerational balance form the basis of a legal obligation of international space law.

Building upon Articles IX and XI OST, Article 5 MA obliges States to share a significant amount of information on their lunar activities and leverage them for the purposes of international coordination. Paragraph 2 of this provision is especially forward-thinking in requiring States to promptly inform each other of the timing and plans for their lunar activities if they become aware that another State Party plans to operate simultaneously in the same area.

Article 6 MA elaborates on Article I (3) OST to reinforce the importance of the freedom of scientific investigation. The most interesting part of this provision is again the second paragraph, which addresses in great detail the collection of Moon samples and the use of minerals and other substances for scientific purposes. Since the object and purpose of Article 6 MA is to promote and reinforce the freedom of scientific investigation on the Moon, this paragraph exempts the use of lunar resources for scientific purposes from the restrictions posed by the international regime envisaged in Article 11 MA.

Article 7 MA builds upon Article IX OST to address the environmental protection of the Moon. In this regard, Article 7 MA certainly goes beyond the prohibition of harmful contamination laid down in Article IX OST by requiring States conducting activities on the Moon to take measures to prevent the disruption of the existing balance of its environment. From the ordinary meaning of the expression "disruption of the existing balance," it seems that Article 7 MA requires lunar activities to be environmentally neutral, i.e., without any prejudice toward the environment around them. In this regard, it is important to note that Article 7 MA does not prohibit *all* disruptions of the existing balance of the Moon, but *only* those that have a somehow negative effect on the legal status of the Moon and its natural resources as the CHM.

Article 9 MA specifically addresses the establishment of robotic or human stations on the Moon, building upon the implicit right to establish stations and installations established under Article XII OST. In line with the restricted approach of the Agreement, Article 9 MA limits the use of the lunar territory only to the area required for the needs of the station and obliges States to establish their lunar stations in such a manner to not impede the right of others to freely access all areas of the Moon.

Another provision of the Agreement significantly expanding the scope of a rule from the OST is Article 15 MA, which builds upon Articles IX and XII OST to regulate the relations among States Parties to the Agreement. According to this provision, each State Party may assure itself that the activities of other States in the exploration and use of the Moon are compatible with the provisions of this Agreement. A State suspecting violations is entitled to request consultations with the accused State, which shall enter into such consultations without delay. If these consultations would not lead to a mutually acceptable settlement which has due regard for the rights and interests of all States Parties, then the concerned States have to take measures to settle their dispute by other peaceful means.

Pursuant to Article 11 MA, the Moon and its natural resources are proclaimed to be "the common heritage of Mankind." This expression creates a new, stricter status for celestial bodies and their natural resources, whose use has to be governed in accordance with the provisions of the Agreement. In international law, the CHM concept made its first appearance in 1967 as part of a speech delivered at the UN by the Maltese Ambassador Pardo. Several decades after, the concept was implemented in the UNCLOS to govern activities in the Deep Seabed, which (together with its resources) was declared "the common heritage of all mankind." Despite using the same terminology, the CHM regime set forth in the MA is very different from the UNCLOS one. This is made clear by Article 11 MA itself, according to which the status of the Moon and its natural resources as CHM "finds its expression in the provisions of this agreement, in particular in paragraph 5 of this article." Pursuant to this paragraph, States Parties to the MA undertake to establish an international regime, including appropriate procedures, to govern the exploitation of the natural resources of the Moon "as such exploitation is about to become feasible." Moving from the premise that States did not know enough to develop a proper governing regime for the use of lunar resources, Article 11 (5) MA hits "pause" on the normative process to avoid the enactment of inadequate regulation. At the same time, the Agreement does not leave the development of the international regime entirely to the future since its paragraph 7 lays down four main purposes influencing its future configuration. These purposes are (a) the "orderly and safe development" of the natural resources of the Moon, (b) the "rational management" of those resources, (c) "the expansions of opportunities" in their use and finally, (d) an "equitable sharing by all States Parties in the benefits derived" therefrom.

Since the purpose of the MA is precisely to regulate the use of the Moon and its natural resources, its consequences on space mining activities and regulations are obviously manifold. For what concerns States Parties to the MA, if and when the international regime of Article 11 MA is established, they will be able to conduct (all) activities on the Moon exclusively under its terms. In the meantime, due to the absence of a moratorium on the use of space resources, these States can engage in space resource activities, provided that they take good faith efforts toward the negotiation of the international regime mentioned in Article 11 MA. In this regard, the teleological dependence of the norms of the MA on the concept of CHM suggests that the concrete application of the whole Agreement to the actual conduct of lunar activities depends on the establishment of the international regime mentioned in Article 11 MA. As such, States Parties to the MA would not be operatively constrained by its various obligations until the entry into force of the international regime mentioned under Article 11 MA, except for the one to take good faith efforts toward its establishment. For what concerns States which are not Parties to the MA, they should take the Agreement into proper consideration in order to learn from its mistakes and leverage its strengths. In this regard, it is worth recognizing the value of the Agreement's provisions on intergenerational balance, information sharing and international designation of special scientific areas.

iv *Key Takeaway from International Space Law*

From the overall assessment of international space law, it is clear that space resource activities will not be conducted in a legal vacuum. Almost all the principles laid down in the *Corpus Iuris Spatialis* have several implications for the conduct of space mining. At the same time, there is also no doubt that space resource activities are testing the system of space law to its very limit. In the majority of cases, the broadness of the norms of international space law leaves the interpreter with too many regulatory options to pick from. This, in turn, determines a serious risk of conflicting interpretations, as different interpreters are likely to derive different rules. This systemic ambiguity needs to be addressed before space resource activities are conducted with a frequency and on a scale that can destabilize the peaceful uses of outer space.

1.2.2 National Space Legislation

To complete the regulatory assessment of the multi-level system of space mining, Chapter 2 moves to consider the only four examples of domestic legislation addressing the private conduct of space mining enacted by the United States, Luxembourg, the United Arab Emirates and Japan. Notwithstanding the various concerns raised, especially in the academic world, all these laws are found to be fully compatible with the *Corpus Iuris Spatialis*. They address an activity which is permitted under Article I OST, and they do so in compliance with their regulatory obligations under Article VI OST. At the same time, these legislations do not include any substantive provision governing the conduct of space resource activities. For example, none of these laws provides that a space mining permit should not exceed a given physical or temporal extension or that certain scarce resources should be prevented from being spoiled by firstcomers. On the contrary, the goal of all these legislations seems to be declaratory in nature. As such, the main contribution provided by these laws to the development of the multi-level regulatory system of space mining is to establish that space resource activities can be conducted by private actors. While the scope of the U.S. and UAE laws is essentially limited to this declaration, the Luxembourgish and Japanese laws provide administrative guidance on how to obtain a space mining permit. The Luxembourgish Law of 2017, in particular, is the only one foreseeing a detailed procedure for the administrative enactment of a space resources license, including a list of specific requirements to be possessed by applicants. Per its part, the JSRA of 2021 includes forward-thinking provisions establishing exemplary international practices on information sharing and on the harmonization between the national and international regulatory levels. Overall, the only notable implication that can be derived from the analysis of the four national legislations on space mining is their existence itself. From a systemic viewpoint, the very existence of these laws confirms the nature of space mining as multi-level regulatory system. However, the lack in these laws of substantive provisions addressing the conduct of space resource activities reduces their normative meaning in a significant manner. Ultimately, the main impact of these legislations at the moment has been to call the attention of the international community to the regulation of space mining, primarily as a reaction against a potential leading role for national regulators in this process. From a practical viewpoint, it is also possible to add that the enactment of these laws has played an enabling role in promoting the establishment of several private companies and research centers dedicated to space mining that would have never been created otherwise.

1.2.3 *Multi-level Interactions*

After looking at both regulatory levels, Chapter 2 moves to assess their interplays within the nascent system of space mining. In this regard, the chapter observes that the combination of the broadness of the principles of international space law and the administrative nature of the national legislation enacted so far creates a normative deficit within the system. This deficit comes from the lack of clear normative solutions that can concretely govern the conduct of space mining activities. To address this deficit or *impasse*, the chapter suggests the establishment of a middle-level framework that can connect the principles of international space law with the concrete rules (that should be) provided by domestic space legislation. In other words, this framework should harmonize the interpretation of the principles of space law so to guide the enactment of operational rules at the national level. Based on this assessment, the chapter presents recent developments in space policy aimed at addressing the normative deficit.

i Policy Developments in UNCOPUOS

In light of the primary importance of the international dimension for the governance of space activities in general, Chapter 2 provides a detailed overview of the debate in UNCOPUOS. As is well-known, the initial prompt was given by the enactment of the U.S. Law in 2015, which rapidly led to the establishment of an agenda item dedicated to space resources in 2017. Since the initial discussions that were held, it was possible to identify two "factions," one in favor of a leading role for national regulation and one calling for direct international governance. Over the last three years, the debate has moved toward more constructive discussions oriented toward the achievement of concrete results. This process started at the 2019 meetings of the LSC when Member States decided to hold informal consultations on the potential establishment of a working group dedicated to space resources. After a first postponement due to the COVID-19 pandemic, the consultations were held during the 2021 meetings and successfully led to establishment of a new working group under the agenda item on space resources. During the 2022 meetings of the LSC, the SRWG completed the enactment of its foundational documents with the approval of its five-year workplan. According to this document, the SRWG will spend the first three years assessing the legal framework applicable to space resource activities with the goal to evaluate its implications and determine the need for further elaboration. Based on the results of this assessment, the SRWG should then spend the last two years of activities drafting an initial set of principles to ensure the peaceful, safe, rational and sustainable conduct of space resource activities. In accordance with the normative process of UNCOPUOS, these principles will be submitted for the consideration of and consensus agreement by the Committee, followed by possible adoption by the General Assembly as a dedicated resolution. As it will be discussed later, the success or failure of the SRWG will have a decisive impact on the future configuration of the multi-level system of space mining.

ii *Policy Developments in Civil Society*

In parallel to the normative developments happening at the United Nations, several stakeholders from the space community have also looked at which policy solutions might help in solving the regulatory deficits of space mining. Accordingly, the chapter provides an overview of the most important contributions provided by international groups and organizations. In this regard, the chapter recognizes a critical role for The Hague International Space Resources Governance Working Group, which has been the first entity to propose the development of a dedicated framework between international space law and national legislation to address space resource activities. Following the conclusion of the activities of the Group, the idea of developing a minimum shared ground at the international level was supported and complemented in further policy documents produced by the OLF, the SGAC and the MVA. In comparison with the approach of The Hague Working Group, these entities look at the regulation of space resources within the broader context of the governance of celestial bodies, with specific reference to the Moon.

iii *Policy Developments in State Practice*

In October 2020, a group of eight Countries announced the AA, a multilateral political commitment to fundamental principles governing the conduct of their civilian space programs beyond Earth orbit. Section 10 of the AA underlines the legality of space resource activities under Article I OST while also emphasizing the importance of conducting them in accordance with all the principles of the OST. In this regard, the chapter found that the AA—which in just two years have increased from eight to nineteen Signatories—have a critical role to play in demonstrating positive State practice for the legality of space resource activities.

iv *Regulatory Scenarios*

Based on the conducted analysis, the chapter indicates three potential scenarios for the further development of space mining as multi-level regulatory system: uncoordinated national legislation, integrated multi-level regulation and direct international governance. All scenarios move from the current starting point: broad principles at the international level and administrative provisions at the national one. In the first scenario, substantive provisions at the domestic level are enacted in the absence of any international guidance. Given the many different ways in which States could interpret the principles of international space law, said domestic provisions would likely end up conflicting with one another, ultimately threatening the peaceful, safe and sustainable uses of celestial bodies. In the second scenario, the domestic enactment of substantive regulation for space mining is based upon a shared starting point agreed upon at the international level. In this scenario, the regulatory potential held by domestic regulation would be channeled within clear international boundaries, thus limiting the risk of divergence and increasing probability of successful regulation. From a systemic viewpoint, this approach needs to be complemented with the development of appropriate procedures for minimum coordination and amicable resolution of disputes. Minimum coordination mechanisms for space resource activities should be based on three pillars: public notification, bilateral coordination and mutual recognition. Potential disputes should be addressed by means of international arbitration before the PCA (or the future Dubai Space Court) so as to benefit from enforcement under the NYC. Finally, in the third scenario, space resource activities are directly governed at the international level. The main issue of this scenario is that, in accordance with the principle of subsidiarity, the regulation of space mining should be fully transferred at the international level only when States are not able to properly ensure its harmonious and efficient development at the domestic one. Only in a similar situation would there be valid reasons to support direct international governance, together with a centralized enforcement structure ensuring the equal, consistent and efficient application of the given rules.

1.2.4 Key Takeaways on the Regulatory Configuration of Space Mining

From the conducted assessment, the chapter draws a number of conclusions. First, there is an evident imbalance within the multi-level regulatory system of space mining. The international level is clearly much more developed than the national one, which so far has only acknowledged the mere legality of space resource activities conducted by private entities. At the same time, the inherent broadness of international space law does not provide the interpreter with any clear direction among the many available regulatory options. In the prolonged absence of international guidance, the responsibility to operationalize these rules law will inevitably fall on national regulators. Since each of these entities will undertake this task based on their own preferences, at present, the multi-level system of space mining is facing a serious risk of regulatory divergence. If left uncontrolled, this divergence will increase up to the point of becoming intolerable and, as a result, conflictual. On the contrary, if the application of international space law is managed through appropriate international guidance, then the multi-level regulatory system of space mining will flourish.

1.3 Enforcement Options and Proposed Reinforcements

Building upon the systemic and regulatory findings developed in Chapters 1 and 2, Chapter 3 sets to identify and evaluate present options and future models for the adjudication and enforcement of its norms. On a preliminary basis, the chapter frames the concept of enforcement as the proceduralized execution of judicial or administrative decisions ascertaining a normative violation and providing instructions on how to remediate non-compliance. Based on this definition and mirroring the multi-level nature of the regulatory system, the chapter looks at available options in both layers and then evaluates them in light of their legitimacy and effectiveness. Due to the unsatisfactory results of this evaluation, the chapter suggests reinforcing the system with the introduction of dedicated mechanisms for coordination, consultation and adjudication. To inspire the design of such mechanisms, the chapter looks at three comparable legal regimes governing other global commons: the UNCLOS, the ITU and the AT. After determining the suitability of the solutions provided thereby, the chapter concludes by delineating their concrete application in the short, medium and long term.

Within the context of the book, the findings developed in Chapter 3 complement and enrich the regulatory analysis with dedicated studies on the options available for the adjudication and enforcement of space law rules, as well as on the potential correctives that could and should be introduced to address their deficiencies.

1.3.1 International Enforcement Options

From the findings above, it is clear that the norms of international space law are not sufficiently precise to be directly enforced, especially with reference to the conduct of space mining. Even though the general principles of international space law laid down in the OST are certainly applicable to the conduct of space mining, their broadness prevents the clear identification of a precise normative solution that could be enforced accordingly. Further to that, there are no dedicated institutions formally entrusted with the adjudication and enforcement of international disputes related to space law. Thanks to the principle of systemic integration provided by Article 31 VCLT, the system of space mining might fill these gaps with the adjudicatory and enforcement mechanisms provided by the legal order of international law. Among the available options, there are reasonable grounds to determine the potential involvement of two international courts: the ICJ, due to its status as the principal judicial organ of the United Nations, and the PCA, due to its reputation as a recognized international tribunal equipped with a dedicated set of rules for space disputes. In light of the fundamental institutional differences between the two institutions, choosing one over the other would trigger the exercise of different enforcement powers.

i Enforcing ICJ Judgments

Under Article 94 (1) ICJ, decisions are binding upon the Parties to its cases. As a result, they might be enforced either by the UNSC under Article 94 (2) UN Charter or by the injured States under Articles 49-54 ARSIWA.

Under Article 94 (2) UN Charter, if one such party fails to perform its obligations under the judgment, the other party may have recourse to the Security Council, "which may, if it deems necessary, make recommendations or decide upon measures to be taken to give effect to the judgment." It is important to note that Article 94 (2) UN Charter subjects the enforcement of international law violations adjudicated by the ICJ to a double layer of discretion, first from the creditor State and then from the UNSC. These two layers of discretion are introduced to preserve the autonomy of both the States involved as well as of the UNSC. While justified within the architecture of the UN Charter, these layers significantly undermine the practical relevance of the mechanism provided under Article 94 (2) UN Charter. Not by chance, this provision has been invoked only in five cases, none of which lead to its concrete application. As argued by Obregon, pursuant to his thorough review of these cases, the enforcement mechanism designed by Article 94 (2) UN Charter seems to be more of a political than legal nature. In terms of legitimacy, the lack of representativeness of the UNSC and the unbalanced distribution of power between its members would suggest a rather negative evaluation of this tool. At the same time, the direct link established by the conduct of space activities and the maintenance of international peace and security under Article III OST partially mitigates these concerns. In terms of effectiveness, the direct involvement of the five permanent members of the UNSC in space matters would paralyze the ability of the Council to take any action, as demonstrated by the case of Nicaragua. Consequently, the evaluation of Article 94 (2) UN Charter as enforcement option for the system of space mining is negative. Overall, it is unlikely that this provision will play any role in the future enforcement of potential space mining disputes adjudicated by the ICJ.

An alternative route for the enforcement of ICJ decisions would be the enactment of countermeasures under the ARSIWA. Since under Article VI OST States are internationally responsible for ensuring compliance of their national space activities with the Treaty's provisions, an ICJ judgment ascertaining their violation would trigger the international responsibility of the responsible State. As a consequence, a State refusing to abide by such judgment would be exposed to the enactment of countermeasures under Articles 49-51 ARSIWA. Through the use of these tools, the injured State may seek to vindicate its rights under the judgment and restore international legality. It is important to note that Article 49 ARSIWA limits countermeasures to the non-performance of international obligations owed to the State committing an internationally wrongful act.

In terms of legitimacy and effectiveness, the lack of dedicated authorities within the system of international space law might suggest a positive evaluation of countermeasures as an enforcement tool. At the same time, the impact of the sanctions taken by a group of western States against the Russian Federation pursuant to its invasion of Ukraine seems to indicate a different answer. As is well-known, in response to these sanctions, Russia has unilaterally suspended its space cooperation with said States and even threatened to stop propelling the ISS in an attempt to use the negative effect of such decision as a deterrent against the sanctions. As a result, a number of space missions planned in cooperation with Russia had to be canceled, with severe implications on the important scientific objectives connected to them. This is to say that countermeasures have the potential to trigger a dangerous escalation that might very well undermine the stability of the entire space environment.

ii Enforcing PCA Awards

Under Article 18 of the Arbitration Convention, States Parties "agree to submit loyally" to the awards rendered by the PCA. As a result, compliance with these awards might again be enforced by injured States under Articles 49-54 ARSIWA.

In addition to that, PCA awards might be enforced by domestic courts under the 1958 NYC. The goal of the NYC is to maximize the circulation of foreign arbitral awards by removing unnecessary obstacles to their recognition and enforcement. To this date, the Convention has been ratified by 157 States, and it is universally considered to be the cornerstone of the international arbitration system. It is important to note that even though the Convention primarily refers to *foreign* arbitral awards, pursuant to Article I NYC, this term includes all awards which are not considered domestic in the State where their recognition and enforcement are sought, including those made by permanent arbitral bodies (like the PCA). The core rule of the Convention is laid down in its Article III, according to which "each Contracting State shall recognize arbitral awards as binding and enforce them in accordance with the rules of procedure of the territory where the award is relied upon, under the conditions laid down in the following articles." Pursuant to this provision, absent a valid impediment under the other provisions of the Convention—and in particular Articles IV, V, VI and VII—international and foreign arbitral awards must always be recognized and enforced in accordance with relevant domestic rules of procedure. Article III NYC expresses a "pro-enforcement bias" that constitutes the object and purpose of the Convention and ensures its successful application over the past sixty years. In terms of legitimacy, enforcement options granted under the Convention meet the highest standards of legitimacy due to its status as international agreement. In terms of effectiveness, thanks to its strong pro-enforcement bias and the direct involvement of national courts, the remedies offered by the NYC have proved to be extremely effective for the enforcement of arbitral awards. For these reasons, the enforcement of PCA awards under the NYC represents the best enforcement option available at the international level.

1.3.2 National Enforcement Options

The national level is affected by the same lack of enforceability previously identified for international space law. Having said that, to better frame the identification and evaluation of adjudication and enforcement mechanisms, it is important to distinguish between "purely domestic" and "transnational" disputes based on the potential involvement of domestic authorities vis-à-vis foreign entities. With regard to domestic disputes, there is no doubt that they will be adjudicated and enforced through the relevant national mechanisms available in the given jurisdiction. Conversely, the applicability of domestic mechanisms for the adjudication and enforcement of transnational disputes would face serious issues of legitimacy and effectiveness due to the exercise of extraterritorial powers. In the future, these issues might be addressed by the application of the JC, a recent instrument for the global recognition and enforcement of domestic judgments. However, the JC is currently not in force and will require several years before reaching the level of acceptance needed to provide a legitimate and effective solution, so its concrete viability as enforcement option remains to be seen.

1.3.3 *Preliminary Conclusions*

Based on the above, it is possible to formulate some preliminary conclusions on the current status of enforcement options for space mining regulations. First, international norms applicable to space resource activities can be legitimately and effectively enforced only to the extent that their violation has been adjudicated by international arbitration. This is because normative violations adjudicated by international courts like the ICJ cannot be enforced in a legitimate and effective manner, except if the involved Court is part of a supranational regime like the EU or the WTO. Second, domestic norms regulating private space mining activities can be enforced in a legitimate and effective manner only against domestic actors. This is because normative violations adjudicated by domestic authorities cannot be legitimately and effectively enforced against foreign actors without the consent of the involved State. Since the majority of space mining disputes will likely be international in nature or present a transnational character, the possibility of legitimate and effective enforcement would vitally depend on the pursuit of international arbitration. This dependence is a critical vulnerability of the system since, at present, there is no guarantee that States will agree to resolve their space mining disputes through arbitration. As a result of this analysis, it is apparent that the system of space mining is particularly exposed to tensions and conflicts connected to the lack of adequate adjudication and enforcement processes. This, in turn, reveals the need to reinforce the system before the occurrence of a major international accident.

1.3.4 *Reinforcing the System: Proposals from Comparable Models*

Based on the above, the chapter suggests reinforcing the system with the development of dedicated adjudication, coordination and consultation mechanisms. In order to form a better understanding of how to design these correctives, the chapter looks at comparable legal regimes dealing with the governance of global commons: the UNCLOS, the ITU and the AT.

i *The United Nations Convention on the Law of the Sea*

The UNCLOS is one of the most important international agreements in the world. At present, the Convention counts 168 States Parties and is universally recognized as the reference instrument for all issues related to the law of the sea. In accordance with the scope of the chapter, consideration of the UNCLOS has been limited to the adjudicatory system designed in its Part XI for disputes related to activities in the Deep Seabed. The main feature of this system is the establishment of a dedicated Seabed Disputes Chamber within the ITLOS. Even though the Chamber is established as a specialized section of the ITLOS and not as a separate entity, it is provided with relative autonomy in terms of composition, access, procedures and jurisdiction. In terms of jurisdiction, the UNCLOS establishes the competence of the Chamber to adjudicate the following types of disputes:

(1) issues of interpretation or application of Part XI and its related annexes among States Parties to the Convention;
(2) disputes between a State Party and the Authority concerning the latter's acts or omissions (exclusive);
(3) certain disputes between the parties to a contract for Deep Seabed mining;
(4) liability disputes under Annex III of the Convention (exclusive);
(5) any other dispute for which the jurisdiction of the Chamber is specifically provided in this Convention (exclusive).

Pursuant to the agreement of all involved parties, disputes concerning the interpretation and application of Part XI *may* also be referred to a special chamber of the ITLOS or to an ad hoc chamber within the Seabed Disputes Chamber. At the request of any party, commercial disputes related to the interpretation or application of a contract for Deep Seabed mining *shall* be submitted to *binding* commercial arbitration at the request of any party. It is important to mention that arbitrators resolving these disputes shall have no jurisdiction to decide any question of interpretation of this Convention and that should such questions of interpretation arise during the dispute, they shall be referred to the Chamber for a ruling. In terms of exclusions, all potential disputes related to matters falling within the scope of the WTO agreements have been subtracted from the jurisdiction of the Chamber. Further, the Chamber shall have no jurisdiction over the exercise of the discretionary and normative powers of the ISA. In these areas, the Chamber's jurisdiction shall be confined to adjudicate, in individual cases, whether the *application* of such rules, regulations and procedures would be in conflict either with relevant obligations under either the contract or the Convention. In terms of enforcement, the decisions of the Chamber are enforceable in the territories of the States Parties in the same manner as judgments or orders of the highest court of the State Party in whose territory the enforcement is sought.

It is worth noting that existing literature assessing the relevance of the UNCLOS as a model for the governance of space mining has always focused on the CHM principle and/or the ISA model. The analysis conducted in Chapter 3 enriches this debate by offering a different approach focused on the UNCLOS adjudicatory mechanisms. In this regard, the chapter found that the model of the Deep Seabed Disputes Chamber might prove to be particularly insightful in inspiring the development of dedicated bodies and procedures for adjudicating international disputes related to space mining. Leveraging the features of the Deep Seabed Chamber model, it would be possible to design an adjudicatory mechanism combining the strengths of international courts and arbitrators, reconnecting with domestic systems, ensuring prompt enforcement and integrating potentially competing jurisdiction from overlapping regimes. Having said that, it is difficult to imagine the design of such a mechanism in a short timeframe, as Member States in UNCOPUOS do not seem eager to engage in institutional developments until the end of the activities of the SRWG in 2027.

ii *The International Telecommunication Union*

After considering potential reinforcements to the adjudicatory processes of the multi-level system of space mining, the chapter moves to consider the suitability of coordination procedures that could reduce the need for *ex post* enforcement. To this end, the chapter looks at the norms and mechanisms established by the ITU and concludes that the principles laid down in its Radio Regulations might provide an excellent inspiration for developing dedicated coordination mechanisms for space resource activities.

The ITU is a specialized agency of the United Nations and one of the oldest international organizations in the world. The ITU sees the participation of all 193 UN Members and is one of the few intergovernmental organizations welcoming the participation of non-governmental entities. The foundations of the ITU legal regime are laid down in its Constitution and Convention, whereas its coordination and notification rules are provided in an international instrument called Radio Regulations. The Radio Regulations are an intergovernmental treaty amended every four years during dedicated events called WRCs. The legal basis justifying the procedures laid down in the Radio Regulations comes from the special legal status of frequencies and associated orbits as limited natural resources established by Article 44 of the ITU Constitution. This legal status justifies the impositions of limitations and procedures for the rational, efficient and economic use of frequencies and orbits, with the goal of guaranteeing their equitable access to all States.

To this end, the Radio Regulations distinguish between "planned services," i.e., those concerning selected geostationary orbital positions and associated frequencies due to their scarcity and strategic relevance, and "non-planned services," which are all the others. Based on this distinction, the Radio Regulations subject the use of orbits and associated frequencies falling under the definition of planned services to special *a priori* planning procedures guaranteeing equitable access in view of their future use. The core mechanism governing these procedures is the allocation of these resources to specific services and their subsequent allotment to ITU Member States, either on a regional or global scale, regardless of their technological capability to bring them into use. Frequencies and orbits falling under the definition of non-planned services are allocated, allotted and assigned through coordination procedures aiming at their efficient use and interference-free operations. Pursuant to the Radio Regulations, the assignment of these frequencies can be notified for international recognition only after exhausting one of two preliminary processes, the advance public information or the coordination procedure. The application of one or the other depends on the use of certain orbital positions and/or specific frequency bands. The difference between the two procedures is that in the coordination procedure, the publishing administration shall identify in advance, to the extent possible, the administrations with which coordination is to be effected and then execute it. In both cases, if an administration alleges the potential causation of unacceptable interference to its existing or planned systems, then both of them shall endeavor to cooperate in joint efforts to resolve any difficulties, with the possible assistance of the Bureau.

After having exhausted the applicable procedure, the publishing administration may notify the frequency assignments to the Bureau for recording within ITU's Master International Frequency Register, through which the assignment obtains international recognition. It is important to note that the Bureau plays an active role in verifying the conformity of the notified assignment with the relevant rules from the Radio Regulation. As a result of this examination, the Bureau may provide a favorable or unfavorable finding. A favorable finding leads to recording the assignment in the Master Registry, which in turn creates the right to international recognition. Conversely, unfavorable findings lead to returning the notice to the concerned administration, with an indication of appropriate action to be undertaken. It is essential to note that recorded frequency assignments have to be brought into use no later than seven years following the start of the relevant preliminary procedure. This rule is of critical importance because any frequency assignment which is not brought into use within the required period shall be canceled by the Bureau.

At the end of the analysis condensed above, the chapter found that the ITU's ability to combine (1) a coordinated *first-come-first-served* mechanism ensuring efficient uses together with (2) a predetermined allotment system ensuring equitable access provides an excellent example for reinforcing the system of space mining, thanks to the minimization of *ex post* enforcement. Learning from the successful experience of the ITU, it would be possible to introduce enhanced coordination practices with the twofold objective of preventing harmful interference while also promoting equitable uses. The only *caveat* is that the establishment of ITU-like coordination practices would need to be coupled with a minimum degree of institutionalization, which in turn might be difficult to achieve in the short term.

iii *The Antarctic Treaty*

To complete its assessment of potential correctives for reinforcing the system of space mining, Chapter 3 looks at the suitability of consultative processes that could reduce the need for adversarial adjudication. To this end, the chapter focuses on the inspection and consultation mechanisms laid down in the AT. From its analysis, the chapter concludes that the introduction of similar processes would reinforce the system of space mining by reducing existing tensions, incentivizing cooperation and allowing for the incremental development of adaptive regulation in a multi-level fashion.

The AT is a regional agreement governing the exploration and use of Antarctica. The Treaty was concluded in 1958 among eight States involved in the early exploration of Antarctica to settle their territorial disputes and cooperate for the scientific investigation of the Continent. To stop the political and jurisdictional conflicts dividing them, the Parties to the AT agreed to freeze any sovereignty claim over the continent for the time that the Treaty remains in force. In time, the AT expanded both in terms of membership and scope in order to keep up with the increased interest and capabilities in the exploration and use of Antarctica. Today, the Treaty counts fifty-four Parties and is now placed at the center of an overarching legal system featuring four other international agreements and is served by a dedicated Secretariat. The substantive rules at the core of the legal regime set forth in the Treaty are that Antarctica shall be used for peaceful purposes only and that the continent shall be free for scientific investigation and international cooperation.

The Treaty implements these goals by developing a trustful and cooperative environment in support of the freedom of scientific investigation of Antarctica. To this end, the Treaty establishes the right to carry out, through designated observers, inspections in all areas of Antarctica, including all stations, installations and equipment located thereby. It is important to note that observers shall have complete freedom of access at any time to any or all areas of Antarctica. At the same time, not all States Parties to the Treaty are attributed the right to designate observers and conduct inspections. These rights are enjoyed by the original eight Parties as well as by any acceding State demonstrating its interest in Antarctica by conducting substantial scientific research activity there. These States are collectively referred to as Consultative Parties due to their right to participate in dedicated consultative meetings (ATCM). The ATCM are established under Article IX AT for the purpose of exchanging information, consulting on matters of common interest pertaining to Antarctica and considering the enactment of additional measures in furtherance of the principles and objectives of the Treaty. The regular organization of the ATCM has ensured the continuing relevance of the AT by enabling the incremental development of additional governance instruments that could complement it. Both the inspection and consultative mechanisms have played an important role in de-escalating potential tensions among the Parties to the AT by offering an institutionalized opportunity for political exchanges and normative development.

From the conducted analysis, the chapter found the successful experience of the AT to be particularly insightful for reinforcing the multi-level system of space mining. Taking inspiration from the inspection and consultative mechanisms, the system could be reinforced through the introduction of dedicated procedures to ensure open access and foster regular consultations among the States practically involved in space resource activities. These mechanisms would minimize the need for adjudication and enforcement by offering an institutionalized procedure for internalizing potential conflicts before they become of an adversary nature.

iv *Reinforcing the System by Combining the Models*

Building upon the discovered findings, the chapter concluded that the examined regimes might very well support the reinforcement of the multi-level system of space mining. Within each of them, there are certain features and elements that seem to be particularly compatible with the needs and goals of the multi-level system of space mining, in particular from an institutional perspective. Learning from the successful experiences of the UNCLOS, ITU and AT, these weaknesses might be addressed by introducing norms and mechanisms ensuring dedicated adjudication, enhanced coordination and institutional consultation. Due to the infant status of the system, the concrete implementability of these solutions varies depending on the time horizon adopted.

In the short term, the lack of political support for major normative or institutional changes suggests a creative use of the existing legal framework for the development of enhanced practices that can function as provisional correctives. Learning from the successful experience of the ITU, it is possible to combine the principle of due regard under Article IX OST and the information-sharing mechanism provided by Article XI OST for the international coordination of space mining activities. Through a systematic application of these articles, it is possible to argue that by sharing information on its planned and/or ongoing space resource activity, a State becomes entitled to conduct them *free* from potentially harmful interference, at least until it receives a request for consultation from another State. For example, a State informing the international community of its intention to prospect the ice located in a given area of the Shackleton crater would create for itself the right to be consulted by those States planning subsequent activities that might harmfully interfere with the one announced. At the same time, this legal protection would be justified only to the extent that the announced activity is conducted with *due regard* to the interests of the other States. For example, a State granting a license to mine the *entire* south pole of the Moon for an indefinite period of time would definitely not pay due regard to the interest of others in accessing and using the resources located thereby. Potential abuses in the application of these coordination rules could be addressed through the introduction of transparency and consultation mechanisms based on the model of the AT. Combining the principle of free access under Article I OST with the rules laid down under Article XII OST for accessing stations and installations, it is possible to argue that a State *operating on a given celestial body* has the right to inspect all space mining sites located thereby *through pre-appointed representatives*. To reduce the risk of conflict, States should regularly exchange information and consult about their respective space mining operations during the annual meetings of the SRWG, similar to what the Parties to the AT do during the ATCM.

In the medium term, the system could be further reinforced through the introduction of a polycentric adjudicatory system for the resolution of space mining disputes. Bearing in mind the importance of international arbitration for legitimate and effective enforcement, this system should foresee a primary role for the PCA. Taking inspiration from the ruling mechanisms designed under Article 188 (2) UNCLOS, this system could also foresee a role for the ICJ in ruling on fundamental interpretation issues of the space Treaties that might arise during these disputes. In accordance with the normative development of modern international space law, this system might be laid down in a dedicated UNGA resolution guiding the adjudication of space mining disputes.

In the long term, if successful, the proposed correctives could be consolidated in an international regime for the governance of space resource activities. If the proposed correctives would not be successful, the lessons learned from their application could orient the optimal design of better adjudicatory, coordination and consultative mechanisms.

1.3.5 *Key Takeaways on the Enforcement of Space Mining Regulations*

At the end of its analysis, Chapter 3 found that the multi-level regulatory system of space mining is not practically ready nor legally suited for enforcement. To begin with, the system does not have any substantive norm to be enforced in the first place. While international space law provides a foundational starting point for the development of further regulation, its principles are too general to *directly* regulate space mining. As seen in Chapter 2, the main result that can be derived from these principles is a series of implications to be taken into account in the development of substantive regulation. While it would be theoretically possible to use these implications to regulate the conduct of space resource activities, in the absence of international guidance, this operation is too unpredictable to be considered normatively significant. Since no State has the authority to impose a particular interpretation or balancing choice over another, the result of this operation would be, at best, the proliferation of *ephemeral* norms and, at worst, a regulatory chaos of conflicting domestic rules. To further complicate the picture, the only four existing pieces of national space legislation dealing with space resource activities do not make a single normative choice on their substantive regulation. As a result of these normative deficiencies, at present, there are no substantive norms ready to be enforced.

There are two ways in which this situation could be remediated. One option would be the enactment of international principles providing shared foundations for further normative developments at the national level. This is the route currently pursued by the SRWG, even though it remains unclear whether or not the Working Group will be able to achieve it. The alternative option would be the issuance of a judgment from an international adjudicatory body that would indicate, among the available interpretative options, which one to uphold for the regulation of space resource activities. Different from the previous option, in this scenario, it is not yet clear *which* adjudicatory body will get to decide on a space mining dispute. As seen, this uncertainty comes from the lack of dedicated institutions tasked with the interpretation, application and enforcement of space law rules, both at the national and international levels. After conducting a thorough systemic analysis of the options available, Chapter 3 narrowed them down to a few possibilities. However, what will happen in practice remains to be seen. Furthermore, in both scenarios, the vague character of the principles of international space law does not allow to anticipate the concrete normative choices that will be made by either the SRWG or an international court. The consequence of this evaluation is that the system of space mining cannot provide predictable and reliable enforcement processes. This is the reason why the ITU and AT models, which both reduce the need for adjudication and enforcement respectively through *ex ante* coordination among operators and *ongoing* review among regulators, are particularly suitable to provide the reinforcing correctives needed in the short term.

2 FUTURE PERSPECTIVES

The combination of the findings developed throughout the three chapters of this book suggests the following reflections. First, in light of the key importance of international law within the multi-level system of space mining, any substantive rule addressing the conduct of space mining will have to comply with its norms and principles. Second, while the SRWG investigates how to apply these principles to space resource activities, the system needs to be reinforced with dedicated coordination and consultation mechanisms to prevent incidents and conflicts during the early stages. These processes should build upon the principles laid down in Articles I, IX, XI and XII OST and be modeled on analog mechanisms from the ITU and AT models. To complement this approach, it would also be advisable that States commit to international arbitration before the PCA for the resolution of potential legal disputes arising from the conduct of space resource activities. Without dedicated mechanisms for coordination, consultation and adjudication, the current normative divergence and mistrust among States are destined to increase up to the point of undermining the possibility of conducting space resource activities in a peaceful, safe, rational and sustainable manner.

The above reflections are in line with the early stages of space mining. As argued multiple times, the community lacks the necessary knowledge to develop detailed rules for the conduct of space mining at either national or international level. However, this is about to change soon. Over the past three years, missions like Chang-e4 and experiments like Moxie have successfully demonstrated foundational technologies for *in-situ resource utilization*. Looking ahead, several missions are scheduled to achieve even more striking results before the end of this decade, including critical demonstrations from commercial players. While these pioneering missions are increasing our ability to develop good regulation, they also entail the inherent risk of setting up bad regulatory precedents.

To mitigate this risk, it is important to keep the scale of early space resource activities at a proportionate level. This means that States should pay extra care in the exercise of their authorization and supervision duties under Article VI OST.

To preserve the stability of international space law, the multi-level regulatory system of space mining needs to evolve rapidly. In the opinion of this author, this evolution critically relies on the advancements made by the SRWG, as this is now universally recognized as *the* forum to discuss the normative implications of existing international space law on the conduct of space resource activities. On paper, these discussions are supposed to lead to the development of an initial set of principles ensuring the safe, rational, peaceful and sustainable conduct of space mining by the year 2027. Whether or not these principles will be enacted and whether their enactment will be successful depends on the level of regulatory and practical coordination that the SRWG manages to foster in the meantime. To this end, the SRWG provides States with a neutral platform to exchange views on their authorization and supervision regimes for private space mining activities so as to keep the regulatory divergence among them within tolerable margins. Complementarily, the SRWG meetings also offer a unique chance to exchange information about planned and ongoing space resource activities in order to proactively identify and address potential cases of harmful interference, as well as to enable unprecedented opportunities for international cooperation. To be sure, this is a lot to expect from a working group that mostly meets only for a few hours per year. Accordingly, it is hoped that States will leverage the intersessional period to keep exchanging information and ideas in order to make the most of the available time during the meetings.

If the regulatory system of space mining fails to achieve the harmonious and timely evolution suggested above, the consequences might be rather unsettling. Most probably, those States convinced of the importance of space resource activities for sustainable space exploration will continue to encourage it through their financing and domestic regulation. In a similar situation, an international incident would only be a matter of time. Due to the lack of agreed adjudicatory mechanisms at the international level, such incidents would likely be dealt with through bilateral negotiations and possibly lead to unilateral measures.

In turn, this would then have repercussions on other domains of space law, starting a cascade effect that might potentially jeopardize the peaceful and sustainable uses of space.

While it is not up to academics to prevent these outcomes, the findings developed in this book suggest the need for further studies addressing a number of important topics. Moving from the key takeaways identified in this book, in the short term, it would be advisable to investigate the following areas:

- how to leverage existing provisions of international space law to coordinate pioneering activities with the view of ensuring their peaceful and safe conduct;
- how to leverage existing institutions of international space law to consult about both the activities in themselves and the rules governing them;
- how to leverage existing international adjudicatory mechanisms to ensure the predictable and peaceful resolution of any dispute that might arise in the next years.

In the long term, additional studies should investigate the usefulness of an approach based on the development of dedicated international institutions performing coordination, consultation and adjudication functions, as opposed to the establishment of a fully fledged governance system attracting all regulatory functions at the international level. From the perspective of this author, the first approach would seem to be more in line with the multi-level nature of international space law. A fully fledged international governance system would, in fact, create a new (unnecessary?) limit to the freedom of exploration and use under Article I OST and further challenge the role attributed to national authorization and supervision by Article VI OST. As such, negotiations for the development of such a system would have to be conducted with a very high degree of care in order to avoid any impact on the foundational rules of international space law.

In this complex context, there are reasons to be optimistic about the future of the multi-level regulatory system of space mining. The SRWG seems to be well equipped to achieve its critical goals, thanks both to the thought leadership of the Bureau and the cooperative spirit of the Member States. Per their part, academics, operators and civil stakeholders are providing positive contributions to complement the diplomatic activities of the SRWG. Whether the system will evolve in the right direction will be revealed, as with all things, only by time.

Bibliography

Books

Anzilotti Dionisio, *Corso Di Diritto Internationale* (3rd ed., 1928).
Beck Peter, *The International Politics of Antarctica* (2015).
Berger Eric, *Liftoff: Elon Musk and the Desperate Early Days That Launched Spacex* (2021).
Bjorge Eirik, *The Evolutionary Interpretation of Treaties* (2014).
Bjorge Eirik & Andenas Mads (eds.), *A Farewell to Fragmentation, Reassertion and Convergence in International Law* (2015).
Bodin Jean, *Six Livres De La Republique* (1577).
Butrica Andrew J., *Beyond the Ionosphere: Fifty Years of Satellite Communication* (1997).
Casanovas Oriol, *Unity and Pluralism in Public International Law* (2001).
Cassese Antonio, *International Law* 168 (2005).
Cheng Bin, *Studies in International Space Law* (1997).
Christol Carl, *The Modern International Law of Outer Space* (1982).
Cohen Jean L., *Globalization and Sovereignty: Rethinking Legality, Legitimacy, and Constitutionalism* (2012).
Combacau Jean & Sur Serge, *Droit International Public* (2004).
Craig Paul, *EU Administrative Law* (3rd ed., 2018).
De Bittencourt Neto Olavo, Hofmann Mahulena, Masson-Zwaan Tanja & Stefoudi Dimitra (eds.), *Building Blocks for the Development of an International Framework for the Governance of Space Resource Activities: A Commentary* (2020).
De Man Philippe, *Exclusive Use in an Inclusive Environment: The Meaning of the Non-appropriation Principle for Space Resource Exploitation* (2016).
De Wet Erika & Vidmar Jure (eds.), *Hierarchy in International Law: The Place of Human Rights* (2012).
Delmas-Marty Mireille, *Le Pluralisme Ordonné* (2006).
Detter Ingrid, *The International Legal Order* (1944).
Diederiks-Verschoor Isabella, *An Introduction to Space Law* (2008).

Djeffal Christian, *Static and Evolutive Treaty Interpretation: A Functional Representation* 27 (2016).
Dupuy Pierre-Marie, *L'unité De L'ordre Juridique International* (2002).
Elagab Omer Yousif, *The Legality of Non-forcible Counter-Measures in International Law* 227-241 (1988).
Elias Daniel, *Erga Omnes and Countermeasures: Countermeasures by Non-injured States in Response to Mass Atrocities* (2014).
Gaeta Paola, Jorge E. Vinuales & Zappalà Salvatore, *Cassese's International Law* (3rd ed., 2020).
Gorove Stephen, *Studies in Space Law: Challenges and Prospects* (1977).
Haanappel Peter, *The Law and Policy of Air Space and Outer Space: A Comparative Approach* (2003).
Hofmann Mahulena & Masson-Zwaan Tanja, *Introduction to Space Law* (2019).
Hofmann Mahulena, Blount P.J., Leterre Gabrielle, Salmeri Antonino & Zarkan Laetitia, *The Space Legislation of Luxembourg: A Commentary* (2022).
Jakhu Ram (ed.), *National Regulation of Space Activities* (2010).
Kaczorowska-Ireland Alina, *Public International Law* (5th ed., 2015).
Kelsen Hans, *General Theory of Norms* (1991).
Lachs Manfred, *The Law of Outer Space: An Experience*, in *Contemporary Law-Making* (Tanja Masson-Zwaan & Stephan Hobe eds., reissued on the occasion of the 50th anniversary of the International Institute of Space Law, 2010).
Lauterpacht Elihu, *International Law: Collected Papers* (1957).
Lengyel David & Newman Steven (eds.), *International Space Station: Lessons Learned for Space Exploration* (2014).
Levan Alexidze, *Legal Nature of Jus Cogens in Contemporary International Law* (1987).
Lewis John, *Asteroid Mining 101: Wealth for the New Space Economy* (2014).
Lyall Francis, *Law and Space Telecommunications* 351 (1989).
Lyall Francis, *International Communications: The International Telecommunication Union and the Universal Postal Union* (2016).
Lyall Francis & Larsen Paul, *Space Law: A Treaties* (2nd ed., 2018).
Luhmann Niklas, *Potere e Complessita Sociale* (1979).
Maccormick Neil, *Institutions of Law: An Essay in Legal Theory* (2007).
Mazarrolli Ludovico & Girotto Dimitri, *Diritto Costituzionale* (2015).
Peters Anne, *The Refinement of International Law: From Fragmentation to Regime Interaction and Politicization* (2016).
Prost Mario, *The Concept of Unity in International Law* (2012).
Rasmussen Hjalte, *On Law and Policy in the European Court of Justice* (1986).
Repetto Giorgio (ed.), *The Constitutional Relevance of the ECHR in Domestic and European Law: An Italian Perspective* (2013).
Romano Bruno, *Sulla Visione Procedurale Del Diritto: Saggio Sul Fondamentalismo Funzionale* (2001).
Rosenne Shabtai & Ronen Yael, *The Law and Practice of the International Court* (4th ed., 2006).
Schermers Henry G. & Blokker Niels M., *International Institutional Law* (5th revised ed., 2011).

Schulte Constanze, *Compliance with Decisions of the International Court of Justice* (2004).

Shaw Malcolm N., *International Law* (8th ed., 2017).

Sicilianos Linos Alexandre, *Les Reactions Decentralises a L'illicte: Des Contre-Mesures a La Legitime Defense* (1990).

Stubbs Timothy J., Richard R. Vondrak & William M. Farrell, *Impact of Dust on Lunar Exploration* (2005).

Teubner Gunther, *Constitutional Fragments: Societal Constitutionalism in Globalization* (2012).

Van Den Berg Albert Jan, *The New York Arbitration Convention of 1958: Towards a Uniform Judicial Interpretation* (1994).

Villiger Mark E., *Customary International Law and Treaties: A Study of Their Interactions and Interrelations with Special Consideration of the 1969 Vienna Convention on the Law of Treaties* (1985).

Von Der Dunk Frans & Tronchetti Fabio (eds.), *Handbook of Space Law* (2015).

Sir Arthur Watts, *International Law and the Antarctic Treaty System* (1992).

Webb Philippa, *International Judicial Integration and Fragmentation* (2013).

Young Margaret A., *Trading Fish, Saving Fish: The Interaction Between Regimes in International Law* 255-256 (2011).

Zoller Elizabeth, *Peacetime Unilateral Remedies: An Analysis of Countermeasures* (1984).

Chapters

Agaba-Jeanty Timiebi, *Realizing a Regional African Space Program,* in *Innovation in Outer Space: International and African Legal Perspectives* (Mahulena Hofmann & P.J. Blount eds., 2018).

Akehurst Michael, *The Hierarchy of Sources of International Law,* in *47 British Yearbook of International Law* (1974-1975).

Andenas Mads, *Reassertion and Transformation of International Law,* in *A Farewell to Fragmentation, Reassertion and Convergence in International Law* (Eirik Bjorge & Mads Andenas eds., 2015).

Azeredo da Silveira Mercédeh & Levy Laurent, *Transgression of the Arbitrators' Authority: Article V (1)(c) of the New York Convention,* in *Enforcement of Arbitration Agreements and International Arbitral Awards: The New York Convention in Practice* (Emmanuel Gaillard & Domenico di Pietro eds., 2008).

Bastid Suzanne, *Sue Quelques Problèmes juridiques de coordination dans la famille des Nations Unies,* in *Le Droit International, Unité Et Diversité: Mélanges Offerts à Paul Reuter* (Paul Reuter ed., 1981).

Besson Samantha, *Sovereignty,* in *Max Planck Encyclopedia of Public International Law* (2011).

Bjorge Erik, *The Convergence of the Methods of Treaty Interpretation: Different Regimes, Different Methods of Interpretation?,* in *A Farewell to Fragmentation, Reassertion and Convergence in International Law* (Eirik Bjorge & Mads Andenas eds., 2015).

Blount P.J., *Innovating the Law: Fifty Years of the Outer Space Treaty,* in *Innovation in Outer Space: International and African Legal Perspectives* (Mahulena Hofmann & P.J. Blount eds., 2018).

Brisibe Tare, *Africa and Common Interests in Outer Space,* in *Innovation in Outer Space: International and African Legal Perspectives* (Mahulena Hofmann & P.J. Blount eds., 2018).

Calhoun Craig, *Politicization*, in *Dictionary of the Social Sciences* (Craig Calhoun ed., 2002).

Crawford James & Nevill Penelope, *Relations Between International Courts and Tribunals: The "Regime Problem,"* in *Regime Interaction in International Law: Facing Fragmentation* (Margaret A. Young ed., 2012).

D'Aspremont Jean, *The Collective Security System and the Enforcement of International Law,* in *The Oxford Handbook of the Use of Force in International Law* (Marc Weller ed., 2015).

Dembling Paul G. & Arons Daniel M., *The Evolution of the Outer Space Treaty,* 33 Journal of Air Law and Commerce (1967).

Ferrazzani Marco, *The Development of a New Space Economy and of Mega Constellations,* in *Innovation in Outer Space: International and African Legal Perspectives* (Mahulena Hofmann & P.J. Blount eds., 2018).

Fouchard Philippe, *Suggestions to Improve the International Efficacy of Arbitral Awards*, in *Improving the Efficiency of Arbitration Agreements and Awards: 40 Years of Application of the New York Convention* (Albert Jan Van den Berg ed., 2009).

Freeland Steven & Jakhu Ram, *Article II,* in *Cologne Commentary on Space Law: Vol. 1* (Stephan Hobe, Bernhard Schmidt-Tedd & Kai-Uwe Schrogl eds., 2009).

Freeland Steven, *Article 7 MOON,* in *Cologne Commentary on Space Law: Vol. 2* (Stephan Hobe, Bernhard Schmidt-Tedd & Kai-Uwe Schrogl eds., 2013).

Freeland Steven, *Article 8 MOON,* in *Cologne Commentary on Space Law: Vol. 2* (Stephan Hobe, Bernhard Schmidt-Tedd & Kai-Uwe Schrogl eds., 2013).

Freeland Steven, *Article 9 MOON,* in *Cologne Commentary on Space Law: Vol. 2* (Stephan Hobe, Bernhard Schmidt-Tedd & Kai-Uwe Schrogl eds., 2013).

Freeland Steven, *Article 15 MOON,* in *Cologne Commentary on Space Law: Vol. 2* (Stephan Hobe, Bernhard Schmidt-Tedd & Kai-Uwe Schrogl eds., 2013).

Gaillard Emmanuel, *The Urgency of Not Revising the New York Convention*, in *50 Years of the New York Convention: ICCA International Arbitration Conference* (Albert Jan Van Den Berg ed., 2009).

Gaillard Emmanuel & Siino Benjamin, *Enforcement under the New York Convention,* in *The Guide to Challenging and Enforcing Arbitration Awards* (J. William Rowley, Emmanuel Gaillard & Gordon E. Kaiser eds., 2019).

Garret Geoffrey & Weingast Barry, *Ideas, Interests, and Institutions: Constructing the EC's Internal Market*, in *Ideas and Foreign Policy* (Judith Goldstein & Robert Keohane eds., 1993).

Geib Robin, *Non-state Actors: Their Role and Impact on the Fragmentation of International Law,* in *Unity and Diversity in International Law* (Andreas Zimmermann & Rainer Hofmann eds., 2006).

Gerhard Michael, *Article VI OST*, in *Cologne Commentary on Space Law: Vol. 1* (Stephan Hobe, Bernhard Schmidt-Tedd & Kai-Uwe Schrogl eds., 2009).

Gilbert Neil, *A Continent for Science and Peace: Governance in Antarctica*, in *Exploring The Last Continent: An Introduction to Antarctica* (Daniela Liggett, Bryan Storey, Yvonne Cook & Veronika Meduna eds., 2015).

Havercroft Jonathan & Duvall Raymond, *Critical Astropolitics: The Geopolitics of Space Control and the Transformation of State Sovereignty*, in *Securing Outer Space* (Natalie Bormann & Michael Sheehan eds., 2012).

Hemmings Alan D., *Antarctic Politics in a Transforming Global Geopolitics*, in *Handbook on the Politics of Antarctica* (Klaus Dodds, Alan D. Hemmings & Peter Roberts eds., 2017).

Hobe Stephan, *Article I OST*, in *Cologne Commentary on Space Law: Vol. 1* (Stephan Hobe, Bernhard Schmidt-Tedd & Kai-Uwe Schrogl eds., 2009).

Hobe Stephan, *Historical Background of the Outer Space Treaty*, in *Cologne Commentary on Space Law: Vol. 1* (Stephan Hobe, Bernhard Schmidt-Tedd & Kai-Uwe Schrogl eds., 2009).

Hobe Stephan & Hedman Niklas, *Preamble of the Outer Space Treaty*, in *Cologne Commentary on Space Law: Vol. 1* (Stephan Hobe, Bernhard Schmidt-Tedd & Kai-Uwe Schrogl eds., 2009).

Hobe Stephan, Stubbe Peter & Tronchetti Fabio, *Historical Background and Context MOON*, in *Cologne Commentary on Space Law: Vol. 2* (Stephan Hobe, Bernhard Schmidt-Tedd & Kai-Uwe Schrogl eds., 2013).

Hobe Stephan & Tronchetti Fabio, *Article 4 MOON*, in *Cologne Commentary on Space Law: Vol. 2* (Stephan Hobe, Bernhard Schmidt-Tedd & Kai-Uwe Schrogl eds., 2013).

Hobe Stephan & Tronchetti Fabio, *Article 5 MOON*, in *Cologne Commentary on Space Law: Vol. 2* (Stephan Hobe, Bernhard Schmidt-Tedd & Kai-Uwe Schrogl eds., 2013).

Hobe Stephan & Tronchetti Fabio, *Article 6 MOON*, in *Cologne Commentary on Space Law: Vol. 2* (Stephan Hobe, Bernhard Schmidt-Tedd & Kai-Uwe Schrogl eds., 2013).

Hobe Stephan & Tronchetti Fabio, *Article 15 MOON*, in *Cologne Commentary on Space Law: Vol. 2* (Stephan Hobe, Bernhard Schmidt-Tedd & Kai-Uwe Schrogl eds., 2013).

Hobe Stephan & Tronchetti Fabio, *Free Determination of Cooperation*, in *Cologne Commentary on Space Law: Vol. 3* (Stephan Hobe, Bernhard Schmidt-Tedd & Kai-Uwe Schrogl eds., 2015).

Hofmann Mahulena, *Space Resources: Regulatory Aspects*, in *Innovation in Outer Space: International and African Legal Perspectives* (Mahulena Hofmann & P.J. Blount eds., 2018).

Hofmann Mahulena & Blount P.J., *Innovation in Outer Space: International and African Legal Perspectives—Lessons Learned*, in *Innovation in Outer Space: International and African Legal Perspectives* (Mahulena Hofmann & P.J. Blount eds., 2018).

Hofmann Rainer, *Concluding Remarks,* in *Unity and Diversity in International Law* (Andreas Zimmermann & Rainer Hofmann eds., 2006).

Jakhu Ram, *Article 10 MOON,* in *Cologne Commentary on Space Law: Vol. 2* (Stephan Hobe, Bernhard Schmidt-Tedd & Kai-Uwe Schrogl eds., 2013).

Jakhu Ram, Freeland Steven, Hobe Stephan & Tronchetti Fabio, *Article 11 MOON,* in *Cologne Commentary on Space Law: Vol. 2* (Stephan Hobe, Bernhard Schmidt-Tedd & Kai-Uwe Schrogl eds., 2013).

Jakhu Ram, *Article 12 MOON,* in *Cologne Commentary on Space Law: Vol. 2* (Stephan Hobe, Bernhard Schmidt-Tedd & Kai-Uwe Schrogl eds., 2013).

Jakhu Ram & Stubbe Peter, *Article 13 MOON,* in *Cologne Commentary on Space Law: Vol. 2* (Stephan Hobe, Bernhard Schmidt-Tedd & Kai-Uwe Schrogl eds., 2013).

Jane Smith Lesley, *Article XII OST,* in *Cologne Commentary on Space Law: Vol. 1* (Stephan Hobe, Bernhard Schmidt-Tedd & Kai-Uwe Schrogl eds., 2009).

Jane Smith Lesley & Kerrest Armel, *Article I LIAB (Definitions), in Cologne Commentary on Space Law: Vol. 2* (Stephan Hobe, Bernhard Schmidt-Tedd & Kai-Uwe Schrogl eds., 2013).

Jankowitsch Peter, *The Background and History of Space Law,* in *Handbook of Space Law* (Frans Von Der Dunk & Fabio Tronchetti eds., 2015).

Kaye Stuart, *Threats from the Global Commons: Problems of Jurisdiction and Enforcement,* in *Global Legal Challenges: Command of the Commons, Strategic Communications and Natural Disasters* (Michael Carsten ed., 2007).

Kerrest Armel, *Outer Space as International Space: Lessons from Antarctica,* in *Science Diplomacy: Antarctica, Science and the Governance of International Spaces* (Paul A. Berkman, Michael Lang, David Walton & Oran R. Young eds., 2011).

Kerrest Armel & Jane Smith Lesley, *Article VII OST,* in *Cologne Commentary on Space Law: Vol. 1* (Stephan Hobe, Bernhard Schmidt-Tedd & Kai-Uwe Schrogl eds., 2009).

Kopal Vladimir, *United Nations and the Progressive Development of International Space Law,* VII Finnish Yearbook of International Space Law (1996).

Kopal Vladimir, *The 1975 Convention on Registration of Objects Launched into Outer Space in View of the Growth of Commercial Space Activities,* in *Air and Space Law in The 21st Century: Liber Amicorum Karl-Heinz Bockstiegel* (Marietta Benkoe & Walter Kroll eds., 2001).

Kröll Stefan, *Recognition and Enforcement of Awards,* in *Arbitration in Germany: The Model Law in Practice* (Karl-Heinz Bockstiegel, Stefan Kroll & Patricia Nacimiento eds., 2007).

Michael W. Lodge, *International Seabed Authority,* in *Max Planck Encyclopedia of Public International Law* (2020).

Mayence Jean-Frangois & Renter Thomas, *Article XI OST,* in *Cologne Commentary on Space Law: Vol. 1* (Stephan Hobe, Bernhard Schmidt-Tedd & Kai-Uwe Schrogl eds., 2009).

Masson-Zwaan Tanja, *Registration of Small Satellites and the Case of the Netherlands,* in *Small Satellites: Regulatory Challenges and Chances* (Imgard Marboe ed., 2016).

Marboe Irmgard, *National Space Law*, in *Handbook of Space Law* (Frans Von Der Dunk & Fabio Tronchetti eds., 2015).

Marchisio Sergio, *Article IX OST*, in *Cologne Commentary on Space Law: Vol. 1* (Stephan Hobe, Bernhard Schmidt-Tedd & Kai-Uwe Schrogl eds., 2009).

Marks Gary et al., *Competencies, Cracks and Conflicts: Regional Mobilization in the European Union*, in *Governance in the European Union* (Gary Marks ed., 1996).

Mcgarry Brian, *Rethinking Compulsory Jurisdiction: The Case for U.S. Reentry into the ICJ's Optional Clause System*, in *American Society of International Law: Proceedings of the Annual Meeting* (Volume 111, 2017).

Mitrany David, *A Working Peace System*, in *The European Union: Readings on the Theory and Practice of European Integration* (Brent Nelsen & Alexander Stabb eds., 1994).

Obregon Edgardo Sobenes, *Recourse to the Security Council under Article 94 (2) of the United Nations Charter*, in *Max Planck Encyclopedia of International Procedural Law* (2017).

Oellers-Frahm Karin, *Multiplication of International Courts and Tribunals and Conflicting Jurisdiction: Problems and Possible Solutions*, in *Max Planck Yearbook of United Nations Law Vol. 5* (Armin von Bogdandy & Rüdiger Wolfrum eds., 2001).

Oellers-Frahm Karin, *Article 94 UN Charter*, in *The Statute of the International Court of Justice: A Commentary* (Andreas Zimmermann, Christian Tomuschat, Karin Oellers-Frahm & Christian J. Tams eds., 2006).

Oeter Stefan, *Regime Collisions from a Perspective of Global Constitutionalism*, in *Contested Regime Collisions: Norm Fragmentation in World Society* (Kerstin Blome et al. eds., 2016).

Rao Patibandla Chandrasekhara, *International Tribunal for the Law of the Sea*, in *Max Planck Encyclopedia of Public International Law* (2011).

Ribbelink Olivier, *Article III OST*, in *Cologne Commentary on Space Law: Vol. 1* (Stephan Hobe, Bernhard Schmidt-Tedd & Kai-Uwe Schrogl eds., 2009).

Rothwell Donald, *Dispute Settlement under the Antarctic Treaty System*, in *Max Planck Encyclopedia of International Procedural Law* (2018).

Sakamoto Mitsushiro, *Radio Regulations and Procedures in Cases of Harmful Interference*, in *Harmful Interference in Regulatory Perspective: Legal Rules for Interference-Free Radio Communication* (Mahulena Hofmann ed., 2016).

Sakamoto Mitsuhiro, *WRC's Challenge to Meet Technology Development*, in *Innovation in Outer Space: International and African Legal Perspectives* (Mahulena Hofmann & P.J. Blount eds., 2018).

Sauveplanne Jean Georges, *Renvoi*, in *International Encyclopedia of Comparative Law: Volume 3: Private International Law* (Kurt Lipstein chief ed., 1990).

Schmidt-Tedd Bernhard & Mick Stephan, *Article VIII OST*, in *Cologne Commentary on Space Law: Vol. 1* (Stephan Hobe, Bernhard Schmidt-Tedd & Kai-Uwe Schrogl eds., 2009).

Schmidt-Tedd Bernhard, Bohlmann Ulrike, Malysheva Natalya, Stelmakh Olga & Tennen Leslie, *The 1975 Convention on the Registration of Objects Launched into Outer Space*, in *Cologne Commentary on Space Law: Vol. 2* (Stephan Hobe, Bernhard Schmidt-Tedd & Kai-Uwe Schrogl eds., 2013).

Schrogl Kai-Uwe, *The Concept of Space Traffic Management as a Basis for Achieving the Fair and Equitable Use of Outer Space*, in *The Fair and Responsible Use of Space: Studies in Space Policy* (Wolfgang Rathgeber, Kai-Uwe Schrogl & Ray Williamson eds., 2010).

Schrogl Kai-Uwe & Neumann Julia, *Article IV OST*, in *Cologne Commentary on Space Law: Vol. 1* (Stephan Hobe, Bernhard Schmidt-Tedd & Kai-Uwe Schrogl eds., 2009).

Seidl-Hohenveldern Ignaz, *Hierarchy of Treaties*, in *Essays on the Law of Treaties: A Collection of Essays in Honour of Bert Vierdag* (Jan Klabbers & René Lefeber eds., 1998).

Shani Yuval, *One Law to Rule Them All: Should International Courts Be Viewed as Guardians of Procedural Order and Legal Uniformity?*, in *The Practice of International and National Courts and the (De)Fragmentation of International Law* (Ole Kristian ed., 2014).

Slaughter Anne-Marie, *Government Networks: The Heart of the Liberal Democratic Order*, in *Democratic Governance and International Law* (Gregory Fox & Brad Roth eds., 2000).

Spencer Ronald L. (jr.), *International Space Law: A Basis for National Regulation*, in *National Regulation of Space Activities* (Ram S. Jakhu ed., 2010).

Stelmakh-Drescher Olga, *Global Space Governance for Space Sustainability*, in *Innovation in Outer Space: International and African Legal Perspectives* (Mahulena Hofmann & P.J. Blount eds., 2018).

Strupp Karl, *Les Regles Generales du Droit International de la Paix*, 47 Collected Courses of the Hague Academy of International Law (1934).

Sundahl Mark, *Financing Space Ventures*, in *Securing Outer Space* (Natalie Bormann & Michael Sheehan eds., 2012).

Treves Tullio, *Historical Development of the Law of the Sea*, in *The Oxford Handbook of the Law of the Sea* (Donald R. Rothwell, Alex G. Oude Elferink, Karen N. Scott & Tim Stephens eds., 2015).

Triggs Gillian, *The Antarctic Treaty System: A Model of Legal Creativity and Cooperation*, in *Science Diplomacy: Antarctica, Science and the Governance of International Spaces* (Paul A. Berkman, Michael Lang, David Walton & Oran R. Young eds., 2011).

Tronchetti Fabio, *Legal Aspects of the Military Uses of Space*, in *Handbook of Space Law* (Frans Von Der Dunk & Fabio Tronchetti eds., 2015).

Tronchetti Fabio, *Legal Aspects of Space Resources Utilization*, in *Handbook of Space Law* (Frans Von Der Dunk & Fabio Tronchetti eds., 2015).

Tzanakopoulos, Antonios *Judicial Dialogue in Multi-level Governance: The Impact of the Solange Argument*, in *The Practice of International and National Courts and the (De)Fragmentation of International Law* (Ole Kristian ed., 2014).

Vidas Davor, *The Protocol on Environmental Protection to the Antarctic Treaty: A Ten-Year Review*, in *Yearbook of International Co-operation on Environment and Development* (Olav Schram Stokke & Øystein B. Thommessen eds., 2002).

Vikari Lotta, *Environmental Aspects of Space Activities*, in *Handbook of Space Law* (Frans Von Der Dunk & Fabio Tronchetti eds, 2015).

Von Der Dunk Frans, *The Origins of Authorisation: Article VI of the Outer Space Treaty and International Space Law*, in *National Space Legislation in Europe* (Frans Von Der Dunk ed., 2011).
Von Der Dunk Frans, *International Organizations in Space Law*, in *Handbook of Space Law* (Frans Von Der Dunk & Fabio Tronchetti eds., 2015).
Von Der Dunk Frans, *International Space Law*, in *Handbook of Space Law* (Frans Von Der Dunk & Fabio Tronchetti eds., 2015).
Zielonka Jan, *Enlargement and the Finality of European Integration*, in *What Kind of Constitution for What Kind of Polity? Responses to Joschka Fisher* (Christian Joerges, Yves Meny & J H Weiler eds., 2000).
Waldock Humphrey, *Third Report on the Law of Treaties*, in *1964 Yearbook of the International Law Commission Vol. II* (1964).
Webb Dave, *Space Weapons: Dream, Nightmare or Reality?*, in *Securing Outer Space* (Natalie Bormann & Michael Sheehan eds., 2012).
Williams Maureen, *Dispute Resolution Regarding Space Activities*, in *Handbook of Space Law* (Frans Von Der Dunk & Fabio Tronchetti eds., 2015).

Articles

Journals

Alter Karen J., *Who Are the "Masters of the Treaty"?: European Governments and the European Court of Justice*, 52 (1) International Organization (1998).
Angelov Ivaylo, *Global Commons and Their Strategic Significance for the European Union and NATO*, 2 (2) Security & Future (2018).
Arnold Rudolph P., *The Common Heritage of Mankind as a Legal Concept*, 9 International Lawyer (1975).
Blount P.J., *Outer Space and International Geography: Article II and the Shape of the Global Order*, 52 (2) New England Law Review (2018).
Capurso Andrea, *The Non-appropriation Principle: A Roman Interpretation*, 2018 (1) Proceedings of the International Institute of Space Law (2018).
Charney Jonathan, *The Proliferation of International Tribunals: Piecing Together the Puzzle*, 31(4) New York University Journal of International Law and Policy (1999).
Cheng Bin, *The 1967 Outer Space Treaty*, 95 Journal du Droit International (1968).
Cocca Aldo Armando, *Property Rights on the Moon and Other Celestial Bodies*, 1996 (1) Proceedings of the International Institute of Space Law (1996).
Davis Ruth, *Enforcing Australian Law in Antarctica: The HSI Litigation*, 8 Melbourne Journal of International Law (2007).
De Maestri Maria Elena & Carbone Sergio, *The Rationale for an International Convention on Third Party Liability for Satellite Navigation Signals*, 14 (1-2) Uniform Law Review (2009).
Diederiks-Verschoor Isabella, *The Development of Financing of Spacecraft*, 1997 (3) Proceedings of the International Institute of Space Law (1997).
Diederiks-Verschoor Isabella, *Environmental Protection in Outer Space*, 30 German Yearbook of International Law (1987).

Dietz Thomas et al., *The Struggle to Govern the Commons*, 302 (5652) Science (New Series) (2003).

Fujii Kojiro, Ishido Shimpei & Mizushima Atsushi, *What Is an Appropriate Interaction Between International Law and Domestic Legal Systems to Promote Space Resources Development?*, 42 Air & Space Law (2017).

Fukushima Masahiko, *Legal Analysis of International Space Station (ISS) Program Using the Concept of "Legalization,"* 24 Space Policy 33-41 (2008).

Galloway Eilene, *Status of the Moon Treaty*, Space News 21-22 (August 3-9, 1998).

Gläser Philippe et al., *Illumination Conditions at the Lunar South Pole Using High Resolution Digital Terrain Models from Lola*, 243 Icarus (2014).

Gorove Stephen, *Interpreting Article II of the Outer Space Treaty*, 37 Fordham Law Review (1969).

Gorove Stephen, *Freedom of Exploration and Use in the Outer Space Treaty: A Textual Analysis and Interpretation*, 1 Journal of International Law and Policy (1971).

Gorove Stephen, *Pollution and Outer Space: A Legal Analysis and Appraisal*, 5 New York University Journal of International Law & Policy (1972).

Gottfried Kurt & Lebow Richard Ned, *Anti-satellite Weapons: Weighing the Risks*, 114 (2) Daedalus (1985).

Hardin Garret, *The Tragedy of the Commons*, 162 (3859) Science (1968).

Hofmann Mahulena, *ITU Instruments under the Perspective of General International Law*, 2013 (3) Proceedings of International Institute of Space Law (2013).

Hofmann Mahulena & Bergamasco Federico, *Space Resources Activities from the Perspective of Sustainability: Legal Aspects*, 3 (4) Global Sustainability 1-7 (2020).

Higgins Rosalyn, *The ICJ, the ECJ, and the Integrity of International Law*, 52 International & Comparative Law Quarterly (2003).

Isnardi Christina, *Problems with Enforcing International Space Law on Private Actors*, 58 (2) Columbia Journal of Transnational Law (2020).

Jaeckel Aline, *Deep Seabed Mining and Adaptive Management: The Procedural Challenges for the International Seabed Authority*, 70 Marine Policy (2016).

Jakhu Ram, *Legal Issues Relating to the Global Public Interest in Outer Space*, 32 Journal of Space Law 31 (2006).

Jakhu Ram & Freeland Steven, *The Relationship Between the Outer Space Treaty and Customary International Law*, 2016 (2) Proceedings of the International Institute of Space Law (2016).

Jakhu Ram, Bhupendra Jasan & Jonathan McDowell, *Critical Issues Related to Registration of Space Objects and Transparency of Space Activities*, 143 Acta Astronautica (2018).

Janis Mark W., *The Law of the Sea Tribunal and the ICJ: Some Notions about Utility*, 16 (2) Marine Policy (1992).

Jensen Michael C. & Meckling William H., *Theory of the Firm: Managerial Behavior, Agency Costs and Ownership Structure*, 3 (4) Journal of Financial Economics (1976).

Koch Jonathan S., *Institutional Framework for the Province of All Mankind: Lessons from the International Seabed Authority for the Governance of Commercial Space Resource Activities*, 16 Astropolitics (2018).

Kornuta David et al., *Commercial Lunar Propellant Architecture: A Collaborative Study of Lunar Propellant Production*, 13 Reach (2019).
Layers Troy, *Law as a Smart Bomb or Just a Limited Tool of Coercion: Considering Extra-Territorial Economic Sanctions*, 146 (5) Royal United Services Institute (2001).
Lang Andrew, *The Role of the International Court of Justice in a Context of Fragmentation*, 62 International & Comparative Law Quarterly (2013).
Lefeber Renè, *The Exercise of Jurisdiction in the Antarctic Region and the Changing Structure of International Law: The International Community and Common Interests*, 21 Netherlands Yearbook of International Law (1990).
Lefeber Renè, *Relaunching the Moon Agreement*, 1 Air & Space Law 41-48 (2016).
Longo Michael, *Reconceptualising Public International Law: Convergence with the European Union Model?*, 25 (1) University of New South Wales Law Journal 88-93 (2002).
Lord Thomas, *The Antarctic Treaty System and the Peaceful Governance of Antarctica: The Role of the ATS in Promoting Peace at the Margins of the World*, 10 (1) The Polar Journal (2020).
Marceau Gabrielle, Izguerri Arnau & Labonnovy Vladyslav, *The WTO's Influence on Other Dispute Settlement Mechanisms: A Lighthouse in the Storm of Fragmentation*, 47 Journal of World Trade (2013).
Masson-Zwaan Tanja, *Article VI of the Outer Space Treaty and Private Human Access to Space*, 2008 (9) Proceedings of the International Institute of Space Law (2008).
Masson-Zwaan Tanja, *Space Law and the Satellite Collision of 10 February 2009*, 174 Space Research Today (2009).
McLachlan Campbell, *The Principle of Systemic Integration and Article 31 (3) (c) of the Vienna Convention*, 54 International and Comparative Law Quarterly (2005).
Megiddo Tamar, *Beyond Fragmentation: On International Law's Integrationist Forces*, 44 (1) Yale Journal of International Law (2019).
Mendes de Leon Pablo, *Crossing Borders in International Air and Space Law*, 3 (1) India Law Journal (2010).
Erik J. Molenaar, *Participation in the Antarctic Treaty*, 11 (2) The Polar Journal (2021).
Monserrat Jose, *Acts of Aggression in Outer Space*, 2001 (4) Proceedings of the International Institute of Space Law (2001).
Moravcsik Andrew, *Liberal Intergovernmentalism and Integration: A Rejoinder*, 33 (4) Journal of Common Market Studies (1995).
Muhammadin Fajri Matahati, *Can International Law Be Enforced Towards Its Subjects Within the International Legal Order?*, 2 Ius Quia Iustum Law Journal of Islamic University of Indonesia (2014).
Mrema Elizabeth, *Protecting the Global Commons: The Challenge of Collective Action*, 18 (1) Georgetown Journal of International Affairs (2017).
Nicolaidis Kalipso & Shaffer Gregory, *Transnational Mutual Recognition Regimes: Governance Without Global Government*, 68 (3-4) Law and Contemporary Problems (2005).

Nikoalidis Kalipso & Tong Joyce L., *Diversity or Cacophony? The Continuing Debate over New Sources of International Law*, 25 (4) Michigan Journal of International Law (2004).

Olleson Simon, *Internationally Wrongful Acts in the Domestic Courts: The Contribution of Domestic Courts to the Development of Customary International Law Relating to the Engagement of International Responsibility*, 26 (3) Leiden Journal of International Law (2013).

Paulson Colter, *Compliance with Final Judgments of the International Court of Justice Since 1987*, 98 American Journal of International Law (2003).

Pelkmans Jacques, *Mutual Recognition in Goods: On Promises and Disillusions*, 14 (5) Journal of European Public Policy (2007).

Petras Christopher, *"Space Force Alpha": Military Uses of the International Space Station and the Concept of "Peaceful Purposes,"* 53 Air Force Law Review (2002).

Petras Christopher, *The Debate over the Weaponization of Space: A Military-Legal Conspectus*, 28 Annals of Air and Space Law (2003).

Pierson Paul, *The Path to European Integration: A Historical Institutionalist Perspective*, 29 (2) Comparative Political Studies (1996).

Pino Paolo et al., *Waste Management for Lunar Resources Activities: Towards a Circular Lunar Economy*, 9 (4) New Space (2021).

Pocar Fausto, *An Introduction to the PCA's Optional Rules for Arbitration of Disputes Relating to Outer Space Activities*, 38 Journal of Space Law (2011).

Poisel Tim, *Deep Seabed Mining: Implications of Seabed Disputes Chamber's Advisory Opinion*, 19 Australian International Law Journal (2012).

Pollack Mark, *Delegation, Agency, and Agenda Setting in the EC*, 51 (1) International Organization (1997).

Raible Lea, *Extraterritoriality Between a Rock and a Hard Place*, 82 Questions of International Law (2021).

Ranganathan Surabhi, *Global Commons*, 27 (3) European Journal of International Law (2016).

Ranjeva Raymond, *Global Justice: Compulsory Jurisdiction and the Role of the ICJ*, 17 (3) Harvard International Review (1995).

Rasche Andras, *Global Policies and Local Practice: Loose and Tight Couplings in Multi-stakeholder Initiatives*, 22 (4) Business Ethics Quarterly (2012).

Roloff Julia, *Learning from Multi-stakeholder Networks: Issue Focused Stakeholder Management*, 82 Journal of Business Ethics (2008).

Salmeri Antonino, *The Integration Between National and International Regulation of Space Resources Activities under Public International Law*, 43 (1) Journal of Space Law (2019).

Salmeri Antonino, *Developing and Managing Moon and Mars Settlements in Accordance with International Space Law*, 2020 (2) Proceedings of the International Institute of Space Law (2020).

Salmeri Antonino, *Collective Space Objects as a New Concept of International Space Law*, 46 (2) Air & Space Law (2021).

Sattler Rosanna, *Transporting a Legal System for Property Rights from the Earth to the Stars*, 6 Chicago Journal of International Law (2005).

Schmidt Susanne K., *Mutual Recognition as a New Mode of Governance*, 14 (5) Journal of European Public Policy (2007).

Schrogl Kai-Uwe, *Space Law and Diplomacy*, 2016 (1) Proceedings of the International Institute of Space Law (2016).

Scott Gary L. & Carr Craig L., *The ICJ and Compulsory Jurisdiction: The Case for Closing the Clause*, 81 (1) American Journal of International Law (1987).

Shahar Keren & Greenbaum Dov, *Lessons in Space Regulations from the Lunar Tardigrades of the Beresheet Hard Landing*, 4 Nature Astronomy (2020).

Sharma-Wallace Lisa, *Adaptive Governance Good Practice: Show Me the Evidence!*, 222 Journal of Environmental Management (2018).

Shaw Lauren E., *Asteroids, the New Western Frontier: Applying Principles of the General Mining Law of 1872 to Incentive Asteroid Mining*, 78 Journal of Air Law & Commerce (2013).

Skagestad Odd Gunnar, *Sovereignty, Jurisdiction, and Cooperation: The Antarctic Treaty, Preconditions, Substance and Future Relevance*, 1 New Ground Research Journal (2013).

Sundahl Mark, *Regulating Non-traditional Space Activities in the United States in the Wake of the USCLCA*, 42 Air & Space Law 29-42 (2017).

Sundahl Mark & Salmeri Antonino, *The Registration of Lunar Activities: Recommendations from the Registration Project*, 2021 (2) Proceedings of the International Institute of Space Law (2021).

Tronchetti Fabio, *The Non-appropriation Principle under Attack: Using Article II of the Outer Space Treaty in Its Defence*, 2007 (5) Proceedings of the International Institute of Space Law (2007).

Tronchetti Fabio, *Private Property Rights on Asteroid Resources: Assessing the Legality of the Asteroids Act*, 30 Space Policy 194 (2014).

Tronchetti Fabio & Hao Liu, *The American Space Commerce Free Enterprise Act of 2017: The Latest Step in Regulating the Space Resources Utilization Industry or Something More?*, 47 Space Policy 1-6 (2019).

Vecchio Valentina, *Customary International Law in the Outer Space Treaty: Space Law as Laboratory for the Evolution of Public International Law*, 66 German Journal of Air and Space Law (2017).

Vlasic Ivan, *Disarmament Decade, Outer Space and International Law*, 6 Annals of Air and Space Law (1981).

Von Der Dunk Frans, *The Moon Agreement and the Prospects of Commercial Exploitation of Lunar Resources*, 32 Annals Air and Space Law (2007).

Walker Brian et al., *Resilience, Adaptability and Transformability in Social-Ecological Systems*, 9 Ecology and Society (2004).

Young Oran R., *Building and International Regime Complex for the Arctic: Current Status and Next Steps*, 2 (1) Polar Journal 391-407 (2012).

Online Articles

Brindestine Jim, *Life on Earth Is Better Because of NASA*, available https://blogs.nasa.gov/bridenstine/2020/09/25/life-on-earth-is-better-because-of-nasa/ (last accessed October 2022).

Brindestine Jim, *Shared Standards Are a Vital Part of Future Space Exploration*, available https://blogs.nasa.gov/bridenstine/2020/10/12/statement-on-international-exploration/ (last accessed October 2022).

Brindestine Jim, *Space Resources Are the Key to Safe and Sustainable Lunar Exploration*, available https://blogs.nasa.gov/bridenstine/2020/09/10/space-resources-are-the-key-to-safe-and-sustainable-lunar-exploration/ (last accessed October 2022).

Christensen Ian & Johnson Christopher, *Putting the White House Executive Order on Space Resources in an International Context*, available https://www.thespacereview.com/article/3932/1 (last accessed October 2022).

Deng Xiaoci, *Lunar Research Station to be Inked by China and Russia This Year, Operational by 2035: CNSA*, January 28, 2022, Global Times China, available https://www.globaltimes.cn/page/202201/1250142.shtml (last accessed October 2022).

Doyle Gerry, Factbox: *Anti-satellite Weapons: Rare, High-Tech, and Risky to Test*, March 27, 2019, Reuters Aerospace and Defence, available https://www.reuters.com/article/us-india-satellite-tests-factbox-idUSKCN1R80UW (last accessed October 2022).

Erwin Sandra, *DARPA to Survey Private Sector Capabilities to Build Factories on the Moon*, February 7, 2021, Space News, available https://spacenews.com/darpa-to-survey-private-sector-capabilities-to-build-factories-on-the-moon/ (last accessed October 2022).

Gamillo Elizabeth, *How Sanctions on Russia Affect International Space Programs*, available https://www.smithsonianmag.com/smart-news/sanctions-on-russia-reach-outer-space-180979679/ (last accessed October 2022).

Gorman Steve, *Buzz Aldrin, Second Man on Moon, Recalls "Magnificent Desolation,"* available https://www.reuters.com/article/us-space-exploration-aldrin-idUSKCN1UC01P (last accessed October 2022).

Hitchens Theresa, *DARPA Space Manufacturing Project Sparks Controversy*, February 12, 2021, Breaking Defense, available https://breakingdefense.com/2021/02/darpa-space-manufacturing-project-sparks-controversy/ (last accessed October 2022).

Jones Andrew, Russia, China to Sign Agreement on International Lunar Research Station, February 17, 2021, Space News, available https://spacenews.com/russia-china-to-sign-agreement-on-international-lunar-research-station/ (last accessed October 2022).

Johnson Christopher, *A First Look at the Artemis Accords*, available https://www.linkedin.com/pulse/first-look-artemis-accords-christopher-johnson?articleId=6722061704605286400#comments-6722061704605286400&trk=public_profile_article_view (last accessed October 2022).

Long Patrick, *Becoming a NASA Astronaut and Military Service*, June 25, 2019, available https://www.thebalancecareers.com/so-you-want-to-become-an-astronaut-3345123 (last accessed October 2022).

Mann Adam, *The Moon May Be Tectonically Active, and Geologists Are Shaken*, National Geographic, available https://www.nationalgeographic.com/science/

article/moon-may-be-tectonically-active-geologists-shaken-apollo-moonquakes (last accessed October 2022).

Mellmann Jan, *Deep Sea Mining: Why Now and How?*, available https://www.wfw.com/articles/deep-sea-mining-why-now-and-how/ (last accessed October 2022).

Newman Christopher, *The Artemis Accords and Lunar Exploration-Revolution and Evolution*, available https://spacewatch.global/2020/10/spacewatchgl-opinion-the-artemis-accords-and-lunar-exploration-revolution-and-evolution/ (last accessed October 2022).

Rothwell Donald, *The Antarctic Treaty Is Turning 60: In a Changed World, Is It Still Fit for Purpose?*, available https://www.downtoearth.org.in/blog/climate-change/the-antarctic-treaty-is-turning-60-in-a-changed-world-is-it-still-fit-for-purpose--77606 (last accessed October 2022).

Salmeri Antonino, *Houston We Have a Law: A Model for National Regulation of Space Resource Activities*, 2019 Proceedings of the 70th International Astronautical Congress (2019).

Salmeri Antonino, *No, Mars Is Not a Free Planet, No Matter What SpaceX Says*, November 16, 2020, Space News, available https://spacenews.com/op-ed-no-mars-is-not-a-free-planet-no-matter-what-spacex-says/ (last accessed October 2022).

Salmeri Antonino, *One Size to Fit Them All: Interoperability, the Artemis Accords and the Future of Space Exploration*, available https://spacewatch.global/2020/11/spacewatchgl-opinion-one-size-to-fit-them-all-interoperability-the-artemis-accords-and-the-future-of-space-exploration/ (last accessed October 2022).

Treiman Allan H. et al., *Sample Return from the Earth's Moon*, available https://www.lpi.usra.edu/decadal/captem/AllanTreimanMoon.pdf (accessed January 2021).

Tronchetti Fabio & Liu Hao, *Australia Between the Moon Agreement and the Artemis Accords*, available https://www.internationalaffairs.org.au/australianoutlook/australia-between-the-moon-agreement-and-the-artemis-accords/#:~:text=On%2015%20October%202020%2C%20Australia,to%20promote%20its%20prosperous%20future (last accessed October 2022).

Xu Fengna, *The Approach to Sustainable Space Mining: Issues, Challenges, and Solutions*, available https://iopscience.iop.org/article/10.1088/1757-899X/738/1/012014/pdf (last accessed October 2022).

Yotsumoto Hiroko, Ishikawa Daiki & Odan Tetsuji, *Hamada Mori & Matsumoto, The Space Law Review: Japan*, available https://thelawreviews.co.uk/title/the-space-law-review/japan#footnote-003 (last accessed October 2022).

Miscellaneous

International Documents

Antarctic Treaty System's Compilation of Key Documents, Measure 1 (2003), available https://documents.ats.aq/atcm43/ww/ATCM43_ww008_e.pdf (last accessed October 2022).

International Seabed Authority's Draft Regulations on Exploitation of Mineral Resources in the Area, available https://isa.org.jm/files/files/documents/isba_25_c_wp1-e_0.pdf (last accessed October 2022).

International Telecommunication Union's Radio Regulations, adopted by the 2019 World Radiocommunication Conference (WRC-19).

United States President's Executive Order on Encouraging International Support for the Recovery and Use of Space Resources, enacted on the April 6, 2020, available https://trumpwhitehouse.archives.gov/presidential-actions/executive-order-encouraging-international-support-recovery-use-space-resources/ (last accessed October 2022).

The Artemis Accords: Principles for Cooperation in the Civil Exploration and Use of the Moon, Mars, Comets, and Asteroids for Peaceful Purposes, available https://gouvernement.lu/dam-assets/documents/actualites/2020/10-octobre/14-luxembourg-nasa-artemis/Artemis-Accords-signed-13102020.pdf (last accessed October 2022).

Optional Rules for Arbitration of Disputes Relating to Outer Space Activities, Permanent Court of Arbitration, Effective December 6, 2011, available https://docs.pca-cpa.org/2016/01/Permanent-Court-of-Arbitration-Optional-Rules-for-Arbitration-of-Disputes-Relating-to-Outer-Space-Activities.pdf (last accessed February 2021).

Specialized Panel of Arbitrators Established Pursuant to the Optional Rules for Arbitration of Disputes Relating to Outer Space Activities, available https://docs.pca-cpa.org/2022/01/2022/01/a42fa03c-pca-184031-v15-current_list_annex_4_sp_outer_space_arb.pdf (last accessed October 2022).

Reports, Studies & Theses

Bergamasco Federico, *The ITU and ICAO Regulating Aeronautical Safety Services and Related Radio Spectrum* (2021).

Bryce Space Technology, *Global Space Industry Dynamics* (2017).

Brycetech, *Projected Exploration Missions (2020-2030)* (2020).

Crawford James, *Articles on Responsibility of States for Internationally Wrongful Acts* (2012), available https://legal.un.org/avl/pdf/ha/rsiwa/rsiwa_e.pdf (last accessed October 2022).

Garcimartín Francisco & Saumier Geneviève, *Explanatory Report on the Convention of 2 July 2019 on the Recognition and Enforcement of Foreign Judgments in Civil or Commercial Matters* (2020).

International Telecommunication Union, *Radio Regulatory Framework for Space Services*, available https://www.itu.int/en/ITU-R/space/snl/Documents/ITU-Space_reg.pdf (last accessed October 2022).

Johnson Kaitlyn, *Fly Me to the Moon: Worldwide Cislunar and Lunar Missions* (2022), available https://csis-website-prod.s3.amazonaws.com/s3fs-public/publication/220215_Johnson_FlyMe_Moon.pdf?eBOSyAKB1ite5cort60IluuBQWvYyADa (last accessed October 2022).

Leterre Gabrielle, *Providing a Legal Framework for Sustainable Space Mining Activities 48-51*, master book available https://wwwen.uni.lu/content/download/102978

/1231496/file/Gabrielle%20Leterre%20Providing%20a%20Legal%20Framework%20for%20Sustainable%20Space%20Mining%20Activities.pdf (last accessed October 2022).
Moon Village Association, *Best Practices for Sustainable Lunar Activities*, available https://moonvillageassociation.org/wp-content/uploads/2020/10/MVA-Best-Practices-Issue-1-19.10.2020-FINAL.pdf (last accessed October 2022).
Open Lunar Foundation, *Lunar Resources Policy*, available https://www.openlunar.org/library/lunar-resources-policy (last accessed October 2022).
Space Foundation, *The Space Report 2022* (2022).
Space Generation Advisory Council, *Effective and Adaptive Governance for a Lunar Ecosystem: Recommendations from the Young Generations at the United Nations—Lunar Governance Report*, available https://spacegeneration.org/wp-content/uploads/2021/12/EAGLE-Report.pdf (last accessed October 2022).
Gabriel Swiney & Amanda Hernandez *(Nasa Office of Technology Policy and Strategy), Lunar Landing and Operations Policy Analysis* (2022), available https://www.nasa.gov/sites/default/files/atoms/files/nasa-otps-lunar-landing-and-operations-policy-analysis-final-report_2.pdf (last accessed October 2022).
The Hague International Space Resources Governance Working Group, *Building Blocks for the Development of an International Framework for the Governance of Space Resource Activities*, available https://www.universiteitleiden.nl/binaries/content/assets/rechtsgeleerdheid/instituut-voor-publiekrecht/lucht—en-ruimterecht/space-resources/bb-thissrwg—cover.pdf (last accessed October 2022).
United Nations Commission on International Trade Law, *Guide on the Convention on the Recognition and Enforcement of Foreign Arbitral Awards of 1958*, available https://newyorkconvention1958.org/index.php?lvl = cmspage&pageid = 10&menu = 729&opac_view = -1 (last accessed October 2022).
United Nations Office for Outer Space Affairs, *Space Supporting the Sustainable Development Goals*, available https://www.unoosa.org/oosa/en/ourwork/space4sdgs/index.html (last accessed October 2022).

Working Papers

De Man Philip, *Luxembourg Law on Space Resources Rests on Contentious Relationship with International Framework (2017)*, available https://ghum.kuleuven.be/ggs/publications/working_papers/2017/189deman (last accessed February 2021).
Falkner Robert, *Global Governance: The Rise of Non-state Actors—A Background Report for the Soer 2010 Assessment of Global Megatrend* (2011).
Koskenniemi Martin, *Fragmentation of International Law: Topic (A): The Function and Scope of the Lex Specialis Rule and the Question of Self-Contained Regimes: An Outline* (2004).

Press Releases, Speeches & Statements

Press Release of the Ministry of Economy of Luxembourg, Luxembourg's New Space Law Guarantees Private Companies the Right to Resources Harvested in Outer Space in Accordance with International Law, available http://www.space

resources.public.lu/content/dam/spaceresources/press-release/2016/2016_11_11PressReleaseNewSpacelaw.pdf (last accessed October 2022).
Press Release of the White House Office of the Press Secretary, Remarks by the President on Space Exploration in the 21st Century (2010), available https://www.nasa.gov/news/media/trans/obama_ksc_trans.html (last accessed October 2022).
Speech by His Excellency Judge Gilbert Guillaume, President of the International Court of Justice, to the Sixth Committee of the General Assembly of the United Nations, The Proliferation of International Judicial Bodies: The Outlook for the International Legal Order, available https://ghum.kuleuven.be/ggs/events/2013/springlectures2013/documents-1/guillaume-proliferation-intnat-judicial.pdf (last accessed October 2022).
Speech by Michael W. Lodge, Secretary General of the International Seabed Authority, to the Max Planck Institute of Procedural Law, The International Seabed Authority and Deep Seabed Disputes, available https://isa.org.jm/files/documents/EN/SG-Stats/mpi_sept2017_0.pdf (last accessed October 2022).
Statement by the Board of Directors of The International Institute of Space Law (IISL), Claims to Property Rights Regarding the Moon and Other Celestial Bodies, available http://iislwebo.wwwnlss1.a2hosted.com/wp-content/uploads/2015/03/IISL_Outer_Space_Treaty_Statement.pdf (last accessed October 2022).

Others

China National Space Administration and Roscosmos, International Lunar Research Station (ILRS) Guide for Partnership (2021), available http://www.cnsa.gov.cn/english/n6465652/n6465653/c6812150/content.html (last accessed October 2022).
Global Governance and Governance of the Global Commons in the Global Partnership for Development Beyond 2015, available https://www.un.org/en/development/desa/policy/untaskteam_undf/thinkpieces/24_thinkpiece_global_governance.pdf (last accessed October 2022).
National Aeronautics and Space Administration's Reference Guide to the International Space Station (2010).
Position Paper on Space Resources Mining Adopted by Consensus by the IISL Board of Directors on December 20, 2015, available https://www.iislweb.org/docs/SpaceResourceMining.pdf (last accessed October 2022).
The International Planetary Protection Handbook (2009), available https://ec.europa.eu/research/participants/documents/downloadPublic?documentIds=080166e5c1c292c4&appId=PPGMS (last accessed October 2022).
Vancouver Recommendations on Space Mining, available http://www.outerspaceinstitute.ca/docs/Vancouver_Recommendations_on_Space_Mining.pdf (last accessed October 2022).

Table of Cases and Advisory Opinions

Court of Justice of the European Union

Case 9/56 (annulment application), (Judgment, June 13, 1958), 1957-1958 E.C.R. 135, 28

Case 120/78 (reference for a preliminary ruling), (judgment, February 20, 1979), 1979 E.C.R. 649, 23

Case C-126/97, (judgment, June 1, 1999) 1999 ECR I-3055, 158

Case C-376/98 (reference for a preliminary ruling), (judgment, October 5, 2000), 2000 E.C.R. 8498, 24

Joined Cases C-404/15 and C-659/15 PPU (reference for a preliminary ruling), (judgment, April 5, 2016), CJEU Digital Reports ECLI:EU:C:2016:198 13, 23

Opinion pursuant to Article 218 (11) on the Accession of the European Union to the European Convention for the Protection of Human Rights and Fundamental Freedoms, (Opinion, December 18, 2014), CJEU Digital Reports ECLI:EU: C:2014:2454, 31

European Court on Human Rights

Al-Dulimi and Montana Management Inc v. Switzerland, (Application no. 5809/08) (Judgment of the Grand Chamber, June 21, 2016), 29

Case of *Bosphorus Hava Yollari Turizm Ve Ticaret Anonim Şirketi v. Ireland*, (Application no. 45036/98), (Judgment, June 30, 2005), 2005-VI E.Ct. H.R. 107, 24

Case of *Hatton and Others v. The United Kingdom* (Application no. 36022/97), (Judgment, July 8, 2003), 2003-VIII ECtHR Report 216, 23

Stichting Mothers of Srebrenica and others v. The Netherlands, (Application no. 65542/12), (Decision on Admissibility, June 11, 2013) 2013 ECHR 739, 29

International Court of Justice

Allegations of Genocide under the Convention on the Prevention and Punishment of the Crime of Genocide (*Ukraine v. Russian Federation*), *(Order*, March 16, 2022), available https://www.icj-cij.org/public/files/case-related/182/182-20220316-ORD-01-00-EN.pdf (last accessed October 2022), 149

National Courts

International Tribunal on the Law of the Sea

Other International Tribunals

Table of Treaties

International Agreements

U.N. Documents

Resolutions of the UN General Assembly

Resolutions of the UN Security Council

Resolution 820/1993 adopted by the Security Council at its 3200th meeting, UN Doc S/RES/820 (April 17, 1993), 146
Resolution 2087/2013 adopted by the Security Council at its 6904th meeting, UN Doc S/RES/2087 (January 22, 2013), 39

Reports of the Committee and Subcommittees of the UN Committee on the Peaceful Uses of Outer Space

Report of the Committee on the Peaceful Uses of Outer Space on its 22nd Session, held in Vienna from June 18 to July 3, 1979, UN Doc A/34/20 (Supplement 20, 1979), 100
Report of the Committee on the Peaceful Uses of Outer Space on its 50th Session, held in Vienna from June 6 to 15, 2007, UN Doc A/62/20 (2007), 77
Report of the Committee on the Peaceful Uses of Outer Space on its 64th Session, held in Vienna from August 25 to September 3, UN Doc A/76/20 (2021), 120
Report of the Legal Subcommittee on its 60th Session, held in Vienna from May 31 to June 11, 2021, UN Doc A/AC.105/1243 (2021), 120
Report of the Committee on the Peaceful Uses of Outer Space on its 62nd Session, held in Vienna from June 12-21, 2019, UN Doc A/74/20 (2019), 120
Report of the Committee on the Peaceful Uses of Outer Space on its 62nd Session, held in Vienna from June 12-21, 2019, *Guidelines for the Long Term Sustainability of Outer Space Activities*, UN Doc A/74/20, Annex II (2019), 77
Report of the Legal Subcommittee on its 56th Session, held in Vienna from March 27 to April 7, 2017, UN Doc A/AC.105/1122 (2017), 4, 119
Report of the Legal Subcommittee on its 57th Session, held in Vienna from April 9 to 20, 2018, UN Doc A/AC.105/1177 (2018), 4, 119
Report of the Legal Subcommittee on its 58th Session, held in Vienna from April 1 to 12, 2019, UN Doc A/AC.105/1203 (2019), 4, 119
Report of the Legal Subcommittee on its 61st Session, held in Vienna from March 28 to April 8, 2022, UN Doc A/AC.105/C.2/L.321/Add.1 3-6 (Draft, 2022), 177
Report of the Chair and Vice-Chair of the working group established under the Legal Subcommittee agenda item entitled "General exchange of views on potential legal models for activities in the exploration, exploitation and utilization of space resources", UN Doc A/AC.105/C.2/2022/SRA/L.1 (2022) (SRWG Report), 4, 120–125, 179, 204, 207

Study Group Reports & Working Papers

Report of the Study Group of the International Law Commission, Finalized by Martti Koskenniemi, *Fragmentation of International Law: Difficulties Arising From The Diversification And Expansion Of International Law,* UN Doc A/CN.4/L.682 (April 13, 2006) (ILC Study), 9–17, 20–22, 25, 30–32, 34
Report of the Study Group of the International Law Commission, *Fragmentation of International Law: Difficulties Arising from the Diversification and Expansion of International Law,* UN Doc A/CN.4/L.702 (July 18, 2006), 9
Working Paper from the Governments of Belgium and Greece, Proposal for the Establishment of an Working Group for the Development of an International

Other UN Documents

National Laws

Index

J

L

T

U

V

AEROSPACE LAW AND POLICY SERIES

1. Erwin von den Steinen, *National Interest and International Aviation*, 2006 (ISBN 90-411-2455-1).
2. Ludwig Weber, *International Civil Aviation Organisation: An Introduction*, 2007 (ISBN 978-90-411-2622-1).
3. Niels van Antwerpen, *Cross-Border Provision of Air Navigation Services with Specific Reference to Europe: Safeguarding Transparent Lines of Responsibility and Liability*, 2008 (ISBN 978-90-411-2688-7).
4. Brian F. Havel, *Beyond Open Skies: A New Regime for International Aviation*, 2009 (ISBN 978-90-411-2389-3).
5. Jiefang Huang, *Aviation Safety through the Rule of Law: ICAO's Mechanisms and Practices*, 2009 (ISBN 978-90-411-3115-7).
6. Marian Hoeks, *Multimodal Transport Law: The Law Applicable to the Multimodal Contract for the Carriage of Goods*, 2010 (ISBN 978-90-411-3246-8).
7. George N. Tompkins, Jr., *Liability Rules Applicable to International Air Transportation as Developed by the Courts in the United States: From Warsaw 1929 to Montreal 1999*, 2010 (ISBN 978-90-411-2646-7).
8. Daniel Calleja Crespo and Pablo Mendes de Leon (eds), *Achieving the Single European Sky: Goals and Challenges*, 2011 (ISBN 978-90-411-3730-2).
9. Donal Patrick Hanley, *Aircraft Operating Leasing: A Legal and Practical Analysis in the Context of Public and Private International Air Law, Third Edition*, 2022 (ISBN 978-94-035-4030-6).
10. Mikołaj Ratajczyk, *Regional Aviation Safety Organisations: Enhancing Air Transport Safety through Regional Cooperation*, 2015 (ISBN 978-90-411-5861-1).
11. Benjamyn I. Scott (ed.), *The Law of Unmanned Aircraft Systems, Second Edition*, 2022 (ISBN 978-94-035-4573-8).
12. Stamatis Varsamos, *Airport Competition Regulation in Europe*, 2016 (ISBN 978-90-411-6831-3).
13. Katarzyna Malinowska, *Space Insurance: International Legal Aspects*, 2017 (ISBN 978-90-411-6784-2).
14. John Milligan, *European Union Competition Law in the Airline Industry*, 2017 (ISBN 978-90-411-6618-0).

15. Dejian Kong, *Civil Liability for Damage Caused by Global Navigation Satellite System*, 2019 (ISBN 978-94-035-1171-9).
16. Pablo Mendes de Leon and Niall Buissing (eds), *Behind and Beyond the Chicago Convention: The Evolution of Aerial Sovereignty*, 2019 (ISBN 978-94-035-1131-3).
17. Neta Palkovitz, *Regulating a Revolution: Small Satellites and the Law of Outer Space*, 2019 (ISBN 978-94-035-1762-9).
18. Federico Bergamasco, Roberto Cassar, Rada Popova & Benjamyn I. Scott, *Cybersecurity: Key Legal Considerations for the Aviation and Space Sectors*, 2020 (ISBN 978-94-035-0110-9).
19. Luis Fernando Fiallos Pazmiño, *The International Civil Operations of Unmanned Aircraft Systems under Air Law*, 2021 (ISBN 978-94-035-2854-0).
20. Merinda E. Stewart, *Freedom of Overflight: A Study of Coastal State Jurisdiction in International Airspace*, 2021 (ISBN 978-94-035-3804-4).
21. Cyril-Igor Grigorieff, *Uniformity and Fragmentation of the 1999 Montreal Convention on International Air Carrier Liability*, 2022 (ISBN 978-94-035-3732-0).
22. Mahulena Hofmann, P.J. Blount, Gabrielle Leterre, Antonino Salmeri & Laetitia Zarkan, *Space Legislation of Luxembourg: A Commentary*, 2022 (ISBN 978-94-035-4381-9).
23. Jacomo Restellini, *Labour Relations in Aviation*, 2022 (ISBN 978-94-035-4561-5).
24. Antonino Salmeri, *The Multi-level Governance of Space Mining*, 2023 (ISBN 978-94-035-1856-5).